Our Daily Breach

6 September 2015

Dear Joe —

Your continued support
of my work means the
world to me.
I am honored to have
your endorsement on my
book —

With affection and
gratitude —

Denis

Our Daily Breach
Exploring Your Personal Myth Through Herman Melville's Moby-Dick

Dennis Patrick Slattery, Ph.D.

Our Daily Breach
Exploring Your Personal Myth Through Herman Melville's Moby-Dick

Published simultaneously in Canada, the United Kingdom, and the United States of America by Fisher King Press. For information on obtaining permission for use of material from this work, submit a written request to:

permissions@fisherkingpress.com

Fisher King Press
109 E 17th St, Ste 80
Cheyenne, WY 82001
www.fisherkingpress.com
fisherking@fisherkingpress.com
+1-307-222-9575

Many thanks to all who have directly or indirectly provided permission to reprint their work. Every effort has been made to trace all copyright holders; however, if any have been overlooked, we will be pleased to make the necessary arrangements at the first opportunity.

Front cover image © is an original photo by Vincent Shay and is used with permission by Vincent Shay Photography.

Vincent Shay is an award winning photographer and videographer from San Luis Obispo, California, focusing on active lifestyle, documentary, and the abstract. For more information about Vincent Shay visit:
www.vincentshayphotography.com

Dedication

To Howard P. Vincent
In gratitude for your passionate mentoring into the subtle
complexities of Melville's magnificent White Whale at Kent State
University in the late 1960s.

and

To all the planet's whales, both living and dead, for the deep wisdom
shrouded in your enchanting songs.

Incipit

To produce a mighty book, you must choose a mighty theme. No great and enduring volume can ever be written on the flea, though many there be who have tried it.

> —Herman Melville, *Moby Dick*,
> Chapter 104, "The Fossil Whale."

I would also include Melville's *Moby Dick*, which I consider to be the greatest American novel, in this broad class of writings.

> —C.G. Jung, *The Spirit in Man, Art, and Literature*.
> Volume 15 of *The Collected Works of C.G. Jung*, p. 88.

When we think of the masterpieces that nobody praised and nobody read, back there in the past, we feel an impatient superiority to the readers of the past. If we had been there, we can't help feeling, we'd have known that *Moby-Dick* was a good book—why, how could anyone help knowing?

> —Randall Jarrell, "An Unread Book," qtd.
> in Dana Gioia's *Can Poetry Matter?*

Contents

Foreword

Have you ever wanted to read Herman Melville's *Moby-Dick* but thought it too daunting? Or maybe you read it in high school or college but are curious to see what more you might learn from it today? Dennis Patrick Slattery's new book, *Our Daily Breach: Exploring Your Personal Myth through Herman Melville's Moby-Dick*, offers a brilliantly conceived strategy for reading Melville's classic while also exploring one's own life story. Professor Slattery, a teacher and scholar who has published widely on psychology, myth, and memory, believes that everyone has a personal story or myth to tell, one that few of us ever bother to discover or recreate. What's so original about his new book is the idea that our own lives and life stories mirror the narratives of the great classic works of literature—they resonate with us personally but often without our being fully aware of it. As readers, we have a natural sympathy with the characters and actions of classic works like *Moby-Dick* that leads us to recall similar, parallel moments and feelings in our own lives. Classics are classics because they hold the potential for a powerful, intimate, personal connection to us—as they have for generations of readers throughout history.

As Slattery explains in his illuminating introduction, we see life deeply through the classics, but the classics help us see our own lives deeply as well. The classic narratives provide a means or mode of self-discovery through the presence of myth because myth captures experience that is universal as well as personal. When we enter imaginatively into what he calls "world narratives," we engage our own "unfolding myth," our own life story, whether we do so consciously or not. Slattery's thinking derives from many sources, including such formidable students of myth as C.G. Jung, Joseph Campbell, Rollo May (*The Cry for Myth*), and James Hillman (*Healing Fiction*), but his application of their theories derives from his own experience and insight into mythic stories, too, which, as he argues, are open ended and can be used for our own purposes as readers. They therefore act as "intermediaries or midwives"; and they can heal. In fact, given the rough-and-tumble, often tragic nature of human experience, all of us have experienced some kind of wound or wounding in our lives; and all of us consequently have reason to hunger for healing—healing that can happen with greater self-understanding.

Taking an important cue from Aristotle, Slattery argues not that we imitate myth but that "we are imitated" by the mythic dimension of classic tales—a discovery we make implicitly but often unconsciously in the process of reading such narratives. Professor Slattery's ingenious strategy for reading *Moby-Dick* with the aid of his book involves the reader responding, informally in writing, to a series of pointed, often probing questions, starting from the beginning and tied to scene after scene in Melville's text, that lead the reader through one parallel personal memory or self-discovery after another and in a way that helps readers to uncover the shape and pulse of their own life story, their own "personal myth."

Moby-Dick, Melville's story of "one Ishmael," Ahab, and the great White Whale is especially appropriate for Slattery's purposes, because Ishmael, the narrator, is himself engaged in a protracted quest for self-understanding, one the reader experiences through him chapter by chapter but also relives for himself or herself in parallel with Ishmael through personal memory. Ishmael goes to sea because, as he explains, the sea holds "the image of the ungraspable phantom of life" which is "the key to it all." In one major instance in the novel, that phantom is instanced by the image of Narcissus, the beautiful youth who became fascinated with the beauty of his own image in the water and drowned. However, the most important instance of this phantom is the image of the great White Whale itself, which is also the novel's most persistent symbol of Ishmael's unfolding, maturing character. Ishmael is so obsessed with learning about whales and the White Whale in particular because he intuits and then confirms, through close analysis and personal soul-searching, that it is an image of his own deeper self or "soul"—the repository or treasure-house of all the strengths and virtues, the angels and demons, within himself. "Meditation and water and wedded forever," as he says, because water—the ocean and the Whale that inhabits it—contains the likeness, and the mystery, of the self we see in every mirror.

In the beginning of his story, Ishmael starts like many of us, or many a wandering hero such as Dante in the *Divine Comedy*, in a state of darkness or uncertainty marked by anger, confusion, and spiritual deadness. We see how widespread, even universal is his longing for self-understanding in the opening scene of the book, when on a Sunday afternoon it seems every working stiff in Manhattan has made their way to the wharf where they can be seen staring out into the watery part of the world, eager to find themselves, eager to gain self-understanding, but afraid of giving up the conventional life, weekdays "tied to counters, nailed to benches, clinched to desks." Among these "crowds" of inexperienced landlubbers, however, only Ishmael dares to heed the "call" to adventure at sea and undertake the journey to self-discovery on the *Pequod*. Luckily, Ishmael has the experienced harpooneer, Queequeg, to serve as his guide through the intricacies and challenges of whaling and the pursuit of the great White Whale under the Pequod's monomaniacal Captain Ahab. Similarly, readers of this book are fortunate in having Dennis Slattery to serve as their savvy teacher and guide through the maze of Melville's *Moby-Dick* and the voyage of self-discovery and personal myth-making he has so skillfully constructed for them.

One final note, an anecdote I hope all adventurous readers of Professor Slattery's book will find encouraging, even inspiring: Writing to his new friend, Nathaniel Hawthorne, in June 1851, while in the late stages of composing *Moby-Dick*, Melville—then in his early 30s--admitted, "Until I was twenty-five, I had no development at all. From my twenty-fifth year I date my life. Three weeks have scarcely passed, at any time between then and now, that I have not unfolded within myself. But I feel that I am now come to the inmost leaf of the bulb, and that shortly the flower must fall to the mould." It is hardly a coincidence that it was in his twenty-fifth year, after returning from several years at sea, that Melville started his career as a writer, and, in writing, began to discover his own story, his personal myth.

Christopher Sten
Author of *Sounding the Whale*
Professor of English, George Washington University

Introduction
Literary Classics and Personal Mythology

The Storied Self

For a good segment of my life I did far more listening than talking. Part of the reason for this reticence was that I did not consider my own story interesting enough to relate; others, I had convinced myself, would not find it very exciting. "Not dramatic enough," I told myself, and so I answered for them and did not tell my own story, much as it yearned to be expressed. Told or not, one's story will find an opening into the world. I now believe, as I reflect back on my own narrative, that one of the strongest desires a human being has is not what we most assume or are told we have: food, clothing, shelter, sexual satisfaction and the like. I believe it is the deep longing to tell our story and in the telling and being witnessed, to retrieve or discover something essential about ourselves. The second, perhaps equally strong impulse, is the wish to be told stories of others by others. In what better way can a relationship begin and grow than through the mutual sharing of one's biography or that of others, *with others*? So our stories are what can create the most intimate bonds between people, and they never take very long to unfurl.

Simply put, we want to reveal our identities through the narratives that compose us and are composed by us. Of all the identities we are, none is more important than our narrative identity, our storied self. Moreover, we tell our tales for reasons we often only dimly comprehend. We may seek at times comfort, sympathy, assurance, recovery of who we are, advice, or another angle on what the story might point to, mean, resemble, and how even to change the narrative in its signal design. We are changed, in addition, by the stories we tell and the stories we listen to in ways that may not be consciously grasped at the moment. Even more attractive, all of our personal narratives can be found, in one form or another, in literary classics. I think that is a significant part of the reason why they perdure with such delicious tenacity for years and, with some, for millennia.

Narratives, I sense, give us much more knowledge than just the content of the literal story. If you want to socialize with someone and get a good sense of who and how they are, share a film with them and then have coffee or a drink or dinner afterward to discuss it. I am always astonished by how much of what constitutes a person surfaces through what s/he says in the discussion. In these moments, you will get two stories: the one from the film and the other from the person as s/he gives you a sense of the film's import. There is nothing better than a story, one discussed, if not told, to draw from the person some response analogous to the narrative and a simulacrum of him/herself. I believe another way of speaking of these stories is through the notion of a personal myth. Myths are the backdrop and the backbone of the stories we hear or read. We can travel backward and down into the narrative to uncover some of the underlying patterns of our or another's personal myth. Storytelling, in other words, is a form of myth-making and shaping. It offers theories of ourselves in narrative form or as Bruce Lincoln defines it, *"ideology in narrative form"* (*Theorizing* xii). In another context I suggested that "a myth includes a way, a *via* or roadway, a path, that allows things of the world to present themselves to me in a particular style of intellectual and emotional presence" (*Riting Myth* 3). The cultural critic Alan Watts believes that "myth…is an imagery in terms of which we make sense out of life" ("Western Mythology" 14). Myths slide us into an "as-if" frame of reference by which we believe what we see, think, remember or feel; they are templates that shape us according to specific categories of awareness. What could be more powerful or worth pursuing, especially through the richness of an epic like Melville's *Moby-Dick*, the focus of this book.

In addition, I sense a deep connection between the act of re-reading and re-storying ourselves to others. In his bold insights into the act of rereading, Matei Calinescu offers that "what rereading does is to add a circular twist (and sometimes more than a mere twist—an imaginatively new, mysterious, mythical dimension) to an otherwise inescapable linearity" (39). I suspect a rich correspondence here between recollecting in order to re-story our plot and rereading the plot of a poem. The linearity of a first reading is replaced with the circular or perhaps more accurately, the spiral twist of rereading.

I have been blessed with re-reading and re-teaching many of the great stories from literature for over 40 years, stories I never tire of re-thinking in the setting of the classroom. Among them: Homer's *Odyssey*, Melville's *Moby-Dick,* the subject of this book, Toni Morrison's *Beloved,* Dante's *Divine Comedy, Inanna, Gilgamesh,* Sophocles' *Oedipus,* and Wole Soyinka's *Death and the King's Horseman.* I am continually fascinated by the connective tissue between classical stories told and our own individual and unique narratives that are uncovered and revealed in new and unique ways through the stories we read and that read us. Reading classics of world literature is both an intense and pleasurable way to learn by seizing on what one did not know before, or in quite the way the classic poem reveals it to us, at this point in our lives. For example, to read *Moby-Dick* at age 18, then at 28 and then at 46 and again at 68 will reveal very different stories and introduce very distinct Leviathans. This and other classic narratives are comprised like Proteus, the shape-shifting god of the sea in Greek mythology; they have something of a liquid quality about them and will fill a vessel according to the dictates of its contours. How is this so? What is the nature of the shifts or changes that renders these narratives so differently? Why do we respond with such different perspectives as we mature into ourselves and into the world? Answering these questions through works of literature is an implicit undertow of the present introduction to the universal importance of Melville's narrative of the White Whale as both a spiritual pilgrimage and a poetic rendering of the myth of America in the 19th century that resonates with today's culture.

Two observations have prompted me to write these words as well as those that will follow and to focus on Melville's epic to explore some questions that fascinate me: first is that many academic programs have entombed literary classics as elitist texts that don't belong in the public sphere, or worse, trivializing them by shellacking them over with theories *about* literature. Both impulses are destructive to poetic insights into the lived experience that the story yields because theory, when given top billing and specialization, often pulls classical literature away from a larger access for an intelligent lay public; the consequence can often block or uncouple these stories from part of the larger fictions of our lives. In this severing, the joy of reading them evaporates, along with the kind of intuitive or sensate knowing that educator James Taylor has called a "sensory-emotional experience of reality" (*Poetic Knowledge* 5).

Can classical works be reclaimed for a larger reading public, one that includes many people who were too young or not sufficiently invited in to discuss these works and consequently dismissed them from their lives, perhaps permanently? Suppose we talk about them in a different way in order to open a few avenues of discussion to give *people a reason for reading or re-reading them now,* a little later in life, when they have been ripened by the pains, sorrows, monotonies, betrayals, losses, fidelities, births and deaths and joys of life. How can we converse about literature that would provoke in people a desire for the insights offered by reading not with the sharp knife and objectivity of analysis but rather with the intimate, personal connectedness to their own narrative lives that meditation encourages? One of our earliest writers on literature, the Greek philosopher Aristotle, believed that there is an intrinsic and deep pleasure in imitating. He discerned that "as human beings, we enjoy seeing a likeness; in contemplating it we find ourselves learning by inference or analogy" (*Aristotle's Theory of Poetry and Fine Art* 17).

The other observation is that in the years I have taught both traditionally-aged undergraduates as well as adult learners who have returned to school after years, even decades away from the classroom, I detect a marked difference in their approaches to learning. Now, in their adult years, they have returned to study at the current institute I teach in. As adult learners they have responded to a call from deep within to study Mythology, Counseling Psychology, Clinical or Depth Psychology, Humanities or Somatics leading to a Masters or Doctoral degree. I have watched with great joy their transformation in working with and having been worked on, by literary classics. They will often say to me regarding *Moby-Dick*, for instance: "I read this novel as an English major 20 or 15 or 10 years ago and saw none of what we have been discussing." Just the other day, one of my mythology students wrote me the following: "*Moby-Dick* became such an incredible experience for me. The richness of Melville's expression and the width and depth of his sensitivity have affected me greatly." What happened? Well, life happened. Reflection happened. Desire to know happened. And perspective happened, namely, an angle by which to see and understand and imagine more deeply, more mythically, what has unfolded in their personal narratives.

Personal Myth and Reading the Classics

Can such a change occur to anyone? I believe anyone reflective and passionate in their desire to learn about themselves as well as harboring a longing to understand both historical and contemporary events swirling around us daily, to make some sense of what has happened throughout human history, as well as to formulate new insights for themselves—all can benefit from reading the classics. They are classical perhaps because the deep experiences imbedded in their stories seem to persist over time, yet inflected uniquely in each of us. We can relate to them, to their own mythology, through the individual myths unfolding in and informing each of us. The Neo-platonic writer, Plotinus, believed that "all knowing comes by likeness" (*Enneads* I.8.1. 56).

This last point needs some clarification. The great quality about classical works of literature is that each harbors its own myth, its own manner of seeing and apprehending the world according to certain values, beliefs, prejudices, shortcomings and discoveries that comprise a developing worldview. When we enter into their territory or their poetic field of influence to read them openly and freely, devoid of prejudice or antagonism, and when we are able, as the poet Samuel Taylor Coleridge advised us, to willingly suspend our disbelief, for that alone constitutes poetic faith (*Biographia Literaria* 171), our own personal myth begins to entwine with the myth that engages us through a classic like *Moby-Dick*. In this very imaginative and complex process, we find ourselves in sympathy not only with the characters and action of the work but in more generous sympathy with our own and others' pilgrimages. The psychologist and lover of literature, Rollo May, observes that "our powerful hunger for myth is a hunger for community. The person without a myth is a person without a home" (*Myth* 45). We need myths to shore up our relationships with ourselves and others. One place that the collective myths, of which we are all players, appear is in classics that stimulate the imagination to explore them in order to increase our own mythic focal length. To see mythically is to be attuned in some measure to what the work seeks to "reproduce [which] is an inward process, a psychical energy working outwards; deeds incidents, events, situations, being included under it…" (S.H. Butcher 123).

My own sense is that we actually begin to experience life differently through the classic. We grasp some truth by means of another mode of knowing. Think of the epic that is the focus of this book, or another that you have enjoyed, even without knowing why, as offering a unique way of knowing *something* as well as a content of knowing—both a *what* and a *how*. Classic poems are like waking dreams, even formed reveries, exquisitely crafted in language that delights and expands our own lexicon; here we can uncover something deeply important to our way of being to reveal what we had not known or only vaguely glimpsed through a rich analogical affiliation. Said another way, our own myth is mimetically altered through the classic narrative that touches us deeply; we enter imaginally into the narrative that replicates on profound levels the particles of our own plot. Our critical faculties are for a moment held in abeyance and what we imagine gains ascendency.

Our own personal myth is stirred deeply by the actions of the classic. We can act on it or by means of it and experience a transformation in our lives, modifying our behavior, discerning events twisted differently, and offering us a new or revised story, a more complex plot and perhaps a greater range of characters. A poem like *Moby-Dick*, moreover, does not carry in its cargo moral lessons or even "hidden meanings"—a phrase I've always disliked as student and teacher. Quite the reverse: it imparts revelations that we can experience by analogy, not head on or head first but through the energy of the oblique angle that metaphors and symbols—indeed all figural language—offers us. In my teaching, I have witnessed students respond and identify with the actions of a Captain Ahab, an Oedipus, or an Antigone. The Swiss psychologist C.G Jung, who turned to literature often in his practice and in his writing over decades of exploring poetry, mythology and the human psyche, discovered that if we are able to discriminate between "objective knowledge and emotional value-judgments, then the gulf that separates our age from antiquity is bridged over, and we realize with astonishment that Oedipus is still alive for us" (*CW* 5: par. 1). Entering this terrain of what seems immortal and ageless in its importance to us for living a reflective life is what the American epic in this book explores. Directly focusing on Melville's masterpiece, Jung went on to write in another volume when he explored the difference between psychological and visionary fiction; he wrote of the latter category: "I would also include Melville's *Moby Dick,* which I consider to be the greatest American novel, in this broad class of writings" (*CW* 15: par. 137). His words appear in the *Incipit* of this book.

Classical works of literature contain a built-in ordering principle that is accessible to us if we dare enter fully into the story with an open and authentic heart and a mind free of judgment and bias. Fiction has a strange power and capacity to order or reorder our lives by allowing us to meditate on complex human actions that we cannot grasp in their fullness as we live them or witness them in personal experiences. We need that second act of contemplation to allow them to gain a richer sense for our own plot. Students have relayed to me that for the first time in their lives, by reading classical poems, they began to discern the contours and the complexity of their own story. Initially, however, they needed to place their personal narrative next to one that had an ordered complexity, even a planned subtlety, so that they could see from an angle in a mirror of imaginative reflection, their own complex and nuanced plot. Their own life narrative became available to them through the indirection of another story's deep intricacy. The literary and Jungian scholar David Miller has observed of classical dramas like Aeschylus' *Oresteia*, "Everything that follows the opening curtain is like a projection of meaning for future living; it is a metaphor of human existence . . . . It is a magic mirror, which teases and tricks man into future possibilities. . . ("Orestes" 37). Such is the value of reading classical literature less through the lens of a distancing theory and more through the prismatic magical glass of one's personal mythology. We discover in the form of the work informing principles of our own narrative identity.

A Personal Story

To make a bit more tangible what I ended with above, I relate here an experience I had over 45 years ago that I can recall in its full emotional recognition as if it happened yesterday. What is important in that last sentence is the "as-if" phrase.

In the mid 1960s I was attending college part time while working as a deputy bailiff in a Municipal Court in Euclid, Ohio, east of Cleveland. I had a new car, a fine job, an area of study that I enjoyed: sociology. I was dating the police chief's secretary and felt a future with her. At the time, I was living at home, was 20 years old and bored out of my skin. During a particular night course at Cuyahoga Community College in Cleveland, I met another student, Denny Collins; we shared a similar temperament. We thus began, like Ishmael, or like Huck, or like anyone who wanted to light out for the territory, to break the mold, to leave all the appendages of security behind and plunge into uncharted seas. We began nosing around the shipping wharfs in Cleveland's port where freighters from around the world docked and dropped their cargo or picked up merchandise and headed out across the Great Lakes, up the St. Lawrence Seaway and out the Gaspe Peninsula into the North Atlantic and destinations around the globe. We thought we could perhaps book passage on a freighter and see some other parts of the world from its deck.

On one visit, towards early summer, as we inquired after what was available, the harbor master informed us that a German freighter arriving soon from Detroit was short-handed and that if we cared to, we might sign on as crews' mess hands and work our passage to Bremerhaven, Germany, the ship's final port. The ship's name was the Transamerica, owned by Poseidon Lines in Hamburg, Germany. We were excited beyond belief and accepted his offer.

We had 15 days to put our lives in order, including the night class we were taking. The professor agreed to advance our final exam so we could finish early and salvage our semester's work. That done, and passports obtained quickly, we made the deadline by 4 days. Then one evening our parents drove us to the docks at Cleveland's waterfront; we boarded the freighter with our duffle bags and sailed on a balmy June night at 1 a.m. As we began to put distance between ourselves and land on the merchant seaman's freighter, we passed within a mile of the beach that was at the end of the street where I had lived for years. We then sailed into the blackness of the night, full face into the warm breeze blowing from the east. I can still hear the pistons of the old crude oil burning engine as we stowed our gear in the small cubby of a locker in our small quarters deep in the ship's hold and prepared to see what the Canadian ports, the North Atlantic and Western Europe had in store. Neither of us had been any farther from home than New York City. We soon joined the dozen or so German merchant seamen fulfilling their military obligation by working for two years on board this cargo ship.

We survived the ordeal of 21 days crossing, including stops at various ports in Canada to discharge and take on new cargo. Our jobs were menial: cleaning bathrooms and cabins of the 10 passengers we had on board as well as the crews' lodgings. We hauled food across deck from the kitchen, often in storms, by holding on to hemp lifelines laced across deck to discourage us from being thrown overboard by aggressive waves breaking over the careening deck. We sailed through iceberg fields, changed course to avoid herds of whales, slowed into gales in the North Atlantic, and witnessed the sheer cliffs of Scotland. At one stretch we were out of sight of land for 9 days. When we finally descended into the port of Germany and disembarked, we struggled to walk on stable land without toppling over.

Our adventures took us hitchhiking through Germany, the Netherlands, England, Wales, and Southern and Northern Ireland, before we had to wire for money to fly home. Our attempts to secure a ship out of Belfast to the United States were futile, in part because so many Irish youth exiting Ireland had first pick of the available jobs and bunks. After a full summer, we gave up our quest to stay away for a year and flew home, a bit disappointed but wide-eyed with our experiences outside the United States.

When we arrived home and settled into our familiar landscape again, we found different jobs, but our main interest was recounting to others our adventures. We were so full of stories yearning to be told. But something did not satisfy us in telling these tales. There existed a palpable gap, even a lack in the telling. Something was missing. Not excitement, exactly, but a plenitude. On impulse, I began buying and reading every tale I could get my hands on that took place on seas or rivers: Richard Henry Dana's

Two Years Before the Mast; Jack London's *Sea Wolf,* Joseph Conrad's *Heart of Darkness, The Secret Sharer* and *Lord Jim;* Mark Twain's *Huckleberry Finn* and the Hornblower series. As a finale, first Herman Melville's *White Jacket* followed by *Moby-Dick* and *Billy Budd.* During the voyage I had written daily, both aft on the ship every night of the voyage and then at home, as I read these sea tales. What fascinated me about the narratives was that they were not my stories; but as I read them, I began to understand my own sea story better, more abundantly, it seems, and in more profound and varied ways through the prism of the prose these tales afforded. I sensed what was at stake in going to sea (which is another way of going to see), what prompted it, what made it such a universal desire in all of us and how we each harbor deep within us a fathomless yearning for a getaway but will often resist the impulse, deny the call, postpone the adventure, perhaps for a short while or a lifetime. Mythically, I was later to discern, my sea adventure became my first profound "see" story, for it enlarged the orbit of my perceptions and pushed me out of the narrow confines of my life up to then.

What occurred to me was that the act of traveling, or journeying, was much like reading a story. They had many analogies fortifying them. Both were actions and forms of learning at the same time. I thought that if stories could, after their fashion, actually fashion my own story more deeply, or disclose it more fully, then they were worth studying. When I enrolled at Kent State University for my last two years of undergraduate work, I knew that I had left home for the long haul. Living there was no longer possible. I also declared an English major, not sociology or psychology, as was my focus of study. In retrospect, I grasped that in voraciously studying stories from the past, that they were in fact not past at all but amazingly and significantly emotionally and intellectually present. Furthermore, they were in no way "vicarious," another misleading word that swirls around literary studies in English course classrooms. These powerful tales were not a substitute or a replacement for something; they were life itself in a shaped, organic, living imaginal form and in their formative structure re-formed my own narratives with a profundity that had been absent. The beautiful and poetic language of the classics contained within their linguistic folds both mythic content and what I was later to learn was a psycho-aesthetic energy. Reading them energized me in the deepest recesses of my being. They appeared as figures of ancestors or elders out of history and seemed more than amenable to instruct me if I remained open enough to allow them in. When I journeyed reading through these magnificent artifacts of the imagination, I was just as intensely exploring my own story, my own mythology, indirectly, by analogy, by attunement and by rich and subtle correspondences. *Moby-Dick* was one of the most forceful adventures that I have studied and taught for many years; its world is the focus of this book as a means for readers to explore their own personal myth, as I have my own over decades.

What an amazing discovery! By entering imaginatively into world narratives, I was simultaneously contacting and engaging my own unfolding myth. There is a term for this I was later to learn: *mythopoesis.* I understand it to be the most deeply experienced imaginative journey doubled, for it occurred simultaneously in my own deep terrain as well as in the world's mysterious literary landscape. In all of their complexity and clarity, as well as in their superbly crafted structures, poetry certified my narrative, endorsed my feelings, charmed me to see more, not less, of life, and to know it on a richer imaginative level. I could remember and envisage my own story through the poetic story I was reading. The poetic work snagged something of the experience my own narrative ability was not strong enough to capture and placed it into a more poetic vessel of knowledge. The high seas were never so exciting as the deep seeing I was imaginatively engaging in my own waters of discernment prompted and provoked by Melville's Leviathan tale.

What slowly dawned on me was that not only are we biological, psychological, spiritual, and emotional beings, we are also mythical mammals whose own mythology is as unique as our voice or thumbprint. Mythical reality, given to us both in world mythologies and in literary classics, prods us into the deepest way of knowing ourselves and the world. As one of my finest teachers, Dr. Louise Cowan, suggested to us in graduate classes with her, we read Homer or Dante or Dostoevsky or Flannery O'Connor not to become Greek or Russian or Italian or Southern, but to become more of who we actually are through the refracting glass of these enduring narratives that satisfied so completely and offered ontological insights so generously. We can easily devote a lifetime growing into them as they grow more deeply down into us.

I found her observation to ring true. I would add a further refrain: one way to understand so many events that unfurl around us, yet have, seemingly, no rhyme or reason for their happening, is through literary classics. Analogously, two somatics instructors, Yuji Oka and Stephanie Gottlob have written of contemporary artists since the beginning of the 19th century—Jackson Pollock, John Cage, Joseph Beuys among them—who shifted the emphasis of the visual arts away from the historical period of their creations and towards "the subjective internal experience" which is paramount. They claim that in the artists mentioned above, "the aesthetic experience becomes largely an internal form of meditation, where it is not the strokes of paint, or notes, or sculptures that matter, but rather the changes they can make inside us" ("Spiral Praxis" 41). Experiencing classics shares this meditative quality: instead of the poem being analyzed, theorized and classified, it is contemplated as a living organism in league with our own internal narrative. Not mastery but a deepening meditation is at work in the energy field of the fiction; moreover, it is powerfully interactive.

Mundus Imaginalis:
The World of Mythic Imagination

What Carl Sagan did to interest the popular mind in science and Steven Hawking achieved in making physics accessible, Joseph Campbell succeeded in returning the study of mythology to the contemporary imagination. In his most cited volume, *The Power of Myth,* a series of interviews with cultural commentator Bill Moyers, Campbell tells the story of Black Elk, a young Sioux boy about nine years old who experiences a dramatic initiation during the course of a life-threatening illness. The family invites a shaman in, a holy, healing man, to remedy the boy's condition. Campbell relates how, in Black Elk's illness, the young boy has a revelation of his tribe's future wherein he envisions his nation's hoop connected to the hoops of many other nations in a vast girdle of community, not unlike the Olympic Games' interconnecting circles or those that appear on the grill of an Audi. He sees that the boy was also pilgrimaging through the hoops of his own interiority, like spiritual stages, and accumulating in the journey their value for himself and his tribe. Then the boy, in his vision, proclaims to those around him: "'I saw myself on the central mountain of the world, the highest place, and I had a vision because I was seeing in the sacred manner of the world.' The sacred central mountain was Harney Peak in South Dakota"(89), but for the young boy the pronounced realization was that the "central mountain is everywhere." It is where one stands in the immediate present. It is the sacred place of understanding itself.

Following Black Elk's experience, the mythologist Joseph Campbell offers the following mythological realization:

> The center of the world is the *axis mundi,* the central point, the pole around which all revolves: the central point of the world where stillness and movement are one. Movement is time and stillness is eternity. Realizing how the movement of your life is actually a moment of eternity

and experiencing the eternal aspect of what you're doing in the temporal experience—this is the mythological experience. (*Power* 89)

When reading and reflecting on a classic, something in us shifts, moves about, and may even be reordered because the imagination allows us to access our interior life more fully when such admission is made available through a story that is both mythic and poetic, as is Melville's epic.

Literary Classics: Re-membering Ourselves

The psychiatrist Robert Coles writes in *The Call of Stories* that the "beauty of a good story is its openness—the way you or I or anyone reading it can take it in, and use it for ourselves"(47). Less manipulation, however, than revelation. They are meant to be used more as disclosures of something shared in us and through us shared with the world, an experience that can actually be richer and more fully understood than the actual event. What goes on here?

When I returned from my ocean voyage to Europe and began reading the tales of ships, rafts and crews, as well as the conflicts and resolutions aboard them, I felt that for the first time, my own story had a home, a context, a place of safe harbor. In other words, I needed some analogous stories, different from but like mine, to get what mine *meant* by anchoring it within meanings that far transcended mine, yet included it. I needed another *as-if* story to put down next to my own in order to see mine through the lens or the filter or web of the mythic story these classics rendered with such power. I then perceived mine more fully and with a greater order and pattern than I would have, had I simply remembered it in a literary vacuum and deployed it to others. I suddenly realized that *seeing by means of* could be more penetrating into what an experience meant in one's life than seeing directly, with no intermediary, no between place or space, no inflected presence. That is it, I thought: these classic tales were intermediaries, midwives even—stories that placed themselves between what I had experienced and what the poet had discovered, perhaps through a vision as Black Elk experienced, in an analogous event. Such was the power of analogy, of correspondence, and complicity, even a co-conspiracy in stories; I began to grasp how, perhaps, the psyche learns best, and even insists on, analogy as a way of knowing something in its more opulent valence.

This power of seeing one's own story by parsing it through another, especially a classic narrative, is what I hope to convey through one passage per day from Melville's sea story; my goal is to highlight common and not so common human experiences in their full emotional, mythic and poetic force by means of passage-ways from his epic tale. Several poets and writers have spoken of the ordering principle inherent in literature. We often forget that while our daily lives generally have a schedule and a format but often no cohering venue, what orders our lives derives from somewhere else, not the least place of which is memory. The deep and often hidden patterns in our lives surface through the patterns of a classic. Our lives can find an order—emotional, psychological, spiritual and embodied—through such timeless poems that are simultaneously timely for any who animates them in the act of reading. Classics of literature offer us new opportunities and means of recalling what we do not realize we have forgotten. Reading and thinking about them is a deeper and more mythically-attuned form of remembering.

The poet C. Day Lewis claims that "the pattern of poetry is the pattern which gives pleasure because it satisfies the human yearning for order and for completeness" (35). Not perfection but completeness. This same yearning hastens to be satisfied often and with some complex elaboration. Simple statements, categorical formulas, stereotyped and clichéd responses simply fail to satisfy.

A Poetic Therapy

Classics like *Moby-Dick* are so powerful in their capacity to transform how we live our own narrative from that first moment of encounter forward. Some writers have asserted that there is even a healing property in stories that can act as a kind of imaginal tonic within us. May the imagination be so powerful that it can heal through narratives? The founder of psychoanalysis, Sigmund Freud, based much of his psychoanalytic therapy on the fact that his patients seemed to improve markedly simply by lying on the couch in his study and giving a voice to their remembered narratives. In the safe retreat of the consulting room, they were free to wander in memory and imagination back as far as they dared, to their origins and then to speak it.

Freud also discovered in listening to these narratives that often fabrication mingled with actual historical events; he began then to discern less how much of a fiction we tell, and more how much of a fiction we are. Relief often came to the analysand in the act of recollection and in speaking his/her narrative. It may be that both in the telling of stories and in hearing or reading them, that something torn or lacerated or afflicted in us finds a balm that soothes the wound. Fiction became a balm for the affliction. The ideas that contour us as well as the beliefs we formulate are part of the mythic structure that provides the foundation for our lives as well as shapes it in unique ways. The early twentieth century philosopher Hans Vaihinger explored and enunciated the elaborate fictions we create to give our life contour and coherence (*The Philosophy of 'As-If'*, xxx-xxxiv). Well before psychology was even an idea as a discipline, literary classics served their culture as forms of therapeutic healing through catharsis; they were stories as treatments which, when entered imaginatively, helped reconcile some psychic wound that might have both collective and personal origins. In addition, these same works still retain that capacity. Perhaps we could say of the classics: Stories that keep on healing; in this regard they have immense utility for us on a daily basis.

More recently, in *Writing For Your Life,* Deena Metzger has beautifully affirmed how "stories heal us because we become whole through them. In the process of writing, and in discovering our story, we restore those parts of ourselves that have been scattered, hidden, suppressed, denied, distorted, forbidden, and we come to understand that stories heal" (71). She further suggests that the act of "re-membering" plays a major role in healing because who we have been may have to be dismantled and then re-membered or reassembled so that we can go "beyond the imagined limits of ourselves" (71). I would add to her fine insight that not only in the mysterious act of writing, but in the equally mythic act of reading, and then rereading, we gain the capacity to undergo a form of alchemical breakdown and reassemblage, not necessarily to construct a new self but rather to let more of who we have already fashioned declare a voice and a place in our lives. This openness to all of who we are is allowed, even supported, through the classics if we only assent as readers to its imaginal landscape.

I would say it this way: by means of entering imaginatively into a classic story, some deep analogy in my own being is forged within the crucible of the narrative. What is most important about my own story resonates with the fiction I have entered, *as if* an imaginal field had been generated to hold both my narrative and the classic's plotline. Gerard Manley Hopkins, a British poet of the last century, wrote the following about the natural world and its analogy within himself as he watched the felling of an old ash tree in his garden: "I heard the sound and looking out and seeing it maimed, there came at that moment a great pang and I wished to die and not to see the inscapes of the world destroyed anymore" (*Poetic Image* 67). The world's inscapes, the interiority of things as well as their outward manifestation, was what he encouraged us to notice. This inscape is part of every literary classic that finds its correspondence in our own backdrop. Literature's purpose is less to give us an escape from our lives and more to offer pathways into its mythic soulscape. There seems then, to be two worlds addressed at the same time: the outer tangible landscape and the inner invisible, but felt and heard, inscape. When we reflect on them both at once, we enter the dominion of "the magical mirror."

A built-in paradox then arises. For these two stories—mine and the narrative I am reading—are different and yet surprisingly similar. What is different about them holds my fascination and allows me to enter another story; what is the same about them allows me to sense my own narrative's relation to it—that my "unique" narrative is in fact the story of the "other" as well. What can emerge from such a recognition is a felt sense of compassion for the plotline of others as well as a growing awareness of the unity of us all in our mysterious diversity. One discerns in this imaginal reading some field of resonance penetrated, or that energy flows between the classic story and me such that I gain some beneficent energy in the experience of that story. I am brought to feel emotions analogous to those felt by the characters whose lives I suddenly enter; in such emotional melding I enter into my own emotional life, with all of its moral complexities, openings, *cul de sacs*, sharp turns and unexpected twists and distortions. Out of this deep relationship, aspects of my personal myth are incarnated.

I have suggested to my students what I wish to share here. When you read, keep pen or pencil handy and pay close attention to what calls to be underlined, highlighted, even read aloud, or those places where you hesitate, go back and reread, write a few words in the margins, or are otherwise arrested by. It may be a passage of dialogue, a description of something or someone, even a small, incidental object like a handkerchief, an old scarf, or a broken cane, that you find significant. My sense is that at just these psychic and mythopoeic junctures—call them psychological crossroads or thresholds—that one's personal myth is stimulated, even disturbed, perhaps outraged in being challenged. However, at these intersections, or revelatory archeological sites, a deeper form of knowing is proffered if one allows time to meditate on the passage through a porous perspective.

Our personal mythologies may often be embellished, enriched, reordered, or transformed in the reading. Readers have discovered that at just these dwellings they are prompted to write about what is taking place, both in the narrative and in themselves, and these points are what I call mythopoeic moments, important reference points as well as reverence points. Such locales in space and time are where things heat up for the reader, gather sense and distill meaning—and we read always to experience these moments—quickening hot spots or sensitive nerve centers in the narrative where psychological and emotional relevance coagulate and stew. Something significant begins cooking. The pudding offers its proof in the pauses we allow, if they are long enough to smell the varied aromas coaxed from the slow heat of the plot's unfolding.

Miming the Myth from Memory

It may seem strange to speak of literary classics as ancestors, but they are. Akin to voices from the past, they have the capacity to shape our present by helping us to discern what in our contemporary world we continue to struggle with: power, violence, murder, vengeance, fidelity, homelessness, excess, slavery, resentments, prejudice, love, family order, rebirth, fate, destiny, freedom, the power of the past, to name a few. Contemplating these human qualities and actions through poems like *Moby-Dick* can be as initiating as they are illuminating and enjoyable.

Some deep psychological, emotional, even spiritual needs may be reclaimed as forms of inheritance that are both personal and communal. They incarnate through their plots' enactments the capacity to order our lives in ways that we cannot muster alone. They are not documents espousing political agendas but exciting mythic enactments of events that take place in all of us on some level of significance that we can attune ourselves to with sympathy and imaginal generosity.

Whose Myth Is It Anyway?

What could be more intriguing, other than learning the meaning of our nocturnal narratives, our dreams, than discovering the contours *as well as* the content of our personal myth. If we think of them for a moment, every story has some form of conflict in it. Something in an individual or even a collective life that seemed to have order and coherence suddenly goes awry, breaks down and shatters. Something in a relationship stumbles off the straight and true path. Dante the pilgrim wakes to discover he is lost in a dark wood; Odysseus finds himself stuck on an island with no way home; Antigone discovers that she is to be buried alive for wanting to give her dead brother a proper burial; Ishmael suddenly finds himself under the spell of a monomaniac captain intent on killing them all if that is the price to avenge his dismemberment by a White Whale.

Suddenly the story seizes our attention, like dreams that we wake up with and muse over for days, so bent and distorted might they have been, where friends attack us, we wear the clothes of the opposite sex, or find ourselves killing family members. Something has slipped off kilter and just as suddenly we have and are in a story. Getting off the track—this is the story's appeal. And does that appeal come on so strongly because we wish to make it right, to fix it? Perhaps. But something deeper is stirred in us by a narrative that goes off track that abruptly gives us a reason for demanding we now pay close and undistracted attention. I am interested, like everyone else, in this action, this insult to the normative, a rupture of the conventional and a deep crease in the everyday. So I ask at the beginning: what is it that insists on breaking through? What wants to be heard? What is it in Oedipus, or Inanna, or Dionysus in Euripedes' *The Bacchae* that struggles to speak out, to voice itself into being, not just in the story we are reading but in the part of the story deciphering us? There would be no interest in, much less attraction to, the story without some identification, by analogy, to our own narrative life.

When we return to a classic like Melville's epic less with the intention to treat it as an historical document informing us how people lived "back then," so it remains distant to our own world, or as grist for literary theory or clever explanation, but rather as a story that imitates and so shapes and forms our own personal mythology, then we read it at the deepest level of usefulness and apprehend something of ourselves in the same imaginative process. Moving to the most subtle and complex part of our nature, this whale tale offers a fuller understanding of our unfolding mythology. It also touches that part of our nature that is spiritual, that seeks after final causes, after the transcendent, the numinous and the invisible. Today we hear it called the sacred. Most all great and sustaining literature sooner or later in their plots implicate this deep sacred element that seems imbedded in us as much as the genes that give us a particular hair color or even contribute to our unique temperament.

I like two words that Thomas Moore offers in his introduction to the extremely successful *Care of the Soul: Care* and *Cultivation*. Without these two qualities in our lives, we run the risk of starving to death on several levels in the midst of plenty. Classic works do illustrate care and cultivation; they are also closer to renderings of deep psychologically-embodied and spiritual experiences that ignite in us these actions of care and cultivation. Some force in the soul is driven by the poetic action of a literary work; when we emerge from under the end of a story, we are somehow different human beings than when we entered the tube of the tale. We now have available to us another way of grasping and apprehending the world. Our world has been tweaked just enough for us to see clearly through the distortion, the curvature of the magic mirror, as it spirals back an image just recognizable enough to make us pause and ponder it.

This is the greatest gift of classic literature and what I hope to convey through an extended exploration of *Moby-Dick* as my paradigm: an alternative way of seeing to augment or shift our previous limited vision. Perhaps rather than "seeing," I should use the world "imagining," because it is not just sight-inflected but a profoundly altered sense of things in their interior life as well as their external vitality.

Moore writes at the end of his introduction to *Care of the Soul:* "Let us imagine care of the soul, then, as an application of poetics to everyday life" (xix). In this statement he ambles closer to what I am proposing by reading classics, these voices from the past that grow in strength for our present lives. Poetics, for the Greeks, meant a "making," or a "crafting." Making something of yourself is a poetic move. There exists an intimate correspondence between psyche and poiesis—a soulful making, through the stories we read and ingest as nutrients for the imaginal ground of our being. They have the capacity to make something of us that had not been kneaded or shaped or molded before. Here one's personal mythology rubs shoulders with the narrative actions of the past—actions that are really quite formidable when engaged in presence.

I am less interested in *explaining* Melville's tale of vengeance on a White Whale than I am in pointing to or alluding to what they seem to be about, what their interests are, what patterns yearn to emerge from them and what mythic structure they offer to some of life's immediate experiences. My intention is to steer you, the reader, to a string of these concerns and then allow you a way in, guided into the thick terrain of each chapter by the large concerns that will often be immediate to your own life and then invite you to engage those writing meditations that seem most pertinent to your unfolding narrative.

Page Structure

For this excursion, use any copy of the epic you find appealing and easy to read. I chose a leather-bound hardback volume published by Easton Press. It is aesthetically attractive, will tolerate many rereadings and its print size is charitable to the eyes. Regarding the pages of this book: each of the 365 entries is divided into four sections. 1. A citation from the epic that seemed to me particularly pertinent to the story's myth-making process; 2. A brief summary of what is taking place in the quoted material; 3. A reflection on the passage to open its implications to an individual life; 4. A suggested writing meditation so that you, the reader, may become the writer and track the implications of the quoted material through your own history.

Begin not necessarily by choosing each one to write on; rather, gravitate to those that carry more allure. Return, if you like, to others that initially had less interest. Use a journal and write in longhand rather than using a computer. Writing cursively invites a level of meditation that I believe typing sidesteps. I offer numerous reasons for writing long hand in my book, *Riting Myth, Mythic Writing: Plotting Your Personal Story* (2012), especially chapter 3: "The (W)riting Self." The trajectory of exploration, then, is from Ishmael's story to a larger meditation to a particular act of remembrance by you, the reader/(w)riter. In a sense, your engagement with the passages and with your own plotted narrative add to and complete the epic in a unique manner, even as you grow more intimate with your own story that will gather into greater presence through the double imaginal acts of reading and writing. In this rich process, not only will you cultivate a keener intimacy with Ishmael's spiritual and creative journey, you will come, I believe, to love more deeply by recollecting more broadly, the enduring outlines of your own unique myth. May Melville's whaling epic mirror your own fathomless depths.

Notes

The five chapter groupings of *Moby-Dick* are taken from Chris Sten's excellent mythological study of the epic: *The Weaver God, He Weaves: Melville and the Poetics of the Novel*. Kent, Ohio: Kent State UP, 1996. Used by permission of the author (11/11/2013).

Part I

Preparation for the Hunt
Chapters 1-23

It is only those who know neither an inner call nor an outer doctrine whose plight truly is desperate; that is to say, most of us today, in this labyrinth without and within the heart.

—Joseph Campbell, *The Hero With a Thousand Faces*, 17.

January 1. Extracts: Supplied by a Sub-sub Librarian

As touching the ancient authors generally, as well as the poets here appearing, these extracts are solely valuable or entertaining, as affording a glancing bird's-eye view of what has been promiscuously said, thought, fancied and sung of Leviathan, by many nations and generations, including our own (xv).

If asked, most readers of *Moby-Dick* will say the first line of the novel is the famous "Call me Ishmael." Not so. Yes, the narrative begins with these liquid three words, but the novel carries two prologues in its hold: "Etymology," the study of words and their histories, specifically the word "whale," and "Extracts" cited from above. Within its considerable pages are citations from world books, journals, memories, holy texts, ships' logs, letters, poems, novels, etchings, biographies, songs and chronicles—all of which vortex around the whale's seemingly ubiquitous presence. An "extract," you recall, is a distillation, a concentrated form of some substance, a primal or originary material of an element out of which flows a less concentrated form of the original intense substance. An extract is an essence. The whale is the extract out of which will flow the entire matter of Melville's alchemical epic.

Seeking our own extract, the substance of our essential nature, is a lifelong whale hunt of the soul to discover ourselves. I think of it as our nuclear core, a divine firm center, what gathers us up each day of our lives. It contains also what we extract from the world to give meaning to our lives. It is the core of our personal myth extracted from all our experiences and constitutes what we are born to steward and sustain. Extract is the ontological center of who we are, carbuncles and barnacles, flukes and tails, as well as the whale soul we each harbor within, always ready, given the right conditions, to breach into view.

Meditation

What three particular elements or qualities comprise your core being?

January 2. Chapter 1: Loomings

Call me Ishmael. Some years ago—never mind how long precisely—having little or no money in my purse, and nothing particular to interest me on shore, I thought I would sail about a little and see the watery part of the world . . . whenever it is a damp, drizzly November in my soul . . . then, I account it high time to get to sea as soon as I can. This is my substitute for pistol and ball (3).

The narrator Ishmael, for it is his story we are invited to enter, recites the terms under which he escapes the land, "a way I have of driving off the spleen and regulating the circulation" (3). He vacates the suffocating monotony of land-locked life to seek a soul adventure to refresh and re-ground him in the maze of daily existence. The sea is a primordial place of profound change and renewal. He is named, as are so many characters in the story, after figures from the Hebrew Bible, here the son of Hagar and Abraham, who will become father of a nation. Ishmael's name means "God shall hear." So he asks us to call him Ishmael. His real name? Perhaps; so we call him and call to him: "Ishmael," as we simultaneously call ourselves.

When I say these three words above I find that I too become the pilgrim whaler. He is anyone of us who answers the call to the strange world of seascape adventure, where the floor beneath is liquid, in motion, never the same from one instant to the next. We long at times to take on the identity of others in fiction; in fact, to leave the comfort of home—where the soul begins a search for open landscapes, new callings, perhaps a novel way of vacating the familiar life that has lost its vitality and purpose. To be called is both a blessing and a severe challenge; heeding it an act of courage. Callings are moments of grace; we relinquish control and clarity and yield to something original.

Meditation

What calling would you respond to in your present circumstances?

January 3: Chapter 1: Loomings

Why did the old Persians hold the sea holy? Why did the Greeks give it a separate deity, and own brother of Jove? Surely all this is not without meaning. And still deeper the meaning of that story of Narcissus, who because he could not grasp the tormenting, mild image he saw in the fountain, plunged into it and was drowned. But that same image, we ourselves see in all rivers and oceans. It is the image of the ungraspable phantom of life; and this is the key to it all (5).

Meditating on the power of water to evoke reveries, Ishmael plunges imaginatively and mythically deep into the element's mystery to enter a rich musing through both water's nature as well as the aperture of the myth of Narcissus and Echo. But not before he surveys the divine figures associated with water's substance, which is the only natural element that can mirror us back to ourselves. The phantom of life we cannot grasp seems to be the self who stares into the water but cannot be possessed. Myths seem to carry less explanation than ways of thinking about the mystery of what cannot be grasped analytically.

Water invites meditation. Sit by a river, cruise on a ship and look over the side, swim well beyond the shoreline of a lake or ocean and feel the daring attraction and danger of water. Water refreshes us, supports us and can entomb us when it swallows us whole or enwomb us when it revives our spirit and purpose. We too consist primarily of water and so carry a natural affinity with its nature. It can beckon us to leave for a time the solidity of the shore and inhabit its constantly shifting substance—ever-changing, moving, able to transform our moods, our inner aquatic landscape, our limpid liquid self. The world opens to us to afford enriching depth through water's aperture.

Meditation

Has a river, an ocean, or a lake played a significant role in your history? Describe its impact on you.

January 4. Chapter 1: Loomings

Though I cannot tell why it was exactly that those stage managers, the Fates, put me down for this shabby part of a whaling voyage, when others were set down for magnificent parts in high tragedies, and short and easy parts in genteel comedies, and jolly parts in farces . . . .

Chief among these motives was the overwhelming idea of the great whale himself. Such a portentous and mysterious monster roused all my curiosity [and] helped to sway me to my wish (7).

Ishmael muses on the forces, impulses and invisible powers guiding and pulling on him to set sail, this time not as a merchant seaman but as a whaler. While he considers his role in the whaling drama to be less than satisfying, he knows that no accident attends his calling; rather, he "found part of the grand programme of Providence" (7) decided long ago. He is part of a pattern of the way the world is destined to unfold and has submitted to fulfilling his small part in the performance enacted with others on the world's vast watery stage. The main protagonist is Leviathan itself, around which the entire production will ripen.

Feeling that one's life is not incidental or arbitrary, much less devoid of meaning or insignificance, but is to the contrary part of a mysterious script, can offer solace in different periods of one's drama. It is worth considering one's life as a literary genre: lyric, tragic, comic or epic, each of which carries the patterned energy of one's life and allows one to consider if one is in the right play and character role in the narrative that will afford the most growth. Each of us lives within a patterned field of thought and action that scripts the large contours of our personal myth; it places us in the world with a sense of dramatic significance as we live out our beliefs, prejudices, desires and dreams.

Meditation

Have you sensed your life is destined, yet allows for free choices?

January 5. Chapter 3: The Spouter-Inn

Upon entering the place I found a number of young seamen gathered about a table, examining by a dim light divers specimens of *skrimshander*. I sought the landlord, and telling him I desired to be accommodated with a room, received for answer that his house was full--not a bed unoccupied. "But avast," he added, tapping his forehead, "you haint no objections to sharing a harpooneer's blanket, have ye? I s'pose you are goin' a whalin', so you'd better get used to that sort of thing" (15).

Ishmael has just entered The Spouter-Inn owned by Peter Coffin. This section of New Bedford is shabby, dark and harbors cheap lodgings. It stands as one of numerous sites of his many initiations. It is a mythic halfway house, between the commerce of the city and the more fluid domain of the whale grounds. This place of the proprietor, Peter Coffin, portends a death—a leaving or divesting of one life in order to don another. The implication is that he will not be alone but will from this time forward be adjusting to a new affiliation with a larger world community, beginning with one unknown mate whose room he will share. Ishmael's spiritual journey begins and ends with a coffin.

When in those moments of our lives that we risk something by taking a step out of the familiar and into what life has in store for us, we begin a voyage of self-discovery through what is initially strange and unpredictable. The world has a freer hand in moving towards us to accommodate our curiousity. We must first, however, take the initial step: to journey across a well-trod threshold into unknown landscapes peopled by those who may be much different from us. Such a transition requires us to hear a calling, then to act on it with faith, courage, trust and a bit of wildness. We can, however, choose to stay at home.

Meditation

What have you done, or are doing, to revitalize and refresh your life?

January 6. Chapter 3: The Spouter-Inn

The more I pondered over this harpooneer, the more I abominated the thought of sleeping with him. It was fair to presume that being a harpooneer, his linen or woolen, as the case might be, would not be of the tidiest, certainly none of the finest. I began to twitch all over . . . . how could I tell from what vile hole he had been been coming?

"Landlord! I've changed my mind about that harpooneer. –I shan't sleep with him. I'll try the bench here" (18).

Worried about the differences between them, Ishmael reconsiders his decision to share the last bed in the inn with a foreign whaler. His fear of the unknown as well as his assumptions persuade him to play it safe and to sleep alone on a downstairs bench rather than in a communal bed. His conventions and stereotypes tumble forward to bolster his decision. All the fears cling to his resolution like barnacles to a ship's hull. Better be safe than sorry. He tells Peter Coffin he will make due on a hard wooden bench alone than in a soft bed with a foreign, and probably filthy, other. Discomfort is less forbidding than uncertainty.

Our assumptions, many well-founded, can often serve to foreclose on the world, especially in its uncertainty. The stronger temptation is to cling to our past experiences rather than risk a breakthrough into the unfamiliar by entertaining the possibility that what we fear could be unfounded. Our images can create roadblocks that may keep us safe and secure but at the expense of sterile familiarity. Risk has its price tag, but playing it safe can eventually exact a higher toll. Overcoming assumptions that stifle risking ourselves into new territory is an act of courage. Complacency can be its own coffin. Security and safety may be two of the many nails that secure the lid for years or a lifetime.

Meditation

When have overriding your assumptions about another pushed you to reassess your judgments of another's character?

January 7. Chapter 3: The Spouter-Inn

But what is this on the chest? I took it up, and held it close to the light and felt it, and smelt it, and tried every way possible to arrive at some satisfactory conclusion concerning it. I can compare it to nothing but a large door mat, ornamented at the edges with little tinkling tags . . . . I put it on, to try it, and it weighed me down like a hamper, being uncommonly shaggy and thick . . . . I went up in it to a bit of glass stuck against the wall, and I never saw such a sight in my life. I tore myself out of it in such a hurry that I gave myself a kink in the neck (22).

Curious about this unseen stranger, Ishmael puts on the skin of the harpooneer, even as he tries to interpret what this animal skin is, so foreign does it seem from anything he has ever seen or worn. Only a doormat comes to mind that he associates with this smelly skin that is decorated, damp and shaggy. The language Ishmael uses--"I put it on, to try it"--is the language of the try-pots on board the whaling ship, in which the whale's flesh is boiled to yield its oily essence. In the mirror the self-reflecting Ishmael repeats part of the Narcissus myth in that the image in the glass is both strange and familiar, both himself and other at the same instant, a strange double which flusters him.

When are we willing to slip on the skin of another, to walk in another's shoes, sandals or moccasins, in order to see the world and one's self from such a novel perspective? Here, the other in one's self-image allows Ishmael for an instant to become the harpooneer. When we acquire a double vision of self and other simultaneously, we enter a mythic way of seeing in both power and perception. We comprehend the new through a familiar aperture and we envision the familiar in a new way. In so doing, our assumptions, if not shattered, are severely shaken. A new vision can then breach into our field of vision to alter our myth.

Meditation

When have you worn the skin of another to see how the other sees?

January 8. Chapter 3: The Spouter-Inn

Meanwhile, he continued the business of undressing, and at last showed his chest and arms. As I live, these covered parts of him were checkered with the same squares as his face; his back too was all over the same dark squares . . . . Still more, his very legs were marked, as if a parcel of dark green frogs were running up the trunks of young palms. It was now quite plain that he must be some abominable savage or other shipped aboard of a whaleman in the South Seas, and so landed in this Christian country. I quaked to think of it (24).

Ishmael meets Queequeg in the darkness of night and in the pale light of ignorance. He perceives the doubled inky shapes on the islander's body and struggles to interpret them according to his own narrow band of categories. It is an important moment because the epic is a "see" voyage of interpretation as well as a whale hunt. Ishmael sees through his fear of the unknown; he thus makes ghastly assumptions about his roommate. No words have yet been spoken between them. Ishmael's conjectures create a phantom reality of Queequeg, one who is not present as himself but a figure of Ishmael's threatened imagination.

Writ large, nations often enter wars with adversaries because their understanding of the other is more fear-based or domination-based than the facts disclose. Fearful, we imagine the unknown or different as a threat to our self-preservation, including preserving familiar prejudices and judgments. How we interpret the unknown mirrors the terms of the myth we are living in and out. What we see as different, however, can, if one opens to it, reveal something of ourselves that is present in the foreignness of the other: "Thou art that." Secure in our own brand of knowing, however, we may deflect the dark double in ourselves.

Meditation

Has fear or prejudice persuaded you to imagine the worst of a person or situation because you anticipated a threat to your safety?

January 9. Chapter 3: The Spouter-Inn

"Who-e debel you?"—he at last said—"you no speak-e, dam-me, I kill-e." And so saying the lighted tomahawk began flourishing about me in the dark.

"Landlord, for God's sake, Peter Coffin!" shouted I. "Landlord! Watch! Coffin! Angels! save me!"

. . . .

"You gettee in," he added, motioning to me with his tomahawk, and throwing the clothes to one side. He really did this in not only a civil but a really kind and charitable way. I stood looking at him a moment. For all his tattooings, he was on the whole a clean, comely looking cannibal. What's all this fuss I have been making about, thought I to myself—the man's a human being just as I am. . . (26).

Terror and desperation soon yield to calm acceptance and even a respectful regard for Queequeg as Ishmael settles down and beds with the cannibal, who still sports his tomahawk. Images of coffins, Lord, Angels, Salvation are prelude to Ishmael gazing at the "terrible other" and seeing through his foreign nature to the goodness below the surface of his inked skin. Fear yields to a fast friendship in embracing what was only moments before fear-engendering and life-threatening.

This comic vignette leads us to consider what we each fear as foreign when the familiar is held in check by the strange, the unruly, the savage that terrifies—be it a person, an idea, an event, a diagnosis, or an image. Might there be something to befriend in what first appears to estrange and unsettle? Perhaps it has the capacity to comfort and guide us if we are willing to bed down with it; instead of hiding under the quilt, we might reach a place of sharing our covers with it.

Meditation

When were you terrified by something or someone that you gradually or suddenly came to befriend and embrace?

January 10. Chapter 4: The Counterpane

Upon waking next morning about daylight, I found Queequeg's arm thrown over me in the most loving and affectionate manner. You had almost thought I had been his wife. The counterpane was of patchwork, full of odd little parti-colored squares and triangles; and this arm of his tattooed all over with an interminable Cretan labyrinth of a figure, no two parts of which were of one precise shade . . . [which] looked for all the world like a strip of that same patchwork quilt (28).

Ishmael muses in the morning light on how the bed cover, with its intricate design, replicates Queequeg's own patchwork pattern tattooed on his arm. A doubling is what strikes Ishmael, even as he feels the affection from this man he has entered the night world with. That he compares it with the Greek mythological image of the Cretan labyrinth reclaims the story of the Minotaur and Daedelus the artificer who initially designed it. When later the Greek Theseus was sent to slay the Minotaur, he was aided by Ariadne into and out of the maze. Perhaps Queequeg is Ishmael's Ariadne who will aid him in his journey into and out of the maze that leads to the Grail: the White Whale. Such a mythic overlay in the scene above provides a rich mythic overlay to the story.

One mythic narrative mirrors or doubles the second and places the Narcissus myth, with its seductive doubling, as the central action in our self-reflective pilgrimage. We may see double, double over, or even double down in our own adventure; double-trouble may seek us out to awaken us in the act of reflection to a doubling of what our life journey means and then orient ourselves to it. When we hear or read stories, we may also sense how they in part double our own life. Such a discovery can reveal the mythic underpinnings of our identity through reflection.

Meditation

What experience in your life revealed two seemingly disparate events or ideas that, upon reflection, were seen as doubles of one another?

January 11. Chapter 6: The Street

In New Bedford, fathers, they say, give whales for dowers to their daughters, and portion off their nieces with a few porpoises a-piece. You must go to New Bedford to see a brilliant wedding; for, they say, they have reservoirs of oil in every house, and every night recklessly burn their lengths in spermaceti candles.

. . . .

And the women of New Bedford, they bloom like their own red roses. But roses only bloom in summer; whereas the fine carnation of their cheeks is perennial as sunlight in the seventh heavens (35-36).

Full of ambition, modern, a locale where races from throughout the world gather is New Bedford, an icon of progress, opulence, commerce and consumption. Ishmael's tone is lighthearted, exaggerated and dark as he describes this place, "a land of oil, true enough" (35). It is lush, playful and excessive in its burning whale fluids, where whales are often an essential part of dowries. The word "recklessly" refers to their abuse of spermaceti candles; it portrays the city as a site of excess, a sense of enormous appetite, even as Ishmael praises its elegance.

New Bedford is a grotesque portrait of over-consumption, of waste and too muchness; it seems devoid of limits and moderation. It feeds on whales and porpoises without restraint and treats the natural order with an aloof disdain. Bloated and consumed by its own wants, it carries the cargo of self-serving excess. New Bedford reflects a modern tendency to short-term satisfaction with a myopic vision of long-term sustainability. America's massive appetite will be satisfied at the expense of the limits of the natural order's resources. Whales are domesticated as dowry gifts for the wealthy. The town's name emphasizes the word "new" and carries the novelty of the most current fad or fashion.

Meditation

Where in your own life might excessive consumption be moderated?

January 12. Chapter 7: The Chapel

Oh! ye whose dead lie buried beneath the green grass; who standing among flowers can say—here, here lies my beloved; ye know not this desolation that broods in bosoms like these. What bitter blanks in those black-bordered marbles which cover no ashes! What despair in those immovable inscriptions . . . . As well might those tablets stand in the cave of Elephanta as here (39).

When he and Queequeg enter the seaman's chapel, Ishmael is attracted to the cenotaphs of sailors whose bodies were never recovered from the sea. The cenotaphs memorialize in words on marble walls those who are absent but not forgotten. "Sacred to the memory of..." (38). Reading the inscriptions leads Ishmael into a reverie on the absence of men's bodies replaced by words; they call up and recover the men's absence in place. No bodies, only words as stand-ins for the missing ashes of flesh. He alludes to the cave of Elephanta on a strip of land close to Mumbai Harbor consisting of both Hindu and Buddhist caves, with the former devoted to the god Shiva, the Hindu deity as destroyer and transformer; a huge stone statue of an elephant guards one of its entrances (www.wikipedia/elephantacave). The words are portable.

Place holds no meaning for the families of dead whalemen; only blankness, a keyword in the lexicon of the whale tale. Words can create out of themselves in the imagination of the reader a presence even when its referent is absent. Words elicit presence in an absent way, as understudies for what is now present imaginally. The epic itself is a recorded passage gathering in the sea of memory. Recollection in words is a powerful imaginal form of re-presencing, re-visioning and re-forming experiences out of the traceless immensity of the sea's surface.

Meditation

What have you written or spoken that reanimated something or someone from the dead to live once again in your and others' memory?

January 13. Chapter 7: The Chapel

Yes, there is death in this business of whaling—a speechlessly quick chaotic bundling of a man into Eternity. But what then? Methinks we have hugely mistaken this matter of Life and Death. Methinks that what they call my shadow here on earth is my true substance. Methinks that in looking at things spiritual, we are too much like oysters observing the sun through the water .... Methinks my body is but the lees of my better being. In fact take my body who will, take it I say, it is not me (40).

Ishmael continues to muse on the cenotaphs, which conjures a larger metaphysical reflection on fundamental realities of life and death. His is an ancient reverie of reversal: what appears as shadow is actual reality, while his seemingly substantial physical flesh is less material than it appears. From here he draws the rich analogy of an oyster looking through its watery context to view the sun while thinking its perception is through "the thinnest of air" (40). The questions of perception and interpretation assume center stage in his imagination as he prepares to embark across the skin of the sea and to peer as best he can into its mysterious depths. His initiation is almost complete.

A philosophical or psychological moment of awakening can perturb our comfortable worldview and astonish us into another mode of seeing. In such revelatory instances what we thought was central in our life can often slide to the margins and what we had relegated to our horizontal perception may suddenly crowd into focus. It is as if we need a jolt of perceiving differently to equip us for a new story or life adventure. The older sustaining vision's shelf life has expired.

Meditation

When has something you read, saw, thought or met suddenly altered your familiar way of understanding into a new angle of vision?

January 14. Chapter 8: The Pulpit

No, thought I, there must be some sober reason for this thing; furthermore, it must symbolize something unseen. Can it be, then, that by that act of physical isolation, he signifies his spiritual withdrawal for the time, from all outward worldly ties and connexions? Yes, for replenished with the meat and wine of the word, to the faithful man of God, this pulpit, I see, is a self-containing stronghold—a lofty Ehrenbreitstein, with a perennial well of water within the walls (42).

Ishmael watches in amazement as the erstwhile whaleman, now preacher, Father Mapple, makes his way to his pulpit, which is shaped like a ship's prow. After climbing into his pulpit-fortress, Mapple turns and pulls his ship's ladder up behind him, sealing himself in his own spiritual citadel. Reference to the Ehrenbreitstein fortress on the banks of the Rhine river across from the town of Koblenz was built in the 19th century to guard the Rhine region from French invasions www.Wikipedia/Ehrenbreitstein/fortress. Ishmael sees Mapple's behavior in a double vision, one visible, the other invisible. The entire epic will follow this doubling, grounded in the double image of the Narcissus myth to allow history and myth to share the same bunk.

Recognizing the invisible realm in correspondence with the visible world locates the epic and our own band of awareness within a spiritual quest: one reality becomes two if we have the eyes to see behind the phenomenal world in what might be called a mytho-poetic angle of vision of the soul's interior motion. The visible world is tinctured by the invisible realities of being. The whale itself is a perfect metaphor for this interplay of visible with invisible forces in nature and human nature. Grasping some dimension of this reality enriches our understanding.

Meditation

Where in your own life have invisible presences played an important role in shaping your beliefs and general development?

January 15. Chapter 8: The Pulpit

Nor was the pulpit itself without a trace of the same sea-taste that had achieved the ladder and the picture. Its paneled front was in the likeness of a ship's bluff bows, and the Holy Bible rested on a projecting piece of scroll work, fashioned after a ship's fiddle-headed beak.

What could be more full of meaning?—for the pulpit is ever this earth's foremost part; all the rest comes in its rear; the pulpit leads the world . . . . Yes, the world's a ship on its passage out, and not a voyage complete; and the pulpit is its prow (43).

Ishmael's poetic and spiritual imagination regularly takes a simple scene or object and discerns in it metaphorical and metaphysical possibilities through likeness or "as-if" analogies. Pulpit becomes ship's prow, the Bible part of the ships ornate scroll work; the pulpit is the forehead of the world and leads it through the seas of experience. The Bible is set forth as a text that guides large segments of the world's population. Ishmael's quest is to dive deep into its pages, interpreting many of its passages, guided largely by religious zeal and the written word of God. As a ship, the world is still executing its maiden voyage.

To see into what is invisibly present is the task of the visionary artist and the mystic, both constellated in the outcast Ishmael, who sees all from the margins. His task as whaler/writer is to instruct us into a similar kind of seeing by analogy. His lucrative imagination reveals to us readers how to discern the passages of the journey. Central to America's mythology is the Bible as the strong ship of state, a text whose passages are to be incorporated into one's spiritual journey. We each inhabit a pulpit from where we survey the seas of our life and speak it.

Meditation

What pulpit do you listen to or speak from? What is the content of the Scripture you embody that serves as an act of faith on your life voyage?

January 16. Chapter 9: The Sermon

"Shipmates, this book, containing only four chapters—four yarns—is one of the smallest strands in the mighty cable of the Scriptures. Yet what depths of the soul Jonah's deep sealine sound! what a pregnant lesson to us is this prophet! What a noble thing is that canticle in the fish's belly! . . . we sound with him to the kelpy bottom of the waters; sea-weed and all the slime of the sea is about us! But *what* is this lesson that the book of Jonah teaches? Shipmates, it is a two-stranded lesson, a lesson to us all as sinful men. . ." (46).

Father Mapple exhorts his congregation to venture with him into the brief but mighty passages of the Old Testament story of one soul who attempted to escape his destiny but who in suffering finally yielded to God's call to speak His word where it was most needed. The Jonah narrative dives fathoms down to touch the deep interior directly in a powerful epic of the lost soul who is revived through God's grace. Few biblical stories touch the profundity of Jonah, who defied God by choosing to obey himself, is devoured and subsequently delivered to fulfill a delayed destiny. He is transformed in Leviathan's belly.

The Hebrew Bible offers us a universal pattern of existence through a fierce devotion to particular narratives. Jonah exists in any of us who have, from fear or simple refusal of one's heroic calling, preferred to slip the knot of destiny and follow one's own self-willing. Anyone who has denied the truth of his/her trajectory, suffered and finally yielded to forces larger than oneself, has ingested the Jonah narrative. Identifying the fish that can or has devoured us offers a deeper insight into the sea journey. The Jonah story is another aperture into the entirety of the whale narrative Ishmael relates to offer a double vision.

Meditation

When have you contrived to escape or default on what you sense deeply is your destiny? Have you, over time, yielded to it?

January 17. Chapter 9: The Sermon

"All dressed and dusty as he is, Jonah throws himself into his berth, and finds the little state-room ceiling almost resting on his forehead. The air is close, and Jonah gasps. Then, in that contracted hole, sunk, too, beneath the ship's water-line, Jonah feels the heralding presentiment of that stifling hour, when the whale shall hold him in the smallest of his bowels' wards.

'Oh! so my conscience hangs in me!' he groans, 'straight upwards, so it burns; but the chambers of my soul are all in crookedness!'" (48-49).

As Father Mapple recounts the narrative, Jonah struggles to free himself from God's command by hiding deep in the bowels of the ship. Perhaps it is the ship's womb, however. But oppression, fear, guilt and shame torque his soul into the same "crooked" condition as the swinging lamp's oscillation in his quarters. The close space appears to reflect the moral condition of his actions when he becomes more fully conscious of what he is doing in such a casket-like space, which doubles as his "berth" place. He shares with Ahab all the torments and scourges of a wounded soul attempting to escape God's destiny. In this cramped space, Jonah suffers both death and birth in a double action.

As readers, we feel the torments of a soul twisted out of context and coherence. When the soul is mangled into an unnatural shape, anguish and anxiety may explode throughout it. Doing his/her own bidding out of fear can twist one into a grotesque distortion of oneself, as any of us has experienced when we deny or recoil from our authentic calling: "Call me Terrified" might be Jonah's rejoinder to Ishmael's assertion earlier. Others may even remain deaf to the call.

Meditation

Describe a life situation in which contemplating an important decision or action left you contorted and crooked.

January 18. Chapter 9: The Sermon

"And now behold Jonah taken up as an anchor and dropped into the sea; when instantly an oily calmness floats out from the east, and the sea is still, as Jonah carries down the gale with him, leaving smooth water behind. He goes down in the whirling heart of such a masterless commotion that he scarce heeds the moment when he drops seething into the yawning jaws awaiting him; and the whale shoots-to all his ivory teeth . . . . Then Jonah prayed unto the Lord out of the fish's belly . . . . He leaves all his deliverance to God . . . . And here, shipmates, is true and faithful repentance" (51).

As the direct cause of the cursed storm that threatens to capsize the ship, Jonah is gathered up by the crew and thrown overboard, an isolato now severed from the human community and cast into the maw of nature's turbulence. All grows calm on the surface while below chaos roils. God's instrument, the whale, swallows Jonah into itself where he is held, in terror, in its belly, there eventually to offer himself to God when he accepts the consequences of his choices. In the briny darkness he is delivered from his own fears and self-willing.

Jonah's story is our story. From chaos to calm, from belligerent rebel to a serene surrender, from acts of willfulness to a more willing yielding—what set of behaviors, often of our own making, bring each of us in life into the belly of Leviathan? Cast off from the human community can be the first instance of our re-integration after a major change of heart, a *metanoia* of intentions and a renewal of our life's true purpose. We hear others' stories of descent and devouring and can be moved, even transformed by such power in the narrative because it affects our own thought patterns and behavior in witnessing them.

Meditation

What has been your experience of finding yourself in the whale's belly? What led you to be finally vomited out onto new or secure land?

January 19. Chapter 9: The Sermon

"But God is everywhere; Tarshish he never reached. As we have seen, God came upon him in the whale, and swallowed him down to living gulfs of doom . . . . Then God spake unto the fish; and from the shuddering cold and blackness of the sea, the whale came breeching up towards the warm and pleasant sun . . . and 'vomited out Jonah upon the dry land;' when the word of the Lord came a second time; and Jonah, bruised and beaten . . . did the Almighty's bidding. And what was that, shipmates? To preach the Truth to the face of Falsehood! That was it!" (52).

Father Mapple's impassioned recounting of one of the most dramatic narratives of the Old Testament unites the natural, supernatural and human orders in an intricately webbed trinitarian tale of remembrances in recollecting the Biblical story and Ishmael's recollection of his own voyage. A double story, as God's word comes a second time, on this occasion to be both heard and heeded. So much of the plot of *Moby-Dick* is composed of the act of doubling, begun with the Narcissus story and now with God's words doubled. Reflection is the key act of imagination, a constant reversion to see and hear anew.

It is not difficult to remember when out of fear, or a sense of failure or willfulness, we tried to deflect our destiny for what *we* desired. Jonah's story reveals the infernal consequences that may be leveled at us in moments of our willful detour. Each of us is given our own vision of "preaching the Truth to the face of Falsehood" that requires enormous courage and self-sacrifice. In our spiritual quests, we may question our motives even while we have revealed to us our own pursuit of what is a fundamental verity of our destiny.

Meditation

What aspect of your Truth do you feel compelled or called to speak in the face of what you believe warrants correction or amending?

January 20. Chapter 10: A Bosom Friend

With much interest I sat watching him. Savage though he was, and hideously marred about the face—at least to my taste—his countenance yet had a something in it which was by no means disagreeable. You cannot hide the soul. Through all his unearthly tattooings, I thought I saw the traces of a simple honest heart; and in his large, deep eyes, fiery black and bold, there seemed tokens of a spirit that would dare a thousand devils .
. . . He looked like a man who had never cringed and never had had a creditor (54).

Returning from the Chapel to the Spouter-Inn, Ishmael comes across Queequeg sitting in solitude by the fire first gently whittling away at the nose of his little negro idol, then turning the pages of a book he picks up. He sees Queequeg again but anew. Ishmael's sight has shifted as a result of his pilgrimage to the Chapel and the story of Jonah. He sees now through what is different about them to what is shared in all humanity: familiarity, a simple honest heart, fearlessness and independence. Both personal experiences as well as narratives themselves have the capacity to alter perception; Ishmael can now see through Queequeg's tattoos, its own text, to a more universal dimension of him. The once strange "other" is now a mirrored double of himself.

Seeing double, revisioning, returning to what one believed one knew, but with an altered consciousness, can reveal something numinously strange in the mundane familiar if one is open and receptive to reconsidering one's judgments and even suspending them for a moment. One sees through in a moment of revelation in reflection what earlier had been catalogued and filed away, diminishing it in the process. Something/someone alters in his/her own presence.

Meditation

Describe a person you thought you had figured out and catalogued away, but who on closer discernment became someone different.

January 21. Chapter 10: A Bosom Friend

I had noticed also that Queequeg never consorted at all, or but very little, with the other seamen in the inn . . . . All this struck me as mighty singular; yet upon second thoughts, there was something almost sublime in it. Here was a man some twenty thousand miles from home, by the way of Cape Horn . . . . and yet he seemed entirely at his ease; preserving the utmost serenity; content with his own companionship; always equal to himself. Surely this was a touch of fine philosophy (55).

Ishmael deepens his vision of and by means of Queequeg, his brother now, who elicits from him some of those same qualities of serenity, equanimity, ease and self-containment, all of which Ishmael lacked when he began his narrative voyage. His vision is now double: he sees the invisible soul through the physical body and its demeanor. He is learning by the example of his guide to become more self-defined, less frantic, less suicidal, less self-absorbed and more in keeping with a soul serene in its own skin. His tutor teaches by example, not by words. Ishmael teaches *us*, however, through the language of narrative which has the capacity to double our own story.

It can be enough to change one's heart from bitterness and resentment, as Ishmael began, to one of grace and largesse simply by reflecting deeply on those qualities lived out incarnately in another; one bears witness to his/her guide's wisdom. To simply witness the virtues of another can be sufficient for our imagination to construct a sense of those qualities through both initiation and emulation. Our hearts can be transformed by the presence of goodness. We have the power to become the things we contemplate, which can initiate us to the good. Narratives themselves can be powerful patterned presences to recruit us as well.

Meditation

When were you transformed by the presence of someone or something you deeply admired?

January 22. Chapter 10: A Bosom Friend

As I sat there in that now lonely room; the fire burning low, in that mild stage when, after its first intensity has warmed the air, it then only glows to be looked at; the evening shades and phantoms gathering round the casements, and peering in upon us silent, solitary twain; the storm booming without in solemn swells; I began to be sensible of strange feelings. I felt a melting in me. No more my splintered heart and maddened hand were turned against the wolfish world. This soothing savage had redeemed it .
. . .

And then we sat exchanging puffs from that wild pipe of his, and keeping it regularly passing between us (55-56).

In a rare moment of solitude and serenity Ishmael experiences a "see change" within his splintered heart. As the sheer presence alone of Queequeg, the soft glow of the coals, the shadowed world's presence against the light of the fire and the vast silence all conspire to transform the soul of one man whose heart had grown, through constant discord, cankerous and brittle against the world. Living antithetically to the world's patterns, Ishmael now melts down and through his spite, isolation, and seething resentments into the softer glow of human friendship coaxed by Queequeg's affection.

At times only the love of another given freely is sufficient to change the course and the construction of our lives. Unconditional acceptance by another can restore and redeem us; it is enough to melt amassed acerbities that deflect us bitterly from life toward impulses of spiritual or physical suicide. Nothing less than a miracle is it for a calcified self and splintered heart to heal in the presence of unconditional love. Not correction but compassion is far more potent.

Meditation

Describe a situation when your accepting another unconditionally or being accepted in the same manner, changed both of you.

January 23. Chapter 10: A Bosom Friend

If there yet lurked any ice of indifference towards me in the Pagan's breast, this pleasant, genial smoke we had, soon thawed it out, and left us cronies. He seemed to take to me quite as naturally and unbiddenly as I to him . . . [as]he pressed his forehead against mine, clasped me round the waist, and said that henceforth we were married, meaning, in his country's phrase, that we were bosom friends; he would gladly die for me, if need should be. In a countryman, this sudden flame of friendship would have seemed far too premature . . . (56).

Once softened, Ishmael is ripe to accept and enter into a lasting friendship with the pagan Queequeg, the most culturally removed from him yet very much his double. When all differences of race, culture, religion and traditions dissolve into one another, subsumed by the powerful enchantment of marital affection and mutual loyalty, the grace of giving one's self over to another becomes a new experience for Ishmael. Queequeg opens his heart to a more universal principle at work in the world: care for another's well-being and a vow of sacrifice to guard that well-being from all harm.

The deep bonds of unconditional affection shared by two people in friendship is often a rare experience; anyone is blessed to be so befriended. An opulent irony occurs when all differences assume a minor key in the larger musical harmony of similar shared affection. The effect can be so profound as to reorient and recalibrate a person's attitudes and even worldview. Feeling that deep relatedness with another may be one way that grace enters one's field to permanently alter it through a mutual sense of shared community.

Meditation

Who has been your most valued friend in life? What predominant qualities drew you to him/her?

January 24. Chapter 10: A Bosom Friend

I was a good Christian; born and bred in the bosom of the infallible Presbyterian Church. How then could I unite with this wild idolator in worshipping his piece of wood? But what is worship? thought I. Do you suppose now, Ishmael, that the magnanimous God of heaven and earth—pagans and all included—can possibly be jealous of an insignificant bit of black wood? Impossible! But what is worship?—to do the will of God? *that* is worship. And what is the will of God?—to do to my fellow man what I would have my fellow man do to me—*that* is the will of God. Now, Queequeg is my fellow man (57).

Ishmael has been watching Queequeg at his evening prayers and feeling a growing unease about how he would respond if his mate asked him to join him in worship. He retreats for a moment to have a conversation with himself in a doubling of his own presence about what God's will consists of. He addresses himself as other, naming himself explicitly. He poses the most fundamental question and arrives logically at a response that captures the largesse of love and generosity: that one treat others as one wishes to be treated, so that the other doubles oneself. Now not God but the individual chooses freely to worship in such an ecumenical manner by following God's will.

Reflecting on how each of us treats others provides a mirror on how we treat ourselves. We are the other mirrored back to us, so to be responsible for the welfare of another is to encourage a like treatment of ourselves. Read the world as double, as reflection in the spirit of the Narcissus myth and one will have a truth revealed, as in a clear glass. The world of worship is an authentic doubling of who I am. It rests on the proposition that finally we are all communally connected.

Meditation

What fundamental principle or attitude guides you in your treatment of yourself and others?

January 25. Chapter 11: Nightgown

The more so, I say, because truly to enjoy bodily warmth, some small part of you must be cold, for there is no quality in this world that is not what it is merely by contrast. Nothing exists in itself . . . . For the height of this sort of deliciousness is to have nothing but the blankets between you and your snugness and the cold of the outer air. Then there you lie like the one warm spark in the heart of an arctic crystal (58).

Ever the philosopher poet, Ishmael wonders about the smallest human experience and extracts from it delightful reflections both fresh and animated. He meditates on the contrasts of opposites that in fact yield an underlying unity, not unlike Ishmael himself and Queequeg together as the genesis of a communal rhizome. Warm and cold are as different and distinct as the two men cozied under covers. When the two opposites conjoin, they form a wholeness of experience wherein one completes the other. Rather than creating dis-ease, for a supple imagination, opposites are necessary. Their contrasts offer a full lived experience. Where he once saw diversity, even antagonism, now under the imaginal presence of two, Ishmael senses a double vision where "nothing exists in itself." Everything in existence is conjoined.

Sensing harmony where once discord ruled one's sensibilities is a major step towards a fuller perception in life. Antagonisms can move to an integrated harmony without either side losing its distinct character. One's nose exposed to the cold offers the rest of the body a delicious warmth. One honors and embraces its opposite. Through the double sensations of warm and cold, a new sensation arises, a third degree, to affirm the existence of contrasts' ability to form a union. Contrast in and of itself need not be oppositional but a place of fresh communion.

Meditation

Explore where in your life a conflict of opposite tendencies or impulses or incidents might be amenable to an arising unity.

January 26. Chapter 11: Nightgown

Be it said, that though I had felt such a strong repugnance to his smoking in the bed the night before, yet see how elastic our stiff prejudices grow when once loves comes to bend them. For now I liked nothing better than to have Queequeg smoking by me, even in bed, because he seemed to be full of such serene household joy then . . . . I was only alive to the condensed confidential comfortableness of sharing a pipe and a blanket with a real friend (59).

Ishmael's earlier "melting" in Queequeg's presence has now opened to the fullness of love for another that includes several effects:
 1. It encourages acceptance of another without conditions.
 2. It evaporates prejudices or puts them in a modulated perspective.
 3. It glories in the pleasures of another.
 4. It connects one to another in joy.
 5. It brings the other to life and into a presence more fully.
All of these qualities and attitudes, though he is now recollecting a voyage long completed, will serve him on the watery road ahead. Queequeg teaches Ishmael how to be "at home" with himself.

Love in its fullness propagates acceptance, participation with one's whole being, a stretching of ourselves in thought and action even as it dismantles the ego, with its attendant appetites and preoccupations, including that of self-absorption. Love both concentrates our attention while it diffuses self-interest. Love also elevates the simplest human interaction to that of a priceless gift given gratuitously to another, free of drawstrings. In love, our greatest joy can be the well-being not of ourselves but of our other-in-love. Generosity would seem to lurk below unconditional love, where no reservations have a foothold.

Meditation

Describe a simple moment with a loved one that afforded each of you great joy and pleasure. What needed to be present for this occasion?

January 27. Chapter 12: Biographical

Queequeg was a native of Kokovoko, an island far away to the West and South. It is not down on any map; true places never are . . . .

His father was a High Chief, a King; his uncle a High Priest; and on the maternal side he boasted aunts who were the wives of unconquerable warriors. There was excellent blood in his veins—royal stuff; though sadly vitiated, I fear, by the cannibal propensity he nourished in his untutored youth (60).

A biography is like an extract of one's life. The first part of the above quote detailing Queequeg's home existing on no map, followed by "true places never are," places him within a mythic rather than a historical neighborhood. The name of his island, moreover, looks and sounds like a double of itself, as does Queequeg's name. He seems a double of Ishmael as well in that both have exhibited a huge hunger for things remote, unfamiliar, yet necessary to explore. Queequeg is akin to a particular form of the imagination itself; he offers up worlds that are plausible yet not literally in the world; he is like a blueprint for imagining life and world within a much larger field. In so being, he opens the world to the once rigid but now flexible Ishmael.

Not infrequently, the strange and different may assume an intimacy in us when once the surface skin is peeled away to expose what is more a complement than a conflict between ourselves and others. This other often appears out of nowhere to change our lives dramatically because it allows to gestate and grow in us something we may have been unaware of or even willfully denied. The heroic part of our being will respond favorably to such newness as an opportunity to increase our orbit of possibilities if we can grow down into it with a measure of pliability.

Meditation

When has an event that initially appeared very "foreign" to you assumed an organic and complementary relation to all that was familiar?

January 28. Chapter 12: Biographical

But by and by, he said, he would return,--as soon as he felt himself baptized again. For the nonce, however, he proposed to sail about, and sow his wild oats in all four oceans. They had made a harpooneer of him, and that barbed iron was in lieu of a scepter now . . . .

I told him that whaling was my own design, and informed him of my intention to sail out of Nantucket, as being the most promising port for an adventurous whaleman to embark from. He at once resolved to accompany me to that island, ship aboard the same vessel . . . (61).

Away from home for years and among Christians who have disillusioned him by their actions, Queequeg has acquiesced to the ways of the West while retaining his own culture's myth. Needing a baptism before returning home a renewed man, he wishes to satisfy the deep itch for travel. Ishmael, ever the apprentice to life, seeks his own adventure yet wants to learn more from his brother about the lore of whaling. Queequeg is as much desirous of remaining Ishmael's companion and "to share my every hap" (62) by keeping his close company. Both agree to companion the other as they plot their whaling adventure.

No telling how our destiny in life may unfold; at times we may use people we meet "by chance" to shape our voyage and our identity in unexpected ways and to draw us along in the currents of our own calling. "Call me Ishmael" is itself a calling, to us. We listen closely to voices of instruction and muster the courage to follow beyond where our map ends and the traceless sea opens with no clear path. Where we sail to next may be the wrong way of grasping the voyage; the destination may be an after-thought to the larger design of a life's pilgrimage. The motion of the journey may double the e-motion of our souls.

Meditation

Where and when have you been called by following chance circumstances to begin a new chapter in your life story?

January 29. Chapter 13: Wheelbarrow

At last, passage paid, and luggage safe, we stood on board the schooner. Hoisting sail, it glided down the Acushnet river . . . .

Gaining the more open water, the bracing breeze waxed fresh; the little Moss tossed the quick foam from her bows, as a young colt his snortings. How I snuffed that Tartar air!—how I spurned that turnpike earth!—that common highway all over dented with the marks of slavish heels and hoofs; and turned me to admire the magnanimity of the sea which will permit no records (64-65).

Like a prologue to signing on board the Pequod, this mini-adventure to Nantucket, leaving the modern consumer-laden town of New Bedford in their wake, Ishmael and Queequeg feel the blood stir in them anew. Ishmael has dared to trade the slavish life of order, obligation and monotony for the traceless tracts of the sea—a landscape that leaves no residue or memory on its surface. Its external skin remains everlastingly virginal, always fresh, free of recollections of who and what had recently or remotely plied its surface. Both men inhale the exuberant, unnerving salty air of freedom.

We can all enter the nervous intoxicating excitement of setting sail across waters to experiences that will shape our memories and our future sense of ourselves, perhaps with a deep permanence. One may even feel a baptism of new life, of renewal, and retrieval wash over one as the sea's great expansiveness articulates its majestic force. Something of the liquid shape-shifting water's significance beckons something deep within us. That we will leave no trace of the voyage but instead have it etched in the footprints of memory and reflection adds to the mystery of water pilgrimages. It is the one element that reflects us back to ourselves.

Meditation

Describe your feelings prior to an important new voyage you once undertook or are in the midst of one you are planning.

January 30. Chapter 13: Wheelbarrow

Shooting himself perpendicularly from the water, Queequeg, now took an instant's glance around him, and seeming to see just how matters were, dived down and disappeared. A few minutes more, and he rose again, one arm still striking out, and with the other dragging a lifeless form. The boat soon picked them up. The poor bumpkin was restored. All hands voted Queequeg a noble trump; the captain begged his pardon. From that hour I clove to Queequeg like a barnacle; yea, till poor Queequeg took his last long dive (66-67).

Having just moments before received insults from the young passenger on board who mocked his appearance, the noble islander risks his life to save the bumpkin knocked overboard by a loose and treacherous boom. Absent self-regard, Queequeg sacrifices all to save the one who mocked him. Connected by their common humanity, Queequeg forgives and forgets as he dives deep, breaching, then diving again to retrieve the young boy, much to the praise of all aboard, including the captain. Ishmael now vows to cling to this whaleman like a barnacle until, he confesses, Queequeg will perish in his last dive.

The unconditional love and a life of sacrifice and service as hallmarks of many religions are here not discussed but incarnated by the "savage." Accepting the differences of another grows easier when it rests on a recognition of a common humanity underpinning surface distinctions. Seeing the other in common action rather than common appearance includes the power to erase variances and dissolve deeply-held, but baseless prejudices, cruelties and superiorities. Freedom allows the different other simply to be in his/her unique way.

Meditation

When have you "seen through" a belief when contradicted by the behavior, attitude or treatment of yourself or another?

January 31. Chapter 14: Nantucket

The Nantucketer, he alone resides and riots on the sea; he alone, in Bible language, goes down to it in ships; to and fro ploughing it as his own special plantation. *There* is his home; *there* lies his business which a Noah's flood would not interrupt, though it overwhelmed all the millions in China . . . . so at nightfall, the Nantucketer, out of sight of land, furls his sails, and lays him to his rest, while under his very pillow rush herds of walruses and whales (69).

Ishmael makes clear the heroic enterprise of the Nantucket whalers, a very different breed from those of New Bedford. From their origin to their expansion outward on the sea, in epic parlance, Ishmael reveals the depth of the quest and the courage that the quest exacts. Connected to the epic venture contained in the Biblical stories like Jonah and Noah, the Nantucket sailors are more at home on sea than land; they treat it as others would a land-locked plantation. Hardy, indefatigable, unconquerable, the Nantucketer is mythic and epic in stature; he is married to the sea and even at night enjoys the aquatic rush of herds swimming like dream figures just beneath his head.

The sea is full of invisible life forms that periodically surface to remind us of the immense, invisible population that uses water as we do air. The whale splits the difference as an air-breathing mammal who plunges deeper than any other living form, yet can breach skyward. A deep mystery attends this nether world that touches a deep part of the aquatic soul in us. Nantucket is a mythical place out from which expands and grows a massive heroic impulse to venture into the unfamiliar, as does the figure of Jonah, one of the most formidable Biblical presences in the novel and our shaman on this journey.

Meditation

Where does greatness, courage and mystery occupy your life? Where is depth present to acknowledge mystery's essential necessity?

February 1. Chapter 15: Chowder

A sort of crick was in my neck as I gazed up to the two remaining horns; yes, *two* of them, one for Queequeg, and one for me. It's ominous, thinks I. A Coffin my Innkeeper upon landing in my first whaling port; tombstones staring at me in the whalemen's chapel, and here a gallows! and a pair of prodigious black pots too! Are these last throwing out oblique hints touching Tophet? (70-71).

Arriving in Nantucket, Ishmael and Queequeg seek out a popular eating establishment when they come on two large black pots hanging from "the cross-trees of an old top-mast, planted in front of an old doorway" (70). He becomes conscious of an accumulating list of images of death. Seeking an analogy for them, he alludes to the Hebrew Bible locale of Tophet. Described in the book of Jeremiah (vii.31,32) it was a place south of the city of Jerusalem dedicated to horrible rites of human sacrifice, including "the immolation of children to Baal and other abominable idols . . . . Tophet was designated as 'the valley of slaughter'"(www.jewishencyclopedia.com/Tophet). Cliffs to one side of the valley are strewn with ancient tombs. Ishmael senses in the signs around him a further chowder of Biblical themes and events.

We seek signs and realize portents of all kinds in our journey through a particular, unique landscape. As we mature, we sense a doubleness of and in life wherein outside events, people and things mirror our interior selves. Later upon reflection we recognize how certain things were pointing us to what came to be. We possess a natural instinct to find analogies of our present experiences in those of the past, either lived out, heard about or read. Such moments provide a container or a vessel of familiarity to situate our life within an existing myth.

Meditation

Where/when has some presentiment or sign of your future life come to pass, perhaps revealing a fundamental pattern?

February 2. Chapter 15: Chowder

Fishiest of all fishy places was the Try Pots, which well deserved its name; for the pots there were always boiling chowders. Chowder for breakfast, and chowder for dinner, and chowder for supper, till you began to look for fish-bones coming through your clothes. The area before the house was paved with clam-shells. Mrs. Hussey wore a polished necklace of codfish vertebra . . . . There was a fishy flavor to the milk too . . . . I saw Hosea's brindled cow feeding on fish remnants and marching along the sand with each foot in a cod's decapitated head . . . (72).

An initiation into the varied species of the aqueous world brings the two whalers into the domain of the deep's denizens. Nourished by chowder is a fine indoctrination. Chowder is comprised of scraps and bits of many forms of sea life—varied, complex, and composed of extracts of fishy flesh in the pot. All is steeped in the life of the sea, now moving inward as Ishmael and Queequeg, surrounded by shells and splinters of sea life, assume a piece of this watery world. The Hebrew Scripture Book of Hosea is imbedded here in the chowder as well; Mrs. Hosea Hussey resonates the adulterous wife of Hosea, herself a hussey. Ishmael will continue to double his voyage with suggestive analogies from the Bible.

Becoming part of a new life may require a complete immersion. To enter a new position, a new role, or a new adventure requires leaving one world behind, or muting it, to clear a space for different furniture, food, patterns of behavior, new skills and adaptations to the unfamiliar. We may shed one skin for another yet remain flexible and open to the new chowder in our life—an amalgam of nourishing flavors to sustain us on the voyage we learn over time to metabolize.

Meditation

When has the world offered you a new chowder to sample?

February 3. Chapter 16: The Ship

After much prolonged sauntering and many random inquiries, I learnt that there were three ships up for three years' voyages—The Devil-dam, the Tit-bit, and the Pequod . . . . *Pequod* you will no doubt remember, was the name of a celebrated tribe of Massachusetts Indians . . . .

She was a ship of the old school, rather small if anything; with an old fashioned claw-footed look about her . . . . Her venerable bows looked bearded . . . . Her ancient decks were worn and wrinkled . . . (74).

In the spirit of a fairy tale in which the hero is given three choices—beds, meals, houses, shells—and asked or forced to choose one, Ishmael is faced with three ships, the choice of which will most fulfill his destiny when he enters uncharted seas. His instincts lead him to the one rooted in a Native American tribe. Their history and legacy contained in the ship's name will carry Queequeg and him over the dark waters to the White Whale. His choice appears influenced in part by the appearance of the aged, bearded and wrinkled old ship that has proven her worth in the world of whales. She appears carrying the status of an ancient and wizened character in the plot.

What brings us to choose certain things, directions, persons and vocations in life while discarding others is no small matter when we think of how those myriad choices have brought us to where and who we are presently. We may feel as well that there existed other influences at play, some invisible phantoms or designs playing their hand in our decisions, with us as one of their cards. Not what looms large before us, but the smaller version, at times almost incidental, becomes the most significant in our life's mythic pattern that we can most affectively grasp through self-reflection.

Meditation

What life choices, seen now in retrospect, appear fated or destined, even though you once believed they were exclusively your decisions?

February 4. Chapter 16: The Ship

She was apparelled like any barbaric Ethiopian emperor, his neck heavy with pendants of polished ivory. She was a thing of trophies. A cannibal of a craft, tricking herself forth in the chased bones of her enemies. All round, her unpanelled, open bulwarks were garnished like one continuous jaw, with the long sharp teeth of the sperm whale, inserted there for pins, to fasten her old hempen thews and tendons to . . . . A noble craft, but somehow a most melancholy! All noble things are touched with that (74-75).

The Pequod is described as a living embodied character with a personality, not simply an inanimate conglomerate of varied objects from previous hunts. From Ishmael's passage we learn she is both female and male, full of history of her earlier whaling voyage, reflecting attributes of a whale, and noble like the cannibal Queequeg. She is composed of parts of what she hunts, as if the whales brought on board left traces of their own anatomy to fuse with hers; whale teeth have become pins to secure her parts that are fleshy, not woody; bones are now thews and tendons. She is, like a whale, a living incarnation, with the emotion of melancholy sinewing her. Her owners have transformed a pod of whale parts to fit her nautical anatomy.

This phenomenon of how we *may become* what we hunt, desire, seek or pursue while maintaining parts of our original rigging expresses a profound psychological insight. Our unique attributes are in part a congregation of what we value enough to seek on the unknown seas of what life experiences sail towards and at times over us. We are also invited here to see things in their more invisible, yet animated, properties. Our personal myth is a conversation between bits and pieces.

Meditation

Describe one dimension of yourself that was inherited by something in life you sought and even perhaps achieved and assimilated.

February 5. Chapter 16: The Ship

Now when I looked about the quarter-deck, for some one having authority, in order to propose myself as a candidate for the voyage, at first I saw nobody; but I could not well overlook a strange sort of tent, or rather wigwam, pitched a little behind the main-mast. It seemed only a temporary erection used in port . . . .

And half concealed in this queer tenement, I at length found one who by his aspect seemed to have authority . . . . He was seated on an old-fashioned oaken chair, wriggling all over with curious carving (75).

Two worlds congeal on board the Pequod: the original Native American world of inhabitants and the white world of discoverers that eventually displaced and marginalized one tribe after another. Ishmael's language in describing himself as a "candidate for the voyage" suggests he is not automatically hired but may first have to endure some entrance exam or initiatory rite to demonstrate his worthiness to sail. He seeks out authority external to himself because he lacks the insight of his own. Called, and responding to it affirmatively, he now must prove his worth, already prepped by his mentor Queequeg. He enters a world half concealed, half revealed, not unlike the whale hunt itself.

The call to adventure that Joseph Campbell highlights so forcefully in *The Hero With a Thousand Faces* is only the beginning. One may--and many do--refuse the call. Preference for the known and familiar deflects many from venturing forth into mystery. Life's adventures have their own standards that we may fail to measure up to, or it may be the wrong adventure for us. Being refused by the mandates of the adventure can rescue us from our own ambitions; yet refusing the call may murder something deep in us, a spark of life that goes out for lack of attention.

Meditation

When has some obstacle blocked you from venturing forth, a circumstance that now you find yourself grateful for or lament?

February 6. Chapter 16: The Ship

There was nothing so very particular, perhaps, about the appearance of the elderly man I saw; he was brown and brawny, like most old seamen, and heavily rolled up in blue pilot-cloth, cut in the Quaker style; only there was a fine and almost microscopic net-work of the minutest wrinkles interlacing round his eyes, which must have arisen from his continual sailings in many hard gales, and always looking to windward . . . .

"Is this the captain of the Pequod?" said I, advancing to the door of the tent.

"I was thinking of shipping."

. . . .

"Well, sir, I want to see what whaling is. I want to see the world." (75-76).

Ishmael's interrogation by Captain Peleg, one of the owners of the Pequod, is a test to see if he is worthy to claim the ship and the voyage. Called to the sea is not a free pass into it, as Peleg reveals. In the wigwam set up on deck to enlist and question possible crew members, Peleg inquires as to what motives have driven the tyro Ishmael to board the vessel that blends, like its name, Native American culture with a stern Quaker temperament. Ishmael responds with a singular intent.

Whaling is less a contrivance for seeing the world and more an analogy *of* the world. Our calling may harbor a double intention. Its motives are twofold. What we choose to see in our life's work is a small analogy for something much larger, grander, nobler but nonetheless sought through the process of a particular "work" in progress. However we might define whaling, it is an instrument that allows the world we inhabit to widen and deepen, with mystery as its center-piece.

Meditation

Do your current pursuits open you to a larger vision?

February 7. Chapter 16: The Ship

Bildad never heeded us, but went on mumbling to himself out of his book, "*Lay* not up for yourselves treasures upon earth, where moth—"

"Well, Captain Bildad," interrupted Peleg, "what d'ye say, what lay shall we give this young man?"

"Thou knowest best," was the sepulchral reply, "the seven hundred and seventy-seventh wouldn't be too much, would it?—'where moth and rust do corrupt, but lay—'"

"*Lay*, indeed, thought I and such a lay! the seven hundred and seventy seventh!" (82).

The Bible furnishes the textual waters that the epic floats upon. Bildad uses scripture to offer Ishmael a tiny percentage of the profits from the impending voyage: 777th part. It is a symbolic number in many belief systems and suggests initiation toward unity for the celestial man. (www.ridingthebeast.com). Bildad, the name of one of Job's comforters in *The Book of Job,* seems a swindler justifying his behavior by quoting scripture. The play on the word "lay" is rich, comic and complex in the lines that follow, as Ishmael begins a series of rich puns on the word. Religion and capitalism, two giant myths within the American soul, breach here in Ishmael's initiation into his worth and worthiness.

Money and soul, Mammon and commerce, are two supporting edifices of our American vision of success: salvation and being selected as a people expresses itself in the doctrine of Manifest Destiny; coveting others as well as coveting what others possess in the name of religion and commerce embrace the core of our democratic ethos. One place that the shadow of money appears is in the overlay of religious beliefs and capitalism when they often breed injustice through greed.

Meditation

Are religion and money sources of conflict in your daily life?

February 8. Chapter 16: The Ship

And, after signing the papers, off I went; nothing doubting but that I had done a good morning's work, and that the Pequod was the identical ship that Yojo had provided to carry Queequeg and me round the Cape.

But I had not proceeded far, when I began to bethink me that the Captain with whom I was to sail yet remained unseen by me . . . .

"And what dost thou want of Captain Ahab? It's all right enough; thou art shipped."

"Yes, but I should like to see him" (84-85).

Unease begins to unsettle Ishmael now that he has elected to sail on the Pequod. He is nervous about what is unseen so he doubles back to ask Peleg to see the Captain. Ahab is present and visible in name only. His name is all that Ishmael has to go on. Like the whales themselves, Ahab is a hidden, unknown and secret entity who nonetheless commands all on board. As such he is like an unknown god that Ishmael wants to face directly in order to believe. Being accepted as a *bona fide* whaleman is insufficient to quench Ishmael's curiosity of who will lead him to sea. But not being able to see Ahab is his main impediment.

We have all had experiences of signing on, committing ourselves, and taking the plunge into what remains invisible and inscrutable, yet present perhaps in name only. But the name both is and is not the reality, as was evident in the cenotaphs where the names were the only tangible referent to the absent remains of men who perished at sea. Yet, as initiates, we are compelled to sign on board to an invisible reality that eventually reveals itself over time. Such is the nature of a spiritual quest that insists we risk ourselves into the unknown. Without accepting what we cannot foresee or control, we may refuse our calling.

Meditation

When have you committed to a future with little to guide you but a calling to an unknown, still invisible venture?

February 9. Chapter 17: The Ramadan

Now, as I before hinted, I have no objection to any person's religion, be it what it may, so long as that person does not kill or insult any other person, because that other person don't believe it also. But when a man's religion becomes really frantic; when it is a positive torment to him, and, in fine, makes this earth of ours an uncomfortable inn to lodge in; then I think it high time to take that individual aside and argue the point with him.

And just so now I did with Queequeg (91).

Exasperated by his friend's meditations all night sitting on the floor of their shared room, Ishmael cannot accept this foreign religious practice. From his more conventional Christian imagination, he believes Queequeg's "prolonged ham-squattings in cold, cheerless rooms" (91) was not good for his health. Queequeg's religious practices are not frantic for *him,* but they are for Ishmael. Queequeg's sustained meditation troubles his roommate, who sees it as fanatical. As he grows increasingly uncomfortable with its strangeness, Ishmael rebels against this annoying otherness of his friend's religious rituals. Because he does not conform to Ishmael's fantasies of religious practices, he needs to be corrected—perhaps converted--by the logic of Ishmael's narrow vision.

Differences in beliefs over politics and religion, to name two prickly subjects, provoke many people's energies as flashpoints of controversy. Beliefs, as substantial elements of myths, dive deeper than skin color or surface tattoos. It is easy for any of us to feel self-righteous in encouraging others to hold beliefs that comply with our own. It is thin tolerance to attempt to change another rather than stretch our own ability to endure and even embrace differences that could enrich our thinking.

Meditation

When in your own past have you insisted or pushed another to conform to your perspective? Have you been pressured to conform to another's?

February 10. Chapter 18: His Mark

Finding myself thus hard pushed, I replied, "I mean, sir, the same ancient Catholic Church to which you and I, and Captain Peleg there, and Queequeg here, and all of us, and every mother's son and soul of us belong; the great and everlasting First Congregation of this whole worshipping world; we all belong to that; only some of us cherish some crotchets no ways touching the grand belief; in *that* we all join hands" (94).

Ishmael responds on board the Pequod to Bildad's questioning how it is that Queequeg, standing at the ready to sign on as whaleman, is a Deacon of the First Congregational Church. Ishmael's response is far more ecumenical in temper than his previous prejudice. We are, he suggests, all members of one congregation—that of a common humanity even though not all are ready to relinquish their grip on cherished religious truths. Ishmael's change of heart, as well as his ability to persuade the two captains to accept his savage friend as crew member, reveals a soul that has abandoned its isolato status and entered into a more communally-inflected tolerance of sameness in difference.

Yielding some safe and security-inducing beliefs to allow a wider orbit of tolerance to enter our lives comprises a large part of our journey into the fullness of who we are. Tolerance and acceptance as elements in a larger image of worship ratifies a greater community adhesion as well as a more elastic soul. One's citadel of favored ideologies gives way as we grow into a more tolerant and accepting disposition towards what is alien. In such a move, the world expands in its mystery as our level of acceptance weathers more diversity.

Meditation

What new belief, idea, behavior or event have you allowed yourself to grow into that altered your attitude to what had once been foreign?

February 11. Chapter 19: The Prophet

"Shipmates, have ye shipped in that ship?"

Queequeg and I had just left the Pequod, and were sauntering away from the water, for the moment each occupied with his own thoughts, when the above words were put to us by a stranger. . . .

. . . .

"Yes," said I, "we have just signed the articles."

"Anything down there about your souls?"

"About what?"

"Oh, perhaps you have'n't got any," he said quickly. "No matter though, I know many chaps that hav'n't got any,--good luck to 'em; and they are all the better off for it. A soul's a sort of a fifth wheel to a wagon" (97).

The figure of Elijah, shabbily dressed, with pock-marked skin, sidles up behind the two new whalemen and begins to interrogate their recent commitment. Named after the Hebrew prophet, he is more concerned with their souls than their share of profits. Elijah implies that Queegueg and Ishmael may have just signed their souls away as well. The cost of sailing under "Old Thunder," Captain Ahab, may exact more from them than simply hunting down leviathans. He implies that being a soulless crew member may be more beneficial. Elijah reveals explicitly that both men are about to embark on a soul journey.

When we sign on to life's voyages generally and to a specific vocation or calling explicitly--partly chosen, partly destined--we cannot measure the cost or have exact knowledge of the terms or foresee its consequences. What exacts a price from us that implicates our souls is determined by both circumstances as well as a fair price tag. "Signing the articles" is a declaration of both cognition and submission.

Meditation

Have you paid out too much or too little for your life's passage?

February 12. Chapter 20: All Astir

But, as before hinted, for some time there was a continual fetching and carrying on board of divers odds and ends of things, both large and small.

Chief among those who did this fetching and carrying was Captain Bildad's sister, a lean old lady of a most determined and indefatigable spirit, but withal very kindhearted . . . . Never did any woman better deserve her name, which was Charity—Aunt Charity, as everybody called her. And like a sister of charity did this charitable Aunt Charity bustle about hither and thither ready to turn her hand and heart to anything that promised to yield safety, comfort and consolation. . . (102).

One of few women to appear in the epic, she is a figure who oversees the ship's larder, assuring its abundant largesse for the voyage. Selfless and tireless, devoted to the welfare of the men, Aunt Charity makes present the feminine energy in the form of goods for the journey. She embodies the opposite attitude of her brother Bildad in that she lives the Christian directive through acts of generosity, stocking the ship and offering a woman's touch to all she handles in the spirit of abundance.

Any preparation for a pilgrimage, a life work, a vacation, a temporary move, or any sustained severance from home requires another way of ordering one's life to both necessities and comforts. Preparing for an extended journey includes a crucial ritual so that needs are in balance with wants within the premium of limited space. The preparation can indicate what quality the journey will have. One must consider carefully what is truly of value and what should be shed. Keeping a sense of generosity for oneself softens the departure and modulates loss.

Meditation

What do you consistently take with you, what leave behind, so as to keep your pilgrimage uncluttered?

February 13. Chapter 20: All Astir

During these days of preparation, Queequeg and I often visited the craft, and as often I asked about Captain Ahab, and how he was, and when he was going to come on board his ship . . . . If I had been downright honest with myself, I would have seen very plainly in my heart that I did but half fancy being committed this way to so long a voyage, without once laying my eyes on the man who was to be absolute dictator of it . . . . But when a man suspects any wrong . . . he insensibly strives to cover up his suspicions even from himself (102-03).

The hero Ishmael is cautious about committing to a journey for which he must face uncertainty about outcomes. He struggles to adjust to what is mysterious and absent. The invisible commander leaves him with an uncomfortable feeling of not knowing what is to be expected of him, yet he refuses to deny himself the adventure. The guide remains imperceptible but the mode of conveyance is starkly present. They can have one but must forego the other. The whaling adventure's terms cannot be known in their entirety; Ishmael recognizes his tendency to gloss over what he feels is amiss in order to inaugurate the voyage.

When we agree to hoist our life sails and begin to tack into foreign waters, we may feel a tug of resistance: something is not right or feels off, amiss, or perhaps dangerous. But do we let this phantom of unease abort the journey? For some it may be a toss-up: continue to plan and then launch into uncharted seas without knowing, or yield to the resistance and retreat. Once one is committed, however, it is difficult to resist lifting all sails into whatever winds that arise. One must ask: if all terms of the voyage were known, would it be worth the effort launching into and yielding to its predictability?

Meditation

Have you ever begun a new journey or a new tack in your life under strong presentiments of doom or disaster? What transpired?

February 14. Chapter 21: Going Aboard

"Holloa!" he breathed at last, "who be ye smokers?"

"Shipped men," answered I, "when does she sail?"

"Aye, aye, ye are going in her, be ye? She sails to-day. The Captain came aboard last night."

"What Captain?—Ahab?"

"Who but him indeed?"

. . . .

Soon the crew came on board in twos and threes; the riggers bestirred themselves; the mates were actively engaged . . . . Meanwhile Captain Ahab remained invisibly enshrined within his cabin (106-07).

Officially now on board, with others regularly appearing on deck, Ishmael and Queequeg have crossed the threshold into another world. But they still wonder about their captain's invisibility, a phantom who again successfully eludes them. His unseen presence disturbs them, as whales' unseen presences can create intense anticipation during the hunts. That Ahab is "enshrined" deep in his cabin below deck suggests a god or priest or some holy object now in the underbelly of the ship. Like Jonah before him, Ahab will assume a powerful presence.

At the beginning of a voyage, some brooding presentiment may make itself present, more potent because invisible. Controlling the terms of the voyage, Ahab is that invisible guide and leader of the journey's trajectory and tone—the manner in which it will unfold and, powerful enough, can muster a creative or destructive journey. Risking these multiple possibilities is part of the texture of any excursion. One can never be certain of one's preparedness because the unseen and unforeseen may find one's skills and disposition wanting.

Meditation

On an important life voyage, has a particular phantom or shadow accompanied your excitement and trepidation?

February 15. Chapter 22: Merry Christmas

At last the anchor was up, the sails were set, and off we glided. It was a short, cold Christmas; and as the short northern day merged into night, we found ourselves almost broad upon the wintry ocean, whose freezing spray cased us in ice, as in polished armor. The long rows of teeth on the bulwarks glistened in the moonlight; and like the white ivory tusks of some huge elephant, vast curving icicles depended from the bows (110).

The Pequod is a living, organic beast on the ocean, part whale, part elephant. The two animals conjoined link earth and sea. Christmas Day is a crucial temporal threshold as the birth of new life; in the Christian myth divine life melts into human existence just past the shortest day of the year. Teeth and tusks, ice and moonlight all conspire to create an atmosphere full of promise and peril, devouring and armored, like a medieval knight. The journey invites a certain jeopardy. The Pequod now sails into the unknown perils of life as it heads to the port of Nantucket, with Captain Bildad, substituting for Ahab, piloting the vessel. His invisible double remains below in the night sea journey.

In our own voyage, when anchor is weighed, the adventure may have a prologue, like a mini-adventure anticipating the major voyage. People telling of their journey often recall the unexpected: how fate intervened or a miracle ensued to fluff the sails in a different direction than that originally sketched out. As a journey unfurls, one often senses other forces being enlisted; they assume control of the rudder for part of the journey. Chance may be the commander with Fate as first mate. It dawns on many early on that yielding to the terms of the voyage may be the best strategy to endure, enjoy and survive its emerging patterns.

Meditation

When you recollect an important voyage taken, what was most surprising, unnerving, unexpected, welcomed or rejected?

February 16. Chapter 22: Merry Christmas

But, at last, he turned to his comrade, with a final sort of look about him,—"Captain Bildad—come, old shipmate, we must go. Back the mainyard there! Boat ahoy! Stand by to come close alongside, now! Careful, careful!—come, Bildad, boy—say your last . . . —good-bye and good luck to ye all—and this day three years I'll have a hot supper smoking for ye in old Nantucket. Hurrah and away!"

"Captain Ahab may soon be moving among ye—a pleasant sun is all he needs, and ye'll have plenty of them in the tropic . . ." (111).

The two owners of the Pequod prepare to relinquish their ship to the high seas, fate, chance and Ahab's command. God willing, he will bring them a profit. Their Quaker ways are left behind, their decisions on who they hired about to be tested. A feeling of finality attends their goodbyes, a presentiment of the journey's tenure. Their final word is of the invisible Captain in his cabin deep in the belly of the ship. He will, like the whales, soon breach on deck to galvanize the crew under the banner of his afflicted obsession. The two owners offer advice to the crew to keep their Captain in the pleasant sunshine and even-keeled.

The moment in a journey when you feel it is truly free from encumbrances and earlier forms of control in the form of people, the familiar, the known is a giddy experience. What is new, strange, exciting, dangerous, uncanny, can now enter the space left by conventions. Especially true is what lurks beneath the skin of the voyage, the hunt, the quest, the grail difficult to attain, the treasure that will involve danger and great risk to acquire. Dread and anticipation may mingle in the soul because of the unknown forces in the future. What would be less satisfying would be to refuse the call to venture.

Meditation

As you embarked on a life-changing voyage, what was your greatest concern as you shipped out?

February 17. Chapter 23: The Lee Shore

The port would fain give succor; the port is pitiful; in the port is safety, comfort, hearthstone, supper, warm blankets, friends, all that's kind to our mortalities. But in that gale, the port, the land, is that ship's direst jeopardy; she must fly all hospitality; one touch of land, though it but graze the keel, would make her shudder through and through. With all her might she crowds all sail off shore; in so doing fights 'gainst the very winds that fain would blow her homeward; (113).

Ishmael has been thinking of the whaler Bulkington who shipped aboard the Pequod. Just returned from a four year hunt, he immediately signs on the Pequod for another long voyage. "The land seemed scorching to his feet" (113) thinks Ishmael. Bulkington evokes a meditation in the narrator: how from one perspective or set of conditions, home port is full of blessings, but in a gale that same port is the ship's greatest peril. He goes on to surmise that Bulkington is like a symbol of the soul, which in her depth must "keep the open independence of her sea," for in landlessness "alone resides the highest truth, shoreless, indefinite as God--" (113).

Being unmoored, existing on the open sea away from most of what is familiar and social in life, disposes the soul to sound its depths. The truth of one's life in its deepest recesses is best discovered in the liquid expanse of water, free of the fixity of land as well as the ports that make the permanence of land available. Treacherous, yes, but in conditions of turmoil a safer setting than the approaching shore. The liquidity of water carries its own safety, though it may seem at first less assuring. But to enter the constant motion of the ocean of our lives puts us in touch with realities out of reach when we cling to the shoreline for safety.

Meditation

In the open rugged waters of your life, what truth have you been given, hooked, or netted?

Part II

Presentation of the Lore of the Whaling Industry
Chapters 24-47

The original departure into the land of trials represented only the beginning of the long and really perilous path of initiatory conquests and moments of illumination.

The Hero With a Thousand Faces, 90.

February 18. Chapter 24: The Advocate

I freely assert, that the cosmopolite philosopher cannot, for his life, point out one single peaceful influence, which within the last sixty years has operated more potentially upon the whole broad world, taken in one aggregate, than the high and mighty business of whaling. One way and another, it has begotten events so remarkable in themselves, and so continuously momentous in their sequential issues, that whaling may well be regarded as that Egyptian mother, who bore offspring themselves pregnant from her womb (116).

As a great apologist for whaling, Ishmael pulls out all the rhetorical circuits to persuade us that whaling is both epic and mythic in its power and range. It carries the freight of many lands and people in its quest to describe the mighty mammals of the deep. He compares it to an Egyptian mythic figure whose pregnancy begets pregnancies in the life force's power to reproduce in abundance. Whaling is strange, extraordinary, and pregnant with possibilities. His wish is to elevate what has been seen as a menial business venture, or cold-blooded killing, to the level of a noble epic enterprise. It can only happen with language that itself is elevated to match the level of the epic action; only then will the poet-philosopher Ishmael reach his goal as writer.

Some inflation can attend what one engages as an adventure or as a profession, so much so that its importance can run away from itself, especially when all boundaries and limits of one's work collapse. Full of pride in one's burgeoning enterprise, one may be easily blinded to the damage or loss to self, others, and to the planet that such mighty work may generate. Yet, something more is epic here: the act of writing itself and its capacity to create an entire world that has not been sung before.

Meditation

What work have you engaged that afforded you great pride and satisfaction in an achievement that benefitted others?

February 19. Chapter 24: The Advocate

The whale has no famous author, and whaling no famous chronicler, you will say.

The whale no famous author, and whaling no famous chronicler? Who wrote the first account of our Leviathan? Who but mighty Job? . . .

No good blood in their veins? They have something better than royal blood there . . . .

Whaling not respectable? Whaling is imperial! By old English statutory law, the whale is declared "a royal fish."

. . . .

No dignity in whaling? The dignity of our calling the very heavens attest. Cetus is a constellation in the south! No more! Drive down your hat in presence of the Czar, and take it off to Queequeg! (118-19).

With not a little droll hyperbole, Ishmael's passionate sense of whaling's nobility dismantles many of the conventional attitudes that belittle this enterprise. His blood boils over any suggestion that whaling lacks epic stature worth immortalizing in the song of this narrative. His range includes the Biblical Job and the astrological constellations. One could not do better, he believes, than to sign on board a whaling vessel. Not the Czar of Russia, but noble savage Queequeg is worth adoration as an imperial example of human nobility and courage which Ishmael is determined to capture and convey mightily in language.

Our work should instill in us a nobility of purpose, even when others may demean or trivialize it. Not they but we assign value to our calling, our craft and our labor. Work may be what sustains us, proffers our life purpose, and prescribes a sense of worth and achievement. Its heroic value relies not on others for acceptance or praise but ourselves.

Meditation

What needs or desires does your chosen work satisfy in constructing your purpose and your identity?

February 20. Chapter 24: The Advocate

And, as for me, if, by any possibility, there be any as yet undiscovered prime thing in me, if I shall ever deserve any real repute in that small but high hushed world which I might not be unreasonably ambitious of . . . . if at my death, my executors, or more properly my creditors, find any precious MSS in my desk, then here I prospectively ascribe all the honor and the glory to whaling; for a whale-ship was my Yale College and my Harvard (119).

Ishmael ends "The Advocate" chapter by expressing a deeply personal sense of what exists nobly in himself: an "undiscovered prime thing," the essence of who he is and what shaped him most formidably—whaling his curriculum and the whale-ship his campus and classroom. He points directly to the task of writing a book but has no guarantee of living long enough to complete it. The passage asserts a minor will of sorts, since he acknowledges now that he owes his formation as a person and as a writer to his student years learning the art and craft of whaling as well as writing. Whaling and writing are kindred grail searches.

Many people work for decades at jobs that corrode, if not steal, their souls. Others more fortunate find careers that shape them into their fullest possibilities. The first group, however, may find fate shifting forces in a craft or a work outside their means of earning a living that provides their life a vibrant meaning. One may, perhaps, seek fulfillment in volunteer work. Another may find her Yale and Harvard in coping with a disease, a great loss or other life-altering events. We all require a work that fulfills us, well beyond material gain. Our satisfaction in our work reflects the unique qualities of our soul as well as the formative principles of our personal myth.

Meditation

Describe the most important, satisfying and self-shaping work you have ever done. What did it develop that remains with you today?

February 21. Chapter 26: Knights and Squires

The chief mate of the Pequod was Starbuck, a native of Nantucket, and a Quaker by descent. He was a long, earnest man, and though born on an icy coast, seemed well adapted to endure hot latitudes, his flesh being hard as twice-baked biscuit . . . . His pure tight skin was an excellent fit; and closely wrapped up in it, and embalmed with inner health and strength, like a revivified Egyptian, this Starbuck seemed prepared to endure for long ages to come . . . .

. . . .

Starbuck was no crusader after perils; in him courage was not a sentiment; but a thing simply useful to him, and always at hand upon all mortally practical occasions (121-22).

Ishmael's descriptions of key crew members are richly metaphorical and revelatory. His portrayal of the first mate moves from skin to soul and back again in a rhythm that reveals the first mate more intimately than we might know our neighbor. Ishmael portrays a moral physiognomy here, not only how Starbuck's flesh is wrapped in tight skin, but how his soul is enshrouded with courage, a practical utensil rather than a moral attribute. Through Ishmael's eyes, each of the mates is drawn richly and complexly. We learn as well a great deal about Ishmael's own poetic prowess through his metaphors.

Describing another person beyond conventional bromides and vague generalities tells us plenty about the one crafting the description. To bring another in flesh and spirit to others in language is a creative expression of subtle fashioning, both physical and mythical. There exists a persuasive force that attends such presencing—a gift to the listener or reader because parts of our hidden self are often stirred to life in fresh vibrating prose that entertains and enlightens.

Meditation

Describe yourself in third person in both literal and metaphorical terms.

February 22. Chapter 26: Knights and Squires

Men may seem detestable as joint stock-companies and nations; knaves, fools, and murderers there may be; men may have mean and meager faces; but, man, in the ideal, is so noble and so sparkling, such a grand and glowing creature, that over any ignominious blemish in him all his fellows should run to throw their costliest robes. That immaculate manliness we feel within ourselves, so far within us, that it remains intact though all the outer character seem gone; bleeds with keenest anguish at the undraped spectacle of a valor-ruined man (123).

Reflecting on his description of Starbuck as a man of firm fortitude and courage, and in part remembering forward to the journey *before us* but *behind him,* Ishmael begins a rich meditation of man in the ideal, one who can, in life's matters, fall well below his capacities, but as an ideal is a noble figure who strives and seeks what is magnificent in life and what in the ideal state sustains him. Ishmael has learned this truth of human beings as a result of his voyage; he grasps that below the blemishes and imperfections of individual men lurks an archetype of goodness, an innate pattern in the soul that far transcends the fallen, fallible and limited designs of any one person. We mourn, he surmises, when any one of us loses valor and honor, tainting our noble nature.

The soul in all of us carries the good, the honorable and courageous, those noble verities of what we maintain in ourselves and strive imperfectly to realize, regardless of life's adulterating circumstances. Our task may be never to lose sight of such inherent dignity but to lean on it in times of darkness and failure so we are not undone by our imperfections. The imagination can reclaim the ideal to buoy us up. Without this yearning, life can lose its meaningful center.

Meditation

To what image, faith, memory, or belief do you turn to strengthen your purpose in life's dark moments of doubt and despair?

February 23. Chapter 26: Knights and Squires

But this august dignity I treat of, is not the dignity of kings and robes, but that abounding dignity which has no robed investiture. Thou shalt see it shining in the arm that wields a pick or drives a spike; that democratic dignity which, on all hands, radiates without end from God; Himself! The great God absolute! The centre and circumference of all democracy! His omnipresence, our divine equality! (123).

Acknowledging implicitly America's split from the British crown, Ishmael extolls the new form of dignity and work ethic of the common man who, even while wielding a pick or laying ties for a railroad track, participates in and embodies a spiritual grandeur and a profound dignity, from God. As Walt Whitman's poetry lauds the common man's nobility of spirit, Ishmael reveals a direct correlation between the self-worth of the worker gifted from God and the pervasive virtue of democracy that glorifies this disposition. In such a truth does democracy reside. We are all equal in the eyes of God. The philosophy of democracy is its sterling witness as well as the individual's innate grandeur.

Our political life and its institutions cannot be separated from our spiritual and moral constitution. It is what we share in common as part of the joint-stock company of humanity; it comprises our legacy and our center. Important enough is it to celebrate what unites us in both its ideal religious attributes and in our political inflections. We are each an amalgam of both under the guidance of a higher authority that confers a munificence on our flawed nobility. Not that such a belief erases differences, but under the veneer of variance is a ground of sameness constituting our true legacy. No one exists in isolation.

Meditation

What is it in your life that unites and binds you to others as a common gift and heritage? How did you come to such a belief or sense?

February 24. Chapter 27: Knights and Squires

Stubb was the second mate. He was a native of Cape Cod; and hence, according to local usage, was called a Cape-Cod-man. A happy-go-lucky; neither craven nor valiant; taking perils as they came with an indifferent air; and while engaged in the most imminent crisis of the chase, toiling away, calm and collected as a journeyman joiner engaged for the year. . . .When close to the whale, in the very death-lock of the fight, he handled his unpitying lance coolly and off-handedly, as a whistling tinker his hammer . . . . Long usage had, for this Stubb, converted the jaws of death into an easy chair (125).

A bit comic, light on his feet and easy-going, Stubb, with his constant "little black pipe" in his mouth and easy demeanor makes him a prototype of a Popeye of the sea. Raw whale steaks rather than cans of spinach are his fuel. Threatened by nothing, at ease within a hair's breath of death's jaws, Stubb seems impervious to danger, indifferent to life's difficulties and uncommonly courageous when danger haunts the stern of his life's ship. Never rattled by circumstance, Stubb, in his stubby solidity, provides stability and order to his world no matter the intensity of the strife he confronts.

Stubb, like all the mates, is a disposition, an attitude and a way of easeful being in the world. We call on the stubbiness of ourselves when in crisis, danger or in unfamiliar terrain that beckons us to risk ourselves. Stubb is our easy-going, unruffled self, smiling in the face of danger as we perform our duties, gently puffing on our pipe of serenity. Stubb, as with all three mates, suggests by analogy dispositions we all carry within; noting what mate appeals most to us may offer insights into that dimension of our personal myth.

Meditation

When has that measurement of your person, the Stubb in you, conserved your serenity in times of crisis or danger?

February 25. Chapter 27: Knights and Squires

The third mate was Flask, a native of Tisbury, in Martha's Vineyard. A short, stout, ruddy young fellow, very pugnacious concerning whales, who somehow seemed to think that the great Leviathans had personally and hereditarily affronted him; and therefore it was a sort of point of honor with him, to destroy them whenever encountered . . . . [for]the wondrous whale was but a species of magnified mouse, or at least water-rat . . . . As a carpenter's nails are divided into wrought nails and cut nails, so mankind may be similarly divided. Little Flask was one of the wrought ones; made to clinch tight and last long (126).

A simple man without a sense of life's mysterious presences, Flask reduces everything to his own meagerness in order to grasp it. He is the antithesis of the epic impulse that Ishmael embodies. Simple and small in both design and form, the third mate will "twist things smaller" than they are in order to navigate their meaning. Stalwart, tough, tenacious, firm, fitting, fearless and largely unconscious, Flask diminishes the things of the world into one dimension, draining them of complexity and wonder. His life remains largely unadorned of any qualities but the most evident and these he clinches tightly to ground him in the world.

Part of ourselves that seeks fun, entertainment, diversion and that reduces nuance or subtlety, mystery or beauty to a simple and small dimension is the Flask impulse in the soul. Lacking much imagination except in its disposition to abridge all into our own image and to cling to it with a fierce tenacity represents a Flasky form of knowing. Reluctance and resistance to change typify qualities Flask personifies.

Our instinct to trivialize or de-mystify events is a Flask compulsion.

Meditation

Where might you now discern mystery, beauty, or complexity where before there was only the obvious surface appearance?

February 26. Chapter 27: Knights and Squires

[I]t is therefore but meet, that in this place we set down who the Pequod's harpooneers were, and to what headsman each of them belonged.

First of all was Queequeg, whom Starbuck, the chief mate, had selected for his squire. But Queequeg is already known.

Next was Tashtego, an unmixed Indian from Gay Head, the most westerly promontory of Martha's Vineyard, where there still exists the last remnant of a village of red men . . . . Tashtego's long, lean, sable hair, his high cheek bones, and black rounding eyes—for an Indian . . . all this sufficiently proclaimed him an inheritor of the unvitiated blood of those proud warrior hunters. . . (127).

The three squires, Queequeg, Tashtego and Daggoo, who appears in the next passage, carry a tradition and mythology reaching deep into the past. Tashtego is close to the last of his line on Martha's Vineyard: a warrior, noble and mysterious, who had been conquered by the white man's expansion. Yet here he and his other squires are, on board the Pequod—part of an inclusive tribe of humanity bearing different and distinct traditions, yet united by the whale hunt as a common, shared pursuit. Each adds a nobility as well as a dark duskiness to the voyage as they expand the range of humanity seeking the invisible White Whale.

Some believe we carry all the tribes of the world within us as archaic, primordial wisdom, and as a presence of the most unfamiliar imbedded deeply in our souls. Our human history, part of our constitution, does not end with our indigenous lineage. Farther down is the primal presence of ages past, often hidden in the folded fathoms of our being. Below the surface of difference resides an ancient unity.

Meditation

What circumstance or revelation might have revealed to you that we are all related in our essential nature?

February 27. Chapter 27: Knights and Squires

Third among the harpooneers was Daggoo, a gigantic, coal-black negro-savage, with a lion-like tread—an Ahasuerus to behold. Suspended from his ears were two golden hoops, so large that the sailors called them ring-bolts, and would talk of securing the top-sail halyards to them .... Daggoo retained all his barbaric virtues, and erect as a giraffe, moved about the decks in all the pomp of six feet five in his socks .... Curious to tell, this imperial negro, Ahasuerus Daggoo, was the Squire of Little Flask, who looked like a chess-man beside him (127-28).

A grand nobility attends Daggoo's presence on board. True to the epic genre that Ishmael is crafting, this Squire embodies a grand stature. Ishmael compares him to Ahasuerus, a noted Persian King (486-465 BCE) who appears in *The Book of Esther* (www.JewishEncyclopedia.com/articles/967Ahas). His reign stretched from "India, even unto Ethiopia." While Ahasuerus remains a controversial historical figure in Biblical history, here his majestic larger-than-life appearance places the white man, Flask, in miniature relief. Slavery was, for Melville, a destructive presence in the United States. Here, Ishmael showcases the grand prominence of the African race to counter the prejudice that blacks were less than human.

Perception is often what allows us to see nobility or savagery in others. One ideology can condemn and exploit an entire people while another can cultivate a benevolent acceptance of Otherness. Fathoms below skin level pigment and a variety of customs and beliefs that differentiate us resides a shared universal humanity. Nobility may be found in figures perceived to be less than us; grandeur is classless.

Meditation

When have you altered your understanding and encouraged a greater acceptance of another who was radically different from you?

February 28. Chapter 27: Knights and Squires

How it is, there is no telling, but Islanders seem to make the best whale-men. They were nearly all Islanders in the Pequod, *Isolatoes* too, I call such, not acknowledging the common continent of men, but each *Isolato* living on a separate continent of his own. Yet now, federated along one keel, what a set these Isolatoes were! An Anacharsis Clootz deputation from all the isles of the sea . . . . accompanying Old Ahab in the Pequod to lay the world's grievances before that bar from which not very many of them ever come back (128).

Ishmael continually writes two narratives: one is the remembered experience aboard the Pequod; the other is historically anchored in analogies that yields a more universal, epic yeast to his voyage through the correspondences he crafts. Here he refers to Anacharsis Clootz (1755-94) formerly named Jean-Baptiste, who was a fervent orator of the Human Race and devoted his life to promoting "humanitarian ideals. When he came to Paris during the French Revolution, he pushed for the liberation of Europe by means of the Revolution's ideals" (www.wikianswers/ColumbiaEncyclopedia). Ishmael's transformation on this voyage, now recollected, was influenced by a vision of a universal humanity that included the world's Isolatoes gathered up in one federation of human fraternity and shared equality.

When we surrender our own little continent of self-interests and self-absorptions in order to enter the magical space of *communitas* that the imagination affords us, and when we agree to "federate along one keel," all its members are raised up. We give up to be raised up by something we collectively dream up. Our borders can swell out to majestic greatness. A shared dream harbors an epic impulse to a dream of equality wherein the good of the whole rests on the value of its parts.

Meditation

When have you constructed something to benefit the many?

February 29. Chapter 28: Ahab

[S]o soon as I levelled my glance towards the taffrail, foreboding shivers ran over me. Reality outran apprehension; Captain Ahab stood upon his quarter-deck.

There seemed no sign of common bodily illness about him, nor of the recovery from any. He looked like a man cut away from the stake, when the fire has overrunningly wasted all the limbs without consuming them, or taking away one particle from their compacted aged robustness. His whole high, broad form, seemed made of solid bronze, and shaped in an unalterable mould, like Cellini's cast Perseus (131).

The entire atmosphere on board changes dramatically with the appearance of Ahab on stage, as if all were witnessing a dramatic performance in which the main character has just appeared. Like Queequeg's presence earlier and Moby Dick's presence later, we hear of these figures in language before they appear substantially in the flesh. Ahab's first marker is his woundedness, struck by lightning, one of nature's harpoons and weapon of the god Zeus. He also seems stark, flinty, unyielding like Cellini's bronze sculpture of 1554 which stands in the Loggie del Lanzi in the Piazza della Signoria in Florence. Perseus gains mythic fame in slaying and beheading the gorgon Medusa by holding a polished shield up to her so she sees herself and perishes.

A nobility of soul and an afflicted body gather in the figure of Ahab. Part of his dismembered self is shared by each of us who has been wounded, dismembered, marked or scarred by life's intrusions. Such afflictions can harden us like bronze or soften us to accept the world on its terms, not ours. We can increase this hardness by shielding ourselves from strife. But that same shield may give us back our own reflection so that we become our own most intense Medusa.

Meditation

Where may an unalterable cold bronze hardness reside in you?

March 1. Chapter 28: Ahab

So powerfully did the whole grim aspect of Ahab affect me, and the livid brand which streaked it, that for the first few moments I hardly noted that not a little of this overbearing grimness was owing to the barbaric white leg upon which he partly stood. It had previously come to me that this ivory leg had at sea been fashioned from the polished bone of the sperm whale's jaw . . . .

There was an infinity of firmest fortitude, a determinate, unsurrenderable wilfulness, in the fixed and fearless, forward dedication of that glance . . . . And not only that, but moody stricken Ahab stood before them with a crucifixion in his face; in all the nameless regal overbearing dignity of some mighty woe (132).

Ishmael's prose alters to accommodate his new theme: the mighty, majestic, titanic and dismembered Ahab who appears on deck as a man-god, already part whale with his prosthetic leg. He stands simultaneously on both land and sea. The jaw of the White Whale that dismasted him is now, in another form, a double of what he stands upon. Such a tragic and imperial irony: part god-like, part wounded Fisher King, part the Leviathan he pursues. Ahab is the icon of one suffering in grand agony in the "overbearing dignity of some mighty woe." His face is imprinted with the crucifixion, yet he is no Christ.

Suffering is a mystery, both complex and nuanced. We do not escape some form of being stricken, dismembered, wounded or otherwise etched by experience. What rejoinders we embody in response to life's afflictions is ours to will. Becoming fixed on reprisal, revenge or obsessing over meting out a counter attack on another, however, can often crucify the self on the main mast of one's own excesses. An Ahab consciousness broods over vengeance until it consumes one completely.

Meditation

When have you been dismembered? What is your prosthesis?

March 2. Chapter 29: Enter Ahab; to Him, Stubb

Some days elapsed, and ice and icebergs all astern, the Pequod now went rolling through the bright Quito spring, which at sea, almost perpetually reigns on the threshold of the eternal August of the Tropic. The warmly cool, clear, ringing perfumed, overflowing, redundant days, were as crystal goblets of Persian sherbet, heaped up—flaked up, with rose-water snow. The starred and stately nights seemed haughty dames in jeweled velvets, nursing at home in lonely pride, the memory of their absent conquering Earls, the golden helmeted suns! (134).

In a wild contrast to Ahab's atmosphere of dark fixity that Ishmael's language captures with persuasive zeal, here a description of Nature's lovely seductive and even mythic beauty prevails in a *tour de force* of poetic transformation. Ishmael's versatility in language is the strongest epic quality of his poetic voyage. Lush, seductive, eternal, perfumed—these comprise qualities of a world which has a lyric texture impossible to resist. The language rises mightily to meet the grandeur of the "helmeted suns" in a rich and delicious description of nature "as crystal goblets of Persian sherbet." From the fixed gloom of the crucified Captain to the perfumed ambience of nature's luxurious delights, Ishmael is a master of world-creating in far-ranging linguistic latitudes.

To be able to delight in the natural order, to suddenly realize that the sun setting before us is a sign of some divine presence, or to feel the still air enwombing one's entire being reveals a supple imagination that can experience joy in celebrating Nature's gifts to buoy us up on the seas of our own scattered sufferings. Language can assist us in seeing into beauty that normal modes of perception cannot deploy. The passage above captures Nature's prelapsarian splendor.

Meditation

What moments and conditions of the natural order delight and comfort?

March 3. Chapter 29: Enter Ahab; to Him, Stubb

"Am I a cannon-ball, Stubb," said Ahab, "that thou wouldst wad me that fashion? But go thy ways; I had forgot. Below to thy nightly grave; where such as ye sleep between shrouds, to use ye to the filling one at last.—Down, dog, and kennel!"

. . . .

"It's very queer. Stop, Stubb; somehow, now I don't well know whether to go back and strike him, or—what's that?—down here on my knees and pray for him? . . . It's queer; very queer; and he's queer too; aye, take him fore and aft, he's about the queerest old man Stubb ever sailed with. How he flashed at me!—his eyes like powder-pans! is he mad! . . . and the pillow a sort of frightful hot, as though a baked brick had been on it? A hot old man! (135-36).

After Stubb has an unpleasant run-in with Ahab on deck, in which the Captain verbally abuses him, the second mate considers either a direct altercation with him, or praying for him—his first time praying. Stubb addresses himself in the third person, as if he were speaking to a double of himself. Ahab behaves like a scorched riddle, an enigma striding a leg of whale bone. Stubb recollects what the Dough-boy has told him of the captain's restless sleep, warring with his covers and leaving the heat of his delirious hot head on his pillow when he rises.

Hot-headed, enraged, impatient, with teeth clenched in frustration and impotence, signal a soul at furious odds with itself. Such rage can scorch anyone who ventures into its fiery field. Wounded, we may try to put a coherent explanation to our violent behavior, to grasp its origin and purpose, through our own victimizing by it. The soul in rage is an open wound that will not heal so long as it smolders so strongly in us.

Meditation

Describe your own experience of rage in a moment when it was inflicted on others, or another's fury that placed you in Stubb's role.

March 4. Chapter 30: The Pipe

For a Khan of the plank, and a king of the sea and a great lord of Leviathans was Ahab . . . .

"How now," he soliloquized at last, withdrawing the tube, "this smoking no longer soothes. Oh, my pipe! hard must it go with me if thy charm be gone! Here have I been unconsciously toiling, not pleasuring—aye, and ignorantly smoking to windward all the while . . . . as if, like the dying whale, my final jets were the strongest and fullest of trouble. What business have I with this pipe? This thing that is meant for sereneness . . . . I'll smoke no more—"

He tossed the still lighted pipe into the sea. The fire hissed in the waves; the same instant the ship shot by the bubble the sinking pipe made (137).

Ahab's meditation in an overheard soliloquy in a one page chapter, reveals him recoiling from what had for years given him great pleasure. He tosses it into the sea where it hisses and bubbles like a try-pot. As a symbol of contentment, equanimity and serenity, even a partner in his solace, the pipe is now abandoned and with it the last remnant of Ahab's non-obsessive nature and any last chip of tranquility. His heated obsession to find and murder the White Whale grows more pronounced the farther from home and hearth he voyages in his isolation.

To strip ourselves of what once afforded pleasure because our hearts are so consumed with feelings of destruction that alienate us from ourselves and others is a form of emotional abandonment and suicide. We dismember ourselves from the human community and isolate ourselves with our wounds that can then multiply their festering damage. Joy is absent, pushed overboard by emotions that shrink life's possibilities. Our afflictions can imprison us from life's joys.

Meditation

When have life's circumstances left you isolated and alienated?

March 5. Chapter 31: Queen Mab

Next morning, Stubb accosted Flask.

"Such a queer dream, King-Post, I never had. You know the old man's ivory leg, well I dreamed he kicked me with it; and when I tried to kick back, upon my soul, my little man, I kicked my leg right off! And then, presto! Ahab seemed a pyramid, and I like a blazing fool, kept kicking at it . . . . 'Why,' thinks I, 'what's the row? It's not a real leg, only a false one.' And there's a mighty difference between a living thump and a dead thump . . . . The living member—that makes the living insult, my little man" (138).

Stubb's dream is revelatory; it brings forth a wisdom about kicking back against a force mightier than any kick could possibly harm. He wonders about the phantom leg of ivory bone vs. the real enfleshed leg as he places the incident in a truer perspective. His wish for vengeance is modulated by his recognition of a living over against a dead thump-stump. That he says he lost his leg in seeking vengeance on the one who affronted him spills his dream over into the conflict/dismemberment between Ahab and the white pyramid, Moby Dick. His dream underscores the power of living flesh against its prosthetic counterfeit.

Dreams have their own wisdom that bypass rational consciousness. They can reveal the truthful underbelly of the soul in conflict or competition with itself, or in a violent exchange with life's presences. Dreams reveal our own compulsive-addictive behaviors, often in symbolic form, and can offer a way out through an oneiric exit strategy that liberates us from the enemy deep within or allows us to integrate the other abiding in us. Dreams are part of our fiction in primal form.

Meditation

Has a dream revealed an event or a quality or an emotion in your life that, in time, surprised you with its wisdom?

March 6. Chapter 31: Queen Mab

"But now comes the greatest joke of the dream, Flask, While I was battering away at the pyramid, a sort of badger-haired old merman, with a hump on his back, takes me by the shoulders and slews me round. 'What are you 'bout?' says he. Slid! man, but I was frightened. Such a phiz! But, somehow, next moment I was over the fright. 'What am I about?' says I at last. 'And what business is that of yours, I should like to know, Mr. Humpback? Do *you* want a kick?'. . . then he turned round his stern to me, bent over . . . . his stern was stuck full of marlinspikes, with the points out. Says I on second thought, 'I guess I won't kick you, old fellow'" (138-39).

This part of the elaborate dream, which he interprets as best he can to Flask, exposes the back side of its content. Now Stubb is Ahab and the mythic merman—Mr. Humpback—is the White Whale. The figure dragging seaweed with him reveals the perilous side of himself one might impale one's foot on if, as Stubb considers, he were to kick against the spikey spine of this wise sea creature. He then instructs Stubb that to be kicked by greatness, as he was by Ahab, and as Ahab was by Moby Dick, should be considered an honor, not an insult. Stubb believes the old merman's presence and his purpose have "made a wise man of me, Flask."

What draws our attention through dreams can result in a complete shift in attitude or a radical change of perspective towards events in waking life. Dreams are perspectival as well as symbolic. They offer another angle of vision from which to gauge our life. Dream consciousness takes us deep into the core of who we are and reveals to us what may have been hidden for decades. They are, then, gifts of the soul from many fathoms down to help us plumb aspects of ourselves.

Meditation

Recall a dream that skillfully instructed you in some action or attitude.

March 7. Chapter 32: Cetology

Already we are boldly launched upon the deep; but soon we shall be lost in its unshored harborless immensities. Ere that come to pass; ere the Pequod's weedy hull rolls side by side with the barnacled hulls of the leviathan; at the outset it is but well to attend to a matter almost indispensable to a thorough appreciative understanding of the more special leviathanic revelations and allusions of all sorts which are to follow.

It is some systematized exhibition of the whale in his broad genera, that I would now fain put before you (141).

A turning point in the story occurs as Ishmael again doubles his image of ship and whale, imagining them floating in concert, mirroring one another in context, design and motion. The entire epic is a sustained litany of doubling, even as Ishmael draws our attention to his epic writing task to re-present his voyage in a language that captures and doubles its design, now in words. His belief is that by laying out to us readers a systematic, formal, scientific series of categories, we will sail closer to the whale's meaning. Crafting a verisimilitude of his quest "upon the deep" is now his epic task.

However we may think so, the mystery of life, even the enigma of any one living entity--here the whale in its scanned measurement--is a distinct "systematized exhibition" whose purpose is to contain it. We seek in our telling to give visible form to what resides largely beneath the aspects of appearance, to what remains elusive and often beyond our grasp. A different level of imagining is required to provoke the whale's presence from below the surface, what remains frustratingly illusive, whatever we designate as the whale's meaning for us.

Meditation

If the whale is an image as well as a double of one's ship of life itself, how have you attempted to schematize its meaning?

March 8. Chapter 32: Cetology

I promise nothing complete; because any human thing supposed to be complete must for that very reason infallibly be faulty . . . . My object here is simply to project the draught of a systematization of cetology. I am the architect, not the builder.

But it is a ponderous task; no ordinary letter-sorter in the Post-Office is equal to it. To grope down into the bottom of the sea after them; to have one's hands among the unspeakable foundations, ribs, and very pelvis of the world; this is a fearful thing. What am I that I should essay to hook the nose of this leviathan! The awful tauntings in Job might well appal me. "Will he (the leviathan) make a covenant with thee? Behold the hope of him is vain!" (143).

Ishmael recognizes his limits and the fallacy of completeness in writing of leviathan, but his epic calling is to attempt such a whale of a feat. He feels a certain futility in grasping with both hands at the world's mystery, the mysterious phantom of life itself that defies conquest. To dare stretch one's arms out to seize the very pelvis of the world is both inflated and infatuating; perhaps the epic hero needs to feed off of both. To write of a mighty theme is not for the faint-hearted or the ordinary author. He sees an intimate kin in the Biblical Job who wonders about a covenant with the whale but feels it is in vain.

Each of us, I suspect, comes to a place in one's life where we may want to lay hands on the body of the world in its deepest depth and bulk, to feel into its sinews, tendons, ribs and cartilage. This moment may be unnerving and audacious, demanding a radical life change. Yet the impulse to do so is equal to a heroic calling. A sense of wonder may seize us and prompt such a daring enterprise. Many refuse the call to grasp the world's mysteries; for others, it originates the journey.

Meditation

Describe what "covenant" with the world you've made or wish to make.

March 9. Chapter 32: Cetology

Finally: It was stated at the outset, that this system would not be here, and at once, perfected. You cannot but plainly see that I have kept my word. But I now leave my cetological System standing thus unfinished, even as the great Cathedral of Cologne was left . . . . For small erections may be finished by their first architects; grand ones, true ones, ever leave the copestone to posterity. God keep me from ever completing anything. This whole book is but a draught—nay, but the draught of a draught. Oh, Time, Strength, Cash, and Patience! (153).

One of the longest chapters in the epic edifice constructed by Ishmael, it details both the classification of whales and the craft of writing. So enormous is his theme that his only hope as a writer is to produce a draught of a draught—a masterful project of endless revision. Try as he may, his systematic compartmentalizing of all whales is in the end futile. Leviathan will not lend itself to such a formal catalogue. Like the magnificent Cathedral of Cologne, Ishmael's edifice is as complex and as impossible to complete in his lifetime. He prays, therefore, never to complete it or anything else, for to do so would be to foreclose on a theme that is inexhaustible in scope and organic in nature.

Not completing life projects rubs against the grain of cultural assumptions that we complete or finish what we begin as a moral imperative. Often considered a failure to leave "unfinished business," we may find a satisfying liberation in not being obsessed with finishings. Worthy projects, like life itself, often defy completing because loose ends may be a permanent part of their design. "Finishing Schools" seem quaint by comparison. Perhaps the process of working and not bringing something to completion harbors its deeper value.

Meditation

Have you ceased a project that seemed very important in the process, but offered a level of satisfaction in its incompleteness?

March 10. Chapter 33: The Specksynder

But Ahab, my Captain, still moves before me in all his Nantucket grimness and shagginess; and in this episode touching Emperors and Kings, I must not conceal that I have only to do with a poor old whale-hunter like him; and, therefore, all outward majestical trappings and housings are denied me. Oh, Ahab! what shall be grand in thee, it must needs be plucked at from the skies and dived for in the deep, and featured in the unbodied air! (156).

In one of the most philosophical and psychological chapters in the voyage, Ishmael attempts to fathom the form of his Captain in his grand "sultanism" (155). He calls him "my Captain" in a tone of affection and awe while keeping alive the image of the shaggy bear he called Ahab earlier. Ishmael imagines two Ahabs: the outward form of "a poor old whale hunter" and an inward formidable majesty of grandeur and tyranny, akin to that of a sultan. But to discover that grandeur requires an ascent and a descent into deepness. It is a phantom self of "the unbodied air." As he earlier struggled to describe the whale through its cetology, Ishmael now grapples to fathom the concealed Ahab's magnitude. Whale and man duplicate one another once again.

Lurking often in our lives is the vague apprehension that beyond or behind the phenomenal world lies an invisible reality that in moments of clarity surfaces beside the tangible and palpable. It is often no more than an intuitive awareness or a phantom presence; nonetheless, it is real, valuable and can feel even numinous. It seeks recognition and acknowledgement in its grand eruption. Intuiting it, we grow aware of a form or an architecture that supports and structures it.

Meditation

Where and when in your life have you discerned a reality or a presence concealed behind the visible structures of experience?

March 11. Chapter 34: The Cabin-Table

Over his ivory-inlaid table, Ahab presided like a mute, maned sea-lion on the white coral beach, surrounded by his war-like but still deferential cubs. In his own proper turn, each officer waited to be served. They were as little children before Ahab; and yet, in Ahab, there seemed not to lurk the smallest social arrogance . . . . Ahab thereby motioned Starbuck's plate towards him, the mate received his meat as though receiving alms; and cut it tenderly . . . . so these cabin meals were somehow solemn meals, eaten in awful silence (158-59).

Order, degree, propriety, solemnity and fear suffuse the cabin meals, with Ahab as both sealion and king, accompanied by his knights of the table. In the captain's presence, his mates seem to lose their identity and regress to the status of children in the company of a stern and silent brooding parent. Each receives his food in silence and servitude, each slipping into his own cocoon to eat, separate from one another even though they gather in a communal setting. There exists no *communitas*, only the silence of alienated souls where each yields his voice to the silence of the Captain's "dumb" melancholy presence.

Awful silence in the presence of a tyrannical, wounded and controlling parent, spouse, boss, or leader steals or suffocates our human impulse toward relationship. The connective tissue of language, conversation and developing friendships, when discouraged, fashions in its silence an insidious expression of control. No intimate or common experiences are shared, no troubles or joys find air vents in language; one becomes a victim of a silent and silencing absolute power. Our words spoken are our bond with others. When conversation is disallowed, some isolating and less-than-human atmosphere prevails.

Meditation

When has your voice been taken from you, made unwelcome, wherein you were reduced to silence and alienated from others?

March 12. Chapter 34: The Cabin-Table

In strange contrast to the hardly tolerable constraint and nameless invisible domineerings of the captain's table, was the entire care-free license and ease, the almost frantic democracy of those inferior fellows the harpooneers. While their masters, the mates, seemed afraid of the sound of the hinges of their own jaws, the harpooneers chewed their food with such a relish that there was a report to it. They dined like lords . . . .

It was a sight to see Queequeg seated over against Tashtego, opposing his filed teeth to the Indian's; crosswise to them, Daggoo seated on the floor . . . . at every motion of his colossal limbs, making the low cabin framework to shake, as when an African elephant goes passage in a ship (160-61).

Ishmael affectionately describes the three harpooneers, how at ease they are with one another, creating a true democracy in their cultural differences, yet united by a common fraternity. They represent the polar opposite political and social structure from the king and his knights of Ahab's suffocating Arthurian table. The former are separate but equal, united thereby in a common brotherhood. Magnificent Daggoo, a giant of a man, hardly fits into their dining room, yet he reveals almost a "dainty" (161) quality to his eating. Ishmael admires this "frantic democracy" in its human joyfulness.

How different is it to enjoy a meal where each can be oneself in the face of differences in culture, traditions and mythologies. To move along a common keel in the spirit of equality with one another bespeaks a mutual respect and an intrinsic value of each member in the life-force of a democratic union. Smacking lips in enjoyment of a fine meal with others in conversation celebrates the nobility of each participant.

Meditation

When have you experienced an authentic democratic spirit?

March 13. Chapter 34: The Cabin-Table

[I]n the cabin was no companionship; socially, Ahab was inaccessible . . . . He lived in the world, as the last of the Grisly Bears lived in settled Missouri. And as when Spring and Summer had departed, that wild Logan of the woods, burying himself in the hollow of a tree, lived out the winter there, sucking his own paws; so, in his inclement, howling old age, Ahab's soul, shut up in the caved trunk of his body, there fed upon the sullen paws of its gloom! (162).

Ishmael's power of language knows few parallels in his majestic tragic description of the bearish captain. Isolated, torqued inward on himself, hibernating in his own wounded shroud, tucked into the tree's hollow described earlier in "Loomings: "There stand his trees, each with a hollow trunk, as if a hermit and a crucifix were within" (4). Ahab "wears a crucifixion in his face" (132). His soul seems crucified on the wood of his deep wound, his body the tree that incarcerates his soul in muted agony. He devours himself in his gloomy wake of hibernation—isolated from all joys of communal fraternity and wrapped in his own misery. This dark pall eventually settles over all those he commands.

This Ahab impulse is foreign to none of us when a wound, an affliction, or an infection closes us inward in self-pity, rage or deep resentment. We may seek to strike out at someone for our afflictions, a form of spiritual dismemberment. We can in the process lose all contact with others that we need for psychic and emotional well-being. Perhaps there exists no greater devourer of our joy in life than the bearishness of our own self-absorption. Licking our wounds may be sorry consolation when we suffer a crucifixion absent redemption.

Meditation

When have you found yourself isolated from the entire human community because of a deep affliction or dismemberment?

March 14. Chapter 35: The Mast-Head

It was during the more pleasant weather, that in due rotation with the other seamen my first mast-head came round.

I take it, that the earliest standers of mast-heads were the old Egyptians; because, in all my researches, I find none prior to them . . . . And that the Egyptians were a nation of mast-head standers, is an assertion based upon the general belief among archaeologists, that the first pyramids were founded for astronomical purposes . . . [and]those old astronomers were wont to mount to the apex, and sing out for new stars, even as the look-outs of a modern ship sing out for a sail, or a whale just bearing in sight (163).

Such a rich historical analogy does Ishmael construct in comparing Egyptian astronomers with whalemen manning the mast head of a ship, where whales and sails are their new stars. Astronomy meets cetology. Later, whales' scars and grooves in their skin will be described as Egyptian hieroglyphs difficult to fathom; Moby Dick himself will be compared to a white pyramid. Whalemen in ships' mast-heads continue the tradition of earlier stargazers, one group looking to the seas, the other seeking in the night sky additional celestial bodies. The White Whale is the white star in the depths.

The perspective the mast-head offers is sublime. There, above the sea, one discerns such distances from that height, above the fray of mere mortals below. It seems a position of transcendence, a wooden elevation to see the blows and breaches of whales that for those on deck remain invisible. As a metaphor, the mast-head allows one a god-like view of the world in its many atmospheres. The pinnacle of a pyramid is an additional rich metaphor for a heightened vision of the world.

Meditation

Have you experienced a heightened view of your life and its trajectory?

March 15. Chapter 35: The Mast-Head

In the serene weather of the tropics it is exceedingly pleasant the mast-head: nay, to a dreamy meditative man it is delightful. There you stand, a hundred feet above the silent decks, striding along the deep, as if the masts were gigantic stilts, while beneath you and between your legs, as it were, swim the hugest monsters of the sea . . . . There you stand, lost in the infinite series of the sea, with nothing ruffled but the waves. The tranced ship indolently rolls; the drowsy trade winds blow; everything resolves you into languor . . . . [while]a sublime uneventfulness invests you; you hear no news; read no gazettes (165).

Yes, *Moby-Dick's* central action is the hunt for the White Whale. But when we read passages like the one above, we realize the orbit of the plot circles out, well beyond an obsessive chase for the afflicting Leviathan. Crucial terms of Ishmael's spiritual pilgrimage breach in this passage; it is the quest of one soul as it traverses and deepens into the *anima mundi*—the soul of the world. A mystical sense of reverence and reverie attends Ishmael's high serenity; his gaze is horizontally improved as he acknowledges the monsters of the deep. His perception is cross-joined—both horizontal and vertical at once. In this visionary state he escapes all the mundane trappings and tracings of mortality.

We each are occasioned moments of sublime detachment from the world's busyness, news, "domestic afflictions, bankrupt securities" (165)—all the sufferings of life. In instances characterized by languor, sublimity and reverie, all melts away like icicles on a warm winter day. What may then emerge is an awareness of one's deeper being as it connects to the soul of things in ecstatic harmony. The natural order offers a perspective and a serenity unattainable in urban landscapes.

Meditation

Recall a moment of detachment and bliss when you felt above the mundane, inhabiting your own mast-head nest of complete contentment.

March 16. Chapter 35: The Mast-Head

Let me make a clean breast of it here, and frankly admit that I kept but sorry guard. With the problem of the universe revolving in me, how could I—being left completely to myself at such a thought-engendering altitude—how could I but lightly hold my obligations to observe all whale-ships' standing orders, "Keep your weather eye open, and sing out every time."

And let me in this place movingly admonish you, ye ship-owners of Nantucket! Beware of enlisting in your vigilant fisheries any lad with lean brow and hollow eye; given to unseasonable meditativeness . . . and this sunken-eyed young Platonist will tow you ten wakes round the world, and never make you one pint of sperm the richer (167-68).

Meditation and contemplation are markers of a philosophic life but fit only narrowly into whaling's active life. Ishmael's metaphysical bent high above the world's fray is not in accord with keeping one's eyes sharpened for whale spouts. Meditating on the forms existing invisibly behind the phenomenal world will not fill the hold with spermaceti. Ishmael knows his spiritual propensities to be weaknesses in whale hunting because "singing out" is outside his reveries. He cautions ship owners to avoid any sunken-eyed Platonists like himself who wander aboard to sign on to kill whales; they will yield few if any.

To seek the "ungraspable phantom of life" (5) is to have the universe revolving within. Our philosophic or meditative reveries may be a way to discover the world's formative principles and tap into the primal, the archaic and eternal forms that lie behind and bestow shape to the earthly matter. To wonder at the way things are and to explore how this is so marks the beginning of philosophy's love of invisibles.

Meditation

As you develop, do you sense in yourself an impulse to wonder about what might lie behind or beyond the things of sense?

March 17. Chapter 35: The Mast-Head

Perhaps they were; or perhaps there might have been shoals of them [whales] in the far horizon; but lulled into such an opium-like listlessness of vacant, unconscious reverie is this absent-minded youth by the blending cadence of waves with thoughts, that at last he loses his identity; takes the mystic ocean at his feet for the visible image of that deep, blue, bottomless soul, pervading mankind and nature; and every strange, half-seen, gliding, beautiful thing that eludes him; every dimly-discovered, uprising fin of some undiscernible form . . . .

Over Descartian vortices you hover . . . . Heed it well, ye Pantheists! (168-69).

Ishmael's mystical reverie melts him into communion with the grand unity of mortals and nature. In his mast head mentality, seeking whales transforms into a discovery of the *anima mundi*, or what Ralph Waldo Emerson termed the "over soul." Like Father Mapple's sermon from his podium, Ishmael is like a *high* priest of the imagination wherein he dissolves into the grand phantasm of life itself by transfiguring into a "no self." In such an expansive disposition he discerns those forms residing majestically behind the world's appearances, only dimly grasped, like a partially-perceived whale.

We are each blessed with moments in which we are given a glimpse behind the veil of daily life to a more potent presence of what finally can't be named, only experienced; not captured or tamed, it is too big, too impersonal and too autonomous. But we can feel something akin to rapture or sublimity when it appears, both hierophanic and grand—as part of us. It may place us on the path of a spiritual awakening. We discern a formative principle resting behind phenomena.

Meditation

When have you sensed reality, like Ishmael's, that permanently altered your worldview, or your depth and breadth of understanding?

March 18. Chapter 36: The Quarter-Deck

Soon his steady, ivory stride was heard, as to and fro he paced his own rounds, upon planks so familiar to his tread, that they were all over dented, like geological stones, with the peculiar mark of his walk.

. . . .

"D'ye mark him, Flask?" whispered Stubb; "the chick that's in him pecks the shell. 'Twill soon be out."

. . . .

"What do ye do when ye see a whale, men?"

"Sing out for him!" was the impulsive rejoinder from a score of clubbed voices.

"Good!" cried Ahab with a wild approval in his tones (170-71).

From the isolated perception of the world's depths in reveries of dissolution of the self in the last entry, the epic now tacks into the first communal gathering on the quarter-deck. Ahab assembles the entire crew composed of members from around the globe—into a mono-maniacal unity. Wherever Ahab walks on the ship, he leaves a prosthetic impression; whenever he gathers the men, he dents their souls into servitude. His wounded force acts like a magnet, his language seductive, his aims self-serving. He disarms his men with feigned camaraderie.

Each of us knows the power of a speaker, a leader, or an acquaintance to seduce, to beguile and to bend our will with the crowbar of a cause that we may only half-consciously understand; we yield nonetheless. We may become subservient and lose ourselves in another's grand design. We may also pull others into service and servitude to promote our own narrow cause. We may recognize the terms of the cult that seized us, or our own cult-driven design on others.

Meditation

When have you been overpowered by another, where you discovered you were serving their cause, not your own well-being?

March 19. Chapter 36: The Quarter-Deck

"All ye mast-headers have before now heard me give orders about a White Whale. Look ye! d'ye see this Spanish ounce of gold?"—holding up a broad bright coin to the sun—"it is a sixteen dollar piece, men. D'ye see it? Mr. Starbuck, hand me yon top-maul."

. . . .

"Whosoever of ye raises me a white-headed whale with a wrinkled brow and a crooked jaw; whosoever of ye raises me that white headed whale, with three holes punctured in his starboard fluke—look ye, whosoever of ye raises me that same White Whale, he shall have this gold ounce, my boys!" (171-72).

The terms of the real purpose of the Pequod's destiny is now exposed on the quarter-deck; money is promised in exchange for information—much like a bounty on the head of a criminal sought for committing violent acts. The gold coin from Quito, Ecuador resting on the equator deploys a numinous energy for Ahab when he hammers it to the main mast, a crucified coin against the wood that bestows on the Pequod its primary intention.

Moby Dick is also wounded, crooked, wrinkled, and punctured, in part like the coin as reward to subdue him. Ahab's three incantations of "whosoever of ye" is both emphatic and startling in its conjuring force.

A monetary reward is a powerful incentive and temptation; it can reveal how often what is most valued is information or data. We can be sucked into another's obsession when money is the grand payoff. We see in our day how greed for more wealth can lead otherwise temperate individuals to be so obsessed with money that they skim off all moderation and common decency in order to win the prize dangling before them, its pursuit bankrupting self and others.

Meditation

Has the promise of greater wealth seduced you to abandon values?

March 20. Chapter 36: The Quarter-Deck

"Who told thee that?" cried Ahab; then pausing, "Aye, Starbuck; aye, my hearties all round; it was Moby Dick that dismasted me; Moby Dick that brought me to this dead stump I stand on now. Aye, aye," he shouted with a terrific, loud, animal sob, like that of a heart-stricken moose; "Aye, aye! it was that accursed White Whale that razed me; made a poor pegging lubber of me for ever and a day! . . . Aye, aye! And I'll chase him round Good Hope, and round the Horn, and round the Norway Maelstrom, and round perdition's flames before I give him up. And this is what ye have shipped for, men! to chase that White Whale . . . . till he spouts black blood and rolls fin out" (173).

The itinerary of the commercial whale hunt is made clear: not the enterprise of profit earned from whale oil but a personal vendetta paid for in its success with one gold coin from a country at the center of the globe. Ahab describes himself as a dismasted ship who now wears an ivory leg of whale bone; he walks with legs both human and animal, becoming a duplicate of what he pursues. The White Whale has made him impotent like the legendary Fisher King and similar to the wounded King Ahab biblically recounted in 1 Kings. Vengeance could not be more fiercely stated than in Ahab's aggrieved words.

Vengeance, revenge, an obsession to get even, or to square the score can consume every ligament of our being. Obsession with exacting pain and suffering in our legitimate or distorted sense of Justice can cripple us further than any retribution could accomplish. Vengeance's energy can incinerate our soul and dismember us further so we eventually have no moral leg to stand on. Our entire self can become a dead stump wherein we live through an emotional prosthetic.

Meditation

Recall when a desire to "even the score" caused great suffering in you and left you even more afflicted and perhaps impotent.

March 21. Chapter 36: The Quarter-Deck

"Vengeance on a dumb brute!" cried Starbuck, "that simply smote thee from blindest instinct! Madness! To be enraged with a dumb thing, Captain Ahab, seems blasphemous."

"Hark ye yet again—the little lower layer. All visible objects, man, are but as pasteboard masks. But in each event—in the living act, the undoubted deed—there, some unknown but still reasoning thing puts forth the mouldings of its features from behind the unreasoning mask. If man will strike, strike through the mask! How can the prisoner reach outside except by thrusting through the wall? To me, the White Whale is that wall, shoved near to me. . . . Talk not to me of blasphemy, man; I'd strike the sun if it insulted me" (174).

Such a powerful statement of a wounded soul whose affliction has birthed a worldview that is narrow, confining and self-defeating. This dismembering encounter with the White Whale permanently altered the terms of Ahab's existence. Physis, nature, and metaphysics gather around his suppurating wound that language poignantly captures. Only an act of violence will free Ahab from his prison, so he believes. Yet, behind the whale wall may be nothing but a void, an abyss, "naught." Ahab is check-mated by his fierce impulse for vengeance. Starbuck's alternative perception runs counter to his Captain's maimed metaphysic.

Some wounds we suffer are permanent. But the deepest affliction resides in not letting it go, as Stubb's dream earlier seemed in its wisdom to encourage. We may at times need our afflictions for our own deepening into who we are; however, relentlessly kicking against the feelings that bubble up from the violence may be far more debilitating. Wounds can become a chrysalis to encase us or liberate us.

Meditation

What wound(s) do you still find necessary to carry and nurture, and to keep open, always draining vengeful bile?

March 22. Chapter 36: The Quarter-Deck

"Drink and pass!" he cried, handing the heavy charged flagon to the nearest seaman. "The crew alone now drink. Round with it, round! Short draughts—long swallows, men; tis hot as Satan's hoof. So, so; it goes round excellently. It spiralizes in ye; forks out at the serpent-snapping eye. Well done; almost drained."

. . . .

"Advance, ye mates! Cross your lances full before me. Well done! Let me touch the axis." So saying, with extended arm, he grasped the three level, radiating lances at their crossed centre; while so doing, suddenly and nervously twitched them (175-76).

Disclosing publicly to the crew the real purpose of the voyage, Ahab rushes to ritualize and so vortex every crew member into his design. His wish is to galvanize them to his monomaniacal scheme: to slay the White Whale at all costs. Bribed now by money and grog, the crew submits to his mania, which is couched in satanic imagery. To complete the ritual, he places his hand symbolically on the lances at their centering connection, blesses them and baptizes them into his obsession. He assumes the role of high priest at a satanic ritual.

Our deepest afflictions can procreate by enlisting others in our vengeful wake to slay the offender, the genesis of the affliction. Nations have historically done so with fierce regulatory. The plot: to create an enemy and then heap one's bile on it, often smothering any chance of its survival. Then the wound suppurates as a communal infection; all are often blindly swept into its maelstrom; in the process they relinquish their own thoughts and values. Afflicted, we convince others that we are right and just in pursuing a violent response.

Meditation

When have you been conscripted as co-signer to another's revenge?

March 23. Chapter 36: The Quarter-Deck

"Now, three to three, ye stand. Commend the murderous chalices! Bestow them, ye who are now made parties to this indissoluble league. Ha! Starbuck! but the deed is done! Yon ratifying sun now waits to sit upon it. Drink, ye harpooneers! drink and swear, ye men that man the deathful whaleboat's bow—Death to Moby Dick! God hunt us all, if we do not hunt Moby Dick to his death!" The long, barbed steel goblets were lifted; and to cries and maledictions against the White Whale, the spirits were simultaneously quaffed down with a hiss (177).

The success of Ahab's baptism and conversion of the crew to his paralyzing design is measured in goblets of grog, chalices in the ritual Mass and final sacrifice of the hosted White Whale. The Captain has, through ritual and rhetoric, turned the collective soul of the crew to destroy one whale demonized as the swimming substance of evil itself. Anxious to please the enigmatic Captain, they gather their barbs around him, united against a common adversary. The community formed is not for its own well-being but rather to spread a malignity in each member. Only Starbuck "paled, and turned, and shivered" (177) when he sees through the sickness so forcefully transmitted on board.

Often only one person can poison the collective pot by creating in the communal imagination of one's group a demonized Other. History is populated by tyrants who turn their people against a scapegoat or an imagined enemy who carries all the wounds and sufferings of the wronged. It is a powerful force in the world, but it needs the cooperation of mass belief and indoctrination to continually nourish it. This accomplished, it gathers its own momentum to assume a life force unto itself, with all its members sucked into its energy field.

Meditation

Have you been swayed by coercion to join in a community that made you surrender your own values to a cause?

March 24. Chapter 37: Sunset

The cabin; by the stern windows; Ahab sitting alone, and gazing out.

I leave a white and turbid wake; pale waters, paler cheeks, where'er I sail. The envious billows sidelong swell to whelm my track; let them; but first I pass.

Yonder, by ever-brimming goblet's rim, the warm waves blush like wine. The gold brow plumbs the blue. The diver sun—slow dived from noon—goes down; my soul mounts up! she wearies with her endless hill. Is, then, the crown too heavy that I wear? this Iron Crown of Lombardy . . . . 'Tis iron—that I know--not gold . . . .

Gifted with the high perception, I lack the low, enjoying power; damned, most subtly and most malignantly! damned in the midst of Paradise! Good night—good night! (*waving his hand, he moves from the window.*) (178).

After the manic excitements of the last chapter, a peaceful tranquility settles over Ahab's soliloquy as the sun dives into the sea from its high noon perch. He absorbs the beauty of the natural order and lyrically expresses it. Yet even in what seems like a solace garnered in the moment, he feels the weight of the crown of Kingship as Lord of his Pequod Kingdom. Legend suggests that the Crown of Lombardy was made from one of the nails of the true cross and was used in coronations of kings of Italy from the 11th century on (http://en.wikipedia.org/wiki/Iron_Crown_of_Lombardy). A surly stiffness creeps into his enjoyment of the sunset, damning him.

Obsessions, resentments, and vengeful thoughts can kidnap from us any joy in the simple moments that our lives and nature gift us. We can sacrifice what Ahab calls "the low enjoying power," so snared are we by our own obsessions and desires. We ransom our own serenity.

Meditation

When do you or have you ransomed your joy in life's simple pleasures?

March 25. Chapter 37: Sunset

Oh, hard! that to fire others, the match itself must needs be wasting! What I've dared, I've willed; and what I've willed, I'll do! They think me mad—Starbuck does; but I'm demoniac, I am madness maddened! That wild madness that's only calm to comprehend itself! The prophecy was that I should be dismembered; and—Aye! I lost this leg. I now prophecy that I will dismember my dismemberer. Now, then, be the prophet and the fulfiller one. That's more than ye, ye great gods, ever were . . . . I will not say as schoolboys do to bullies—Take some one of your own size; don't pommel *me!* (178-79).

Rarely is Ahab as candid and clear about his wound and his desire for fixed vengeance than in this extended tortured soliloquy that recalls characters in Shakespeare's tragedies. He knows that his behavior will be destructive, but as he has placed himself above the gods and even fate itself, it seems a small matter. This moment of calm contemplation is akin to the eye of an emotional cyclone. He has created himself as the sole force of his fate; he will mirror his own wound by wounding the Other with like mind. But mocking the gods is a dangerous business, as dangerous as striking the sun if one feels insulted by it.

There are so many ways to respond to being attacked, afflicted and crucified by the world. The Queen Mab chapter revealed the prudence in refraining from kicking back at forces well beyond one's prowess when seized by them. To mock the invisible presences that one assumes had a hand in one's wounding is itself a form of dismemberment. Madness maddened seems so extreme that perhaps in such a condition self-annihilation appears as the only plausible consequence. Rigid responses with no elasticity can turn a wound into a tragic cataclysm.

Meditation

When has a rage for vengeance threatened to swallow every part of you and may in instances have succeeded?

March 26. Chapter 37: Sunset

No, you've knocked me down, and I am up again; but *ye* have run and hidden. Come forth from behind your cotton bags! I have no long gun to reach ye. Come, Ahab's compliments to ye; come and see if ye can swerve me . . . . Swerve me? The path to my fixed purpose is laid with iron rails, whereon my soul is grooved to run. Over unsounded gorges, through the rifled hearts of mountains, under torrents' beds, unerringly I rush! Naught's an obstacle, naught's an angle to the iron way! (179).

Ahab's extended soliloquy clusters images of hardness, metal and iron rails as earlier he described himself as "one cogged circle fits into all their various wheels, and they revolve" (176). He will not be deterred from what drives him unswervingly like a locomotive, the land's mechanical leviathan. He seeks the hidden beast deep in the grooves of the sea and tempts it out of hiding by asking it to swerve him. In his imagination Ahab desires Moby Dick, like divinity, to emerge from seclusion so he can confront and subdue him. His iron will is perfectly matched to his brittle metallic reason. The trappings of a tragic unyielding are present, akin to an arthritic soul.

We are told that when knocked off course or have suffered a defeat, we should get back up, brush ourselves off and try again. But might there be occasions when being knocked down occasions a reassessment of what might be driving us, that what we are so obsessed with achieving is finally not the most constructive pursuit? Shifting what we doggedly pursue as well as the intensity of that goal is not a sign of failure. Being elastic enough to swerve may put us on a truer path than what we had convinced ourselves was the only way.

Meditation

When, after suffering a temporary defeat, have you shifted what you were pursuing? What was the consequence?

March 27. Chapter 38: Dusk

By the Mainmast; Starbuck leaning against it.

My soul is more than matched; she's over-manned; and by a madman! Insufferable sting, that sanity should ground arms on such a field! But he drilled deep down, and blasted all my reason out of me! I think I see his impious end; but feel that I must help him to it. Will I, nill I, the ineffable thing has tied me to him; tows me with a cable I have no knife to cut. Horrible old man! . . . Oh! I plainly see my miserable office,--to obey, rebelling; and worse yet, to hate with touch of pity! (180).

In facing chapters, Ahab's madness is answered by Starbuck's surrender to his captain's obsession. Seduced by Ahab's will power and persuasion, Starbuck has not only surrendered but now feels he has no will but the Captain's and so must be an accomplice to his revenge. This "ineffable thing" is the heart beat of Starbuck's imprisonment. They are tied together as one; the first mate is fully conscious of the enterprise he has yielded to, yet he lacks the courage to break free from Ahab's iron grip; this recognition breeds misery within a leaden heart.

Even when we know better, we may succumb to the malicious intention of another while convincing ourselves we have no options but to follow it. So powerful can the charisma or force of another be that we dissolve into it and further feed its ravenous appetite. It is a moment of will-lessness to be overpowered by a belief, a force or an overriding fantasy of another. Caught in another's webbing, we cease struggling to reclaim our own freedom. Our cowardice controls our behavior. We then follow dictates that may run counter to our values and right order.

Meditation

Recall a life event when you either pulled someone into your scheme against his/her will or surrendered to another, knowing it was wrong.

March 28. Chapter 38: Dusk

[A burst of revelry from the forecastle.]
Oh, God! to sail with such a heathen crew that have small touch of human mothers in them! Whelped somewhere by the sharkish sea. The White Whale is their demigorgon. Hark! the infernal orgies! that revelry is forward! mark the unfaltering silence aft! Methinks it pictures life. Foremost through the sparkling sea shoots on the gay, embattled, bantering bow, but only to drag dark Ahab after it . . . . Oh, life! 'tis now that I do feel the latent horror in thee! but 'tis not me! that horror's out of me, and with the soft feeling of the human in me, yet will I try to fight ye, ye grim, phantom futures! Stand by me, hold me, O ye blessed influences! (180-81).

Starbuck's soliloquy counters Ahab's self-enclosed disposition. His first mate reflects on the world he finds himself fastened to while the crew carouse in the forecastle like untamed beasts. They follow the wake of the White Whale as a god. Starbuck clings to the soft pulp of his humanity in order to avoid being vacuumed into the maelstrom of Ahab's obsession. His cowardice fades into courage; he convinces himself to take a stand against the ship's fate. To counterbalance the blind conformity Ahab demands, he prays to what is sacred in life.

We pause at various junctures in life, perhaps lower the sails some to catch less of the breezes of our desires, even obsessions, and to more closely scrutinize life's lineaments. We might ask what webs we are caught in, what whale(s) we pursue and what the grand payoff may actually be. In such instances we may reclaim our lost humanness and call on what is most sacred to sustain us in the face of life's horrors.

Meditation

What is it you pursue or flee from that either increases or diminishes life's value?

March 29. Chapter 39: First Night Watch

(*Stubb solus, and mending a brace.*)
Ha! ha! ha! ha! hem! clear my throat!—I've been thinking over it ever since, and that ha, ha's the final consequence. Why so? Because a laugh's the wisest, easiest answer to all that's queer; and come what will, one comfort's always left—that unfailing comfort is, it's all predestinated . . . . I know not all that may be coming, but be it what it will, I'll go to it laughing. . . .

A brave stave that—who calls? Mr. Starbuck? Aye, aye, sir—(*Aside*) he's my superior, he has his too, if I'm not mistaken. Aye, aye, sir, just through with this job—coming (182).

Stubb's attitude towards the unknown is: all is predestined so why fight it? Little can be done about what is to come except to treat it all as a joke and maintain a comic disposition toward it. Now matter what "horribles" lurk in the unknown, laughing at it and toward it keeps its intensity at a lower burn. Earlier in "Stubb's Dream" he learned not to kick back at life's mysterious pummelings; here he affirms that laughter is a means of escaping life's magnitude, even malice, of an unknown but predestinated future. Laughter carries its own wisdom.

For some, all life deserves a continuous laugh track, for there lurks in everything, especially the unknown, a comic quality. Stubb's heart is by nature light and simple so life's *gravitas* cannot hook him. Certainly laughter can ward off what threatens us, but it may also guarantee that something's depth never becomes available to us. The trade-off is risky, however. Laughing life off can keep us out of depth's way so we never deepen our understanding of ourselves or life's mysteries.

Meditation

Have you protected yourself from a looming unknown by keeping a comic sense about it or treating it lightly through laughter?

March 30. Chapter 40: Midnight, Forecastle

MALTESE SAILOR (*Reclining and shaking his cap*)

It's the waves—the snow's caps turn to jig it now. They'll shake their tassels soon. Now would all the waves were women, then I'd go drown, and chassee with them evermore! There's naught so sweet on earth—heaven may not match it!—as those swift glances of warm, wild bosoms in the dance, when the over-arboring arms hide such ripe, bursting grapes.

SICILIAN SAILOR (*Reclining*)

Tell me not of it! Hark, ye, lad—fleet interlacings of the limbs—lithe swayings—coyings—flutterings! lip! heart! hip! all graze: unceasing touch and go! . . . Eh, Pagan? (*Nudging.*) (185-86).

Crew members have been dancing and singing on deck to provide some levity and entertainment for one another. Their ranks are from all over the world, yet what they share is a deep longing for feminine beauty and fruitfulness that would enrich their merriment. They tease one another with fantasies of buxom women; they celebrate women and their erotic bodies—lip, heart, and hip. Their teasings of one another as they conjure delicious sights of women's bodies adds layers of libido to their festivities. They crave the feminine in this too masculine world.

The presence of beauty and the lure of the opposite sex can be intoxicating and refreshing, desire-enhancing and rejuvenating. The fantasies both sexes engage about the other suggest a deeper attraction and longing for communion that elevates the differences between them as well as acknowledges their mutual desires for one another. It is one manifestation of a desire for union and communion with others. In revelry the energies of the body and desire coalesce.

Meditation

Recall the enjoyment you sensed when attracted by the lure and presence of another's embodied splendor.

March 31. Chapter 39: Midnight, Forecastle

PIP (*Shrinking under the windlass*)

Jollies? Lord help such jollies! Crish, crash! There goes the jib-stay! Blang-whang! God! Duck lower, Pip, here comes the royal yard! It's worse than being in the whirled woods, the last day of the year! . . . But those chaps there are worse yet—they are your white squalls, they. White squalls? White Whale, shirr! shirr! . . . Oh! thou big white God aloft there somewhere in yon darkness, have mercy on this small black boy down here; preserve him from all men that have no bowels to feel fear! (188).

The crew's mess boy possesses an uncanny radar for the future and for seeing below the surface of things. His thought is analogical as he free associates the white squall with the white squalls of the sailors and more, the white race squalling over the seas dismembering whales. He then associates the squalls with Moby Dick that will eventually squall up from the depths to splinter the ship. His imagination moves then to the white god above, to match the White Whale below. Pip then offers his blackness to the dark night and prays for deliverance from those who are reckless and fearless. His imaginative seeing is extraordinary.

Sensing in signs from sources various connections to an impending disaster is not alien to any of us. We all have moments of great clarity and presence about certain events that may be personal, cultural or global, smelling in the air a doom unless restraint or deflection occurs. Such precognition is not felt necessarily as a gift but a burden of insight into the foreboding future. We may each be at various times a bellwether to what is haunting the horizon.

Meditation

When have you clearly intuited with some precision the trajectory of the future, be it personal, cultural or global?

April 1. Chapter 41: Moby Dick

I, Ishmael, was one of that crew; my shouts had gone up with the rest; my oath had been welded with theirs; and stronger I shouted, and more did I hammer and clinch my oath, because of the dread in my soul. A wild, mystical, sympathetical feeling was in me; Ahab's quenchless feud seemed mine. With greedy ears I learned the history of that murderous monster against whom I and all the others had taken our oaths of violence and revenge (189).

In a retrospective confessional tone, Ishmael admits his own surrender to the forceful persuasion of his maimed captain. His language is telling, with words like "welded," "hammer," "clinch," "violence" and "revenge." The hard metaled steel, the unyielding quality of it, the inflexible and unforgiving dimension of violence and revenge—all attest to the fierce animosity the majority of the crew accepted based on a story they offer full allegiance to. So powerful is this story, Ishmael admits, because it corresponds to a mirrored "dread in my soul." Ahab has successfully tapped an analogous archetype in each of his crew. Far from the melting in him that Queequeg's presence promoted, Ishmael has hardened his heart in line with Ahab's brittle scheme.

Being hijacked and willingly yielding to the ferocity of another's design is something many have experienced. We may have thought or done something under the potent force of another that, alone, we might never have contemplated, much less agreed to and fused with. Falling under the wheels of a cult-like figure can be intoxicating when done within a mob mentality. Imprisoned in another's reality, we experience the voice of the "other" become our own. Seduced by injured mania, we yield our deeper identity on the altar of a hypnotic enthusiasm.

Meditation

When have you lost yourself in the emotional force field of another? What consequences did you reap?

April 2. Chapter 41: Moby Dick

And as the sea surpasses the land in this matter, so the whale fishery surpasses every other sort of maritime life, in the wonderfulness and fearfulness of the rumors which sometimes circulate there . . . in such latitudes and longitudes, pursuing too such a calling as he does, the whaleman is wrapped by influences all tending to make his fancy pregnant with many a mighty birth.

No wonder, then, that ever gathering volume from the mere transit over the wildest watery spaces, the outblown rumors of the White Whale did in the end incorporate with themselves all manner of morbid hints, and half-formed foetal suggestions of supernatural agencies, which eventually invested Moby Dick with new terrors . . . (190-91).

Ishmael's reflections on superstitions and fancies of the whaleman, including outblown rumors gathering like barnacles on the skin of Moby Dick all suggest this leviathan is a composite, mosaic and amalgam for many terrors, hearsays and innuendoes that have coagulated in its wake. It sounds as if it becomes well nigh impossible to extract the phantom fictions from the facts of the whale's true nature and behavior. Ishmael "sees through" in retrospect, the stories to what the White Whale may be: an elaborate fiction of the sea and of life itself, ungraspable, full of attributions and descriptions that insinuate themselves in imagination.

What is this impulse in the soul to make sense of life's enigmas by ascribing something concrete and historical with supernaturally remarkable attributes in order to craft a coherent meaning from it? We can murder to correct the disparate mysteries of life by harpooning one image and uniting all these qualities into a comprehensible object. Yet something remains ungraspable, mysterious and enigmatic to the end.

Meditation

Have you discovered that what you thought was a correct understanding of something was actually more fabrication than fact? Did it matter?

April 3. Chapter 41: Moby Dick

One of the wild suggestions referred to, as at last coming to be linked with the White Whale in the minds of the superstitiously inclined, was the unearthly conceit that Moby Dick was ubiquitous; that he had actually been encountered in opposite latitudes at one and the same instant of time.

Nor, credulous as such minds must have been, was this conceit altogether without some faint show of superstitious probability . . . so the hidden ways of the Sperm Whale when beneath the surface remain, in great part, unaccountable to his pursuers . . . (192).

The White Whale in Ishmael's imagination begins to acquire greater epic proportions in part because of the stories that cling to him "as if" they deployed the truth of the leviathan. As readers we watch a legend in its foetal form begin to ripen into something as large as the whale itself: like a phantom, ineffable, ubiquitous and an assortment of "mystic modes" written just below the above description. Such an omnipresent phantom is the stuff of legend: part historical, part fictional, part mythical. Because it is not known what the Sperm Whale does in its invisible life, narratives to contain it begin to blossom like flowers in a garden. We witness myth-making in its embryonic impulse.

Like anything in our lives that is partly visible, partly hidden, the more its invisibility, the more the imagination pursues its own version of its reality through a series of emergent projections. The object assumes over time an exaggerated lore to haunt us as we sense its power in its phantom wake. Its uncertainty and at times its terror exist when a mixture of fiction is shellacked with a veneer of fact. When we don't know or can't identify the leviathan in our imaginations, it gains power.

Meditation

Because it was not fully known or revealed, what presence in your life gained substantial shape and persuasive force?

April 4. Chapter 41: Moby Dick

[I]t cannot be much matter of surprise that some whalemen should go still further in their superstitions; declaring Moby Dick not only ubiquitous, but immortal (for immortality is but ubiquity in time). . . .

But even stripped of these supernatural surmisings, there was enough in the earthly make and incontestable character of the monster to strike the imagination with unwonted power. For, it was not so much his uncommon bulk that so much distinguished him from other sperm whales, but, as was elsewhere thrown out—a peculiar snow-white wrinkled forehead, and a high, pyramidical white hump. These were his prominent features . . . [wherein] he revealed his identity (193).

The narratives that gather around and cling to the White Whale, even though its large bulk remains invisible except for its brief surfacing, is analogous to what transpires in us: the lore and lure of Moby Dick without our seeing it, except perhaps in the lividly whitish scar and bone white prosthesis of Ahab, as well as in the language with which Ishmael invests the whale's reality; it is currently a figure more of the imagination than of history: unique and peculiar enough in its appearance, yet as enigmatic as the silence of Egyptian pyramids docked permanently in the oceans of sand, like ships at anchor.

What breaches in our imagination that might have successfully gained preeminence in our life over time as it tightens its barnacle hold on us? The White Whale may be construed as a symbolic presence for us—powerful, invisible, ubiquitous, clearly recognizable when it appears, yet inscrutable in bulk and intention. We wonder if it is a benevolent force or a recognizable threat to our survival, or both. In one sense, we each harbor our own White Whale in our interior seas.

Meditation

What strange presence do you recognize in your own uncharted waters?

April 5. Chapter 41: Moby Dick

Nor was it his unwonted magnitude, nor his remarkable hue, nor yet his deformed lower jaw, that so much invested the whale with natural terror, as that unexampled, intelligent malignity which, according to specific accounts, he had over and over again evinced in his assaults . . . . For, when swimming before his exulting pursuers, with every apparent symptom of alarm, he had several times been known to turn round suddenly, and, bearing down upon them, either stave their boats to splinters or drive them back in consternation to their ship (194).

Implicit in the whalemen's shock and surprise is that leviathan, far from being a hapless victim to their barbs and harpoons, can aggressively turn on them in its deep instinct for survival. A sea change seems to occur here. Nature has an intelligence; it wishes to survive and multiply in abundance and therefore resists any attempts at her extermination. The natural order has a wisdom and a force in pulling its pursuers up short in their greed to hunt down, dismantle and sell nature's produce. The passage presages what is to occur at hunt's finale.

What an awakening can attend us when we are forced, often through violence and wounding, to reassess our practical perspective or worldview, towards something we thought we understood and that we could with impunity behave toward in a certain way. Some shock of recognition attends such a tack in the sails of our sensibility. Wisdom can emerge from under the canopy of prudence as a result of such an encounter. Realizing how limited was our understanding of an idea, a figure, an event, or a person can sober us into a new consideration, especially when we initially thought it had no intelligence, will or design of its own. We see life in what we once thought was inert matter.

Meditation

When were you taken aback on learning that something you had treated or understood through certain assumptions recoiled?

April 6. Chapter 41: Moby Dick

His three boats stove around him, and oars and men both whirling in the eddies; one captain, seizing the line-knife from his broken prow, had dashed at the whale, as an Arkansas duelist at his foe, blindly seeking with a six inch blade to reach the fathom-deep life of the whale. That captain was Ahab. And then it was, that suddenly sweeping his sickle-shaped lower jaw beneath him, Moby Dick had reaped away Ahab's leg, as a mower a blade of grass in the field. No turbaned Turk, no hired Venetian or Malay, could have smote him with more seeming malice (194).

At the short end of his own life line, Ahab stretches out in fury and desperation to stick a mountain with a pin prick, a response out of all proportion to the adversary's power, so fully can rage engulf one. Ahab's revenge on the whale at this moment of remembered dismemberment is an impotent gesture leveled at an unknown phantom. The whale's jaw may recollect for us the sickle carried by the medieval image of Father Time. Reduced to insignificance is his dismembered leg no more relevant than a clipped blade of grass. Ahab strikes out in a miserable gesture in hopes of retribution. The word "seeming" to define malice makes us pause over Moby Dick's actual "intention."

Cut down, dismembered, or violated by what we pursue, our natural impulse may be to get even, to suffer an eye for an eye, to level the field of battle, or to exact an affliction on the wounder. If that is our only response—to seek an eye for a leg, then sustained conflict, even total annihilation, may be inevitable. When we do battle, then risking dismemberment should not surprise us. However, our desire not to yield may be our tragic undoing.

Meditation

When were you attacked, afflicted, even dismembered or crucified by a desire you sought to consummate?

April 7. Chapter 41: Moby Dick

The White Whale swam before him as the monomaniac incarnation of all those malicious agencies which some deep men feel eating in them, till they are left living on with half a heart and half a lung. That intangible malignity which has been from the beginning . . . . All that most maddens and torments; all that stirs up the lees of things; all truth with malice in it; all that cracks the sinews and cakes the brain; all the subtle demonisms of life and thought; all evil, to crazy Ahab, were visibly personified and made practically assailable in Moby Dick. He piled upon the whale's white hump the sum of all the general rage and hate felt by his whole race from Adam down . . . (194-95).

Ahab transports in his dismembered body the history of ages; he projects upon the White Whale all that provokes and disturbs us as a species. His projections are both titanic and personal. Moby Dick is here raised to the level of an epic malignity present in the world and in history from the beginning of human existence. Ahab co-signs, with the blood of his wound for ink, all the "general rage and hate" that has ever been roused in the hearts of mortals, from our genesis in the Garden. His fever is all-inclusive, deep and self-devouring. Is it only his projection?

Perhaps the wounds we receive can bring us to believe we are righting the universe by seeking our vision of justice, so all-consuming can its affect be on us. Our rage can assume the capacities of an entire cosmos in its ferocious and totalizing outlook. As an archetypal reality, rage/hate can incarcerate and incinerate entire nations, even alter history and consume all individuals' sanity. Its force field is expansive and unsparing. Once the object of our projections is fixed in place, we can heap on it our negative vengeful attitudes for a lifetime.

Meditation

Under what conditions have you heaped on another, a situation, a condition or yourself years or a lifetime of immense stored-up rage?

April 8. Chapter 41: Moby Dick

Yet, when by this collision forced to turn towards home, and for long months of days and weeks, Ahab and anguish lay stretched together in one hammock, rounding in mid winter that dreary, howling Patagonian Cape; then it was, that his torn body and gashed soul bled into one another; and so interfusing, made him mad . . . at intervals during the passage, he was a raving lunatic; and, though unlimbed of a leg, yet such vital strength yet lurked in his Egyptian chest . . . . In a strait-jacket, he swung to the mad rockings of the gales . . . . Ahab, in his hidden self, raved on. Human madness is oftentimes a cunning and most feline thing (195-96).

The climate, geography and inner landscape of turmoil all collude as a trinity of suffering in a chaos of emotions; an inner climate of rage, as he marinates in his loss, conspires in the dismembered King. His body in a straitjacket rolls to the motions of the sea, as Jonah did in the Biblical version of this scene earlier. Ahab bleeds internally as body and soul, now wounded and severed, stream into one another. Boundaries dissolve while a chaotic flow of human elements congeal in a desire for vengeance. Reference to Ahab's Egyptian chest links him to the pyramidal white object of his pursuit as he doubles Leviathan.

So potent can be a physical and psychic dismemberment, be it a flow of emotions—anger, resentment, fear, victimhood, pity and despair--that combine to form a hurricane of devastation. Such a deep trauma can foster as well a turning on one's self in agony and at the outer world seeking retribution. In such a knotted condition, one is capable of almost any thought or action, however unreasonable or mad it seems to us looking in from outside.

Meditation

Recall a time when you were maddened to the brink of sanity. What set of conditions pushed you towards such an emotional brink?

April 9. Chapter 41: Moby Dick

Now, in his heart, Ahab had some glimpse of this, namely; all my means are sane, my motive and my object mad. Yet without power to kill, or change, or shun the fact; he likewise knew that to mankind he did long dissemble; in some sort, did still. But that thing of his dissembling was only subject to his perceptibility, not to his will determinate. Nevertheless, so well did he succeed in that dissembling, that when with ivory leg he stepped ashore at last, no Nantucketer thought him otherwise than but naturally grieved, and that to the quick, with the terrible casualty which had overtaken him (196-97).

The grass blade of a leg the White Whale mowed down from below creates a permanent split in Ahab, as if his entire being had been dismembered: outer grieving appearance and an inner vindictive rage for revenge. The word "dissemble" that Ishmael calls attention to, carries the sense of dis-assemble, as something once whole is splintered into parts such that many realities are made of the one. He realizes that only by appearing well enough to remain capable of commanding a ship will he ever retrieve an opportunity to confront the source of his rage within the infinite expanse of the sea, where his sanity was splintered.

None of us can completely avoid "faking it" at times by concealing our suffering, our true feelings or our hidden motives and desires. We may need the charade to help us through the day, to keep our job, to avoid a family explosion; however, such tension can dismember us further, leaving a vast fractured life in its wake. We may in the emotional energy it requires to keep the fake awake, exhaust ourselves and those around us. We must decide where to make the cut between revealing a wound and keeping its deeper split concealed.

Meditation

When have you been forced, or chose, to dissemble because life's circumstances demanded it? What were the long-term consequences?

April 10. Chapter 41: Moby Dick

Such a crew, so officered, seemed specially picked and packed by some infernal fatality to help him to his monomaniac revenge. How it was that they so aboundingly responded to the old man's ire—by what evil magic their souls were possessed, that at times his hate seemed almost theirs; the White Whale as much their insufferable foe as his; how all this came to be—what the White Whale was to them, or how to their unconscious understandings, also, in some dim, unsuspected way, he might have seemed the gliding great demon of the seas of life,--all this to explain, would be to dive deeper than Ishmael can go (197-98).

The writer Ishmael admits here his limits as he plunges deeper into his Captain's woundedness. As he recollects Ahab's unbridled rage to persuade, to have an entire collective willingly give itself over to a destructive vengeance as a single mind, he feels his rhetorical and poetic powers reach their end point. He does not use "I" but refers to himself as a double in the third person by naming himself as Other. How contagious is Ahab's affliction and desire for a blistering vengeance gains clarity when Ishmael suspects the infection has successfully spread to the entire crew like a moral virus.

What takes place in the soul of the collective in a massive move to scapegoat is as mysterious as it is menacing. Leaders can pollute their entire people and nation by convincing them that vengeance, retribution and retaliation through violence is the only appropriate form of justice available to them. In the process we can each succumb to propaganda that strips from us our own beliefs and interpretations, making us servile accomplices. Such turmoil also robs us of any serenity and sense of balance as well as a clear and unfettered vision of what is true.

Meditation

Where and when have you witnessed a massive takeover of the collective soul by beliefs and convictions of those in power?

April 11. Chapter 42: *The Whiteness of* The Whale

What the White Whale was to Ahab, has been hinted; what, at times, he was to me, as yet remains unsaid.

[A]nd though among the holy pomps of the Romish faith, white is specially employed in the celebration of the Passion of our Lord; though in the Vision of St. John, white robes are given to the redeemed, and the four-and-twenty elders stand clothed in white before the great white throne . . . yet for all these accumulated associations, with whatever is sweet, and honorable, and sublime, there yet lurks an elusive something in the innermost idea of this hue, which strikes more of panic to the soul than that redness which affrights in blood (199-200).

Ishmael attends to one of the most dramatic features of Moby Dick: its color. White is associated with the congregation of all colors as well as the absence of any color. He points out its contrary nature in a psychological way as well, being both sweet and savage and having the capacity to induce in the soul both sublimity and panic. He first offers that this quality of the whale makes him "almost despair of putting it in comprehensible form" for the color, he continues, "above all things appalled me" (199). To situate whiteness historically, he describes its place in Christian rituals as well as other contexts that witnesses whiteness positively and negatively as its own force field.

The quality of the White Whale in a larger sphere can be part of anything that in color, texture, appearance or nature may repel, frighten and appall. Its energy is in its conjuring extreme opposite emotions in the viewer; some repellant presence lurks in it—ineffable and disconcerting, troubling and terrible. Even in something that attracts us can this negative quality be felt in a quality as apparent as its color. How something appears to us colors our understanding of it.

Meditation

Has the color of something or someone both attracted and repelled you?

April 12. Chapter 42. *The Whiteness of* the Whale

But there are other instances where this whiteness loses all that accessory and strange glory which invests it in the White Steed and Albatross.

What is it that in the Albino man so peculiarly repels and often shocks the eyes, as that sometimes he is loathed by his own kith and kin! It is that whiteness which invests him, a thing expressed by the name he bears. The Albino is as well made as other men—has no substantive deformity—and yet this mere aspect of all-pervading whiteness makes him more strangely hideous than the ugliest abortion. Why should this be so? (202).

Ishmael meditates deeply into this color that attracts and repels many of its viewers. He taps a mystery in a thing's appearance that can abhor when its color is beyond range of its normal presentation. The only distinction between an Albino man and others is his color; only *it* is ghastly. Beneath his being repelled by the man's color is a deeper profundity on why one's skin pigment would be enough to make him and all like him an outcast. The skin's tincture becomes the criterion of his value. Entranced by "the all pervading whiteness" of the Albino, Ishmael's question at the end may make us think more deeply about our condemnation of difference, especially when based on skin color.

What is it that allows us to accept and even love the appearance of some people and things while recoiling from others? Is it simply cultural conditioning? Does something deeper lurk in our responses? If our understanding of another is simply skin-deep we can justify our harsh judgment, whatever the "deformity." Yet that same unnaturalness or deformity in someone we have grown to know, as Ishmael has Queequeg, can transform the initial horror into generous acceptance.

Meditation

When has an initial repulsion of someone or thing turned to acceptance?

April 13. Chapter 42: *The Whiteness of* the Whale

It cannot well be doubted, that the one visible quality in the aspect of the dead which most appals the gazer, is the marble pallor lingering there; as if indeed that pallor were as much like the badge of consternation in the other world, as of moral trepidation here. And from that pallor of the dead, we borrow the expressive hue of the shroud in which we wrap them . . . .

Therefore, in his other moods, symbolize whatever grand or gracious thing he will by whiteness, no man can deny that in its profoundest idealized significance it calls up a peculiar apparition to the soul (203).

The cast of whiteness assumes a different hue in Ishmael's Meditation: its intimacy with death, the pellucid texture of the corpse and the shroud used to blanket the body for eternity. In the alchemical process of medieval alchemists, the albedo state of whitening follows the nigredo or darkening of the soul, a depression and a dissolution. "With whitening comes a purification" (von Franz 222) that goes beyond matter. Ishmael's language of the soul's apparitions invites an alchemical reading, as he himself is being purified during the entire spiritual voyage which began in his depression of the nigredo.

Each of our soul's journeys is an alchemical voyage through the various stages of matter's substance as well as the soul's presence as it suffers towards wholeness. The process requires trust in service to the imagination, as Ishmael states later in the above passage. To confront death itself, not as a horror but more in keeping with life's cyclical motion, can both purify and liberate the soul in its pilgrimage. We enter the world's matter as a vehicle for exploring the deep interiority of our nature, where spirit and matter both congeal and converse.

Meditation

Have you at this stage of your life acknowledged your own mortality?

April 14. Chapter 42: *The Whiteness of* the Whale

Nor even in our superstitions do we fail to throw the same snowy mantle round our phantoms; all ghosts rising in a milk-white fog—

. . . .

Can we, then, by the citation of some of those instances wherein this thing of whiteness--...is found to exert over us the same sorcery, however modified;--can we thus hope to light upon some chance clue to conduct us to the hidden cause we seek?

Let us try. But in a matter like this, subtlety appeals to subtlety, and without imagination no man can follow another into these halls (203).

Ishmael instructs us on what important component is present in his methodology to grasp meaning. His exploration is down and through, first by citing historical-cultural uses of whiteness, then moving subtly into "some chance clue" as guide. His strongest certainty is the imagination's power to expose both subtlety and complexity in ever-widening spirals of understanding: find examples, meditate on them, amplify what one sees, deepen into whiteness for its treasures, and rely on what has been thought and imagined before as guides into the hidden fabric of the phenomenal world of appearance. Therein lies revelation.

Some never sense the hidden cause that moves the world's phenomena, often along certain patterned channels. We each develop a method, a *mythology* of sorts, by which we piece our narrative identity together into a meaningful whole. We splice line by line into patterns of awareness and significance. It is a poetic act based on constructing one analogy after another into an ordered pattern that confers on life direction and purpose. Without such a method our life would be incoherent, absent a meaningful narrative pattern or purpose.

Meditation

Cite one pattern in your life that helps you experience coherence.

April 15. Chapter 42: *The Whiteness of* the Whale

Or why, irrespective of all latitudes and longitudes, does the name of the White Sea exert such a spectralness over the fancy, while that of the Yellow Sea lulls us with mortal thoughts of long lacquered mild afternoons on the waves, followed by the gaudiest and yet sleepiest of sunsets? Or, to choose a wholly unsubstantial instance, purely addressed to the fancy, why, in reading the old fairy tales of Central Europe, does "the tall pale man" of the Hartz forests, whose changeless pallor unrustlingly glides through the green of the groves—why is this phantom more terrible than all the whooping imps of the Blocksburg? (204).

Ishmael's pursuit of whiteness's terror migrates from two seas of differing colors to the act of reading illustrations in fairy tales where terrible figures roam the mountains. He rests on "the unsubstantial instance" of the tall pale traveler who emerges from the words on the page as a phantom for us to experience. In the Hartz Forest of Germany are "mountains called Blockberg or Blockenberg" where demons, witches and apparitions populate the surrounding landscape, enhanced by the miners and forresters who live in the region and "are prone to superstition." This range is haunted by a "tutelary demon in the shape of a wild man of huge stature" ("The Demon of the Hartz" www.gutenbergnet.au/books06/0606291h.html.)

Reading is an imaginal act of creation and recreation in which what seems "unsubstantial" or phantom-like, under the power of imagination assumes a reality to rival or surpass those appearances in our quotidian world. Words themselves are the stars of the show; they conjure into presence by art what is absent in fact. The imagination makes present an entire world in both image and affect, for us to move about in.

Meditation

What narrative have you read that altered your perceptions?

April 16. Chapter 42: *The Whiteness of* the Whale

First: The mariner, when drawing nigh the coasts of foreign lands . . . let him be called from his hammock to view his ship sailing through a midnight sea of milky whiteness—as if from encircling headlands shoals of combed white bears were swimming round him, then he feels a silent, superstitious dread; the shrouded phantom of the whitened waters is horrible to him as a real ghost; in vain the lead assures him he is still off soundings; heart and helm they both go down; he never rests till blue water is under him again (205).

By stacking one rich illustration after another on the permutations of whiteness, Ishmael creates several patterns of perception: the distinction between what seems objectively true and what is subjectively imagined; fact over against phantom; the power of whiteness to increase dread and terror by conjuring life's sea of phantoms. They assume a reality out of all proportion to their unsubstantial nature—"the fear of that hideous whiteness" (205) that so stirs the imagination to deeper dreads. Whiteness weds objective reality with horrible imaginings.

What unnerves us may coax to the surface feelings of dread; the soul and the world's substances conspire to create panic because we sense the invisible presence of something ungraspable and unnamed that steals our comfort, our confidence and our feeling of life's secure continuity. Some of these we may share, while others are unique to our own narrative identity. Beneath the calm surface waters of our daily existence roil the monstrous, repellant and terrifying life forms that threaten our equilibrium. These imagined figures or circumstances seem more powerful than any actual event or person we encounter. They gain enormous power precisely *because* of their phantom nature.

Meditation

What dread, fear or alarm do you sense hiding behind life's visible masks?

April 17. Chapter 42: *The Whiteness of* the Whale

But not yet have we solved the incantation of this whiteness, and learned why it appeals with such power to the soul; and more strange and far more portentous—why, as we have seen, it is at once the most meaning symbol of spiritual things, nay, the very veil of the Christian's Deity; and yet should be as it is, the intensifying agent in things the most appalling to mankind.

Is it that by its indefiniteness it shadows forth the heartless voids and immensities of the universe, and thus stabs us from behind with the thought of annihilation, when beholding the white depths of the milky way? . . . is it for these reasons that there is such a dumb blankness, full of meaning, in a wide landscape of snows . . ? (206).

Ishmael deepens his grasp of this phantom whiteness by enlarging the orbit of his reflections to include the vast expanse of the Milky Way and the entire created order. Such a simple element as the color white exposes him to a vast, epic meditation on its infinite meanings and paradoxes, perhaps even extending to the absence of meaning, a fullness as well as an emptiness containing both a sacredness and the demonic at once. The words "and yet" gather around the halo of whiteness to disarm us with its intention of another order of Being lying behind the "pasteboard mask" (174) of reality. It perplexes, bewilders, and terrifies.

Facing paradoxes inherent in our becoming can both terrify and console, upset and calm, disconcert and delight. The color, tincture and hue of our becoming is whitened by our growing consciousness that more there is than meets the eye of matter. Some invisible force of reality enshrouds the known world, putting us in contact with a divine force that can dismember as well as deliver us. Whether we identify it as our White Whale or another presence speaks to the tint of our myth.

Meditation

When in your life has an enigmatic presence breached to unsettle you?

April 18. Chapter 44: The Chart

While thus employed, the heavy pewter lamp suspended in chains over his head, continually rocked with the motion of the ship, and for ever threw shifting gleams and shadows of lines upon his wrinkled brow, till it almost seemed that while he himself was marking out lines and courses on the wrinkled charts, some invisible pencil was also tracing lines and courses upon the deeply marked chart of his forehead . . . .

Ahab was threading a maze of currents and eddies, with a view to the more certain accomplishment of that monomaniac thought of his soul (210).

Few instances reveal the constant action of doubling that permeates the epic. The wrinkled brow of Moby Dick, Ahab's wrinkled brow, the wrinkled charts together create a rumpled Trinity of map, whale and Ahab's monomaniacal devisings. The passage also reveals the Captain's being marked; he is a marked man at the same instant he marks the map in tracing his path to the White Whale. The lamp swaying above his head in the bowels of the ship recalls Jonah's position below deck before he is swallowed by Leviathan. The Biblical story doubles Ahab's current tortured path as it traces the Biblical story into his own narrative.

The world continues to mark each of us every day. We arrive home with the residues of our experiences clinging to us, even as we leave our own mark, dent, trace or record on the world's wrinkled forehead. To be marked is to live; to attempt to remain unmarked is a form of death. No one escapes life unscarred. Impressions are markers on each of our journeys, even as we struggle to chart our course often through unmarked waters. Sometimes the map we create has little resemblance or connection to the particular meanderings of our journey. We might also note from what source emanates the light from our lamp.

Meditation

Have you been able to follow the planned markings of your life?

April 19. Chapter 44: The Chart

So that though Moby Dick had in a former year been seen, for example, on what is called the Seychelle ground in the Indian ocean, or Volcano Bay on the Japanese Coast; yet it did not follow that were the Pequod to visit either of those spots at any subsequent corresponding season, she would infallibly encounter him there . . . . And where Ahab's chances of accomplishing his object have hitherto been spoken of . . . when all possibilities would become probabilities, and, as Ahab fondly thought, every possibility the next thing to a certainty. That particular set time and place were conjoined in the one technical phrase—the Season-on-the-Line (212).

Ahab's design is to chart his way back to the origin of his affliction, there to enter once more "the Season-on-the-Line," where for several years running the White Whale lingered. But no guarantees attend his intuition, however carefully mapped out, because it is impossible to eliminate "chance" in the equation that bends toward certainty. But "Ahab thinking" wishes to wrest from "possibility" a more hopeful "probability" to move his chances of success closer to "certainty" in an unholy Trinitarian alliance to regulate the future.

Charting our life course, especially when guided by a grand design, is a natural impulse that offers hope to our purpose. But when this charting serves only the renewal of a former affliction such that sailing towards it again, in effect to double the wound, is our goal, we perhaps challenge the forces, if not the phantoms of life, that may shatter us on life's hidden shoals. Kicking against injury with the boot of resentment or vengeance invites further persecution and escalating war against forces that may undo us. Willful, however, we can ignore all caution.

Meditation

Does your current life course include avenging a wrong done to you?

April 20. Chapter 44: The Chart

Ah, God! what trances of torments does that man endure who is consumed with one unachieved revengeful desire. He sleeps with clenched hands; and wakes with his own bloody nails in his palms . . . .

[A]nd when, as was sometimes the case, these spiritual throes in him heaved his being up from its base, and a chasm seemed opening in him, from which forked flames and lightnings shot up, and accursed fiends beckoned him to leap down among them; when this hell in himself yawned beneath him, a wild cry would be heard through the ship; and with glaring eyes Ahab would burst forth from his state room, as though escaping from a bed that was on fire (213-14).

Ishmael's language expands magnificently to grasp the titanic suffering of his Captain in the hellish torment of obsession. He first addresses God in his eternal form, then offers a potent and grotesque image of a distorted Christ, perhaps an impotent one, who has failed to achieve vengeance, and who self-crucifies in the agony on the cross of his own consuming desire. The image is one of Christ in hell bedeviled by the torment of demons of frustrated desire. Ishmael's point of view appears to give him access to the fires burning in another man's soul.

Obsession, possession, self-consumption by one desire in life can swallow any of us in its incinerating flames, leaving us spent like a fading ember: exhausted and self-immolated. We can exist without any boundaries and be scattered over the whole world, so powerful is the energy that creates in us a titanism out of all proportion to our earthly limits. We are then taken over by phantom forces timeless in their terror, autonomous in their design and universal in their effect. Possessed by a single design or impulse, we self-consume.

Meditation

When were you consumed by an uncontrollable desire that completely possessed you? What remnants did it leave in its wake?

April 21. Chapter 44: The Chart

Therefore, the tormented spirit that glared out of bodily eyes, when what seemed Ahab rushed from his room, was for the time but a vacated thing, a formless somnambulistic being, a ray of living light, to be sure, but without an object to color, and therefore a blankness in itself. God help thee, old man, thy thoughts have created a creature in thee; and he whose intense thinking thus makes him a Prometheus; a vulture feeds upon that heart for ever; that vulture the very creature he creates (214-15).

Ishmael's understanding of Ahab's self-devouring, creature-creating imagination, as well as his superb language to capture it, is profound. He compares the specter of the Captain to Moby Dick's blankness in "*The Whiteness* of the Whale" chapter. Whale and hunter are locked in a fatal embrace. Ahab's brilliant light has no object in the world to illuminate, so it curls back on its own blankness. The White Whale is a creation of the Captain's imagination. He has charted his creation on the wrinkled map of his own soul and in the process, emptied himself of substantial reality. In the titan Prometheus' success in stealing fire from the gods, a vulture feeds on the chained figure's liver as punishment. In this passage Ahab's heart is eaten; the vulture feasting on him is, like Moby Dick, his own creation.

We each have the capacity to create a living reality of our psychic and emotional life and to form in the depths of our souls a living image that often far excels what we desire or yearn to destroy. The living event pales in comparison to what our "as if" reality, forged in the blast furnace of our imagination, can summon. Then, the created image, person or event can imprison us in its design; we are held hostage.

Meditation

When has a thought that obsessed you ended by creating a presence in you powerful enough to gnaw obsessively at your heart?

April 22. Chapter 45: The Affidavit

So far as what there may be of a narrative in this book . . . the foregoing chapter, in its earlier part, is as important a one as will be found in this volume . . . .

I care not to perform this part of my task methodically; but shall be content to produce the desired impression by separate citations of items, practically or reliably known to me as a whaleman; and from these citations, I take it—the conclusion aimed at will naturally follow of itself.

First, I have personally known three instances where a whale, after receiving a harpoon, has effected a complete escape (216).

Ishmael pauses in his narrative to speak about its construction. Whaling and writing here touch fluke to pen. The quill replaces the harpoon in a "twisted smaller" version of the hunt, now one for words. He informs us of a shift in rhetorical method—less one of classification and more anecdotal--in order to offer another venue by which to grasp the phantom leviathan. The term "whaleman" unites two life forms that combine in one word, for Ishmael is writing of both. The how of our understanding can be equal to the what of our concentration.

The passage evokes something in our style and manner of understanding an important element in our lives and then deploying the best rhetorical expression to convey that knowing. How we choose the style of our subject's delivery either fortifies or fails that reality, depending on our artistic ability to give our subject a formative shape. Succeeding or failing depends on the appropriate delivery system we employ. We sense that the deeper voyage is one of remembering aright; our method of remembering points us to our personal mythos.

Meditation

Recall a time when you forcefully and successfully expressed an important moment in your life, either to yourself or to others.

April 23. Chapter 45: The Affidavit

I do not know where I can find a better place than just here, to make mention of one or two other things, which to me seem important, as in printed form establishing in all respects the reasonableness of the whole story of the White Whale, more especially the catastrophe. For this is one of those disheartening instances where truth requires full as much bolstering as error. So ignorant are most landsmen of some of the plainest and most palpable wonders of the world . . . . they might scout at Moby Dick as a monstrous fable, or still worse and more detestable, a hideous and intolerable allegory (218).

Determined to underscore the veracity of his narrative, Ishmael's intent is partly to lift the veil hiding leviathan and the destructive qualities of the White Whale by exposing the truth claims of his story. He does not wish it to be confused with or confined to fable and allegory. It is, however, both, full of varied and subtle meanings, connections and invisible presences. Ishmael is as fascinated by the nature of the story he is crafting, and being crafted by, and of telling it well and with conviction, as he is with the events of which it is composed. His task is to raise the story to the elevated level of epic splendor. History and fiction congeal right along this fabrication line.

When we tell our stories to one another, it is impossible to know all the subtle fictions that can slip into our historical account of events to shape it into a persuasive, compelling whole. Our narratives are part literal truth and part fabricated "as if" fictions—not lies. We tell stories in a collaborative relationship with truth and what is manufactured, shifting the story's details and emphasizing certain elements to suit our audience and our intentions to achieve narrative veracity.

Meditation

Recall when you have told your story to another; did you sense that another force or presence was also guiding the telling?

April 24. Chapter 45: The Affidavit

The Sperm Whale is in some cases sufficiently powerful, knowing, and judiciously malicious, as with direct aforethought to stave in, utterly destroy, and sink a large ship; and what is more, the Sperm Whale *has* done it.

First: In the year 1820 the ship Essex, Captain Pollard, of Nantucket, was cruising in the Pacifica Ocean. One day she saw spouts, lowered her boats, and gave chase to a shoal of sperm whales . . . when, suddenly, a very large whale escaping from the boats, issued from the shoal, and bore directly down upon the ship. Dashing his forehead against her hull, he so stove her in, that in less than "ten minutes" she settled down and fell over. Not a surviving plank of her has been seen since (219).

At 8:30 a.m. on 20 November, 1820 this incident occurred. Ishmael identifies the historical event that births the fiction he is crafting from memory—a double of this historical incident. History and fiction pool in this instance, wherein the Essex's sinking evokes the story we are reading which now recounts an incident outside the narrative proper that evokes the fiction we are traversing as readers. Lines and boundaries collapse completely between historical event and fictional likelihood. Ishmael's epic achievement will be to mythologize in poetic form this historical confrontation between mortals and nature.

So much of our lives comprise a sustained blend of factual events and fictional accounts of them. At times, what we read about takes on a double life by becoming part of our own narrative development and identity, prompting us to consider what the true boundaries and landscapes of our lived reality actually are. We seem in profound ways to be an amalgam of history and myth in a unique coalition.

Meditation

Has an historical event assumed for you a new form by narrating it?

April 25. Chapter 45: The Affidavit

But I must be content with only one more and a concluding illustration; a remarkable and most significant one, by which you will not fail to see, that not only is the most marvelous event in this book corroborated by plain facts of the present day, but that those marvels (like all marvels) are mere repetitions of the ages; so that for the millionth time we may say with Solomon—Verily there is nothing new under the sun (223).

Ishmael's reminiscence trips upon an ancient pattern in the world's events and in the souls of individuals: some configuration that repeats itself eternally through history's temporality has been called an archetype, an ageless pattern, or "underlying potential form" (*Living Myth* 48) in the world soul and individual psyche. Literal history is densely populated with eternal recurrences that expose both a constant in the world's deepest fabric and a universal form in our immortal souls. Infinite variety in the specific details marries the universal design to a local habitation in time; these specifics point in their expression to the wisdom of Solomon in the *Book of Ecclesiastes* that everything in the world is a reiteration or a memory of what has already been.

When we reflect on our own history, we may begin to discover that the best and worst of our own temporal and particular uniqueness participates in a sea of universal patterns that can guide the personal myth that enwombs us. Noting such an interplay may reveal that we are part of a grand design whose origin we may call by a divine name. World mythologies deploy these timeless narratives through their particular incarnation in specific cultures and societies, but they are finally further iterations of patterns and energies present even before recorded history. They live on in our own plotted pilgrimages.

Meditation

What grand design or pattern in your life continues to shape you?

April 26. Chapter 46: Surmises

To accomplish his object Ahab must use tools; and of all tools used in the shadow of the moon, men are most apt to get out of order. He knew, for example, that however magnetic his ascendency in some respects was over Starbuck, yet that ascendency did not cover the complete spiritual man any more than mere corporeal superiority involves intellectual mastership; for to the purely spiritual, the intellectual but stand in a sort of corporeal relation. Starbuck's body and Starbuck's coerced will were Ahab's, so long as Ahab kept his magnet at Starbuck's brain (225).

"Surmises" is laden with Ishmael's psychological insights on controlling another. Tools to control others and the magnet suggest hard, metalled instruments. Ahab's magnetism, he believes, will continue to control the crew, but Starbuck offers a more mettled challenge. Portrayed as the ship's conscience and its consciousness, Starbuck poses a stiffer challenge to the Captain. The first mate's spiritual tensile strength creates the greatest worry for the Captain. As a tyrant of the imagination, Ahab knows he must be vigilant in how he *appears*.

None of us has escaped the attempted or successful control by another: a spouse, a boss, a friend, a system, or a complex of beliefs. Subterfuge may have been enlisted to keep us fooled, buttoned up, or fastened to a certain belief. Cult leaders are great adepts at such persuasion. But we can and often do regain consciousness and discover where we have been unconscious of this slippery reality. Sometimes a fine line appears between what we think we are choosing and what is chosen for us. Tyranny, we learn, requires constant vigilance to keep the subjects' compasses pointing in the direction of the tyrant.

Meditation

Have you awakened to some controlling force and successfully freed yourself from it?

April 27. Chapter 46: Surmises

Not only that, but the subtle insanity of Ahab respecting Moby Dick was noways more significantly manifested than in his superlative sense and shrewdness in foreseeing that, for the present, the hunt should in some way be stripped of that strange imaginative impiousness which naturally invested it; that the full terror of the voyage must be kept withdrawn into the obscure background (for few men's courage is proof against protracted meditation unrelieved by action); that when they stood their long night watches, his officers and men must have some nearer things to think of than Moby Dick (226).

Coercive techniques in order to sustain Ahab's single-minded design must be cultivated to hide his intention. Knowing the crew may tire of his blueprint for vengeance against the White Whale, he plots to keep his men distracted with cash from the relentless hunt so they will feel the voyage is well-earned. Keeping the crew busy and their attention away from the White Whale's presence, he believes, will buy him more time to seal his success. Ahab's psychology is astute; he knows that during long night watches they will have ample time to rethink their commitment to his monomania and perhaps rebel against it.

World leaders possessing an Ahab imagination often cultivate the cleverness to deceive their people for long periods by portraying one set of noble ideas while in the secrecy of their souls embracing destructive, self-serving intentions. Appearance is naively taken for the only authentic reality. We may be showered by our leaders with the language of noble aims and causes, when in effect we later find ourselves acquiescing to contrary, less magnanimous purposes. Such a discovery may awaken people to demonstrate for a major regime change.

Meditation

Have you awakened from deluded thinking originating in wishing to believe the best and most noble of intentions put to you by others?

April 28. Chapter 46: Surmises

For all these reasons then, and others perhaps too analytic to be verbally developed here, Ahab plainly saw that he must still in a good degree continue true to the natural, nominal purpose of the Pequod's voyage; observe all customary usages; and not only that, but force himself to evince all his well known passionate interest in the general pursuit of his profession.

Be all this as it may, his voice was now often heard hailing the three mastheads and admonishing them to keep a bright look-out, and not omit reporting even a porpoise. This vigilance was not long without reward (227).

Ahab has sunk into a routine of living a double life: Captain of an industrial whale vessel and vengeful, wounded monomaniac in search of unlimited revenge. One must remain concealed so to offer the appearance of a respectable whaling venture. The other, deep in his soul gnawing at him day and night, energizes the more subterranean engines of his brittle desire. He knows he cannot sustain the crew's allegiance to him unless they are kept busy hunting, then processing whales and making money. Ahab hides, like a submerged whale, his true intentions.

History is densely populated with leaders living Ahab's double life. Outwardly, they claim a certain grand ideal, while personally they deploy another agenda crafted for self-gain. We each may find ourselves living a split myth: outward respectable life while in our deeper selves we feel scalded by the boiling water of wounds still festering, resentments full of vital energies, addictions and disappointments in a life dissociated and bilious. Such a split and disingenuous way of being will eventuate in a muddled sense of who we actually are.

Meditation

When in your life did you mask rage, disappointment, or anger behind a cloth of cheerful respectability until you could "settle the score"?

April 29. Chapter 47: The Mat-Maker

I was the attendant or page of Queequeg, while busy at the mat. As I kept passing and repassing the filling or woof of marline between the long yarns of the warp, using my own hand for the shuttle . . . I say so strange a dreaminess did there then reign all over the ship and all over the sea, only broken by the intermitting dull sound of the sword, that it seemed as if this were the Loom of Time, and I myself were the shuttle mechanically weaving and weaving away at the Fates (228).

The act of weaving what is called "a sword mat" used to lash their whale-boat with greater support, gives rise to a rich reverie that places Ishmael in a dreamscape of Time, Fate and the weaving fabric of the self to form a trinity that includes metaphysical, mythic and material worlds. The richness of what the whaling voyage allows clarifies in this somnolent scene of serenity and deepening, where analogies lace back and forth in an "as-if" cosmos. Ishmael dreams of the physical action evoking the foundational qualities of life that engage "chance, free will, and necessity" (228). Words like "page," "yarn" "and "hand" speak also of the shuttling from left to right on the page in writing the story he plaits for us here.

We can relate easily to this moment of calm repose in the sense of a dreamy repetitive act of making something, where the imagination is allowed to disengage in order to dive fathoms down to connect with some essential part of ourselves; here we recognize for a moment the larger mythic patterns present in the unfolding plot of our lives and the texture of our text. A rich fabrication leaves us open to universal forces governing the human soul and modulating our belief in our independent thoughts and actions. Fate itself becomes palpably present.

Meditation

Recall when, for a short time you felt consciously engaged in the deeper patterns of your existence that mat-ter most.

April 30. Chapter 47: The Mat-Maker

Thus we were weaving and weaving away when I started at a sound so strange, long drawn, and musically wild and unearthly, that the ball of free will dropped from my hand, and I stood gazing up at the clouds whence that voice dropped like a wing. High aloft in the cross-trees was that mad Gay-Header, Tashtego. His body was reaching eagerly forward, his hand stretched out like a wand, and at brief sudden intervals he continued his cries.

As he stood hovering over you half suspended in air . . . . you would have thought him some prophet or seer beholding the shadows of Fate, and by those wild cries announcing their coming.

"There she blows! there! there! there! she blows! she blows!" (229).

Ishmael offers two kinds of existence in these passages: the contemplative life and the active life. His reverie is set aside by the musical rhythms of Tashtego's shouts when he spots Sperm Whales on the horizon. Free will collides with Fate as prophecy outruns the present. Like a crucified Christ with one arm free, Tashtego announces the purpose of the Pequod's quest to slay and dismember whales. But when Ishmael addresses us directly with "you," we sense more is at stake than running down a whale. Fate is below us, ready to breach.

We live much of our lives between contemplation and action, repose and motion, reverie and movement. Each signals and invites different realities to surface: one metaphysical, concerned with the soul of things, the other more practical, focused primarily on the phenomenal world. Both are necessary, both fruitful. But action without contemplation is shallow and often reactive; contemplation without action invites stasis.

Meditation

Is your life generally weighted more towards contemplation or action?

Part III

The Pursuit of the Whale
Chapters 48-76

The problem of the hero is to pierce himself (and therewith his world) precisely through that point: to shatter and annihilate that key knot of his limited existence.

The Hero With a Thousand Faces, 125.

OUR DAILY BREACH

May 1: Chapter 48: The First Lowering

The phantoms, for so they then seemed, were flitting on the other side of the deck, and, with a noiseless celerity, were casting loose the tackles and bands of the boat which swung there . . . . The figure that now stood by its bows was tall and swart, with one white tooth evilly protruding from it steel-like lips. A rumpled Chinese jacket of black cotton funereally invested him . . . . Less swart in aspect, the companions of this figure were of that vivid, tiger-yellow complexion peculiar to some of the aboriginal natives of the Manillas;--a race notorious for a certain diabolism of subtilty. . . (231).

These "five dusky phantoms" breach from below deck at the same instant the Sperm Whale surfaces. Appearing as Ahab's secret hidden weapon in the hunt for the White Whale, they emerge, led it seems, by Fedallah, who Ahab commands to lower his boat. The language of "evilly," "steel-like lips," and "diabolism" are qualities that swirl around the Captain. They surface as apparitions of his interiority with qualities Ahab has assigned to Moby Dick. The crew is startled by their abrupt emergence, but they quickly turn their attention to the task of the hunt. In their history and cultural connection these phantoms could not be more different from the medley of nations that comprise the vast diversity of the crew.

Phantom realities populate the entire life adventure and point to realities that are shadowy, insubstantial, powerful and always surprising, even as our own thoughts are composed of phantom realities and figures that may reflect our most recalcitrant obsessions, resentments, desires, needs and fantasies. They gather round us and feed our fixations further. We call them up in moments of obsession, in loosening restraints, and in times of powerful reactions to life's challenges and surprises.

Meditation

What phantom do you call on or that surfaces in your desires?

May 2. Chapter 48: The First Lowering

"Pull, pull, my fine hearts-alive; pull, my children; pull, my little ones," drawlingly and soothingly sighed Stubb to his crew, some of whom still showed signs of uneasiness. "Why don't you break your backbones, my boys? What is it you stare at? . . . Pull, then, do pull; never mind the brimstone—devils are good fellows enough. So, so; there you are now; that's the stroke for a thousand pounds; that's the stroke to sweep the stakes! Hurrah for the gold cup of sperm oil, my heroes! . . . Bite something, you dogs! So, so, so, then: softly, softly! That's it—that's it! long and strong. Give way there, give way!" (232).

For the first time, whaling has officially begun with the lowering. All boats churn into action, each with a leader. Stubb coaches, coaxes, coerces and cajoles his men to row until their backs snap. His is the language of jollity and hyperbole. He does not see the dusky phantoms as impediments, even if they are devils serving their Captain. For Stubb, the more the merrier. The prize he puts before his men has the feel of the grail cup from a medieval pilgrimage. Calling his men "dogs" may remind us of the canines that lick the dripping blood of the Old Testament King Ahab, in 1 Kings. Many allusions cross wakes in Stubb's exhortations.

We each find ourselves at certain nodal points of our lives where we are driven beyond our means for a grand prize. Our entire being is in its service. Limits and moderation fall away. We are commanded to over-reach, perhaps to the detriment of our health. We find ourselves being pushed to the brink by a Stubb-force; we risk it all. We pay close attention to what we are lured to quest for. The treasure that seems so necessary may on closer inspection prove to be of inferior worth.

Meditation

When have you been driven beyond the brink in your pursuit of what you have identified as a grail cup of great value?

May 3. Chapter 48: The First Lowering

"What think ye of those yellow boys, sir!"

"Smuggled on board, somehow, before the ship sailed. (Strong, strong, boys!)" in a whisper to his crew, then speaking out loud again: "A sad business, Mr. Stubb! (seethe her, seethe her, my lads!) but never mind, Mr. Stubb, all for the best . . . . There's hogsheads of sperm ahead, Mr. Stubb, and that's what ye came for. (Pull, my boys!) Sperm, sperm's the play! This at least is duty; duty and profit hand in hand."

"Aye, aye, I thought as much," soliloquized Stubb, when the boats diverged, "as soon as I clapt eye on 'em, I thought so" (233-34).

Starbuck and Stubb converse as their whaleboats cross one another in the hunt. Starbuck's optimism crosses with Stubb's suspicions of devils infiltrating the Pequod. Starbuck can dismiss them because his two goals are being realized in the present action: duty and profit. His practical virtues surface in his exchange with Stubb. He in turn deduces "the White Whale's at the bottom of it. Well, well, so be it" (234) and gives himself over to it as Fate decreed.

Perhaps good and evil are always present hand-in-hand as mixed motives in life's events. Shall we accept this as "the way of the world" and host the mix or fight against it and try to purify the motives present? Our phantoms can come from below to aid us in achieving our goals, but they can also threaten to override our pursuit of the grail cup. The above conversation reveals how we may push ourselves to overlook some menacing evil as we pursue the virtuous good. One wonders if life will eventually push us to recognize our blind side after the fact. In hindsight we grasp the error of judgment in the moment. With eyes intent on the "sperm ahead" we may lose track of all other alternatives.

Meditation

In any of life's pursuits, have you discovered your motives were not as pure as you originally intended or believed?

May 4. Chapter 48: The First Lowering

To a landsman, no whale, nor any sign of a herring, would have been visible at that moment; nothing but a troubled bit of greenish white water, and thin scattered puffs of vapor hovering over it, and suffusingly blowing off to leeward, like the confused scud from white rolling billows. The air around suddenly vibrated and tingled, as it were, like the air over intensely heated plates of iron. Beneath this atmospheric waving and curling, and partially beneath a thin layer of water, also, the whales were swimming . . . . [and]the puffs of vapor they spouted, seemed their forerunning couriers and detached flying outriders (236-37).

An atmosphere not unlike magical realism attends Ishmael's description of two worlds present simultaneously, a doubling of reality, one above, one below with a churning energy between wedding them. In the visible traces of an invisible life form, one must learn to read the visible signs that guide the imagination to a deeper reality of the whale world. His use of an analogy-- "intensely heated plates of iron"-- conjures the hard world of steely knives, penetrating harpoons, cracked backbones, and of course Ahab's inflexible posture. The whales' soft blubbery enormous flesh is in stark contrast to such molten rigidity.

The double reality of the whales' presence offers a rich metaphor for what life forms swim below the radar of our consciousness. We often sense a turmoil deep beneath our more placid conscious life. We can call it the "confused scud from white rolling billows" and may learn to surmise the nature of the turbulence roiling beneath. Gaining skill at spotting and interpreting this turbulence signals a deeper consciousness able to fathom the mysterious invisibles. When we can recognize the field we sail in, we awaken to new riggings of ourselves.

Meditation

When has visible turbulence led you to a deeper motion of meaning in your inner seas?

May 5. Chapter 48: The First Lowering

"That's his hump. *There, there,* give it to him!" whispered Starbuck.

A short rushing sound leaped out of the boat; it was the darted iron of Queequeg. Then all in one welded commotion came an invisible push from astern, while forward the boat seemed striking on a ledge; the sail collapsed and exploded; a gush of scalding vapor shot up near by; something rolled and tumbled like an earthquake beneath us. The whole crew were half suffocated as they were tossed helter-skelter into the white curdling cream of the squall. Squall, whale, and harpoon had all blended together; and the whale, merely grazed by the iron, escaped (239).

Ishmael's description reveals the heart of the epic's action: the ancient hunt of man subduing Nature and Nature escaping his iron resolve to kill, dismember and distribute the whale's parts for commerce. For an instant, however, an almost mystical unity surfaces wherein "squall, whale, and harpoon had all blended together" such that behind the antagonism exists a universal sympathy of all parts: nature, mortals and life itself. A form of grandeur emanates from such a majestic fight for survival. On the whale's turbulent turf, its pursuers are easily tossed out of their element into the sea and rendered temporarily harmless.

What we hunt in life may be in one instant futile and in other fruitful. Our essential action is a constant tension between life and death, between hunter and hunted, between achievement and defeat. With growing technology arises a greater power and a more severe loss of boundaries. What we hunt and conquer may also turn on us at the instant of our anticipated victory. Where we thought we were secure, we suddenly find ourselves fragile and vulnerable in a foreign element.

Meditation

Describe a whale in your life that pitched you into new waters.

May 6. Chapter 48: The First Lowering

The sound came nearer and nearer; the thick mists were dimly parted by a huge, vague form. Affrighted, we all sprang into the sea as the ship at last loomed into view, bearing right down upon us within a distance of not much more than its length.

Floating on the waves we saw the abandoned boat, as for one instant it tossed and gaped beneath the ship's bows like a chip at the base of a cataract . . . . Again we swam for it, were dashed against it by the seas, and were at last taken up and safely landed on board (240).

Nature's forces seem to conspire to save the whales from industrial annihilation. The boats cut their whales loose. The squall turns on the whalemen and creates such a mist that the Pequod, abandoning hope, bears down on the boat and splinters it to the tiniest chip, even as Moby Dick will bear down and splinter the Pequod into tiny shards in its final assault. Queequeg in this instance saves them by hearing the mother ship before it bursts, like a phantom presence, out of the fog.

An old pattern of life sails into our midst here: what was protective and as secure as home can reverse course to destroy our projects and ourselves when we are most vulnerable. Losing our way, we can be crushed inadvertently by what the Fates decree to roll over us, leaving us swimming for our lives. Yet, in another ironic twist, it may indeed save us from itself, a lumbering force field so blinded that it strikes at what relies on it and saves the same people it only moments ago sought to destroy. Such is the way we find danger where we thought safety was imminent and where we find a saving presence when we assumed we were doomed.

Meditation

When have you been attacked by what you were certain offered you assured security?

May 7. Chapter 49: The Hyena

There are certain queer times and occasions in this strange mixed affair we call life when a man takes this whole universe for a vast practical joke, though the wit thereof he but dimly discerns, and more than suspects that the joke is at nobody's expense but his own. However, nothing dispirits, and nothing seems worth while disputing. He bolts down all events, all creeds and beliefs, and persuasions, all hard things visible and invisible, never mind how knobby; as an ostrich of potent digestion gobbles down bullets and gun flints . . . . There is nothing like the perils of whaling to breed this free and easy sort of genial, desperado philosophy; and with it I now regarded this whole voyage of the Pequod, and the great White Whale its object (241).

Such a magnificent moment of pause after narrowly avoiding drowning by the Pequod. Ishmael steps back into a meditative moment to reflect on mortals universally considered. A comic sensibility enters in the wake of near-catastrophe, where life itself seems a barely graspable phantom. Trying to take in all the beliefs, attitudes and what is both visible and invisible in a desperate attempt to make sense of it all, individuals gobble up all the hard things indiscriminately in a sustained struggle to make sense of the illusive phantom--Life.

When we experience a narrow escape or trauma or near fatal moment, we may be compelled to take stock of what our life is for and to question what our role in it is or should be. What does this ungraspable thing called life mean? What does it seek, especially in the aftermath of a crisis averted or surrendered to? Something occurs to knock us off our conventional, comfortable beliefs and prejudices with such force that our vision alters and our direction shifts in an instant.

Meditation

What crisis, averted or experienced fully, shifted your point of view or perhaps your entire life's course?

May 8. Chapter 49: The Hyena

[T]aking all things together, I say, I thought I might as well go below and make a rough draft of my will. "Queequeg," said I, "come along, you shall by my lawyer, executor, and legatee." . . . .

After the ceremony was concluded upon the present occasion, I felt all the easier; a stone was rolled away from my heart. Besides, all the days I should now live would be as good as the days that Lazarus lived after his resurrection . . . . I survived myself; my death and burial were locked up in my chest. I looked round me tranquilly and contentedly, like a quiet ghost with a clean conscience sitting inside the bars of a snug family vault (242-43).

Having narrowly escaped a shattered annihilation by the Pequod's prow, Ishmael has decided, with Queequeg his legal witness, to face his mortality in the form of a written will. Doing so will aid him in relinquishing his hold on all things mortal and ephemeral. His process resurrects something deep within the vault of his soul, a double now, of Lazarus. A calm and serene peace brushes over him; his phantom nature rises to the surface and his point of view enlarges and deepens on his spiritual voyage into himself and outward to the world's uncertainties.

Such a crisis that threatens our existence gives pause to the busy pursuits of life's whaling tasks. We pull back, wonder, reassess, take stock and perhaps allow death's reality to enter us, so closely were we brushed by it through, for instance, illness, accident, wound or loss. Such a moment modifies our imagination, deepens our vision and even engenders gratitude for the finite and imperfect life bequeathed to us. "Going below," we contemplate and then sign off on our willingness to relinquish all that we have in the dead giveaway of a will. Such an intense moment of liberation can transform our attitude toward life.

Meditation

Recall an incident that brought you to contemplate your own death.

May 9. Chapter 50: *Ahab's Boat and Crew*. Fedallah

[C]ertain it is that while the surbordinate phantoms soon found their place among the crew . . . yet that hair-turbaned Fedallah remained a muffled mystery to the last . . . . He was such a creature as civilized, domestic people in the temperate zone only see in their dreams, and that but dimly, but the like of whom now and then glide among the unchanging Asiatic communities . . . . when the memory of the first man was a distinct recollection, and all men his descendants, unknowing, whence he came, eyed each other as real phantoms, and asked of the sun and moon why they were created and to what end . . . when the angels indeed consorted with the daughters of men... (247).

Ishmael attends closely to the others on board the Pequod as deserving of acknowledgement and respect. Fedallah is an emblem of difference, an ancient presence from a history foreign to the white race. He is closer to the genesis of mortals and exudes an aura of a primordial presence on board. He also conjures the image of a phantom presence, of which the White Whale may be the most majestic analogy. A hierarchy exists on board, and Ishmael believes these figures have a place and a purpose in the grand scheme of humanity.

Fear often accompanies a confrontation of difference because it makes what we know and have grown comfortable with feel strangely unnerving, if not threatening. Difference can engender powerful unease, even a wish to destroy or maim such a manifestation. But the suggestion above is simply one's self in different skin or garments. From the presence of Others we are offered an opportunity to see ourselves in an altered, even more authentic form. The experience can be exhilarating, debilitating, or a combination of the two.

Meditation

Has an experience with an Other—a person, place or thing—shifted your perception or understanding of who you are and what you believe?

May 10. Chapter 51: The Spirit-Spout

Days, weeks passed, and under easy sail, the ivory Pequod had slowly swept across four several cruising grounds. . . .

It was while gliding through these latter waters that one serene and moonlight night, when all the waves rolled by like scrolls of silver; and by their soft suffusing seethings, made what seemed a silvery silence, not a solitude; on such a silent night a silvery jet was seen far in advance of the white bubbles at the bow. Lit up by the moon, it looked celestial; seemed some plumed and glittering god uprising from the sea (248).

Ishmael's lyric passage invites us into dream, reverie, meditation and a cool mingling of one's soul with the *anima mundi,* the world soul. The delicious alliterative repetition of the "s" sound creates a gentle hissing whisper out of nature. We sense a presence of a supernatural order emerging from the deep darkness of the sea, an uprising of silvery whiteness, a ghostly presence of what has been concealed until now, appearing in a hierophany in a minor key. The "silent night" and the "silvery jet" may remind us of the birth of Christ; surely divinity suffuses the dreamy light of whiteness in moon glow.

At various intervals in our life we are gifted by the natural order with what might be called a vision rather than an appearance, or a phantom presence rather than a clear reality that is more concrete but does not stir the imagination with delight. Feminine nature for a moment overrides a more masculine presence and we intuit that mystery itself has just abrupted into our midst. We may resist the temptation to lower our boat to seek it, content rather to immerse ourselves on deck in its foretaste. In these moments we detect a reality that rests like a sleeping shadow offering an image of beauty to buoy our spirits. Like an apparition, these moments in life arrest us with their natural beauty.

Meditation

When has the natural order gifted you with its mysterious presence?

May 11. Chapter 51: The Spirit-Spout

Walking the deck with quick, side-lunging strides, Ahab commanded the t'gallant sails and royals to be set, and every stunsail spread . . . .The strange, upheaving, lifting tendency of the taffrail breeze filling the hollows of so many sails, made the buoyant, hovering deck to feel like air beneath the feet; while still she rushed along, as if two antagonistic influences were struggling in her—one to mount direct to heaven, the other to drive yawingly to some horizontal goal. And had you watched Ahab's face that night, you would have thought that in him also two different things were warring . . . [as] every stroke of his dead limb sounded like a coffin-tap. On life and death this old man walked (249).

The previous entry quoted "the ivory Pequod" (248). Here Ahab is again doubled with the ship as he walks on twin struts of life and death. The whale vessel assumes the status of a character in the journey. More, it is a double of her captain; she mimics and mirrors Ahab's disposition. Both are warring between two contrary tendencies: heaven and earth and death and life. The ship and captain are welded together in a tension that will intensify until their showdown with the White Whale, their nemesis and fulfillment.

We can often sense a similar tension in our own lives when we feel the assault of two contrary impulses, each seeking an absolute claim on us. We may spend years in a moral, emotional or physical tug-of-war. It could end in a stalemate wherein we reconcile ourselves to the constant tension without resolution yet may benefit in creative ways from the vertiginous pressure. Whatever the origin of our own "spirit-spout," it may occasion a more conscious awareness of the dual nature we inhabit. We move through our lives in the tug of vertical and horizontal forces.

Meditation

Describe a long-standing tension between two forces in your life.

May 12. Chapter 51: The Spirit-Spout

Close to our bows, strange forms in the water darted hither and thither before us; while thick in our rear flew the inscrutable sea-ravens. And every morning, perched on our stays, rows of these birds were seen . . . . [They] obstinately clung to the hemp, as though they deemed our ship some drifting, uninhabited craft; a thing appointed to desolation, and therefore fit roosting-place for their homeless selves. And heaved and heaved, still unrestingly heaved the black sea, as if its vast tides were a conscience; and the great mundane soul were in anguish and remorse for the long sin and suffering it had bred (250).

The Pequod carries a grave and heavy cargo of melancholy in one hold, restlessness in another and homelessness in a third. Beneath it rolls the dark ocean waters "as if its vast tides were a conscience," its soul suffering for what it had created, as all life suffered its genesis therein. The language opens up and out to a moral liquid landscape in full epic grandeur. The ship's voyage is a mesocosm of what has haunted humanity from Adam on down. All aboard represent humankind on a journey of and within the soul, as if the grail, the elixir of life in its mystery, were the prize. Depth and height surround the Pequod as it whitens the waters leading toward the White Whale.

At some moments in our pilgrimage we may know or intuit that we are engaged in some cosmic action that far transcends, but still includes us, in its motion. We may acquiesce to it or kick against it, but its heaving power under our feet sweeps us along in its ceaseless motion. This voyage may indeed yield strange forms and life shadows so unfamiliar as to incite fear and uncertainty. Then we know we are on *our* voyage rather than replicating that of another.

Meditation

When have you felt directly called or involved in some grand design, or that you were part of some unearthly action that defies naming?

May 13. Chapter 52: The Albatross

"Ship ahoy! Have ye seen the White Whale?" . . . .

While in various silent ways the seamen of the Pequod were evincing their observance of this ominous incident at the first mere mention of the White Whale's name to another ship, Ahab for a moment paused . . . . "Ahoy there! This is the Pequod, bound round the world! Tell them to address all future letters to the Pacific ocean! and this time three years, if I am not at home, tell them to address them to—" (252-53).

The first of at least five meetings, or gams, with other whaling ships begins with the Goney (Albatross), out four years hunting whales and now home-bound to Nantucket. Ahab's only question to them is if they had spotted Moby Dick on their passage. Such an announcement stirs the crew, for their secret mission is given public language to another ship. The epic grandeur of their undertaking Ahab expresses in their voyage around the entire globe. It signifies a monumental expedition and carries with it a smell of destiny in his instructing their mail to be delivered to an enormous PO box—the Pacifica ocean!

Aside from the expanse the entire hunt will traverse, there is a mystery too on naming something for a larger public that has been vaulted in secrecy amidst a small community of initiates. A sea change in their quest the crew feels when the object is named. We sense in our own lives the power of naming what is forbidden, taboo or cloaked. In the naming, something shifts in us as well as in the nature of the thing publicly named. It advances and intensifies in the power of its presence. When what was private goes public, its nature changes; it gains independence and perhaps even further authority.

Meditation

When something secret in your life, perhaps even some pursuit, assumed public naming, did it change or modify your quest?

May 14. Chapter 52: The Albatross

Round the world! There is much in that sound to inspire proud feelings
. . . .

 Were this world an endless plain, and by sailing eastward we could for
ever reach new distances, and discover sights more sweet and strange than
any Cyclades or islands of King Solomon, then there were promise in the
voyage. But in pursuit of those far mysteries we dream of, or in tormented
chase of the demon phantom that, some time or other, swims before all
human hearts; while chasing such over this round globe, they either lead
us on in barren mazes or midway leave us whelmed (253).

We have seen already ways in which the whale voyage is a nuanced and
complex analogy for Life itself. This passage penetrates the heart of the
pilgrimage/hunt—a voyage at once both across the oceans of the world
and deep into the fathoms of the human heart. It is a double expedition
wherein each of us pursues some variant of the White Whale. This is the
story of Ahab's and Ishmael's pursuit of what will satisfy and complete
each. He tells us this demon phantom eventually "swims before all human
hearts." No one escapes its terrifying and numinous presence. No one can
fully grasp its definitions or its myriad inflections.

We could ask ourselves: what White Whale do you or have you pursued?
Where are you in the chase? Have you been dismembered yet? Has your
boat been stoved? What does your whale look like? Has it turned to attack
and tried to end your pursuit? How much of your life has been contoured
to accommodate pursuing its fleeting presence? Have you in your hunt
been led into "barren mazes" or been lost in a funhouse or arrested in a hall
of mirrors? These questions over time may find a range of responses that
evolve as your whale breaches anew. Elements of our personal myth draw
us into the vortex of leviathan's energy.

Meditation

Identify your own White Whale and describe its origin.

May 15. Chapter 53: The Gam

[T]hen, how much more natural that upon the illimitable Pine Barrens and Salisbury Plains of the sea, two whaling vessels descrying each other at the ends of the earth . . . . how much more natural, I say, that under such circumstances these things should not only interchange hails, but come into still closer, more friendly and sociable contact . . . and not a few of the men are personally known to each other; and consequently, have all sorts of dear domestic things to talk about.

For the long absent ship, the outward-bounder, perhaps, has letters on board. . . (254-55).

An abrupt change of atmosphere ushers in this chapter. The tone is social, affable, communal and fraternal. From the isolato to the social impulses within human beings to connect with one another, the Gam is a human acknowledgement of one another as well as an opportunity to be informed of the latest news of the world, both personal and collective. Ishmael mentions both the Pine Barrens, a heavily forested coastal plain of New Jersey, which remains today rural and undeveloped (www.wikipedia.org/wiki/Pine_Barrens_(New_Jersey) and the Salisbury Plains, home of Stonehenge and one of Great Britain's best known open spaces (www.algebra.com). So there is a gam between the two nations here as well.

Our nature is to be drawn to others, either singly or collectively. Being connected to others in our humanity, however briefly, can renew us, allow us to be more of who we are, and learn and be entertained by others with unfamiliar and diverse narratives. We enjoy planning these events with friends, but often some of our richest connections happen seemingly by chance, or spontaneously; we gain immensely from such unforeseen encounters with strangers.

Meditation

When did a chance encounter yield a great bounty for both of you?

May 16. Chapter 53: The Gam

As touching Slave-ships meeting, why, they are in such a prodigious hurry, they run away from each other as soon as possible. And as for Pirates, when they chance to cross each other's cross-bones, the first hail is—"How Many skulls?"—the same way that whalers hail—"How many barrels?" And that question once answered, pirates straightway steer apart, for they are infernal villains on both sides, and don't like to see over-much of each other's villainous likenesses (256).

Ishmael points out the social traffic between ships on the high seas; with great subtlety he brings our attention to slave ships and Pirate ships who want nothing to do with one another because they each know they are trafficking in human cargo, dead or alive, and do not want to be reminded of their evil business by seeing a double of themselves in such close waters. Both recoil from a duplication of their duplicity. The seas are full of violations and injustices; many will avoid the hell of their own likeness reflected in others. We hear the Narcissus myth present once more.

Some conscience is pricked when evil eyes its brother and has one mirrored back to oneself. Left to one's own self image, one can justify all forms of injustice. But when it rises up into consciousness through the image of the violating other as oneself, the urge to escape it quickens. It is as if a light is shone on another so they see their true nature and purpose. The double is an ancient image in history and its presence, as with Narcissus, first reveals a stranger, but in time one recognizes one's self reflected in the waters of consciousness and feels the often unsettling elements of one's true nature. Our double is a great instructor, for what we cannot face or fathom in ourselves is more difficult to avoid when we confront our twin on the high seas of life.

Meditation

When have you had your own shadow or your own destructive thinking or behavior mirrored back to you by a double of yourself?

May 17. Chapter 54: The Town-Ho's Story

(As told at the Golden Inn)

It was not very long after speaking the Goney that another homeward-bound whaleman, the Town-Ho, was encountered. She was manned almost wholly by Polynesians. In the short gam that ensued she gave us strong news of Moby Dick . . . . Interweaving in its proper place this darker thread with the story as publicly narrated on the ship, the whole of this strange affair I now proceed to put on lasting record.

For my humor's sake, I shall preserve the style in which I once narrated it at Lima, to a lounging circle of my Spanish friends, one saint's eve, smoking upon the thick-gilt tiled piazza of the Golden Inn (259-60).

Ishmael focuses on the style of storytelling as much as its content to unite the tenor of narration with its matter. News of Moby Dick is the rudder that directs the ship of the tale, but the story's uniqueness emanates from mimicking its format in the same manner originally shared with his Spanish friends. The "darker thread" involves a lengthy and detailed account of the animosity of two whalemen, Radney, from Martha's Vineyard, and Steelkilt, a "Lakeman and desperado from Buffalo" (261) in perhaps the longest chapter of the epic.

Storytelling is its own art form. It relies on attending to who one's audience is. Listeners will have an effect on how the story is bent and torqued to accommodate particular receptions; as hearers we must adjust ourselves to the delivery in order to participate not just in the narrative but in the style of the story's personality as it unfolds along cultural lines. Stories are that organic; they can expand or contract, emphasize one or the other particulars, depending on the likes and propensities of the audience. Delivery influences our memory and shapes meaning.

Meditation

How does your audience influence your style of storytelling?

May 18. Chapter 54: The Town-Ho's Story

"It was just between daybreak and sunrise of the morning of the second day, when they were washing down the decks, that a stupid Teneriffe man, drawing water in the main-chains, all at once shouted out, 'There she rolls! there she rolls!' Jesu, what a whale! It was Moby Dick."

. . . .

"No need, gentlemen; one moment, and I proceed.—Now gentlemen, so suddenly perceiving the snowy whale within fifty yards of the ship— . . . . All was now a phrensy. 'The White Whale—the White Whale!' was the cry from captain, mates, and harpooneers, who, undeterred by fearful rumours, were all anxious to capture so famous and precious a fish; while the dogged crew eyed askance, and with curses, the appalling beauty of the vast milky mass. . . "(274-75).

Once again Moby Dick appears in narrative form, not in the flesh, which here in the story "shifted and glistened like a living opal in the blue morning sea" (275). It appears as destiny at this precise hour of the day between daybreak and sunrise. Its presence stirs the souls of the crew into a frenzy. The stories and rumors of the whale gather around its glistening mass, a splendid terrifying sight, having been prompted by its history that the men know well. It is a white mass seen in the imagination well before it breaches in blubbery brilliance.

Stories themselves can enhance and even surpass the reality of the presence of something only heard about; such an occurrence can bequeath something or someone a potent celebrity status. Story and sighting come together to create something akin to a numinous reality. The real presence has been infused with a mythical penumbra so that when it appears, finally, its stature and atmosphere are all-consuming.

Meditation

Describe when something narrated appeared in the flesh. How different?

May 19. Chapter 54: The Town-Ho's Story

"'Are you through?' said Don Sebastian, quietly.

"'I am, Don.'

"'Then I entreat you, tell me if to the best of your own convictions, this your story is in substance really true? It is so passing wonderful! Did you get it from an unquestionable source? Bear with me if I seem to press.'

. . . .

"'Is there a copy of the Holy Evangelists in the Golden Inn, gentlemen?'"

. . . .

"'Let me remove my hat. Now, venerable priest, further into the light, and hold the Holy Book before me that I may touch it.

"'So help me Heaven, and on my honor the story I have told ye, gentlemen, is in substance and its great items, true'" (277-78).

Telling this extensive tale, Ishmael dons the hat and persona of the person he assumed when he originally told it to a group of men in Lima about the conflict between two whalemen, Radney and Steelkit. What emerges are questions of the narrative's veracity and authenticity. Only his swearing on a Bible satisfies his Lima audience. They call for a priest who arrives carrying the Holy Book of stories. Ishmael swears to seeing and talking to Steelkit since Radney's death.

This complex narrative of "The Town Ho" interrogates the truth of a narrative as a faithful mirror, or doubling, of a historical reality. It also implicates the place of trust the audience must allow the story. All true stories require a fidelity in the speaker or writer. What then, is the truth claim of *Moby-Dick* itself? And whatever stories we witness, do we question all of them as to their level of veracity, even if partly fictional?

Meditation

What is your current response to the truth claims of *Moby-Dick*?

May 20. Chapter 55: *Of the Monstrous* Pictures of Whales

I shall ere long paint to you as well as one can without canvas, something like the true form of the whale as he actually appears to the eye of the whaleman when in his own absolute body the whale is moored alongside the whaleship so that he can be fairly stepped upon there. It may be worth while, therefore, previously to advert to those curious imaginary portraits of him which even down to the present day confidently challenge the faith of the landsman. It is time to set the world right in this matter, by proving such pictures of the whale all wrong (279).

Almost halfway through the narrative Ishmael comes to the defense of the whale as it is experienced by whalemen and by artists of myth, legend and religion. They got it wrong, he claims, thus the truth of the whale must surface now. Coming on the heels of the last chapter's questioning of the truth of the Steelkit-Radney story, Ishmael's timing is perfect. He depicts for us two whale realities: one in which a whale in all its grandeur is tethered to the side of a whale ship, and those whales rendered in art. The living fleshly whale in its truth is measured incorrectly by imaginal depictions of leviathan that distort its nature. Ishmael's epic initiative as whale writer is to portray the whale rightly.

Ishmael's heroic task advances interesting questions about the nature and purpose of art. Should it depict its subject matter as a realistic representation? Can it not be after other fish in distorting this realistic image in favor of revealing other qualities of it? A realist seeks an exact imprint of the object while the artist may prefer to distort in order to inflect certain characteristics of the object and thereby reflect its true nature. We ask: can de-formation in art yield a "truer" rendering?

Meditation

Describe an object, person, situation or emotion you consciously distorted in order to reveal some inherent truth in it.

May 21. Chapter 55: *Of the Monstrous* Pictures of Whales

But these manifold mistakes in depicting the whale are not so very surprising after all. Consider! Most of the scientific drawings have been taken from the stranded fish; and these are about as correct as a drawing of a wrecked ship, with broken back, would correctly represent the noble animal itself in all its undashed pride of hull and spars. Though elephants have stood for their full lengths, the living Leviathan has never yet fairly floated himself for his portrait. The living whale, in his full majesty and significance, is only to be seen at sea in unfathomable waters; and afloat the vast bulk of him is out of sight. . . (282).

Ishmael's conviction is that the whale can be known only in its living reality in the sea. But precisely that environment keeps him hidden from mortal sight, except for a small part of him, or a fleeting glance when it breaches—hardly enough time to paint or draw him accurately. So the very conditions in which the whale should be painted is exactly the circumstance that keeps him enticingly hidden. Some deep paradox lines the skin of the whale and leaves it a mystery submerged in the sea, its true habitat and home. We grasp its mystery piecemeal.

We can't help but think of rich analogies in our own life wherein to truly understand something it must occur on its terms and terrain, not ours. But these terms can make what we seek only partly visible on the clearest of days, if we wish to know it in its full authentic presence. Anything short of that, we perceive and paint it in a counterfeit manner; the result is a distortion of its true or accurate nature. It is an act of supreme imagination and courage to be willing to see what we wish to grasp, even in its phantom presence, where its being exists in the deepest fathoms of what contains it. It is a rich analogy for life's hiddenness.

Meditation

Describe a life event or a quality that illustrates for you the above reflection.

May 22. Chapter 55: *Of the Monstrous* Pictures of Whales

For all these reasons, then, any way you may look at it, you must needs conclude that the great Leviathan is that one creature in the world which must remain unpainted to the last. True, one portrait may hit the mark much nearer than another, but none can hit it with any very considerable degree of exactness. So there is no earthly way of finding out precisely what the whale really looks like. And the only mode in which you can derive even a tolerable idea of his living contour, is by going a whaling yourself; but by so doing, you run no small risk of being eternally stove and sunk by him . . . . [so]you had best not be too fastidious in your curiosity touching this Leviathan (283).

Ishmael continues his meditation on knowing the whale in its authentic nature, which then precludes it from being artistically rendered. Some have approximated it in their art, but finally it cannot be depicted fully. One wonders how exact Ishmael's painting in words of the whale in this epic approaches the mark. The terms "earthly" and "eternally" in the passage suggest the whale is an image that bridges both realms. Nothing short of whaling itself will bring Leviathan into credible view in all its grandeur. But such a pursuit is not without the risk of death or dismemberment. Art and Nature are not incompatible; the former may always be a phantom image of the latter.

Sometimes, risking everything in order to pursue what draws us to it is the only real choice in life. Actually entering the world on its terms while yielding ours may be fraught with dangers and uncertainties, but may accurately reveal what we seek. "Follow your bliss," writes mythologist Joseph Campbell. We add "and attend to your blisters" that will surely arise in hazarding such a journey. Speaking from a position of insight and hindsight, we more accurately assess the cost.

Meditation

Describe one instance where you took great risks to follow your bliss.

May 23. Chapter 56: *Of the Less Erroneous* Pictures of Whales *and the True Pictures of Whaling Scenes*

The natural aptitude of the French for seizing the picturesqueness of things seems to be peculiarly evinced in what paintings and engravings they have of their whaling scenes . . . . For the most part, the English and American whale draughtsmen seem entirely content with presenting the mechanical outline of things, such as the vacant profile of the whale; which . . . . is about tantamount to sketching the profile of a pyramid (286).

Ishmael's cosmopolitan imagination surveys national ways of seeing aesthetically in their art, each taking up a certain angle of vision to capture the authentic lines of the whale, some with greater success than others. Tendencies, habits of seeing, perceptual prejudices each yields a different Leviathan while imparting a slice of the truth of its existence. He entertains ways of seeing and making sense of the whale through art. Styles of vision then develop part of a country's national myth. The whale is a rich image by which to gauge a nation's soul as it makes creative sense of such a ubiquitous mystery.

On a national and personal level, perspective is deeply psychological and mythical; it reveals how we know what we purport to grasp. This viewpoint can freeze so that for a nation or an individual, no other angles of vision are possible or acceptable. We can freeze-frame the world through a narrow perspective that accommodates no elasticity and respects no other points of view. Ideologies can then grow like encrusted barnacles on the soul of seeing. The seduction is that we can convince ourselves that our point of view represents the only true perspective or fashion of belief, so we spurn all others.

Meditation

What dominant perspective on the world either frees or incarcerates your vision? Are there any other optional optics for understanding?

May 24. Chapter 57: Of Whales *in Paint; in Teeth; in Wood; in Sheet-Iron; in Stone; in Mountains; in Stars*

Throughout the Pacific, and also in Nantucket, and New Bedford, and Sag Harbor, you will come across lively sketches of whales and whaling scenes, graven by the fishermen themselves on Sperm Whale-teeth, or ladies' busks wrought out of the Right-Whale bone, and other like skrimshander articles . . . .

. . . .

Wooden whales, or whales cut in profile out of the small dark slabs of the noble South Sea war-wood, are frequently met with in the forecastles of American whalers. Some of them are done with much accuracy (289-90).

Ishmael offers attempts by mortals to render artistic form and scope to the whale, including objects of usefulness made from whale parts. The geographic locales from where most whale ships launch are populated with artifacts meant to capture its form, and by means of it, Leviathan's nature. Having these talismans on board whaleboats often serve as good luck totems to ensure successful hunting. The business of slaying whales runs directly into the wind of crafting whale images as symbolic forms of Leviathan. Both are methods of crafting its nature.

The impulse to replicate, in an imitative or mimetic act, the object of one's livelihood or desire, rests deep in our souls. A creative response less interested in killing mystery and more in cultivating its image, even using the ivory of a whale to imprint its presence, sounds its own mystery. Where mystery, paradox, contradiction or ambiguity abound, there the force of creation may breach into view. The cry to create is built into our desire to mark the world we inhabit and leave a trace on it. Each wishes to make some "impression" on the world while here.

Meditation

What circumstances have engendered in you a deep desire to create?

May 25. Chapter 57: Of Whales *in Paint; in Teeth; in Wood; in Sheet-Iron; in Stone; in Mountains; in Stars*

Nor when expandingly lifted by your subject, can you fail to trace out great whales in the starry heavens, and boats in pursuit of them; as when long filled with thoughts of war the Eastern nations saw armies locked in battle among the clouds . . . .

With a frigate's anchors for my bridle-bitts and fasces of harpoons for spurs, would I could mount that whale and leap the topmost skies, to see whether the fabled heavens, with all their countless tents really lie encamped beyond my mortal sight! (291).

Waxing both lyrical and epic in his imaginative leap to the heavens, Ishmael launches into a vision worthy of Elijah, of the whale's presence beneath the earth's unfathomable waters, beyond it in the starry vaults and in his own whale-inflected fantasies. The whale seems more a perspective, a point of view, an expanded vision of the wholeness of the created order, as well as a corridor into the invisibles by means of its majestic blubbery mystery. The whale is a method of seeing, of apprehending and of imagining. Mounting it as one would a horse, Ishmael believes it might allow him celestial visions.

We ponder of what the subject matter of our lives consists and what vision, understanding, revelation or insight they may or have offered us. "To see by means of" is a ticklish and rewarding proposition. We may discern that our subject matter allows a gateway to the transcendent, to the realm of the invisibles, to areas of existence that cannot be proven or measured in quantitative ways. We may instead distinguish the presence of a deeper myth animating our insights, provoking our thoughts and shaping our interpretations.

Meditation

What interests in particular subjects or activities led you to new discoveries or new ways of seeing?

May 26. Chapter 58: Brit

Steering north-eastward from the Crozetts, we fell in with vast meadows of brit, the minute, yellow substance, upon which the Right Whale largely feeds. For leagues and leagues it undulated round us, so that we seemed to be sailing through boundless fields of ripe and golden wheat.

. . . .

Indeed, in other respects, you can hardly regard any creatures of the deep with the same feeling that you do those of the shore . . . where, for example, does the ocean furnish any fish that in disposition answers to the sagacious kindness of the dog? The accursed shark alone can in any generic respect be said to bear comparative analogy to him (292-93).

Ishmael's overall intuition is to designate and distinguish the world of the shore from that of the sea. Some may claim that the two realms are approximate to one another; others like Ishmael imagine the sea in its unique and unanological glory, mystery and might. Second, while human advances and discoveries in science may confer a sense of mastery of the oceans, the sea will inevitably prove the stronger by dashing our infant inventions against its aboriginal force. He also points out the complementary workings of Nature wherein the largest of its population in the sea relies on the smallest for its sustenance.

Some have experienced Nature's power first hand, most specifically in the force of great bodies of water. The Titanic comes to mind as an invention engineered to be indestructible, yet it was wounded and swallowed by the sea on her maiden journey. Our battle to dominate Nature may rebound back to us through her primal intelligence and profound resistance, if not overt rebellion. We have the capacity to destroy both and so afflict our own nature beyond healing.

Meditation

When have you encountered the force or mystery of the natural order?

May 27. Chapter 58: Brit

[T]hough we know the sea to be an everlasting terra incognita, so that Columbus sailed over numberless unknown worlds to discover his one superficial western one; though, by vast odds, the most terrific of all mortal disasters have immemorially and indiscriminately befallen tens and hundreds of thousands of those who gone upon the waters; though but a moment's consideration will teach that however baby man may brag of his science and skill . . . . yet for ever and for ever, to the crack of doom, the sea will insult and murder him, and pulverize the stateliest, stiffest frigate he can make . . . (293).

One of the first meditations on the sea is presented here in the chapter outlining the tiny sea life on which the Right Whale feeds. Ishmael compares man's puny victories and discoveries against the timeless qualities of the world's oceans and inhabitants. More than just a different element than the land, the sea carries a shifting power and dreadful potential to destroy any manmade contrivance that sails on its surface. A majesty and fierce energy is inbred in the ocean's nature, ready to reduce humanity's superior feeling to bits and pieces. Moreover, it carries within her invisible mysterious life forms that roil beneath her heaving skin.

A humbling often occurs when people confront the fierce seas or any terrible force of nature that can snuff out the life of an individual, a town, or a region in stormy chaos. Disrespect for the force of the natural order—whether from hubris or ignorance, can end life and property in an instant. Nature requires a certain deference towards her as well as a vigilance respecting her sometimes contrary ways. Ignoring her potential power as well as her limited resources can lead to exhausting all life forms. Recognizing her limits may moderate our pillaging of her.

Meditation

How have you directly experienced Nature's limited bounty?

May 28. Chapter 58: Brit

The first boat we read of, floated on an ocean, that with Portuguese vengeance had whelmed a whole world without leaving so much as a widow. That same ocean rolls now; that same ocean destroyed the wrecked ships of last year. Yea, foolish mortals, Noah's flood is not yet subsided; two thirds of the fair world it yet covers.

Wherein differ the sea and the land, that a miracle upon one is not a miracle upon the other? Preternatural terrors rested upon the Hebrews, when under the feet of Korah and his company the live ground opened and swallowed them up for ever; yet not a modern sun ever sets, but in precisely the same manner the live sea swallows up ships and crews (293).

Ishmael uses the tiniest of sea life—brit--to launch into a series of thoughtful meditations on the eternal patterns of the ocean which exist in time but also harbor a timeless quality because it allows no permanent traces to exist on its deceptive skin. It swallows up history, indeed all events of humankind, with an attitude of calm indifference. His language is already preparing us for the last image of the epic prior to the Epilogue. Moreover, Ishmael understands the sea as a reflective double of the land, as if the two formed a *coniunctio,* a sacred wedding of earth and water. All actions that mortals attempt on the seas are eventually effaced by the eternal impulse of the immortal oceans.

A humbling disposition often arises when people confront the fierce seas or any destruction that arises from them and their capacity to disintegrate a coastline in only hours. Disrespect for the force of the natural order emerges from hubris and/or ignorance in mortals who think they can defend against its infinite power. Nature requires a certain humility and respect in approaching her, as one would an untamed beast.

Meditation

In what way is the natural order a constant presence in your life?

May 29. Chapter 58: Brit

Consider the subtleness of the sea; how its most dreaded creatures glide under water, unapparent for the most part, and treacherously hidden beneath the loveliest tints of azure. Consider also the devilish brilliance and beauty of many of its most remorseless tribes, as the dainty embellished shape of many species of sharks. Consider once more, the universal cannibalism of the sea; all whose creatures prey upon each other, carrying on eternal war since the world began (294).

Ishmael's orbit of vision continues to expand and deepen to include the sea as its own galaxy, deep beneath the surface teeming with mysterious creatures waging their own eternal wars of eating and being eaten. He teases us with a series of "considerations" about what kinds of creatures lurk actively below us. Using "dainty" to refer to sharks hammers home his amusing juxtaposition of worlds. Nature is at war with itself: life feeds on life. Nothing sentimental prevails in the writer's description of Nature's subliminal ways and her recurring plot line.

We too may reveal "the loveliest tints of azure" of the surface but beneath moves a roiling profusion of treachery, resentment, anger, and conflicting feelings like various species of sea life, each fighting to survive. The analogy of surface and depth of the sea with our own internal life is implicit but clear. Like the sea, our own unconscious life teems with contradictions, warring impulses and conflicting beliefs. Part of the whaling voyage we all undertake is fraught with mysteries that may rupture on the horizon or next to the hull of our ship, its forces unfathomable. Like the whale, our lives must remain "unpainted to the last" (283). These mysteries can provoke panic, peace and wonder.

Meditation

Describe one element in your own surface-depth world that mirrors Ishmael's depiction.

May 30. Chapter 58: Brit

Consider all this; and then turn to this green, gentle, and most docile earth; consider them both, the sea and the land; and do you not find a strange analogy to something in yourself? For as this appalling ocean surrounds the verdant land, so in the soul of man there lies one insular Tahiti, full of peace and joy, but encompassed by all the horrors of the half known life. God keep thee! Push not off from that isle, thou canst never return! (294).

A fatedness attends this extended and deepening penetration into the world and into soul—actually into the world soul, the *anima mundi,* that we each participate in to various degrees. Ishmael calls us to analogy, the most profound being between spirit and matter, soul and substance. The land is calm, stable and fixed most of the time; the sea is fluid, shape-shifting, malleable and open to the influences of wind, moon and currents. All are attributes of our human nature. The land, surrounded by water, carries a complex metaphor of mystery, familiarity and ambiguity enfolding certainty. Once one leaves the land, Ishmael cautions, one cannot go home again. To enter the half known sea is to risk everything on one's spiritual pilgrimage.

Seeming a bit like a morality play in its expression, Ishmael's words carry an ontological inflection. To be safe, stay on shore; don't venture out. Once the decision is made to gamble, and one acts on it, the land one leaves disappears forever. The sea and its creatures alter everything; all life's terms shift. We must be certain on some level that given our goals, pushing off is worth the risk. In retrospect we can judge our "push-offs" through the mirror of memory. To remember such life events changes them because imagined from another perspective.

Meditation

When have you pushed away from your insulated life and entered the "terra incognita" of adventure?

May 31. Chapter 59: Squid

But one transparent blue morning, when a stillness almost preternatural spread over the sea, however unattended with any stagnant calm; when the long burnished sun-glade on the waters seemed a golden finger laid across them, enjoining some secrecy; when the slippered waves whispered together as they softly ran on; in this profound hush of the visible sphere a strange spectre was seen by Daggoo from the main- mast head.

In the distance, a great white mass lazily rose, and rising higher and higher, and disentangling itself from the azure, at last gleamed before our prow like a snow-slide, new slid from the hills (295).

The wonder and enchantment of the natural world beams forth in this lyric rendering of an animated nature, given superb language in league with the wonder of it by the poet Ishmael. The triple clauses beginning with the repetitious adverb "when" exact a mesmerizing effect on us readers as we enter "the profound hush," prelude to a moment of ecstatic revelation: the sight of a mysterious white mass dramatically misinterpreted as the energizing presence of the White Whale. Such is the power of this apparition to stir an imaginal presence.

Thinking back, we can all recall an amazing moment, on sea or land, when the natural world was allowed expression on its own terms, when the elements conspired in a symphony of mesmerizing matter and we were drawn into the vortex of such a peaceful verisimilitude. Our life was put on hold for a moment. We grasped the indelible presence of an enchanted world and were transported thereby to another realm of consciousness by imagining creation anew. But first we must be open and vulnerable to mystery in nature's wonders to disclose itself.

Meditation

When in Nature have you felt enchantment through one of its creatures, including yourself?

June 1. Chapter 59: Squid

Almost forgetting for the moment all thoughts of Moby Dick, we now gazed at the most wondrous phenomenon which the secret seas have hitherto revealed to mankind. A vast pulpy mass, furlongs in length and breadth, of a glancing cream-color, lay floating on the water, innumerable long arms radiating from its centre, and curling and twisting like a nest of anacondas, as if blindly to catch at any hapless object within reach. No perceptive face or front did it have; no conceivable token of either sensation or instinct; but undulated there on the billows, an unearthly, formless, chance-like apparition of life.

. . . .

"The great live squid, which, they say, few whale-ships ever beheld, and returned to their ports to tell of it" (296).

The almost supernatural apparition of the great "white ghost" (296) pulls all the men two ways: into bracketing the White Whale from consciousness, and into a reverie of a white phantom, a ghost-like presence in that place where the tentacles of imagination and reality intermingle. It is itself as well as a presence of the absent Moby Dick. Wonder, not vengeance, stirs in the hearts of all those who gaze on this formless host of the deep seas—where the cost of perceiving it signals the destiny of the Pequod as a ship that attends the squid but will not return to port. Starbuck's words to Flask transport us to journey's end.

Natural phenomena can connect us immediately to the numinous, to the other-worldly and to the mystical substrate that undergirds the phenomenal world. For a moment we are citizens of two realms, where the mystery of one exposes us to the enchantment of the other in feelings of delight and dread. We grasp that below conscious awareness teems another entire cosmos of life, often in strange dreamy forms.

Meditation

Have you experienced an apparition in life that transformed you?

June 2. Chapter 60: The Line

With reference to the whaling scene shortly to be described, as well as for the better understanding of all similar scenes elsewhere presented, I have here to speak of the magical, sometimes horrible, whale-line.

. . . .

Of late years the Manilla rope has in the American fishery almost entirely superseded hemp as a material for whale-lines . . . and I will add (since there is an aesthetics in all things), is much more handsome and becoming to the boat, than hemp. Hemp is a dusky dark fellow, a sort of Indian; but Manilla is as a golden-haired Circassian to behold (298).

Down to the minutest detail, Ishmael is determined to describe the entirety of whaling, hook, hemp and line. It is as well an aesthetic enterprise, both whaling and writing, with coiled lines and coiled letters crafted into words and twisted sentences. Hemp, too, can be horrible and is now out of fashion; it is associated with the dusky phantoms that surround Ahab; it will eventually find its place around his neck at journey's end, uniting him with the White Whale. The Circassian reference is to the people who lived in the northwestern region of the Caucasus, which saw heavy trading by the ancient Greeks along its coast. By 1875, under Peter the Great, it had become a Russian province.(www.britannica.com/EBchecked/topic/118238/Circassian).

What holds things together and binds them in a unity is the very object that can violently separate them because of its uncoiling nature. The line fastens and separates. Its coiledness may spring into action in an instant, endangering and confusing, like life's own spiralic circumstances. The line is a powerful presence in our existence. It offers a measure of security as well as danger in a single through line of our plot. It has the capacity to tether us to what inhibits our freedom.

Meditation

Think of a coiled rope in your life line now. Help or hindrance?

June 3. Chapter 60: The Line

Thus the whale-line folds the whole boat in its complicated coils, twisting and writhing around it in almost every direction. All the oarsmen are involved in its perilous contortions; so that to the timid eye of the landsman, they seem as Indian jugglers, with the deadliest snakes sportively festooning their limbs.

. . . .

[S]o the graceful repose of the line, as it silently serpentines about the oarsmen before being brought into actual play—this is a thing which carries more of true terror than any other aspect of this dangerous affair. But why say more? All men live enveloped in whale-lines. All are born with halters round their necks (300-301).

The line enjoys a snaky life of its own and conjures fear in the whalemen more in its static, silent, spiralic repose than when it springs into taut action. Ishmael's customary style of seeing expands the image of the fastening line by suggesting all of us are enveloped in lifelines of one form or another; some constrict us, determine us, restrain us and free us. No one escapes the lines of fate and destiny. Life is a package deal, tied with the bows of hemp or Manilla lines that bind us to our Fate.

We speak of our lifelines, sometimes read in the lining of our palms where our characteristics and destiny are outlined, or in the lines of our face that trace a life lived. We think too of the lines of our story, the plot line of our lives. Ishmael's descriptions give us a line on who he is, whether fictional or factual, though these lines are often so entangled we cannot clearly follow one line before it interweaves with others. Paying attention to our life's lines yields insights into our past and our future. What lines of thought we engage is also part of our mythic pattern and substructure that guides us in and out of life's labyrinths.

Meditation

Describe two or three lines your life follows and/or is entangled within.

June 4. Chapter 61: Stubb Kills a Whale

It was my turn to stand at the foremast-head; and with my shoulders leaning against the slackened royal shrouds, to and fro I idly swayed in what seemed an enchanted air. No resolution could withstand it; in that dreamy mood losing all consciousness, at last my soul went out of my body; though my body still continued to sway as a pendulum will, long after the power which first moved it is withdrawn . . . .

    The waves, too, nodded their indolent crests; and across the wide trance of the sea, east nodded to west, and the sun over all (302).

Just before the explosive action that follows a whale sighting, Ishmael describes another dreamy, meditative trance-like condition in which waves, whales and winsome nature conspire in a moment of blissful, enchanted triune serenity. The gently rolling scene signals an opportune atmosphere for reverie to engage Ishmael's consciousness. He enters the immense void not unfamiliar to mystics, wherein the soul leaves the body and one experiences a pervasive sense of oneness. Everything succumbs to the energies of a mystical trance that is both ubiquitous and intense. Consciousness itself descends into the deep.

Such moments can be rare. One slides into a warm bath of one-ness with the natural order; all strife suffuses into waves and evaporates. No boundaries exist between self and world. One feels the shift from one's substantial being into a subtle body and melds into the natural order, beyond all opposition and conflicts. One's ego is muted. In the condition described above, a full accord with our surroundings permeates the atmosphere. The soul's barometric pressure holds steady to prolong this condition. In such transcendent moments we feel in accord with all that is and perhaps with who we are in our deepest caverns.

Meditation

When have you felt this feeling of oneness in joyful serenity?

June 5. Chapter 61: Stubb Kills a Whale

Suddenly bubbles seemed bursting beneath my closed eyes; like vices my hands grasped the shrouds; some invisible, gracious agency preserved me; with a shock I came back to life. And lo! close under our lee, not forty fathoms off, a gigantic Sperm Whale lay rolling in the water like the capsized hull of a frigate, his broad, glossy back, of an Ethiopian hue, glistening in the sun's rays like a mirror. But lazily undulating in the trough of the sea, and ever and anon tranquilly spouting his vapory jet, the whale looked like a portly burgher smoking his pipe of a warm afternoon. But that pipe, poor whale, was thy last (302-03).

Such great affection pleats Ishmael's description of the sea's tranquil giant lounging in a self-enclosed joy. The whaleman has been awakened by "an invisible gracious agency" that protects him from falling. His loving description reveals his most authentic feelings towards the whales. Something magnificent and innocent enshrouds leviathan—a giant gracefulness, full of serenity and joy in living; it is a mirrored testament to the marriage of sun and water. Ishmael's simile of a burgher smoking his pipe humanizes the whale still further and draws an intimate analogy with mankind and with Stubb. The whale's jet appears as a misty sigh on the sea's surface.

Seeing the natural world so adorned in its own rhythms and graceful appearance is a gift of life itself. A sympathetic union between our own nature and the animal world breaches from our depths to touch the depth of a moment's encounter with the double world of our own. We rejoice in such moments and may retrieve them from memory in dark times when we yearn to feel connected to the larger world.

Meditation

Describe a moment in Nature when you experienced a deep intimacy with some specific part of her world and your own.

June 6. Chapter 61: Stubb Kills a Whale

Soon ranging up by his flank, Stubb, firmly planting his knee in the clumsy cleat, darted dart after dart into the flying fish . . . .

The red tide now poured from all sides of the monster like brooks down a hill. His tormented body rolled not in brine but in blood, which bubbled and seethed for furlongs behind in their wake. The slanting sun playing upon their crimson pond in the sea, sent back its reflection into every face, so that they all glowed to each other like red men.

. . . .

At last, gush after gush of clotted red gore, as if it had been the purple lees of red wine, shot into the frightened air . . . . His heart had burst! (305-06).

Insufferable is the kill for Ishmael; his language mirrors the violence, the grief and the loss of such a magnificent sea creature. Its death is ghastly, messy, massive and murderous. All the crew's faces dyed red in the reflected blood color of the sea accuses them all of such carnage in conspiracy. "Clotted red gore" streaming from the whale's blow hole mirrors the horror of its death at the hands of Stubb, followed by other whalemen. No victory attends this carnage, only a massive extermination of a whale as commodity now to be dismembered.

The carnage done to Nature continues unabated today as the world population exhausts and exterminates her creatures by pillaging her treasures and extinguishing her many species to satisfy insatiable human appetites. Addicted to spoiling, polluting and depopulating the natural order, mortals exact a toll for their behavior: the diminished beauty, diversity and bounty of our environment, our own home. Industry is a new mythos in the 19th century as technologies globally accelerate their rapacity. The air itself expresses fear at the clotted carnage.

Meditation

Where have you witnessed the tormenting or death of Nature?

June 7. Chapter 63: The Crotch

Out of the trunk, the branches grow; out of them, the twigs. So, in productive subjects, grow the chapters.

The crotch alluded to on a previous page deserves independent mention. It is a notched stick of a peculiar form, some two feet in length, which is perpendicularly inserted into the starboard gunwale near the bow, for the purpose of furnishing a rest for the wooden extremity of the harpoons . . . . It is customary to have two harpoons reposing in the crotch, respectively called the first and second irons.

. . . .

All these particulars are faithfully narrated here, as they will not fail to elucidate several most important however intricate passages, in scenes hereafter to be painted (309-310).

Ishmael calls our attention once again to a doubling quality of his narrative. He lives within a sea of doubles from first to last. He reveals a redundancy in whaling by having two harpoons ready in the crotch to hurl in quick succession at the hunted prey. A connection emerges between the lines of his narrative, the lines attached to the harpoons and the "intimate passages" yet to be written. The narrative, then, is double-lined to convey a second reality below the water line.

The lines of our fatedness are at least in part connected to the lines of our own crotch-supported harpoons we wait to hurl at what we hunt, desire, or wish to hold fast to, to target, impact, or penetrate. What our life's desire is comprises what our harpoons seek to fasten us to, as well as the line, thread or threat of our plot line. The whales we seek in life constitute our double. We may double down now on what we reject later. We might ask what the weapons we hold ready look like.

Meditation

What do you wish to, or have harpooned, so to remain connected to your life's quest?

June 8. Chapter 64: Stubb's Supper

Very soon you would have thought from the sound on the Pequod's decks, that all hands were preparing to cast anchor in the deep; for heavy chains are being dragged along the deck, and thrust rattling out of the port-holes. But by those clanking links, the vast corpse itself, not the ship, is to be moored. Tied by the head to the stern, and by the tail to the bows, the whale now lies with its black hull close to the vessel's, and seen through the darkness of the night . . . . the two—ship and whale, seemed yoked together like colossal bullocks, whereof one reclines while the other remains standing (311-12).

Some inverted double of ship and whale converge in an intimate fastening of one to the other. When darkness obscures the Pequod's rigging, the two masses appear as inverted mirrors of one another, The Pequod's purpose rests serenely beside the goal of that purpose. The language to describe the whale is of the ship. Doubling one another in the darkened air, they blur the boundary of the pursuer and the pursued. They appear as compatible partners in their bonds, as Ahab will be bound, finally, by ropes and rigging to the White Whale.

We might imagine in our own life how what we pursue reproduces who and what we are composed of. Our desires double our deepest mythos by reflecting our interior life as an outer perceived image of an invisible deep interior disposition. We see ourselves most forcefully in what attracts us to it in the outer world. Our destiny is tied by massive invisible chains to what we crave with such a keen appetite that it may blot out all other options. At rest, however, what were once pursuer and pursued may reflect an intimate compatibility. What arises is a recognition of sameness within seemingly irreconcilable differences.

Meditation

Reflect on one thing, person, or life situation you pursue. Consider how it mirrors, or is a double, of something in your own essential nature.

June 9. Chapter 64: Stubb's Supper

Mingling their mumblings with his own mastications, thousands on thousands of sharks, swarming round the dead leviathan, smackingly feasted on its fatness. The few sleepers below in their bunks were often startled by the sharp slapping of their tails against the hull, within a few inches of the sleepers' hearts . . . . and turning over on their backs as they scooped out huge globular pieces of the whale of the bigness of a human head . . . . How at such an apparently unassailable surface, they contrive to gouge out such symmetrical mouthfuls, remains a part of the universal problem of all things (312-13).

The sharks in a feeding frenzy imitate or double the action of Stubb as he munches his rare whale steak. Roiling together in such a feast, the sharks devour the whale in massive chunks just inches away from the hearts of men who captured it. They eat most effectively by inverting and tearing off chunks the size of a human head. Sharks, this passage reveals, are aligned with us in their savage appetites. Something mysterious and universal slips into Ishmael's description, sending him deep into a meditation on how the sharks can penetrate with such precision the bulk of the whale to violently dismantle and consume it.

We are to think of the sharks feasting on the kill as counterpart to humankind's feasting in excess of the natural order. We seem implicated in Ishmael's critique. Our enormous appetites to devour Nature in huge symmetrical and methodical clumps promises to annihilate her bounty even as the whale industry almost extinguished the species they pursued. The universal problem to which Ishmael alludes refers to the enormous appetite of the shark and its reversing itself to lay claim to such large gobbets. In a Stubb-like attitude we can remain oblivious to our claims.

Meditation

Have you exhibited the shark's excessive consuming appetite?

June 10. Chapter 64: Stubb's Supper

"Cook, cook!—where's that old Fleece?" he cried at length, widening his legs still further, as if to form a more secure base for his supper; and, at the same time darting his fork into the dish, as if stabbing with his lance; "cook, you cook!—sail this way, cook!"

. . . .

"There are those sharks now over the side, don't you see they prefer it tough and rare? What a shindy they are kicking up! Cook, go and talk to 'em; tell 'em they are welcome to help themselves civilly, and in moderation, but they must keep quiet . . . . Here, take this lantern," snatching one from his sideboard; "now then, go and preach to them!"

Sullenly taking the offered lantern, old Fleece limped across the deck to the bulwarks . . . (314).

Stubb's desire for a peaceful meal confronts the rapacious frenzy of the sharks consuming the whale like masticating machines. They require correcting in the form of a sermon to civilize their table manners. Old Fleece is roused from his bed; he shuffles to do the second mate's bidding. As an on-board replica of Father Mapple's sermon earlier, Fleece's parishioners are the congregation of gluttonous sharks creating a racket in their hedonist feasting. Fleece's sermon may moderate them.

The sharks often represent at various events in the epic the excess of appetite devoid of restraint as well as dangerous impulses deep in us, including limitless cravings to consume. Sharks carry the power of cunning and wolfing with appetites that defy boundaries. Sharks swim deeply within us, rapacious and heedless of moderation. Their speed, cunning and consuming power display excessive appetites as a norm. Wise counsel may modulate such fierce longings.

Meditation

Have you been preyed on by predators or victimized yourself and others with a sharkish display of appetite?

June 11. Chapter 64: Stubb's Supper

"Fellow-critters: I'se ordered here to say dat you must stop dat dam noise dare. You hear? Stop dat dam smackin' ob de lips! Massa Stubb say dat you can fill your dam bellies up to de hatchings, but by Gor! You must stop dat dam racket!"

"Cook," here interposed Stubb . . . . That's no way to convert sinners, cook!"

. . . .

"Well, den, Belubed fellow-critters:"—

"Right!" exclaimed Stubb, approvingly, "coax 'em to it, try that," and Fleece continued.

. . . .

"You is sharks, sartin; but if you govern de shark in you, why den you be angel; for all angel is not'ing more dan de shark well goberned . . . . Don't be tearin' de blubber out your neighbour's mout, I say" (314-15).

Fellowship, community, treating your neighbors as you wish to be treated—all are constant virtues in the order of the epic that Fleece comically but with serious intent uses in his desire to convert the sharks to generous virtues. Not by the terrible guilt sermon of Father Mapple, but by a more loving approach that persuades with kindness, and more akin to Queequeg's disposition toward Ishmael. Once again, a marginal figure delivers one of the epic's central cautions to unruly obsessions.

Even the shark can suffer redemption in the epic journey. The gap between the rapacious and angelic is a thin one; it is easily crossed if one relinquishes self-absorption. Being well-governed can shift life's equation; a conversion or change of heart is always possible. Hearing nothing but the sound of smacking lips denies any change.

Meditation

When has a rapacious shark within you become well-governed?

June 12. Chapter 64: Stubb's Supper

"Well, then, cook, you see this whale steak of yours was so very bad, that I have put it out of sight as soon as possible; you see that, don't you? Well, for the future, when you cook another whale-steak for my private table here . . . Hold the steak in one hand, and show a live coal to it with the other; that done, dish it; d'ye hear? . . . There, now you may go."

. . . .

"Wish, by gor! Whale eat him, 'stead of him eat whale. I'm bressed if he ain't more of shark dan Massa Shark hisself," muttered the old man, limping away, with which sage ejaculation he went to his hammock (318).

The full import of this long chapter on Stubb feasting on raw whale meat surfaces at the end. He has admonished Fleece for his beliefs, his lack of church-going and his conviction that he will enter heaven (317). Now Stubb corrects Fleece's cooking the whale steak and insists on "whale-balls for breakfast—don't forget" (318). Fleece, mortified, imagines Stubb's attack on him not unlike sharks feeding wildly on the whale. He even surpasses their voracious appetite in his reprimands.

"Shark attack" can signify another's ridicule in the form of condemning or demeaning who one is. The shark in us finds fault with another and eats the other alive through corrections and rebukes. One may have to stand as helpless as a dead whale and suffer the bites and chunks out of oneself with no recourse except to escape being "chewed out and up." We may show the worst side of ourselves in proclaiming self-righteous corrections of others. We can easily mirror the very actions we descry if we aren't conscious of this doubling.

Meditation

Think of a time when you were chewed out or you chewed another out, or when you felt eaten alive by another's sharky fierceness.

June 13. Chapter 65: The Whale as a Dish

But what further depreciates the whale as a civilized dish, is his exceeding richness. He is the great prize ox of the sea, too fat to be delicately good. Look at his hump, which would be as fine eating as the buffalo's (which is esteemed a rare dish), were it not such a solid pyramid of fat. But the spermaceti itself, how bland and creamy that is; like the transparent, half-jellied, white meat of a cocoanut in the third month of its growth, yet far too rich to supply a substitute for butter . . . .

In the case of a small Sperm Whale the brains are accounted a fine dish. The casket of the skull is broken into with an axe. . . (320).

One hears two voices in Ishmael's description. One is the matter-of-fact narrative of the whale or the buffalo as an abundant food source, its killing a natural process to reduce them to edible parts. The other voice carries the subtler tonality of man's slaughtering Nature at an unprecedented rate that almost extinguishes both animals, one on the prairies of the Western lands and the other on the more fluid fields of the world's oceans. They are reduced to commodities for consumption while driven to the edge of extinction. Growing up out of such a utilitarian disposition is a tendency to objectify the natural order. Here is Ishmael's version of Irish satirist Jonathan Swift's "Modest Proposal."

In an appetite of consumption, everything is defined as something to ingest. Appetite can replace any admiration or wonder for life forms other than our own. Appetite can become the only element worth satisfying as it transforms all life into market place medallions. Consuming is a fundamental myth; a certain egoism attends this impulse that alienates us from the mystery or the dignity of the other. When we reduce or are reduced to one quality, commodity, statistic, fact or use, we lose all complexity and wonder that comprises us.

Meditation

What or who have you turned into a commodity?

June 14. Chapter 65: The Whale as a Dish

i.e. that a man should eat a newly murdered thing of the sea, and eat it too by its own light. But no doubt the first man that ever murdered an ox was regarded as a murderer; perhaps he was hung; and if he had been put on his trial by oxen, he certainly would have been; and he certainly deserved it if any murderer does. Go to the meat-market of a Saturday night and see the crowds of live bipeds staring up at the long rows of dead quadrupeds. Does not that sight take a tooth out of the cannibal's jaw? Cannibals? who is not a cannibal? . . .

But Stubb, he eats the whale by its own light, does he? and that is adding insult to injury, is it? (320-21).

Ishmael's observing Stubb eating a whale steak soon after its killing spirals out to a vibrant social commentary on the nature of cannibalism in our devouring so many animals, then utilizing what is left over. Not exactly a clarion call to become vegetarians, yet Ishmael exposes a rapacious consumption of nature wherein we are alienated from the animals except when we dine on them. We are the same ones "who nailest geese to the ground and feastest on their bloated livers in thy pate-de-foie-gras" (321). His intention is to encourage us to look closely at our own behavior/relation to the natural order's animal population as more than dishes to hunt down; they are kin.

While we speak of being civilized, in the area of appetite and understanding, our progress is often less than laudable. If we explore our "civilized" behavior closely, we often find a murderous impulse sinewing it. The shadows of our civilization can then become visible. What we choose to slaughter and consume mirrors our prevailing myth of consumption. One writer claims that "a myth can make a cow sacred in one culture and hamburger meat in another" (Sam Keen xi).

Meditation

What "civilized" behavior do you rebel against or wish to delete?

June 15. Chapter 68: The Blanket

True, from the unmarred dead body of the whale, you may scrape off with your hand an infinitely thin, transparent substance, somewhat resembling the thinnest shreds of isinglass, only it is almost as flexible and soft as satin; that is, previous to being dried, when it not only contracts and thickens, but becomes rather hard and brittle. I have several such dried bits, which I use for marks in my whale-books. It is transparent, as I said before; and being laid upon the printed page, I have sometimes pleased myself with fancying it exerted a magnifying influence. At any rate, it is pleasant to read about whales through their own spectacles, as you may say (326).

Ishmael offers a description of whale skin that is part observation and part reverie that doubles the whale as part object to be seen as well as a way of seeing, a medium of perception. He describes the whale both contracting and expanding, twisted smaller and magnified, through its skin. His pilgrimage to grasp the whale in its blubbery presence as well as its essence continues by getting to the skin, or "the skin of the skin" (326) then below or beneath it. Our blanket is our sleep skin. To see the words on whales in his whaling texts through the spectacles of whale membrane imagines Leviathan anew.

The skin of anything offers a rich boundary between its interior life and the external world. The skin is two-faced, with surfaces of interiority and one facing the external world. To see another only skin deep is a shallow perception. We have a natural impulse to penetrate beneath the skin of something or someone to know it deeply. Perhaps our personal myth resides right where our skin divides the world from our interior life; what markings occur at the skin line further define who we are. Tattooed, wounded, scarred or otherwise altered, our skin identifies us.

Meditation

What circumstances thicken your skin? Which reveal its thinness?

June 16. Chapter 68: The Blanket

In life, the visible surface of the Sperm Whale is not the least among the many marvels he presents. Almost invariably it is all over obliquely crossed and re-crossed with numberless straight marks in thick array, something like those in the finest Italian line engravings . . . . Nor is this all. In some instances, to the quick, observant eye, those linear marks, as in a veritable engraving, but afford the ground for far other delineations. These are hieroglyphical; that is, if you call those mysterious cyphers on the walls of pyramids hieroglyphics, then that is the proper word to use in the present connexion . . . . Like those mystic rocks, too, the mystic-marked whale remains undecipherable (327).

In his continued pilgrimage with his pen to trace both surface and depth of the whale's substance and nature, Ishmael draws comparisons between the whale's scarred markings, Italian line engravings, pyramidal hieroglyphics and a form of writing. The text he is creating with his own ink scratchings on white pages finds its place in his machinations and analogies to help us imagine the whale more deeply and inclusively. In the process he reminds us of our own bodies marked by life's plot lines; surface scars point to deeper wounds.

No one's body escapes being marked, wounded, lined, scarred, mutilated, dismembered or tattooed to represent our own novel story line. Even a "birth mark" is an indelible tattoo initiating us into the world. To be born is to invite being marked. Lines in our palms map our history and destiny. To read is to enter the markings of a wounded surface. Reading moves us out from the page to a world of analogies and correspondences that enrich our lives with threaded connections. All we read or mark in our lives may not be immediately clear to us.

Meditation

What marking do you carry as a remnant of an earlier event in your life's story?

June 17. Chapter 68: The Blanket

It does seem to me, that herein we see the rare virtue of a strong individual vitality, and the rare virtue of thick walls, and the rare virtue of interior spaciousness. Oh, man! admire and model thyself after the whale! Do thou, too, remain warm among ice. Do thou, too, live in this world without being of it. Be cool at the equator; keep thy blood fluid at the Pole. Like the great dome of St. Peter's, and like the great whale, retain, O man! in all seasons a temperature of thine own.

But how easy and how hopeless to teach these fine things! Of erections, how few are domed like St. Peter's! of creatures, how few vast as the whale! (328).

The whale, as part of the natural order, continues to expand its meaning in Ishmael's dynamic imagination, into ever-richer analogies. Vital, thick-skinned and interior spaciousness are qualities we might emulate and imitate; it can be as grand as St. Peter's massive cathedral dome in Rome. The whale is an emblem of a virtuous life, even a sacred life of noble generosity. The whale exudes a disposition and an attitude for our complex interiority. Be constant, moderate, detached and serene; like St. Peter's dome, retain a sacred aesthetic presence in the face of life's contraries. The whale, like a sacred architecture, provides a model disposition for humankind to imitate. It schools Ishmael and us.

Two worlds collude in this passage: the whale's exterior features signal the soul's inner disposition. The material imagination weds the moral imagination to reveal an accord between the soul's condition doubled by leviathan's life as model for imitation. Our journey in life is not to be constantly tossed about in the sea of circumstances but to gain a certain serenity in one's daily round. The whale by its behavior can instruct us as it serenely journeys the globe in full self-possession.

Meditation

In the above passage, what analogy draws your interest?

June 18. Chapter 69: The Funeral

"Haul in the chains! Let the carcase go astern!"

The vast tackles have now done their duty. The peeled white body of the beheaded whale flashes like a marble sepulcher . . . . It is still colossal. Slowly it floats more and more away, the water round it torn and splashed by the insatiate sharks, and the air above vexed with rapacious flights of screaming fowls, whose beaks are like so many insulting poniards in the whale. The vast white headless phantom floats further and further from the ship, . . . while that great mass of death floats on and on, till lost in infinite perspectives.

There's a most doleful and most mocking funeral! (329).

The ship has devoured those parts of the whale most valuable to it. It cuts the remainder loose to be fed upon by creatures of both sea and air gnawed with insatiable appetites. A sadness envelopes Ishmael's description as the dignified leviathan, now stripped of its skin, suffers insults since reduced to a headless phantom. The scene brings Ishmael to exclaim: "Oh, horrible vulturism of earth! from which not the mightiest whale is free" (329). Both grief and disgust as well as a fatalistic tone crease his despairing observations about extreme appetites.

Dismantling and consuming something for its valued cargo, with no thought of gratitude, no ritual of thanksgiving, attends the industry of whaling, or the animals that feed off the carcase so life may continue. It signals as well an inescapable harshness of life. "Vulturism" is the term for exploiting the magnificence of nature by a rapacious craving that consumes what it has stripped of its dignity. No presence of the sacred attends the world's victims whose carcasses are cast off as detritus with no thought of their value. Some among us, the passage intimates, must be witness to the grief that insists on being expressed.

Meditation

Have you experienced "a horrible vulturism" that changed you?

June 19. Chapter 69: The Funeral

Nor is this the end. Desecrated as the body is, a vengeful ghost survives and hovers over it to scare . . . . And for years afterwards, perhaps, ships shun the place; leaping over it as silly sheep leap over a vacuum, because their leader originally leaped there when a stick was held. There's your law of precedents; there's your utility of traditions; there's the story of your obstinate survival of old beliefs never bottomed on the earth, and now not even hovering in the air! There's orthodoxy!

. . . .

Are you a believer in ghosts, my friend? (329-30).

A situation threading through the center of the epic is that of absent presences. Things have a power when not physically present, as we witness in the White Whale's phantom existence. Ishmael spins off this idea to survey a history of beliefs when something that once had a power of presence is no more; however, its knee-jerk residue continues to inform and influence an individual's or a nation's values and behaviors. Traditions, orthodox beliefs and rituals now empty of meaning may still carry the force of an absent stick over which habitual thoughts leap. How obstinately can ideas create a "powerless panic" (330).

Often we continue to accept and believe in ideas, "truths," events or interpretations that in fact no longer hold sway in our lives but are nonetheless still successful in infecting and inflecting thought and behavior. When questioned, we may have no clue as to their origins, but there they stand, manipulating our thoughts and decisions. Mindlessness can kidnap us and hold us hostage to a past that is now both impotent and formidable. Such psychic and emotional phantoms can fixate us.

Meditation

What idea, attitude or belief do you sense it is time to relinquish because it no longer serves your development or promotes peace of mind?

June 20. Chapter 70: The Sphynx

When first severed, the head is dropped astern and held there by a cable till the body is stripped. That done, if it belong to a small whale it is hoisted on deck to be deliberately disposed of. But, with a full grown leviathan this is impossible; for the sperm whale's head embraces nearly one third of his entire bulk . . . .

. . . .

When this last task was accomplished it was noon . . . . Silence reigned over the before tumultuous but now deserted deck. An intense copper calm, like a universal yellow lotus, was more and more unfolding its noiseless measureless leaves upon the sea (331-32).

The matter-of-fact objective tone of the first part of Ishmael's description captures the horrific butchering of the sperm whale, large or small. Its head now hangs by cables alongside the ship in plain view. But as the business of severing it is completed, the atmosphere shifts markedly from frenzied work to a mystical, even eastern silence and serenity. Nature herself seems becalmed and in a lingering mood of anticipation and repose. Copper and yellow create a strange tincture to the air so that another cosmos altogether envelopes the ship and its crew.

Often, after a taxing period of intense labor, we may be invited into a calm center of inactivity where rest and reflection are encouraged to step forward and cloak us in their mantles; we can yield to this center of renewal and recovery no matter how ghastly or unpleasant former duties have exhausted us. Without these revolutions of respite we can lose ourselves altogether in the addiction of work that will digest us part by part, inch by inch. Through these gaps in the work, we can enter a calm sea that lavishes on us the sense of well-being.

Meditation

When an unpleasant or exhausting brand of work is completed, what actions help you to reclaim yourself?

June 21. Chapter 70: The Sphynx

A short space elapsed, and up into this noiselessness came Ahab alone from his cabin . . . . [where] he took Stubb's long spade—still remaining there after the whale's decapitation—and striking it into the lower part of the half-suspended mass . . . . so stood leaning over with eyes attentively fixed on his head.

It was a black and hooded head; and hanging there in the midst of so intense a calm, it seemed the Sphynx's in the desert. "Speak, thou vast and venerable head," muttered Ahab, "which though ungarnished with a beard, yet here and there lookest hoary with mosses; speak mighty head, and tell us the secret thing that is in thee. Of all divers, thou has dived the deepest" (332).

The calm space and silence of the whale's majestic head churns up a reverie in the captain that the Sphynx-like emblem held suspended is like a Sybil or seer in the air, ready to impart divine secrets of the deep. Ahab approaches like an impatient suppliant with a prod to encourage a response to his commands. He approaches the bodiless whale seeking oracular knowledge; observant and defiant, he challenges the head to yield the deepest secrets held by the oceans' fathoms. Ahab hungers for a depth of understanding, a knowledge that might heal his wounded revengeful nature if he could only know what lay below.

Ahab's quest to know expresses a deep impulse in us that what we do know is insufficient, that depth is a journey to quench a thirst and that knowing deeply is not a matter of the head but of the embodied heart. We yearn to know the terms of the mystery of our deepest lives and selves and to gain what our current depth does not fathom. We seek and may be driven to know what our limits cannot plumb; the search may enliven us, change the course of our pursuits and open us to enigmas.

Meditation

What depth of knowing do you seek at this period of your journey?

June 22. Chapter 70: The Sphynx

"Where unrecorded names and navies rust, and untold hopes and anchors rot; where in her murderous hold this frigate earth is ballasted with bones of millions of the drowned; there, in that awful water-land, there was thy most familiar home . . . . O head! thou hast seen enough to split the planets and make an infidel of Abraham, and not one syllable is thine."

. . . .

"Better and better, man. Would now St. Paul would come along that way, and to my breezelessness bring his breeze! O Nature, and O soul of man! how far beyond all utterance are your linked analogies; not the smallest atom stirs or lives on matter, but has its cunning duplicate in mind" (332-33).

Ahab's metaphysical reverie uncoiling in the whale's presence offers a profound expression of the entire voyage. His frustration grows because he is in the presence of the deepest diver of the seas, but it remains speechless. Hunting whales orbits out to include a quest for life itself, for its purpose and hidden designs. Ahab feels that if he can approach this mystery of life, the White Whale that dismasted him, he might grasp by analogy the doubled relationship between matter and mind: "the ungraspable phantom of life" (5).

Something resonates in us as we watch Ahab discover the existence of "linked analogies" between man's mind and God's created matter. We may seek such a knowledge in entertaining the possibility that the entire natural order is mirrored microcosmically within each of us. Such a revelation places the White Whale within me as well as deep in the ocean. We sense the metaphysical contours of the whale voyage; it is what our interior ecology is composed of. The whale breaches within.

Meditation

Relate what part of Ahab's monologue stirred you the most.

June 23. Chapter 72: The Monkey-Rope

It was a humorously perilous business for both of us. For, before we proceed further, it must be said that the monkey-rope was fast at both ends; fast to Queequeg's broad canvas belt, and fast to my narrow leather one. So that for better or for worse, we two, for the time, were wedded; and should poor Queequeg sink to rise no more, then both usage and honor demanded, that instead of cutting the cord, it should drag me down in his wake . . . . Queequeg was my own inseparable twin brother; nor could I any way get rid of the dangerous liabilities which the hempen bond entailed (342).

Ishmael relates how the blubber hook is inserted into the whale's back to hold it fast. Because Queequeg is supported on the whale's slippery skin, the monkey-rope gives him a connection to the ship, like a life line or umbilical cord. It unites the two men in a brotherhood of mutual survival; both risk their lives to dismantle the whale's blubber in rolling strips. Ishmael imagines in this life line, dependent on one another to service the ordeal, that they are wedded in a "joint stock company" of two, a mini-community of human interdependence and trust; by contrast, Ahab's solitary impulse is to cut the line from the humanity of others and remain an isolato on board his own ship.

We are each tied to so many others, either with thick or thin monkey-ropes. Some are thick to keep us fast to a few; others are thin and fragile, susceptible to snapping at the slightest pressure. Still others perhaps should be consciously severed to detach us from the behaviors of others who threaten to pull us into the deep vortex of their own pathos. We find ourselves in human communities that nourish us or deplete us of our energies. Cutting certain ropes would liberate us.

Meditation

Describe a monkey-rope that keeps you fastened to something or someone. Is it a healthy or harmful bond?

June 24. Chapter 72: The Monkey-Rope

Suspended over the side in one of the stages, Tashtego and Daggoo continually flourished over his head a couple of keen whale-spades, wherewith they slaughtered as many sharks as they could reach . . . . They meant Queequeg's best happiness, I admit . . . [but] those indiscreet spades of theirs would come nearer amputating a leg than a tail. But poor Queequeg, I suppose, straining and gasping there with that great iron hook—poor Queequeg, I suppose, only prayed to his Yojo, and gave up his life into the hands of his gods . . . .

Are you not the precious image of each and all of us men in this whaling world? That unsounded ocean you gasp in, is Life; those sharks your foes; those spades, your friends . . . (343).

With each chapter Ishmael contours the terms of this rich and liquid allegory for us to contemplate. His poetic way of seeing continually extracts correspondences to life itself through the fierce particularity of the whaling voyage, as if contained on board the Pequod were all the insights and necessities by which to distill or try-out a practical metaphysics of existence. We watch in the process his ripening into deeper and more sophisticated consciousness; as readers, we gather the wisdom with him. In the particulars of whaling he intuits a general pattern or life structure that allows him to scribe such a provocative plot.

We sometimes move through life dancing with our feet to avoid the sharks snapping from below at our progress; at times we are aided by spade-whalers who come to our aid as blessings or angels because beneath the surface is a universal awareness that we are all fastened to one another by invisible monkey-ropes that share one universal soul. Finally, we are each a mirror or a communal image of all others.

Meditation

What life event placed you directly between sharks and spades? Was there someone at the other end of your monkey-rope?

June 25. Chapter 73: *Stubb and Flask Kill a* Right Whale; *and Then Have a Talk Over Him*

It must be borne in mind that all this time we have a Sperm Whale's prodigious head hanging to the Pequod's side. But we must let it continue hanging there awhile till we can get a chance to attend to it. For the present other matters press, and the best we can do now for the head, is to pray heaven the tackles may hold.

. . . .

Nor was this long wanting. Tall spouts were seen to leeward; and two boats, Stubb's and Flask's, were detached in pursuit. Pulling further and further away, they at last became almost invisible to the men at the masthead (346).

Ishmael again offers one of his effective rhetorical strategy's clearest tokens. The Pequod's hunting whales and pursuing Moby Dick is one journey. The second is Ishmael's poetic/historical writing of the first journey. The third journey is our reading the story "as if" we were on board witnessing everything Ishmael describes. So the three are indeed one in the above passage. Experience itself is insufficient for understanding. It needs be remembered and told in a form sufficient to make us embark on the reading voyage, to gather what boons Ishmael offers us in his poetic remembrance. Writing and reading are actions as important as those of seeking whales to kill and process.

Our lives are full of events in minor and major keys. Sometimes what we may have experienced as a minor event, in recollection and re-creation looms much larger in the fabric of our evolving life's weave. Recollection offers a perspective by which to evaluate and value each event according to its merit *within* the larger plot line of our voyage; we see it more clearly and mythically when expressed in language.

Meditation

When did what seemed a small incident in your life become seminal?

June 26. Chapter 73: *Stubb and Flask Kill a* Right Whale; *and Then Have a Talk Over Him*

"I don't know, but I heard that gamboge ghost of a Fedallah saying so, and he seems to know all about ships' charms. But I sometimes think he'll charm the ship to no good at last. I don't half like that chap, Stubb. Did you ever notice how that tusk of his is a sort of [sic] carved into a snake's head, Stubb?" . . . .

"Flask, I take that Fedallah to be the devil in disguise . . . . He's the devil, I say. The reason why you don't see his tail, is because he tucks it up out of sight; he carries it coiled away in his pocket, I guess" (348).

Stubb and Flask intuit something real or imagined in Fedallah's nature. Flask, a man of few words, confesses that Fedallah will harm the ship with his charms. Ahab has made a pact with the musky savage, "striking up a swap or a bargain, I suppose" (348) believes Stubb. Their pact echoes the ageless one of a man whose desires are so powerful he will wager his soul if the devil himself aids in its achievement. Flask in conversation is "coiling some spare line in the boat's bow" to reveal how at night Fedallah sleeps on deck "in a coil of rigging" (348).

Evil does not always arrive with fanfare as an obvious and formidable presence. Often more subtle, it can appear as an accomplice to desires and obsessions, promising a smoother delivery than one can accomplish solo. The persuasive power of evil is in its mirroring back to us what we are convinced is a desired good. Evil can accommodate such a fantasy with great patience, knowing we will often risk everything when we believe the object of our desire is in reach. We wonder as well why it is that we often assign evil designs to the "other" that exists out of our comfortable territory.

Meditation

What form of attraction has evil bargained with you?

June 27. Chapter 73: *Stubb and Flask Kill a* Right Whale; *and Then Have a Talk Over Him*

In good time, Flask's saying proved true. As before, the Pequod steeply leaned over towards the sperm whale's head, now, by the counterpoise of both heads, she regained her even keel; though sorely strained, you may well believe. So, when on one side you hoist in Locke's head, you go over that way; but now on the other side, hoist in Kant's and you come back again; but in very poor plight. Thus, some minds for ever keep trimming boat. Oh, ye foolish! throw all these thunder-heads overboard, and then you will float light and right (350-51).

Ishmael's analogy is both witty and profound. He imagines the Pequod as an individual listing to one side from the weight of one philosophic school, then to the other side from the weight of another. One could spend a lifetime entertaining one philosophical perspective after another and miss the experience of life itself. By jettisoning these interpretations of the mind, one gains a freedom and mobility they mute. The whale heads are absent their bodies, having been truncated by the cutting poles. So, Ishmael suggests, can an individual be split, made less whole, by "heady thought" devoid of a connection to matter.

Beliefs or belief systems can be a help and a hindrance to living a life joyfully enfleshed. Beliefs can flatten mystery, diminish matters of the world and disengage us from the journey. We are able to gain a delicious freedom in engaging everyday occurrences and being finally present to them if our beliefs don't act as a novocain to life, where thinking splits us by abandoning feeling. One can expend a lifetime listing into this or that philosophical school and suffocate life's experiences in the process. Then one's myth hardens into fixity.

Meditation

What beliefs do you hold that may insulate you from lived experiences?

June 28. Chapter 74: The Sperm Whale's Head—*Contrasted View*

Is it not curious, that so vast a being as the whale should see the world through so small an eye, and hear the thunder through an ear which is smaller than a hare's? But if his eyes were broad as the lens of Herschel's great telescope; and his ears capacious as the porches of cathedrals; would that make him any longer of sight, or sharper of hearing? Not at all.— Why then do you try to "enlarge" your mind? Subtilize it (354).

The particularities of the whale's body continue to evoke rich responses as they spiral out from its flesh and skeleton to analogies with life, mind and imagination. Ishmael imagines through the matter of the whale that covers many disciplines. Matter is the medium into a metaphysics of knowing. First remarking earlier that because the whale's eyes exist on opposite geographies of its great head, it can process two realities simultaneously within a brain "much more comprehensive, combining and subtle than man's. . ." (354). His point includes a paradox: such an enormous body perceives the world largely through tiny eyes and miniscule ears, yet both organs of perception function superbly in their compactness.

"Bigger is better" is challenged here because subtlety, nuance, and shading are deep psychological realities seeking cultivation. The small, at times insignificant gestures, realities, events and incidents carry the hefty within them. We pay attention to nuance, often with great insights into ourselves and others; such is whale wisdom. To "subtilize" is to see with a darker eye, to hear with a nuanced ear to what is missed by more massive intake organs that avoid a deeper, poetic presence.

Meditation

When has subtlety uncovered for you a much larger awareness than you could have imagined?

June 29. Chapter 75: The Right Whale's Head— *Contrasted View*

Crossing the deck, let us now have a good long look at the Right Whale's head.

. . . .

But as you come nearer to this great head it begins to assume different aspects, according to your point of view. If you stand on its summit and look at these two f-shaped spout-holes, you would take the whole head for an enormous bass viol, and these spiracles, the apertures in its sounding board. Then again, if you fix your eye upon this strange, crested, comb-like incrustation on the top of the mass—this green, barnacled thing . . . fixing your eyes solely on this, you would take the head for the trunk of some huge oak, with a bird's nest in its crotch (357).

Ishmael leads us reader-whalers across the deck to reveal another perspective as he continues to contrast two examples of the same species of cetaceans. His goal is to reveal a shifting perspective of understanding, depending from where and whence we fix our gaze. The Right Whale's head can become a number of things, serving a wealth of analogies relative to our point of view; the reality of the thing becomes perspectival and thus shape-shifting, with one reality competing with others for preferred veracity. The whale is the world writ smaller.

How something appears to us is influenced by both attitude and by altitude: seeing from a high purchase looking down, or seeing from below. The word "understanding" means to stand under; perspective is situational. It yields a different image of the same ostensible reality. What we know is dependent on from where and when we gaze. Angle of vision influences, if not defines, depth of meaning. The psychology of seeing implicates a mythology of the gaze to uncover multiple meanings.

Meditation

When has shifting perspective yielded a different understanding?

June 30. Chapter 75: The Right Whale's Head— *Contrasted View*

To sum up, then: in the Right Whale's there is no great well of sperm; no ivory teeth at all; no long, slender mandible of a lower jaw, like the Sperm Whale's. Nor in the Sperm Whale are there any of those blinds of bone; no huge lower lip; and scarcely anything of a tongue . . . .

Look your last now, on these venerable hooded heads, while they yet lie together; for one will soon sink, unrecorded, in the sea; the other will not be very long in following.

Can you catch the expression of the Sperm Whale's there? . . . Does not this whole head seem to speak of an enormous practical resolution in facing death? This Right Whale I take to have been a Stoic; the Sperm Whale, a Platonian, who might have taken up Spinoza in his latter years (359-60).

A comic yet serious eulogy Ishmael offers of both hooded phantoms soon to be liberated into the deep. Their matter has valence for consumption on land, yet their visage reflects philosophical import, even schools of thought and behavior with contrasting perspectives. Two sets of approaches to Being surface and hang in the balance aboard the stable Pequod where whales as lovers of philosophy are available. It has what Ishmael calls "the savor of analogical probability" (358). One philosophy leans toward praising matter; the other rests comfortably in the field of eternal forms. Biology and ontology find common ground.

The philosophy of matter weds with the matter of philosophy to suggest that the two are continually intertwined in the mind as it seeks to know the nature of reality and its relation to both spiritual and philosophic jurisdictions. The philosophies that guide us are central to establishing our personal myth; they are not just matters of mind. We might think of schools of philosophical thought as analogy-makers.

Meditation

What philosophic belief grew from engaging the world's matter?

July 1. Chapter 76: The Battering-Ram

Now, mark. Unerringly impelling this dead, impregnable, uninjurable wall, and this most buoyant thing within; there swims behind it all a mass of tremendous life, only to be adequately estimated as piled wood is—by the cord; and all obedient to one volition, as the smallest insect. So that . . . . when I shall show you some of his more inconsiderable braining feats; I trust you will have renounced all ignorant incredulity; and be ready to abide by this . . . . For unless you own the whale, you are but a provincial and sentimentalist in Truth . . . . What befel the weakling youth lifting the dread goddess's veil at Lais? (362-63).

Ishmael describes the forehead which "presents an almost wholly vertical plane to the water" (361) and appears as a battering ram, a truth to become more apparent in the joustings with Moby Dick. He reveals the wood-hard well of the whale's bow, capable of splintering anything in its path. He challenges us to "own" the whale, to know it from the inside out--deep cavity to external skin--else we remain sentimentally ignorant of its cunning and power. Reference to the "dread goddess at Lais" invites references to Calypso, Circe and Aphrodite; to lift the veil is to discover what is behind the mask of the phenomenal world in a divine interior, what Ahab could not imagine or reach.

Experience wedded to a philosophic means of meditation and reflection are twin paths to knowing something of the world in its material and metaphysical features. Philosophy alone is inadequate, as is experiencing the vents of the whale. A life of action and contemplation imaginatively blended offers a much fuller avenue of understanding. The whale is a mythic emblem as well as a commercial commodity.

Meditation

When has direct involvement, coupled with contemplation, yielded greater insight into someone or thing?

Part IV

Capturing the Whale Chapters 77-105

What the hero seeks through his intercourse with them is therefore not finally themselves, but their grace, i.e., the power of their sustaining substance.

The Hero With a Thousand Faces, 155.

July 2. Chapter 77: The Great Heidelburgh Tun

Now comes the Baling of the Case. But to comprehend it aright, you must know something of the curious internal structure of the thing operated upon.

. . . .

The upper part, known as the Case, may be regarded as the great Heidelburgh Tun of the Sperm Whale . . . . Moreover, as that of Heidelburgh was always replenished with the most excellent of the wines of the Rhenish valleys, so the tun of the whale contains by far the most precious of all his oily vintages; namely, the highly-prized spermaceti, in its absolutely pure, limpid, and odoriferous state (364).

Ishmael continues his poetic pilgrimage through the whale's anatomy and its fluids, journeying now into its enormous head to locate this "unalloyed" substance found only here. His comparison with fine German wines connects this precious fruit with the spermaceti, an elixir of great value and renewal. The Sperm Whale's head is like a vessel or Grail cup, both massive and sacred, into which one dips a ladle to extract the precious cargo. Ishmael makes it more vivid through a rich analogy to the land and vineyards flowing through the Rhenish valleys.

The analogy here may send us swimming in reveries of containers, cargo holds, Grail legends, the treasure found inside the leviathan—imaginings of interiorities, precious liquids, renewal, refreshment, the treasure difficult to attain, the crushing of grapes into transformed bottles of wine. All these and more cluster around this rich and fragile alchemy of the heady whale. We find ourselves refreshed and renewed as we inhabit the comparison. The whale's bounty may strike in us a feeling of abundance and gratitude for both sea and earth's life. When we see comparatively we sense an underlying unity in all matter.

Meditation

What does Ishmael's description/comparison allow to arise in you?

July 3. Chapter 77: The Great Heidelburgh Tun

Though in life it remains perfectly fluid, yet, upon exposure to the air, after death, it soon begins to concrete; sending forth beautiful crystalline shoots, as when the first thin delicate ice is just forming in water. A large whale's case generally yields about five hundred gallons of sperm . . . .

. . . .

As in decapitating the whale, the operator's instrument is brought close to the spot where an entrance is subsequently forced into the spermaceti magazine; he has, therefore, to be uncommonly heedful, lest a careless, untimely stroke should invade the sanctuary and wastingly let out its invaluable contents (364-65).

Spermaceti is an extraordinary liquid. Like blood, it coagulates and clots when allowed to surface from its hold in the Sperm Whale's head. It has a delicacy and hardness as it migrates from an encased liquid to a concrete firmness when exposed to air. The head must therefore be approached with respect and precision, like a priest entering a sanctuary where the sacred wine waits in the chalice. The word choice of "sanctuary" lifts the description to another level of meaning: the head is a sacred container of value, of a precious commodity needing precision and care for the numinous liquid's extraction (365).

Reverence for the values in life surface in this decapitation. What is "invaluable" is preserved through great care and precision. Spermaceti is life's elixir. The whale's head is a sanctified locale. Not just in churches, synagogues and mosques is holiness present, but in many other natural places we encounter. Spermaceti conjures what is valued in life, what requires great care to extract and preserve; it provides richer meanings to our experiences in a holy oil of meaning.

Meditation

What sanctuaries do you enter for respite, rest and renewal?

July 4. Chapter 78: Cistern and Buckets

Almost in the same instant, with a thunder-boom, the enormous mass dropped into the sea, like Niagara's Table-Rock into the whirlpool; the suddenly relieved hull rolled away from it . . . [while] Daggoo, through a thick mist of spray, was dimly beheld clinging to the pendulous tackles, while poor, buried-alive Tashtego was sinking utterly down to the bottom of the sea! . . . when a naked figure with a boarding-sword in his hand, was for one swift moment seen hovering over the bulwarks. The next, a loud splash announced that my brave Queequeg had dived to the rescue (368).

Queequeg is once again the epic's life preserver. As he saved the young boy who mocked him on the boat transporting them to Nantucket, and as he saved Ishmael from his own self-destruction, he now dives deep to pull Tashtego from out the whale's head sinking quickly to the ocean's bottom. Ishmael praises Queequeg's prowess and his generous spirit; he repeatedly acts selflessly. He sacrifices his own wellbeing to save others. He practices in his natural unassuming grace the central tenet of many religions: to give of self, to treat others as you seek to be treated. Queequeg cuts through all boundaries in self-sacrifice.

Generosity towards others creates a communal bond between all people. Acting on that generosity in unconditional surrender to another's needs is grace in motion. Christ-like in attitude, we can each skirt past all artificial and culturally-induced prejudices towards others' offenses if we can view them under the aspect of a "joint stock company" of intimate acquaintances. We are naked in such moments of generosity because liberated for a time from self-absorption and safety.

Meditation

When have you received or been the agent of a gratuitous generous act towards another that alleviated danger or crisis?

July 5. Chapter 78: Cistern and Buckets

Now, how had this noble rescue been accomplished? Why, diving after the slowly descending head, Queequeg with his keen sword had made side lunges near its bottom, so as to scuttle a large hole there; then dropping his sword, had thrust his long arm far inwards and upwards, and so hauled out poor Tash by the head. He averred, that upon first thrusting in for him, a leg was presented, but well knowing that that was not as it ought to be, and might occasion great trouble;—he had thrust back the leg, and by a dexterous heave and toss, had wrought a somerset upon the Indian; so that with the next trial, he came forth in the good old way—head foremost. As for the great head itself, that was doing as well as could be expected (368-69).

Ishmael's description is comic, ironic, clever and detailed in describing two heads, expanded and contracted, two head-strong worlds with Queequeg the mediator, midwife and medium who saves Tashtego from a breached and botched birth. Always the go-between, like Hermes, is Queequeg. Instinctive, intuitive, and initiating, his power serves the preservation of life. Out of the mother head heads Tashtego, a second birth that renews his life. Without Queequeg's skill as a midwife, two heads would have sailed as one to the ocean's bottom.

Sacrifice is often comic; seeking to save another is comic, for life itself in any form is preferable to its alternative. Without Queequegs in the world, the number of lives lost would be immeasurably higher. To risk one's life for another recoils against all instincts for self-preservation, yet it is a keen impulse in us to preserve another at our own risk. Queequeg is a motif for that deep desire in us to respond without concern for one's own survival to salvage the life of another.

Meditation

When has the impulse to act selflessly risen up in you? When has someone stepped forward selflessly to aid you in a time of distress?

July 6. Chapter 79: The Prairie

Champollion deciphered the wrinkled granite hieroglyphics. But there is no Champollion to decipher the Egypt of every man's and every being's face. Physiognomy, like every other human science, is but a passing fable. If, then, Sir William Jones, who read in thirty languages, could not read the simplest peasant's face in its profounder and more subtle meanings, how may unlettered Ishmael hope to read the awful Chaldee of the Sperm Whale's brow? I but put that brow before you. Read it if you can (373).

Ishmael addresses us as readers/whalers directly concerning how we might interpret the whale's inscrutable nature. The rich recurring image of Egyptian hieroglyphics, with its strange characters and figures, is nothing in comparison to the character of the whale's awe-ful nature, a wrinkled text that challenges our ability to decipher it. He alludes to the Egyptologist Jean Francis Champollion (1790-1832), who at a young age examined texts from Egypt and discerned relationships between hieroglyphic and non-hieroglyphic scripts, which initiated a breakthrough in deciphering their complex grammar (www.bbc.co.uk/history_figures/champollion_jean.shtml).

Inscrutability, Ishmael suggests, is the dominant sinew we confront in the mystery of every person's face.

Can we know the invisible interior of a person through his/her visage? Physiognomy comprises invisible mysteries, motives and desires that lurk in the deep waters of each of us. Appearances are deceptive, we learn; the masked characters of a face can camouflage the most sinister motives or generous blessings. Gaze for a moment at your own face in a mirror and ask what is written there. Can you fathom the deep interior of yourself through this reflective medium?

Meditation

Reflect on your own face. What remains invisible and inscrutable?

July 7. Chapter 80: The Nut

If the Sperm Whale be physiognomically a Sphinx, to the phrenologist his brain seems that geometrical circle which it is impossible to square.

In the full-grown creature the skull will measure at least twenty feet in length . . . . The brain is at least twenty feet from his apparent forehead in life; it is hidden away behind its vast out-works, like the innermost citadel within the amplified fortifications of Quebec . . . .

It is plain, then, that phrenologically the head of this Leviathan, in the creature's living intact state, is an entire delusion. As for his true brain, you can then see no indications of it, nor feel any. The whale, like all things that are mighty, wears a false brow to the common world (374).

The analytical Ishmael continues to wrestle with the poetic, philosophical Ishmael in his ongoing hermeneutical or interpretive quest of the whale's true nature: through analogies with history, myth, science, phrenology, and fictions Yet it remains as silent and inscrutable as a Sphinx, wrapped in mystery while presenting a hard, broad impenetrable head to the world. Phrenology cannot penetrate its fortifications; mystery is its essential bulwark, inscrutability its outer lining. Its majestic power and silence harbors invisible meanings.

The passage may make us wonder what true or false notions reside behind any face the world puts before our vision. We may deploy several varied structures which promise a penetration into its truth, yet all theories and descriptions fail or fall short of offering a comprehensive vision of what resides behind its ambiguous visage. The whale's mystery is a potent metaphor for the puzzling appearance of any mighty presence of the phantom of life that bewilders us.

Meditation

In your experience, what "whale" has left you dumbfounded in wonder?

July 8. Chapter 80: The Nut

For, viewed in this light, the wonderful comparative smallness of his brain proper is more than compensated by the wonderful comparative magnitude of his spinal cord.

But leaving this hint to operate as it may with the phrenologists, I would merely assume the spinal theory for a moment, in reference to the Sperm Whale's hump. This august hump, if I mistake not, rises over one of the larger vertebrae, and is, therefore, in some sort, the outer convex mould of it . . . . I should call this high hump the organ of firmness or indomitableness in the Sperm Whale. And that the great monster is indomitable, you will yet have reason to know (376).

Ishmael's description combines the physical with the metaphysical dimensions of the Sperm Whale. Phrenology is inadequate for imagining the whale's physiology. Measurement and quantification pale in the presence of the imaginal, or in dreaming the whale into being. Ishmael sees in the hump a mirror of another reality that molds its features. The hump is a quality, not a quantity; it is the image of indomitableness itself, a seminal feature of the whale's character it carries on its back as a showing forth, or revelation. Physical feature exudes a character trait that cannot be measured but can be seen through resemblance. The whale's deeper nature exists through the power of analogy.

Our individual features reveal some important dimensions of our character. Distinguishing aspects of our being gather in physiognomy so that one mirrors or evokes the other. *What* and *who* advance together in our outward appearance as a mold for inner realities and other interior landscapes that impress our character into its unique shape. While never completing or exhausting our interior profile, our bodies yield to the world important qualities we inhabit and live by.

Meditation

What in your external appearance mirrors a quality of your character?

July 9. Chapter 81: *The Pequod Meets* The Virgin

It so chanced that almost upon first cutting into him with the spade, the entire length of a corroded harpoon was found imbedded in his flesh, on the lower part of the bunch before described . . . . But still more curious was the fact of a lancehead of stone being found in him, not far from the buried iron, the flesh perfectly firm about it. Who had darted that stone lance? And when? It might have been darted by some Nor' West Indian long before America was discovered.

What other marvels might have been rummaged out of this monstrous cabinet there is no telling (385).

Ishmael relates the history of a whale and its longevity through the discovery of a stone lancehead. The age of this whale indicated by the substance of the lancehead astonishes. As he has been so intent on the physical matter of the whale in space, he now turns to the endurance of the whale in time. We sense in reading it that Ishmael means more than simply relaying the whale's age. The stone lancehead conjures up a feeling of the whale's long lasting presence *in* the world and *as* the world. Like a god or hero in myth, the whale conveys an enormous staying power; something eternal gathers around its enduring presence.

Discovering the ancient lancehead buried in the whale conveys an image that incites dreams of antiquity, of first mortals and of immortality's shades. It carries as well echoes of the wounded Fisher King, who when the lancehead that afflicts him is removed, one discovers a grail signature inscribed on it. We discern in this momentous event a connection with both history and myth that carries our imagination well beyond the whale's physical presence; it opens the imagination to a wider orbit of discovery more inclusive in design.

Meditation

Have you discovered in an object or person in the present a rich and lengthy legacy imbedded therein?

July 10. Chapter 81: *The Pequod Meets* The Virgin

It was not long after the sinking of the body that a cry was heard from the Pequod's mast-heads, announcing that the Jungfrau was again lowering her boats; though the only spout in sight was that of a Fin-Back, belonging to the species of uncapturable whales, because of its incredible power of swimming. Nevertheless, the Fin-Back's spout is so similar to the Sperm Whale's, that by unskillful fishermen it is often mistaken for it. And consequently Derick and all his host were now in valiant chase of this unnearable brute . . . .

Oh! many are the Fin-Backs, and many are the Dericks, my friend (387).

Ishmael speaks directly to us as "friend" in conveying how those unskilled in distinguishing kinds of whales may confuse those that can be captured from those that are ungraspable. Because of their lack of experience and discernment, the crew of the Jungfrau futilely head out to chase the uncatchable. The name of their ship reflects their inexperience. So off they go. Derick and the Fin-Back are types, both of what cannot be captured and those who confuse it with what they believe can be.

Moments in the epic like the one above open us to a lower layer of meaning where a whaleman and his crew chasing after a far-too-swift whale conveys the metaphor for all of us who have at various moments in our lives decided to pursue the unattainable. Such a hunt can be short-lived or it can last for years, even a lifetime. The caution here: beware what you choose to pursue because it could be something or someone far exceeding one's grasp or constructed on faulty perspectives. We are cautioned to know accurately the whale we pursue before lowering our boat in a chase that could consume all our energies.

Meditation

What have you pursued in life but eventually realized was well beyond your reach?

July 11. Chapter 82: *The Honor and Glory of* Whaling

There are some enterprises in which a careful disorderliness is the true method.

The more I dive into this matter of whaling, and push my researches up to the very spring-head of it so much the more am I impressed with its great honorableness and antiquity; and especially when I find so many great demi-gods and heroes, prophets of all sorts, who one way or other have shed distinction upon it, I am transported with the reflection that I myself belong, though but subordinately, to so emblazoned a fraternity.

The gallant Perseus, a son of Jupiter, was the first whaleman (388).

Ishmael's encomium to whaling lore and practice from a historical and mythical perspective introduces us to a long line of heroes, gods and historical figures who engaged whales. Hunting the whale or being pursued by it spirals back to the origin of creation itself; Ishmael proudly places himself within the noble lineage of such an epic congregation. His community membership expands out from Queequeg to the ship's personnel to the history of such a noble quest. His other journey, then, is to pilgrimage to the wellspring of such a confrontation, to hunt it to its source, even if at times he might have to rotate or rewrite history or legend to carry the lineage seamlessly back into pre-history. His quill rather than a harpoon is the sharp instrument of his calling.

Becoming conscious of one's place in history by seeing one's task in life as a noble enterprise, perhaps as ancient as life itself, can bestow esteem on what might seem mundane: parenting, journeying into the unknown, serving others, pursuing a noble end, teaching, or creating something new. All have a potent history or tradition to be carried forward with pride as it links one to such an ancient *communitas.*

Meditation

What engaged work has united you to a much larger community?

July 12. Chapter 82: *The Honor and Glory of* Whaling

Akin to the adventure of Perseus and Andromeda—indeed, by some supposed to be indirectly derived from it—is that famous story of St. George and the Dragon; which dragon I maintain to have been a whale . . . . Any man may kill a snake, but only a Perseus, a St. George, a Coffin, have the heart in them to march boldly up to a whale . . . .

Thus, then, one of our own noble stamp, even a whaleman, is the tutelary guardian of England; and by good rights, we harpooneers of Nantucket should be enrolled in the most noble order of St. George. . . .

Whether to admit Hercules among us or not, concerning this I long remained dubious. . . .

. . . .

Perseus, St. George, Hercules, Jonah and Vishnoo! there's a member-roll for you! What club but the whaleman's can head off like that? (389-90).

Ishmael's specific members of his fraternity of nobility descending from mythic figures down to present day Nantucketers offers a lineage of noble, courageous hearts committed to the epic enterprise of whaling by forging a heroic tradition into which Ishmael now casts himself as an active member. He extends this heredity to the legend of Vishnoo, Hindu god of all creation who, to salvage the Vedas lying at the bottom of the sea, "became incarnate in a whale" (390) to descend to retrieve them.

Whaling seems synonymous with creation itself. The whale is that being at the very foundation of the world and seems the origin and analogy of the heroic impulse in the soul as well as in nature. Whaling offers us nobility fashioned from a pure heart. What we pursue marks us with the opus we define our lives within as well as gauges the quality of our actions and the nobility of our souls. By it we are elevated.

Meditation

What have you engaged that bequeathed your life a nobility?

July 13. Chapter 83: Jonah Historically Regarded

Reference was made to the historical story of Jonah and the whale in the preceding chapter. Now some Nantucketers rather distrust this historical story of Jonah and the whale. But then there were some sceptical Greeks and Romans, who, standing out from the orthodox pagans of their times, equally doubted the story of Hercules and the whale, and Arion and the dolphin . . . .

One old Sag-Harbor whaleman's chief reason for questioning the Hebrew Story was this:--He had one of those quaint old-fashioned Bibles, embellished with curious, unscientific plates; one of which represented Jonah's whale with two spouts in his head—a peculiarity only true with respect to a species of the Leviathan (the Right Whale, and the varieties of that order). . . (391).

Biblical allusions and references are cast continually on to the waters of this epic. Of them, Jonah, Job, Ishmael and Ahab are most prominent. How should they be understood? As fact, fiction, history, myth, and/or legend? One person's Bible may take one in a certain direction, while another rendering offers another interpretation. The historical accuracy of Biblical narratives may be of supreme importance for one reader, far less so for another. What to believe? The passage asks us implicitly: what history fits our own faith, what facts constitute our faith, and what myth orders our sense of history and current reality?

Interpretations shape our world as well as our worldview. What we take as "gospel" places us in a certain attitude towards the past and so by extension, the future. We create "as if" fictions of ourselves and our surroundings based as much on the attitudes we cultivate as on the information we absorb and beatify to be true. Taking our stories literally or symbolically makes a big difference in our myth's perspective.

Meditation

Name two assumptions you carry out of bed with you each morning.

July 14. Chapter 83: Jonah Historically Regarded

Nor have there been wanting learned exegetists who have opined that the whale mentioned in the book of Jonah merely meant a life-preserver—an inflated bag of wind—which the endangered prophet swam to, and so was saved from a watery doom.

. . . .

But all these foolish arguments of old Sag-Harbor only evinced his foolish pride of reason— . . . . I say it only shows his foolish impious pride and abominable devilish rebellion against the reverend clergy . . . . Besides, to this day, the highly enlightened Turks devoutly believe in the historical story of Jonah. And some three centuries ago, an English traveler . . . . speaks of a Turkish Mosque built in honor of Jonah, in which Mosque was a miraculous lamp that burnt without any oil (392-93).

Ishmael continues his critique of scriptural interpretation. If one reads by reason alone, then one can disprove the logic of some biblical passages, assuming thereby that all stories are to be read literally. History then dominates as the instrument of understanding. But the story of the Turks mixes the historical story with a place of worship in honor of the whale as a divinity reflected in the oil-less burning lamp. Is whale oil's absence suggesting how miracle and myth mingle with history?

We often include in our understanding of something both fact and fiction, history and myth, literal and figural, "as if" the two combined might warranty a surer view of what we focus on to grasp a meaning that satisfies. The soul may need both, since facts and reason allow us to plunge only so far into mystery. Something of the miraculous also attends things of the world if our dominant mythology allows it in. We cannot "know" what something means through only one fixed lens.

Meditation

When in your life has the miraculous mingled with the historical?

July 15. Chapter 84: Pitchpoling

To make them run easily and swiftly, the axles of carriages are anointed; and for much the same purpose, some whalers perform an analogous operation upon their boat; they grease the bottom. Nor is it to be doubted that as such a procedure can do no harm, it may possibly be of no contemptible advantage; considering that oil and water are hostile; that oil is a sliding thing, and that the object in view is to make the boat slide bravely. Queequeg believed strongly in anointing his boat, and one morning . . . . took more than customary pains in that occupation . . . . working in obedience to some particular presentiment (394).

Most of Ishmael's descriptions on matters pertaining to whaling carry analogies to life in all its haunting complexities. So is it with Queequeg's preoccupation of anointing the bottom of his whaling boat with oil "as though diligently seeking to insure a crop of hair from the craft's bald keel" (394). Because oil and water are hostile, in many instances they actually complement one another's behaviors. Oil makes the hull slide with less friction because the water is not disposed to absorb the oil into itself. The unction is a blessing to the boat because it increases its efficiency with ease. The word "anointing" connotes several meanings related to the sacramental as part of whaling.

Pouring oil on the troubled waters of our own life is a well-known metaphor. Having a particular oil to rub onto our life's surfaces can ease the friction of any single day. A prayer, a good thought, a favorite memory anoints the burden of any task by encouraging an ease and flow where we might otherwise scrape along. Not a great deal of oil is needed; only enough to slick the surface to ensure a smoother glide. Stories themselves can act as a salve on our scratched surfaces.

Meditation

What oil or grease do you employ to ease the keel of your everyday life or when friction develops in relation to self or others?

July 16. Chapter 85: The Fountain

That for six thousand years—and no one knows how many millions of ages before—the great whales should have been spouting all over the sea, and sprinkling and mystifying the gardens of the deep, as with so many sprinkling or mystifying pots . . . that all this should be, and yet, that down to this blessed minute (fifteen and a quarter minutes past one o'clock P.M. of this sixteenth day of December, A.D. 1851), it should still remain a problem, whether these spoutings are, after all, really water, or nothing but vapor—this is surely a noteworthy thing.

Let us, then, look at this matter, along with some interesting items contingent (397).

This chapter is as much about time as it is the breaching spout of the whale, its ability to remain submerged for an hour or more and the exact nature of the vapor that emanates like a vertical geyser from its exhalation. Ishmael offers us the exact second of these lines'creation, even as he speculates that whales have been circling the globe for millions of years. He will now meditate deeply on the whale spout to discover any analogies to our humanness, since the whale, like us, breathes with lungs. Revealing likenesses rather than differences between us and whales is his intention; a grand nobility surrounds leviathan as a mirror held up to our own noble nature in grand outlines.

All of us are daily preoccupied with time as an ordering principle. We see ourselves in the vapor of time and within this temporal structure we attempt to make sense of what engages us, draw analogies to deepen comprehension and see ourselves in some measure by what draws us to it. Some things, however, no matter how much we contemplate them, will remain unfathomable and phantom-like. Water-laden or vapor-smitten, some concerns will be argued until time evaporates.

Meditation

What element, person or event's meaning continues to elude you?

July 17. Chapter 85: The Fountain

But the Sperm Whale's food is far beneath the surface, and there he cannot spout even if he would . . . .

But why pester one with all this reasoning on the subject? Speak out! You have seen him spout; then declare what the spout is; can you not tell water from air? My dear sir, in this world it is not so easy to settle these plain things. I have ever found your plain things the knottiest of all. And as for this whale spout, you might almost stand in it, and yet be undecided as to what it is precisely (400).

Ishmael possesses an uncanny ability to hone in on a quality or element of the whale as a metaphor for life itself, for what is enigmatic in our existence, and to discern in any one part of the whale's anatomy or behavior a series of rich correspondences for our own lives that breach into view. Here he admonishes us to understand the vapor's nature even as it scuttles between water and air. Its qualities, he asserts, can't be known by reason alone. The plainest makings of life can be the most mysterious when brought into imaginal presence. One can be in the mist of the whale's fountain and still not gauge the right measure of its nature. Further into life's mystery these meditations lead us.

Moments attend our waking life wherein for an instant we ponder the ordinary as it becomes extraordinary before our gaze. We begin to wonder at it, perhaps for the first time, like time itself, for instance. We may gain a heart knowing about it and feel deeply into its furtive presence. One's life may take on a strange tincture. What we find so ordinary can, with a shift of the imaginal eye, assume characteristics of both the strange and the numinous. It is as if we are viewing it with a child-like wonder, with new optics and full attention to its mystery.

Meditation

When you began to wonder about something common and familiar, what shifted in your perception to see in a new way?

July 18. Chapter 85: The Fountain

The wisest thing the investigator can do then, it seems to me, is to let this deadly spout alone.

Still, we can hypothesize, even if we cannot prove and establish. My hypothesis is this: that the spout is nothing but mist. And besides other reasons, to this conclusion I am impelled, by considerations touching the great inherent dignity and sublimity of the Sperm Whale; I account him no common shallow being, inasmuch as it is an undisputed fact that he is never found on soundings, or near shores; all other whales sometimes are. He is both ponderous and profound. And I am convinced that from the heads of all ponderous profound beings, such as Plato, Pyrrho, the Devil, Jupiter, Dante and so on, there always goes up a certain semi-visible steam, while in the act of thinking deep thoughts (401).

Ishmael marvels from the misty spout to the heads of powerful historical figures the degree of depth and profundity the Sperm Whale both possesses and engenders. Nothing shallow attends its nature; it evokes instead deep thinking, profound utterances in its great bulk, almost like a divinity from deep below who spouts a ferocious vapor when he rises to exhale. Ishmael's meditation is itself profound and steamy; he compares the whale's fountain as analogous to the effects of deep thought by figures as diverse as the Devil and Dante.

Profundity, dignity and sublimity are to be wished for, if not partly achieved. We seek depth in our pilgrimage, even if faintly realized. Most of us do not want to feel or be called shallow. We often yearn for a profound quality in our lives to be realized, if not recognized, by others. Seeking it in our work and thoughts makes us more fully human; it attaches us to a greater mystery in the mi(d)st of our pilgrimage.

Meditation

Share a deep meditation that afforded you a remarkable insight.

July 19. Chapter 85: The Fountain

For d'ye see, rainbows do not visit the clear air; they only irradiate vapor. And so, through all the thick mists of the dim doubts in my mind, divine intuitions now and then shoot, enkindling my fog with a heavenly ray. And for this I thank God; for all have doubts; many deny; but doubts or denials, few along with them, have intuitions. Doubts of all things earthly, and intuitions of some things heavenly, this combination makes neither believer nor infidel, but makes a man who regards them both with equal eye (401).

Ishmael creates a beautiful analogy to end the chapter on the whale's spout. Mist is central to the metaphor. As the vapor of mist forms out of the whale's spout to create a rainbow with the sun's cooperation, so is his own foggy thinking occasionally shot through with a heavenly intuition. He addresses both the creative process and epistemology while entertaining ideas that shoot through the foggy pages of his epic-in-process. Here heaven and earth wed with rays of doubt and intuition. One neither gains nor loses faith in the process but is perhaps made whole if one regards both domains with double vision.

At times most of us can find ourselves doubting even what we have been certain about. We may take the next step into denial, but regardless of both, many lack the intuitions from a more divine realm, from where the creative spark may emanate. Like Ishmael, we might well thank God or some transcendent force for gifting us with these intuitions. We may be skeptical of our earthly beliefs yet remain open and receptive to celestial intuitions which wed our clayey part to the sacred, often through analogies, as well as to the mystery of nature's order which we participate in, however mystily.

Meditation

What intuition of mystery, or of some things sacred, have you experienced or realized in your life?

July 20. Chapter 86: The Tail

Other poets have warbled the praises of the soft eye of the antelope, and the lovely plumage of the bird that never alights; less celestial, I celebrate a tail . . . .

In no living thing are the lines of beauty more exquisitely defined than in the crescentic borders of these flukes . . . .

. . . .

But as if this vast local power in the tendinous tail were not enough, the whole bulk of the leviathan is knit over with a warp and woof of muscular fibres and filaments, which passing on either side the loins and running down into the flukes, insensibly blend with them, and largely contribute to their might. . . (402-03).

Ishmael's poetic description of leviathan's tail is yet another occasion for him to express the beauty of the whale. Punster that he is throughout the epic, he plays on the words *tail* and *tale*; his entire narrative is a celebration on one level of the power of story itself to unite disparate elements and people into a communal woven textile. His whale tale mirrors the anatomy of the whale. The instrument of the whale's propulsion and the story that unfolds in the telling are one. Descriptions of the flukes fan outward to include the entire body, knitted like a crafted tale, with the warp and woof of fibres and filaments. In such a description, the whale assumes the shape of a complex allegory.

Fibrous fictions comprise our own tales, full of sinewy intricacy, overlaps and filaments woven by a controlling myth. Each thread of these tales wrap around our entire lives from first thread to last yarn. Nothing is loosely tied; all members of our narrative congeal through an overarching plot that encourages our personal myth to breach into view. Our tales propel us forward with many flukes and turns of fortune.

Meditation

Describe two or three of the fibrous sinews that comprise your tale.

July 21. Chapter 86: The Tail

Nor does this—its amazing strength, at all tend to cripple the graceful flexion of its motions; where infantileness of ease undulates through a Titanism of power. On the contrary, those motions derive their most appalling beauty from it. Real strength never impairs beauty or harmony, but it often bestows it; and in everything imposingly beautiful, strength has much to do with the magic . . . . As devout Eckerman lifted the linen sheet from the naked corpse of Goethe, he was overwhelmed with the massive chest of the man, that seemed as a Roman triumphal arch. When Angelo paints even God the Father in human form, mark what robustness is there . . . .

Such is the subtle elasticity of the organ I treat of, that whether wielded in sport, or in anger . . . . its flexions are invariably marked by exceeding grace (403).

Such a beautiful chapter on strength and aesthetics the narrator weaves around the whale's tail. He continues its comparison with Roman architecture and with both human and divine forms of body and spirit. Most often, Ishmael will discover in the whale's anatomy and movements a grace, strength, and noble beauty that corresponds to the human and/or divine order. The qualities he adumbrates raise humankind to the grand noble level of whales. Both share a sinewy intimacy, a grace in motion and a noble presence in the world order.

When we witness or discover beauty in natural creatures, we are entranced by their grace and nobility. Then we are less their masters, more their equals. Their mirroring us and we them enables both of us to gracefully form a single dimension of an organic and priceless creation in need of sustained stewardship. We reclaim the deep sense of interdependence based on mutual respect for the life of the other.

Meditation

Where has nature mirrored back to you your own unique beauty?

July 22. Chapter 86: The Tail

The more I consider this mighty tail, the more do I deplore my inability to express it. At times there are gestures in it, which, though they would well grace the hand of man, remain wholly inexplicable. In an extensive herd, so remarkable, occasionally, are these mystic gestures, that I have heard hunters who have declared them akin to Free-Mason signs and symbols; that the whale, indeed, by these methods intelligently conversed with the world. Nor are there wanting other motions of the whale in his general body, full of strangeness, and unaccountable to his most experienced assailant (406).

Ishmael expresses his signal frustration in interpreting and expressing such an enigmatic animal. The whale is the *prima materia* that continues to defy, in its mystical, magical and majestical presence, being fully exposed by the instruments of human understanding. His vision is double: he refers to the tail and to his own tale that, in its epic profile, challenges all his poetic prowess to give it shape and form. He learns that the experience of something is no guarantee of expressing with any authentic accuracy its mystery and complexity. The whale's hieroglyphic unfathomable self will remain intact; dissection is deflected at the surface of its skin, its phantom nature never fully plumbed.

As a metaphor for life itself in all its breaching enigmas, the whale contains too many conundrums, strange attributes and qualities, and an infinite number of signs and symbols that resist persuasively rendering it. Self-contained in its own mythology, it occasionally opens just enough to allow an initiate a peek within. Then it closes its spout, sends flukes up, and dives deep into fathomed hiddenness, leaving us to wonder at its design, its meaning and the mystery of its matter. We contemplate our own nature at the same time. Such is life's pattern.

Meditation

What in your own whale life elicits wonder over its enigmatic presence?

July 23. Chapter 86: The Tail

Dissect him how I may, then, I but go skin deep. I know him not and never will. But if I know not even the tail of this whale, how understand his head? much more, how comprehend his face, when face he has none? Thou shalt see my back parts, my tail, he seems to say, but my face shall not be seen. But I cannot completely make out his back parts; and hint what he will about his face, I say again he has no face (406).

Ishmael's final feeling of futility in this crucial chapter of knowing and expressing the whale carries the language of the Bible in which it is written that finally Yahweh cannot be known. He addresses Moses, saying "You cannot see My face; for no man shall see Me, and live" (Exodus 33:20). Like God, the whale is faceless; therefore, he cannot be known from a rational vantage point. The entire spiritual pilgrimage the epic explores is one passage after another into not-knowing. But not knowing and not believing are two very different attitudes. The whale hunt may be one of journeying from non-belief to belief, from isolation to a full sense of relationship with others. Ishmael's shifting disposition towards forms of knowing is a major achievement in his pilgrimage.

Evaluating, assessing, slicing and dicing what eludes our understanding is a common impulse of the grasping ego. Another response is to yield completely to the presence of the Other in wonder by accepting its un-graspable mystery. "Skin deep" is insufficient but may be as far as one can penetrate in this lifetime. Yielding to what remains ineffable can be a way to join with it in a marriage to its own mystery. To adopt a stance of fully accepting not knowing seems a wise yielding to grace, which offers its own mode of apprehension.

Meditation

What in your present life defies comprehension? Can you accept it?

July 24. Chapter 87: The Grand Armada

As marching armies approaching an unfriendly defile in the mountains, accelerate their march, all eagerness to place that perilous passage in their rear . . . even so did this vast fleet of whales now seem hurrying forward through the straits; gradually contracting the wings of their semicircle, and swimming on, in one solid, but still crescentic centre . . . .

And who could tell whether, in that congregated caravan, Moby Dick himself might not temporarily be swimming, like the worshipped white elephant in the coronation procession of the Siamese! So with stun-sail piled on stun-sail, we sailed along, driving these leviathans before us (410).

Never before has the Pequod journeyed into such a rich congress of whales, such a vast "host of vapory spouts" (410). The crew is giddy to begin slaying them for their valuable oil. Inside this vast armada, they further sense, may be lurking the White Whale, the ultimate object of their pursuit. A treasure of excessive riches swims before them, with the Pequod in full sail to close in and begin the slaughter. The comparison Ishmael constructs, with Moby Dick like a white elephant in a coronation procession, layers a level of royalty to the chase, with the thick vast horde blowing white vapors above them in celebration.

Those moments in our lives when what we pursue that has remained scarce or elusive suddenly appearing in abundance, may bring great delight. We accelerate our pursuit, intent on cashing in while the field is rich and abundant. What we may sense too is the possible treasure of a gold nugget lying in the thicket of our desires, wants and cravings. We put up all sails to catch the wind and temporarily delete all other interests that fail to promote such a heated pursuit.

Meditation

What promise of abundant riches has blocked out all other concerns?

July 25. Chapter 87: The Grand Armada

Had these Leviathans been but a flock of simple sheep, pursued over the pasture by three fierce wolves, they could not possibly have evinced such excessive dismay. But this occasional timidity is characteristic of almost all herding creatures. Though banding together in tens of thousands, the lion-maned buffaloes of the West have fled before a solitary horseman. Witness, too, all human beings, how when herded together in the sheepfold of a theatre's pit, they will, at the slightest alarm of fire, rush helter-skelter for the outlets, crowding, trampling, jamming, and remorselessly dashing each other to death . . . . for there is no folly of the beast of the earth which is not infinitely outdone by the madness of men (412).

Ishmael's study of herd behavior in whales, land animals and mortals italicizes the dissolution of individual will in the face of danger, where whales and humankind share a similar herd instinct. A kind of madness overtakes both the whales the Pequod pursues and the panic of a full house of theatre-goers at the sound of an alarm. Beneath this comparison we may hear as well a critique of the entire crew who has buckled under the tyrannous obsession of their Captain in his consuming pursuit. None of what is witnessed in nature can even begin to compare to the madness of human beings in their basic nature.

Giving up individual choice and behavior when swallowed by the power of herd instinct is not unusual. We can easily be persuaded by status quo thinking and actions, by pressures to conform to behavior not agreed upon but that we follow to appease differences. Later, we may ask ourselves, as if coming out of a dream: what made us do or think that? We may feel shame for what we have collectively thought or done. But in the moment, another field of influence successfully seduced us.

Meditation

Have you surrendered to a herd impulse, giving up your own beliefs?

July 26. Chapter 87: The Grand Armada

It had been next to impossible to dart these drugged-harpoons, were it not that as we advanced into the herd, our whale's way greatly diminished; moreover, that as we went still further and further from the circumference of commotion, the direful disorders seemed waning. So that . . . . we glided between two whales into the innermost heart of the shoal, as if from some mountain torrent we had slid into a serene valley lake. Here the storms in the roaring glens between the outermost whales, were heard but not felt. In this central expanse the sea presented that smooth satin-like surface, called a sleek, produced by the subtle moisture thrown off by the whale in his more quiet moods. Yes, we were now in that enchanted calm which they say lurks at the heart of every commotion (414).

From chaos to calm, from turbulence to serenity comprise the alternating moods of whale hunting. Some enchanted space opens to a select few whalers at this moment, a calm dish amidst a stew of turmoil where suddenly and at close range all the debris of panic in the whales harmed by the thrashing of "the iron leech" (412) fastened to one of them fell away to reveal a sleek serenity. Two whales pose as threshold guardians, allowing Ishmael, Queequeg and Starbuck sharing the same boat to enter the lustrous liquid unmolested. They have passed into a sea of tranquility, there to be given a vision few are graced with.

A rich metaphor opens to us wherein storms of inflicted wounds and panic surrender to a calm center within the hurricane of afflictions. We immediately participate in these moments of relief and renewal in our own hunts. When such gifts of grace are given to us amidst the busy turmoil of our daily lives, we can pause, replenish and renew ourselves in a moment of gracious wonder. They revitalize the soul.

Meditation

Describe a gifted sleek experience that replenished you.

July 27. Chapter 87: The Grand Armada

[H]owever it may have been, these smaller whales—now and then visiting our becalmed boat from the margin of the lake—evinced a wondrous fearlessness and confidence, or else a still becharmed panic which it was impossible not to marvel at. Like household dogs they came snuffing round us, right up to our gunwales, and touching them . . . . [as] Queequeg patted their foreheads; Starbuck scratched their backs with his lance; but fearful of the consequences, for the time refrained from darting it (415).

Ishmael recalls who was gifted with entrance into such a serene and safe watery alcove, there to be greeted by the wonder and hospitality of whale cubs and their mothers: Queequeg, Starbuck and Ishmael himself. They comprise the trinity of the elect, the chosen ones, who are bequeathed a glimpse of the inner sanctum of new life nurtured: first past the two whales as threshold guardians, then into the hearth of hospitality of enchantment and tranquil calm. Not harpoons but hand-petting, not penetrating lances but restraint and respect in meeting the whales on their terms, who are no longer imagined as commodities to slay. The three men are initiated into such a softened realm for a deeper vision in this sleek dominion of imagination's power.

Within the full, busy and often rushed days we live, on rare gifted occasions we are allowed a respite; for a few moments we are invited to step into a more serene terrain, there to be visited by a curious calmness that makes us wonder at life in a mood of reflective gratitude. All tasks that seem so important moderate, all acerbic feelings, resentments, inadequacies and goals liquefy. We are free to wonder at the life around us. In deep contemplation our vision is enlarged and deepened.

Meditation

When were you invited to share a special occasion that altered your perceptions of yourself, others, or life generally?

July 28. Chapter 87: The Grand Armada

But far beneath this wondrous world upon the surface, another and still stranger world met our eyes as we gazed over the side. For, suspended in those watery vaults, floated the forms of the nursing mothers of the whales, and those that by their enormous girth seemed shortly to become mothers. The lake, as I have hinted . . . . was exceedingly transparent; and as human infants while suckling will calmly and fixedly gaze away from the breast, as if leading two different lives at the time; and while yet drawing mortal nourishment, be still spiritually feasting upon some unearthly reminiscence;--even so did the young of these whales seem looking up towards us, but not at us, as if we were but a bit of Gulfweed in their newborn sight (415).

Point of view shifts radically in this passage so that the three men in the whaleboat are viewed through the gaze of the nursing whales. The men are the objects, not the subjects, of the whales' attention. Perspective shifts within the peace and tranquility of the newborn and their nurturing mothers. They reveal themselves in their intimate vulnerability with no fear, as if they wished to contact the human order in friendly repose. The scene may remind us of a return to the Great Mother, origin of all life. Two worlds coalesce in this tender moment of fecundity. The vision is double, unified and differentiated; the Narcissus myth is reflected when the men look into the depths and see themselves.

We are each given occasions of seeing through the phenomenal world into a deeper, more primal constellation of forms. If we are ready and deserving, they will be revealed, but they cannot be willed, constructed or purposefully conjured. However, they offer a rare glimpse into worlds behind worlds, forms behind substances; they can be conversion moments in our way of understanding that transforms us.

Meditation

Describe a moment when you were given access to a deeper world.

July 29. Chapter 87: The Grand Armada

Some of the subtlest secrets of the seas seemed divulged to us in this enchanted pond. We saw young Leviathan amours in the deep.

And thus, though surrounded by circle upon circle of consternations and affrights, did these inscrutable creatures at the centre freely and fearlessly indulge in all peaceful concernments; yes, serenely reveled in dalliance and delight. But even so, amid the tornadoed Atlantic of my being, do I myself still for ever centrally disport in mute calm; and while ponderous planets of unwaning woe revolve around me, deep down and deep inland there I will bathe me in eternal mildness of joy (416).

Ishmael seems closer to the heart of the epic's goal in this lyric passage that is as poetic as it gets in his spiritual pilgrimage. It depicts a sacred vision gifted to him that for a moment resists the wounded claims and vengeful impulses of Ahab's afflictions and dissolves instead into an occasion of rare joy. The vision of new life in tranquil waters engages his imagination, as did Queequeg initially. Ishmael depicts his central core of courageous tranquility, unfettered by worries, anxieties, fears and resentments. The whale mothers and their cubs nursing have healed some deep splintered part of the orphan-poet.

Not beauty so much as a serene presence, a loving dependence and a wondrous bond of mother and child can be especially strong in us as we shift our habitual way of seeing and understanding as individuals into a greater communal awareness with and of others. Feelings of gratitude as well as an acknowledgement may envelope us, so that what is savage and tornadoed in our own turmoiled seas finds a calm port in the soul through a rejuvenated spirit in the epic quest.

Meditation

When has a vision or insight offered you a serenity you may have thought was unattainable?

July 30. Chapter 87: The Grand Armada

So that tormented to madness, he was now churning through the water, violently flailing with his flexible tail, and tossing the keen spade about him, wounding and murdering his own comrades.

This terrific object seemed to recall the whole herd from their stationary fright. First, the whales forming the margin of our lake began to crowd a little, and tumble against each other, as if lifted by half spent billows from afar; then the lake itself began faintly to heave and swell; the submarine bridal-chambers and nurseries vanished; in more and more contracting orbits the whales . . . . began to swim in thickening clusters. Yes, the long calm was departing (417).

Such mild intervals in life that yield a vision of tranquility and rejoicing over new life often cannot be sustained. They will assuredly collapse around the three men as the calm lake within the terrible mutilation by the whale's tail, with the sharp spade attached to it by a line begins to contract and collapse. The whales thicken in mass as they cluster to avoid lethal wounding. The chaos of the cutting overtakes the serenity of the interior sea, yet for a moment the two are suspended in one instant of cohabitation and joyous communion.

We cannot expect these moments of harmony, tranquility and joy to last long in the external world, for they are always just on the fringe of our clustered chaotic days where threats to our well-being are only a breach away. But the memory of these moments rests in their offering us a powerful alternative vision, one that can save and sustain us against the sharp spades in life that threaten and often succeed in wounding us. When we recall these brief glimpses of serenity and joy, we deflect the potent counterweights of stormy conflicts and adversities we confront.

Meditation

What image of tranquility do you harbor in memory that sustains you in times of turmoil?

July 31. Chapter 88: Schools and Schoolmasters

The same secludedness and isolation to which the schoolmaster whale betakes himself in his advancing years, is true of all aged Sperm Whales. Almost universally, a lone whale—as a solitary Leviathan is called—proves an ancient one. Like venerable moss-bearded Daniel Boone, he will have no one near him but Nature herself; and her he takes to wife in the wilderness of waters, and the best of wives she is, though she keeps so many moody secrets (421).

Ishmael offers a history of the male Leviathan who escorts and protects his harem of lovely ladies and drives off any "Lothario" (420) who dares to intervene into his treasury. But, as with mortals, in old age the Sperm Whale departs all contact with his species and travels as an isolato with only Nature herself as his feminine companion. He has, like our American loner and hunter, Daniel Boone in the wilderness, separated in serene detachment to wander as he will, free of all responsibilities and burdens of vigilant protection.

We continually see the close relation, through Ishmael's imagination, between whales and us in their respective peculiarities. When we hold a steady mirror up to Nature, we see ourselves in a wondrous communal profile. Killing the whales for their bounty is akin to slaying some treasure in our own nature. We are diminished in worth when we eliminate life forms of Nature simply for self-satisfaction in consuming their benefits. Alienation from, not marriage to, Nature is our forlorn legacy when she should be our constant nurturance, not another commodity to exhaust. We forfeit the chance of being changed by her wisdom when she is reduced to cellophane-packaged goods.

Meditation

What practice do you, or might you, exercise in creating a more secure regard and relation with the natural order?

August 1. Chapter 89: Fast-Fish and Loose-Fish

I. A Fast-Fish belongs to the party fast to it.

II. A Loose-Fish is fair game for anybody who can soonest catch it.

But what plays the mischief with this masterly code is the admirable brevity of it, which necessitates a vast volume of commentaries to expound it.

First: What is a Fast-Fish? Alive or dead a fish is technically fast, when it is connected with an occupied ship or boat, by any medium at all controllable by the occupant or occupants,--a mast, an oar, or a nine inch cable, a telegraph wire, or a strand of cobweb, it is all the same. . . .

These are scientific commentaries; but the commentaries of the whalemen themselves consist in hard words and harder knocks. . .(423-24).

The judicial Ishmael wrestles with the terms of the whale's ownership at sea. At first it seems simple enough; but then he moves to specific court cases which rock the above unassuming descriptions with enormous ambiguities. His tongue-in-cheek description of a whale held to a ship by a cobweb mocks the attempt of the law to cover all contingencies, even all possible definitions, of Fast-Fish. His discussion will soon ripple out to engulf entire nations as either fast or loose.

What makes anything in our lives fastened to us as if we owned it, and what would it take for that same possession to become a Loose-Fish? May it be a grand illusion that anything is actually fast to us or we to it? What are the terms of such fasteners? What, in addition, are we fastened to but may prefer to be a Loose-Fish and take our chances in the deep waters of life, unmoored from anything secure? Fastness may foster death in security as we hang limp alongside another's ship.

Meditation

Where are you a Fast-Fish presently?

August 2. Chapter 89: Fast-Fish and Loose-Fish

Is it not a saying in every one's mouth, Possession is half of the law: that is, regardless of how the thing came into possession? But often possession is the whole of the law. What are the sinews and souls of Russian serfs and Republican slaves but Fast-Fish, whereof possession is the whole of the law? What to the rapacious landlord is the widow's last mite but a Fast-Fish? (425).

Extrapolating from two kinds of whales—claimed and unclaimed—Ishmael's method swells an idea outward to reveal a whole series of linked analogies. From the sea to civilizations, he envisions justice and injustice, slavery and freedom in the dialogue he constructs from whales to world, from a particular form of property ownership on the seas to owning possessions as well as an entire people. The "door-plate of a waif" (425), that is, food and unclaimed property to Russian serfs, reveals the range and magnitude Fast and Loose Fish can implicate. Ishmael's way of imagining is enriched by the whale as a fountainhead of relatedness.

From the physical to the metaphysical is Ishmael's *mythology*. As readers, we can discern correspondences, analogies, accords and connections of one reality with another. To read a classic poem as this one invites us to ponder--provoked by the variety of prose--wider orbits of understanding and comprehension. The truth claims of Fast and Loose-Fish place us a-sail in an archetypal field of profound and universal meanings that are timeless. Whales transform everything about them into models of understanding. Through poetic knowing, we begin to grasp intuitively the invisible interconnectedness of all the world's particular parts as a rich, unified organic web.

Meditation

What prejudice, resentment, joy or possession is a Fast-Fish in your life?

August 3. Chapter 89: Fast-Fish and Loose-Fish

What was America in 1492 but a Loose-Fish, in which Columbus struck the Spanish standard by way of waifing it for his royal master and mistress? What was Poland to the Czar? What Greece to the Turk? What India to England? What at last will Mexico be to the United States? All Loose-Fish.

What are the Rights of Man and the Liberties of the World but Loose-Fish? What all men's minds and opinions but Loose-Fish? What is the principle of religious belief in them but a Loose-Fish? . . .What is the great globe itself but a Loose-Fish? And what are you, reader, but a Loose-Fish and a Fast-Fish too? (426).

Ishmael's global litany of Loose-Fish is an indictment of one nation kidnapping another to colonize it in the victor's image. By imagining a country to exploit through control as a Loose-Fish, permission is granted to tie it along side the ship of state intent on exploiting its resources and expanding one's empire through acquiring as many Loose-Fish as possible, by force if necessary. The right to one's own sovereignty does not apply in the global hunt for expansion. Ishmael sees the global gobbling of smaller fish by larger ones a dissolution of justice and freedom, as well as the belief in a country to be its own Loose-Fish. We must ponder our own nature as fast or loose.

The planet itself, if configured as a Loose-Fish, is ripe for exploitation by corporate-led appetites. Consumption's power can turn the globe into a Fast-Fish feeding field, to be devoured without boundaries or restraint. Nothing is considered loose; all is fast, waiting to be hijacked and consumed. Each of us must decide if our relation to our planet will be operated by a Fast or Loose-Fish mindset. If it is Fast, then the planet will fast exhaust itself through exploitation.

Meditation

Describe one way you can treat the planet as a Loose-Fish.

August 4. Chapter 91: *The Pequod Meets* the Rose-Bud

"In vain it was to rake for Ambergriese in the paunch of this Leviathan, insufferable fetor denying not inquiry." —Sir T. Browne, V.E.

It was a week or two after the last whaling scene recounted, and when we were slowly sailing over a sleepy, vapory, mid-day sea, that the many noses on the Pequod's deck proved more vigilant discoverers than the three pairs of eyes aloft. A peculiar and not very pleasant smell was smelt in the sea.

. . . .

Presently, the vapors in advance slid aside; and there in the distance lay a ship, whose furled sails betokened that some sort of whale must be alongside. As we glided nearer, the stranger showed French colors from his peak . . . [and]it was plain that the whale alongside must be what the fishermen call a blasted whale, that is, a whale that has died (430).

The Rose-Bud is smelled before fully seen because strapped to its side is a rotting Loose-Fish. They have turned it into a most unpleasant Fast-Fish yet believe it a real find. A French ship commanded by an inexperienced captain, it is ripe to be relieved of its decomposing cargo. Not knowing what they have beyond a whale easily captured, the Rose-Bud will soon and voluntarily surrender its putrid corpse containing a treasure within, to the Pequod's more experienced crew.

The Rose-Bud is a rich metaphor for those times in our life that stink: rotten luck, a smelly situation, the foul odor surrounding an event that sails right toward us from the horizon. The stench in life is unpleasant but not without value. What stinks gains our attention, even demands it; it must be reckoned with. Our life heating up in decay may allow us to discover something we should attend to immediately.

Meditation

When has life decomposed, its stench demanding your full attention?

August 5. Chapter 91: *The Pequod Meets* The Rose-Bud

"Why, since he takes it so easy, tell him that now I have eyed him carefully, I'm certain that he's no more fit to command a whale-ship than a St. Jago monkey. In fact, tell him from me he's a baboon."

. . . .

Instantly the captain ran forward, and in a loud voice commanded his crew to desist from hoisting the cutting-tackles and at once cast loose the cables and chains confining the whales to the ship.

. . . .

Presently a breeze sprang up; Stubb feigned to cast off from the whale; hoisting his boats, the Frenchman soon increased his distance, while the Pequod slid in between him and Stubb's whale (434-35).

Using a translator, Stubb mocks the captain's inexperience and naivete concerning the blasted whale. The translator turns Stubb's words into a warning that clinging to the decaying carcass may sicken the crew. The captain, grateful and frightened, commands his men to cut the whale loose. The Pequod sails between the Rose-Bud and the now Loose-Fish, pretending to be sailing away from the rotting whale. But all is a ruse to lay hands on the corpse to excavate the most valuable substance it carries in its head: the coveted ambergris. Stubb immediately goes to work with his spade to break into the carcass.

What, to carry out the metaphor, might the stench in our life situation harbor, contain or camouflage? Something precious may lie below the surface stink, where the offal of an event or a fetid quality blankets a treasure hard to reach and claim. We may, as the French captain, be naïve to its presence and be tempted to cut it loose. Our discernment and intuition are called into play to transform rot into riches, rank odors into a new bouquet of insights.

Meditation

When did life's stink harvest something of real value?

August 6. Chapter 91: *The Pequod Meets* the Rose-Bud

Stubb was beginning to look disappointed, especially as the horrible nose-gay increased, when suddenly from out the very heart of this plague, there stole a faint stream of perfume, which flowed through the tide of bad smells without being absorbed by it . . . .

"I have it, I have it," cried Stubb, with delight, striking something in the subterranean regions, "a purse! a purse!"

Dropping his spade, he thrust both hands in, and drew out handfuls of something that looked like ripe Windsor soap, or rich mottled old cheese; very unctuous and savory withal. You might easily dent it with your thumb; it is of a hue between yellow and ash color. And this, good friends, is ambergris, worth a gold guinea an ounce to any druggist. Some six handfuls were obtained (436).

The stealthy Stubb reveals his whale acumen by locating this mottled solution congealed within the rotting whale's carcass. Willing to tolerate the putrid smell of the whale and to persevere long enough until a soothing aroma of perfume issues from the decay, Stubb coaxes the valuable treasure to the surface and scoops it out as one might find a stash of cool water in the desert landscape. Taking advantage of those ignorant of the treasure within, Stubb claims the precious cargo.

This episode reveals several possibilities in our own lives: the ability to stay with and tolerate the stench of life with the conviction that in a certain situation's difficulty may reside a pearl of great value; holding one's nose in a given encounter until its potential beauty reveals itself; shifting one's attitude toward what is putrefying to reveal a value perhaps sought, or perhaps a complete surprise; scooping from the dissolution or offal of an event or condition another quality even more to be embraced and celebrated. Out of decay may arise a priceless gift.

Meditation

What unpleasant life situation did you tolerate and learn from?

August 7. Chapter 92: Ambergris

Though the word ambergris is but the French compound for grey amber, yet the two substances are quite distinct. For amber, though at times found on the sea-coast, is also dug up in some far inland soils, whereas ambergris is never found except upon the sea. Besides, amber is a hard, transparent, brittle, odorless substance, used for mouth-pieces to pipes, for beads and ornaments; but ambergris is soft, waxy, and so highly fragrant and spicy, that it is largely used in perfumery, in pastiles, precious candles, hair-powders, and pomatum.

Who would think, then, that such fine ladies and gentlemen should regale themselves with an essence found in the inglorious bowels of a sick whale! Yet so it is (437).

Ishmael reveals the capacity of a word with the same etymology to name two opposing qualities and substances, as if words themselves grasped the psychology of a tension of opposites held energetically by the strength of the same term. In addition, he offers us in the two substances—hard and soft—a reverie of texture and quality. Both have their unique uses, both are made to be consumed by the land-bound culture, and both are reduced to commodities for consumption. Ambergris is especially alienated from its origin; it issues from "the inglorious bowels of a sick whale!" for a consumer culture.

Amber and ambergris are a unity in their diverse and contrary states. They unite in difference, share a common heritage in their opposition, and create something whole and complete through their differing realities. What makes them opposites is what unites them; their qualities inversely replicate one another. Perhaps precisely where we find contraries is also the locale of a treasure of a third order wherein diversity lies in wait to be discovered.

Meditation

Where have two opposing elements found a unity in your life?

August 8. Chapter 92: Ambergris

Now that the incorruption of this most fragrant ambergris should be found in the heart of such decay; is this nothing? Bethink thee of that saying of St. Paul's in Corinthians, about corruption and incorruption; how that we are sown in dishonor, but raised in glory. And likewise call to mind that saying of Paracelsus about what it is that maketh the best musk. Also forget not the strange fact that of all things of ill-savor, Cologne-water, in its rudimental manufacturing states, is the worst (438).

Ishmael calls on two thinkers and healers: St. Paul (5-67) and the alchemist, botanist and physician Paracelsus (1493-1541) to entertain a fundamental quality in matter and in life: the relation of corruption to incorruption—an alchemical process that takes place in matter and in spirit. In this ancient process we move as mortals, carrying within us immortal coils as well as two contraries in the paradox of existence. Some truth of the property of things is aired here; we each engage a process that, like Cologne-water, with its aromatic pleasant scent, only arrives at such a condition through a process of putrefaction which yields an unsavory aroma. His observations bear on the alchemical process, both physical and spiritual, from putrefaction to purification.

Ambergris is a material that can be excavated from a galaxy of decay. It becomes a central metaphor for the development of the soul from sin to salvation, corruption to purity, stench to perfume, miasma to musk. It follows the process of a life from fragmentation to wholeness. Ambergris is an elixir, the contents of the grail cup, a metaphor for finding in the most offensive human person or situation something salvific, serene, precious, priceless and vital. A discerning nose for the smell of paradox and contraries can detect its presence.

Meditation

Where or when have you discovered ambergris in corruption or decay?

August 9. Chapter 92: Ambergris

The truth is, that living or dead, if but decently treated, whales as a species are by no means creatures of ill odor; nor can whalemen be recognized, as the people of the middle ages affected to detect a Jew in the company, by the nose. Nor indeed can the whale possibly be otherwise than fragrant, when, as a general thing, he enjoys such high health; taking abundance of exercise; always out of doors, though, it is true, seldom in the open air . . . . What then shall I liken the Sperm Whale to for fragrance, considering his magnitude? Must it not be to that famous elephant, with jeweled tusks, and redolent with myrrh, which was led out of an Indian town to do honor to Alexander the Great? (439).

Ishmael lives two lives in his epic pilgrimage: as tracker of whales to slay and as defender of their magisterial existence on the planet. Whenever there exists an opportunity, he extols their fragrant virtues, as he does here. To further his praise he calls on history for analogies while swatting at the prejudice held in the middle ages of detecting a Jew by smell. Fragrant, healthy, engaged in constant aerobics, the Sperm Whale is to be emulated for its healthy life, not assassinated for its cargo. Nobility and majesty accompany the magnificent creature; Moby Dick will be the apotheosis of such nobility and "spangled" grandeur.

Through our manner of describing something we can create of it a reality of splendor or an image of slander. What analogies we draw in expressing our reality of a presence can persuade others that our image is the true one. What particulars we leave out and include will render an "as-if" reality that for some or many may be the defining characteristics of what we contemplate. We choose to implicate the fragrance or the stench of something as a way to define its reality. We may learn to grasp something by its *likeness* to another reality.

Meditation

What principles are at work when you judge the quality of things?

August 10. Chapter 93: The Castaway

Pip, though over tender-hearted, was at bottom very bright, with that pleasant, genial, jolly brightness peculiar to his tribe; a tribe, which ever enjoy all holidays and festivities with finer, freer relish than any other race . . . . But Pip loved life, and all life's peaceable securities; so that the panic-striking business in which he had somehow unaccountably become entrapped, had most sadly blurred his brightness . . . .

It came to pass, that in the ambergris affair Stubb's after-oarsman chanced so to sprain his hand, as for a time to become quite maimed; and temporarily, Pip was put into his place.

The first time Stubb lowered with him, Pip evinced much nervousness . . . .

Now upon the second lowering, the boat paddled upon the whale . . . (440-41).

Though Pip is referred to at the chapter's beginning as "the most insignificant of the Pequod's crew" (440), his experience is most monumental. A good-natured fellow, he seems directed by "chance" to fill in for an injured crewman; in that position, like Ishmael later, he undergoes an initiation that transforms his soul. Solitarily immersed in the sea, he finds himself terrified and unsure of himself. Sensitive and ever-alert to his new position, Pip feels both jittery and insecure.

Thrust suddenly into a new position on our life's voyage, we can identify with Pip and his fear. When our familiar life is put on hold because "chance" guides us into unfamiliar topography, who we are emerges from the depth of ourselves, swimming with all its virtues and shadows. We may feel less competent, unskilled and more vulnerable. But that is part of the cost of moving into a vision of life that changes us.

Meditation

When has "chance" hurled you into an unfamiliar condition or role?

August 11. Chapter 93: The Castaway

"Damn him, cut!" roared Stubb; and so the whale was lost and Pip was saved.

So soon as he recovered himself, the poor little negro was assailed by yells and execrations from the crew . . . . "Stick to the boat, Pip, or by the Lord, I won't pick you up if you jump; mind that. We can't afford to lose whales by the likes of you". . . .

But we are all in the hands of the Gods; and Pip jumped again . . . .

Pip was left behind on the sea, like a hurried traveller's trunk. Alas! Stubb was but too true to his word . . . . Out from the centre of the sea, poor Pip turned his crisp, curling, black head to the sun, another lonely castaway, though the loftiest and the brightest (442-43).

Pip's fear of the whales so close to him below the more vulnerable whale-boat overpowers him not once but twice, doubling his fear. It sends him compulsively leaping from the boat when a whale is in reach. Each whale-boat assumed another would pick him up; none did. The young tambourine player finds himself in the enormous immensity of the ocean, an insignificant dot on the vast blueness above immeasurable depths. For an instant, his curly black head is the center of the sea—the still point amid constant flux. As a castaway, he points us to his brother solitary on the sea, Ishmael, at epic's end.

Jumping ship out of panic, terror, anxiety or worry is not an uncommon occurrence for any of us. We have all "gone over the side" in our lives: when something we fear mightily begins to loom close by, our fantasies of this threat may compel us toward a quick and instant escape. We bail out and over and into what could become far more menacing, but in the moment we imagine it to be a place of respite. We realize that what we leaped for embraced a worse insecurity.

Meditation

When have you gone over the side of your life's boat in fright or terror?

August 12. Chapter 93: The Castaway

Pip's ringed horizon began to expand around him miserably. By the merest chance the ship itself at last rescued him, but from that hour the little negro went about the deck an idiot; such, at least, they said he was. The sea had jeeringly kept his finite body up, but drowned the infinite of his soul. Not drowned, entirely, though. Rather carried down alive to wondrous depths, where strange shapes of the unwarped primal world glided to and fro before his passive eyes; and the miser-merman, Wisdom, revealed his hoarded heaps. . . (443).

From the still point of his visible head, with the remainder of his body underwater, Pip's horizon ripples out, travelling across the vast expanse to waiting shores. Pip inhabits, like the whale itself, two worlds simultaneously. Such vastness brings him to an altered consciousness some christened idiocy. He speaks henceforth in what sounds like gibberish. But the passage suggests he was made privy to another galaxy of figures, a more intense version of the vision granted Ishmael, Queequeg and Starbuck in the previous chapter; but Pip is alone. He sees the shapes of an earlier time, primal and originary, as if his vision returns him to genesis, to the world's birth, and to the godhead of Wisdom itself.

The power inherent in returning to the origins, to the *arche*, to the primal shapes of the world below the surface of conventional consciousness, is remarkable and miraculous. Like Pip, we may have experienced a like encounter: in the midst of danger for our own safety, something new, unfamiliar and wondrous unlocked and revealed itself—an insight, an image, or an awakening that it took a moment of peril in our lives for it to gleam forth. To have such an experience in isolation, however, can disorient, terrify and unhinge one by its power.

Meditation

When has your life been put at risk, but through it a crucial revelation was bequeathed to you?

August 13. Chapter 93: The Castaway

[A]nd among the joyous, heartless, ever-juvenile eternities, Pip saw the multitudinous, God-omnipresent, coral insects, that out of the firmament of waters heaved the colossal orbs. He saw God's foot upon the treadle of the loom, and spoke it; and therefore his shipmates called him mad. So man's insanity is heaven's sense; and wandering from all mortal reason, man comes at last to that celestial thought, which, to reason is absurd and frantic; and weal or woe, feels then uncompromised, indifferent as his God.

For the rest blame not Stubb too hardly. The thing is common in that fishery; and in the sequel of the narrative, it will then be seen what like abandonment befell myself (443-44).

A transformation of great magnitude envelopes Pip in the vast eternal waters of the deep. He is gifted with an epic vision where time and eternity's boundaries collapse momentarily to expose a mystical sense of the origin of creation. His perspective is permanently altered; it has been deepened into a profound revelation as he touches the origin of the created order and its Maker. He reverses the conventional into what seems insane grasping, yet in the process he gains a priceless wisdom that grows from an extraordinary vision. However, his language is beyond the reach and comprehension of all others to discern his meaning, so Pip's utterances remain "idiotic" and unfathomable.

We may have had a similar moment in our lives when we were thrown from our conventional habits of being into a new galaxy of awareness, a deepening insight that penetrated the phenomenal world and gifted us with the power of a vision that transformed us at once. It may have even altered the way we speak to express our familiar habits of apprehension, and left us without an ability to convey it.

Meditation

What life encounter transformed your speech unalterably?

August 14. Chapter 94: A Squeeze of the Hand

It [sperm] had cooled and crystallized to such a degree, that when, with several others, I sat down before a large Constantine's bath of it, I found it strangely concreted into lumps, here and there rolling about in the liquid part. It was our business to squeeze these lumps back into fluid. A sweet and unctuous duty! No wonder that in old times sperm was such a favorite cosmetic. Such a clearer! such a sweetener! such a softener; such a delicious mollifier! After having my hands in it for only a few minutes, my fingers felt like eels, and began, as it were, to serpentine and spiralize (445).

The tone and atmosphere of the narrative alters remarkably as a counterweight to the lonely, isolated experience of Pip. Here the task is to communally break down the lumpy, waxy sperm, to return it to a more liquid substance. It is a magical cleanser and has the capacity, in Ishmael's imagination, to melt the fingers thrust into it, to dissolve the finger bones so that spiralizing eels are more akin to their condition. He senses another melting in him as the mollifying sperm seeps through his skin to change his interior complexion. Feeling the sperm dissolving him in a cleansing, as did the ancient baths of Rome under Constantine, he loses his hold on the world as all acerbities melt away.

Some experiences we encounter harden us; others mollify us, making us more malleable, more able to blend and bend into the world in a more cooperative largesse. We may find ourselves more social, more tolerant and fluid in our relations with others. Our sperm may consist of a kind word spoken, a compliment bestowed, or a favor performed without being asked. The sperm is present periodically if we can only detect its unctuous aroma and enjoy its cleansing qualities.

Meditation

When have you been given a chance to liquefy, soften, or blend with another softening element that cleansed you, or made your life fresher?

August 15. Chapter 94: A Squeeze of the Hand

As I sat there at my ease, cross-legged on the deck; after the bitter exertion at the windless; under a blue tranquil sky; the ship under indolent sail, and gliding so serenely along; as I bathed my hands among those soft, gentle globules of infiltrated tissues, wove almost within the hour; as they richly broke to my fingers and discharged all their opulence, like fully ripe grapes their wine . . . I declare to you, that for the time I lived, as in a musky meadow; I forgot all about our horrible oath; in that inexpressible sperm, I washed my hands and heart of it . . . . while bathing in that bath, I felt divinely free from all ill-will, or petulance, or malice, of any sort whatsoever (445-46).

The slowly evolving effects of such a spermy emollient further loosen the grip of Ahab's vengeful oath to slay the White Whale. The sperm of life and generosity breaks open the oath and dissipates its strangulating hold, at least on Ishmael. Not only the hardened oath but all ill-will melts from his soul; he is liberated by the chunky fluid from the depths. It has surfaced to redeem him. His heart is cleansed of the corroding acids of resentment, ill-will, anger, petulance and poisoned feelings fueled by his captain's destructive force field.

We know what those moments of liberation from all negative thoughts, corrosive feelings and acidic attitudes feels like, where because of some spermy reality entering our own gates of self-protection and self-incarceration, we find that we have stepped out of and beyond erosions of the soul that bind us to our defective, often unforgiving selves. We willingly let the debilitating emotions slide from us; the barnacles comprised of emotional acids are allowed to dissolve in the air. It offers a powerful unguent of liberation.

Meditation

When were you liberated from corrosive emotions and became more flexible and fluid in your emotional life? What changed?

August 16. Chapter 94: A Squeeze of the Hand

Squeeze! squeeze! squeeze! all the morning long; I squeezed that sperm till I myself almost melted into it; I squeezed that sperm till a strange sort of insanity came over me; and I found myself unwittingly squeezing my co-laborers' hands in it, mistaking their hands for the gentle globules. Such an abounding, affectionate, friendly, loving feeling did this avocation beget; that at last I was continually squeezing their hands, and looking up into their eyes sentimentally . . . . Come; let us squeeze hands all round; nay, let us all squeeze ourselves universally into the very milk and sperm of kindness (446).

A feeling of universal affection overcomes Ishmael when he kneads the globules into a softer substance and feels simultaneously the hands of his brothers. Far from his original isolato impulses, a further melting occurs in him, like an alchemical change of heart, as he surrenders to a feeling of compassion, kindness and universal comradeship with all the disparate whalemen from many countries, all engaged in a tribal ritual squeezing of the sperm. The whale fluid creates a universal harmony in Ishmael; he loses all sense of separateness and melts into the universal soul of humanity. *Communitas* replaces chaos.

A feeling of at-oneness with all the diverse uniqueness of others is a gift we can be alert to, but it cannot be orchestrated or contrived. It occurs when a third thing or presence enters between two entities to dissolve for a moment all distinctions; the many are imagined into one. Space collapses and all find themselves sharing and breathing as a single corpus in joint kindness and love. Not sentimental, it touches in all a zone of relationship to reveal we are finally not only not alone, but truly one in spirit. This impulse of communal connection invigorates all into a common sympathy for one another's humanity.

Meditation

Recount an experience of melting into others in a felt sense of unity.

August 17. Chapter 94: A Squeeze of the Hand

Would that I could keep squeezing that sperm forever! For now, since by many prolonged, repeated experiences, I have perceived that in all cases man must eventually lower, or at least shift, his conceit of attainable felicity; not placing it anywhere in the intellect or fancy; but in the wife, the heart, the bed, the table, the saddle, the fire-side; the country; now that I have perceived all this, I am ready to squeeze case eternally. In thoughts of the visions of the night, I saw long rows of angels in paradise, each with his hands in a jar of spermaceti (446).

The matter of the whale and Ishmael's intimate hands-on feature in breaking it down, opens him to a vision that is terrestrial, timeless, paradisal and comic. Not thoughts of happiness but instead in relation to the domestic presences of common and intimate persons and objects that encapsulate an entire range of shared verities. "Country" suggests both countryside and nation. A vision unfurls from his relation with whales' sperm that unites him to his fellows in a union part mystical, part matter-based. All acerbities break down in an alchemical dissolution of the clots of sperm. His vision is like that of the Hebrew prophets: angels too are squeezing the sperm of human kindness. The internal treasure of the whale has united one soul to all.

Perhaps not space and time but perspective can unite the temporal realm of our active life to the eternal realm of both contemplation and angelic bliss. One sees through matter to this other realm of being existing side-by-side with the ephemeral ground of earthly becoming. We may experience a breakthrough into an eternal region where an angelic order of being appears, squeezed right alongside our daily round where Paradise exists if we can see it. By analogy, we have the capacity to envision the eternal realm in accord with our earthly temporality.

Meditation

When have you connected with a sense of peace and tranquility?

August 18. Chapter 95: The Cassock

Had you stepped on board the Pequod at a certain juncture of this post-mortemizing of the whale; and had you strolled forward nigh the windlass, pretty sure am I that you would have scanned with no small curiosity a very strange, enigmatical object, which you would have seen there, lying along lengthwise in the lee scuppers . . . longer than a Kentuckian is tall, nigh a foot in diameter at the base, and jet-black as Yojo, the ebony idol of Queequeg. And an idol, indeed, it is; or rather in old times, its likeness was. Such an idol as that found in the secret groves of Queen Maachah in Judea (449).

One of the shortest chapters in the epic centers on the penis of the whale, along with the history of this appendage as an idol for worship. In 1 Kings, 15:13, Queen Maachah, mother of King Asa, who was eliminating all unsavory idols from his land, had made an idol in a grove in her son's king-dom and for it was stripped of her royal title (www.theseason.org). If Ish-mael's intention is to voyage through all the parts of the whale's anatomy, then the penis cannot be sidestepped. The source of vitality, reproduction, symbolic ritual and idol of worship, it is a crucial energy font of all they hunt. Related to the little idol, Yojo, it gathers more power because related to the divine. The incident on deck will assume a comic turn as the mincer, with assistance, "heavily backs the grandissimus" and carries it off (449).

Our relation to sex organs can stimulate many fantasies. The great sex organ of the male described above puts us in touch with the enormity of the sperm of life, the vital principle and the continuation of the species. Its dismemberment and its lifelessness are qualities that may arrest us for a moment as well as invite fantasies of titanism. Our prowess or its absence in procreating is brought front and center.

Meditation

What fantasies gather for you around the image in this passage?

August 19. Chapter 95: The Cassock

Extending it upon the forecastle deck, he now proceeds cylindrically to remove its dark pelt, as an African hunter the pelt of a boa . . . . then cutting two slits for arm holes at the other end, he lengthwise slips himself bodily into it. The mincer now stands before you invested in the full canonicals of his calling. Immemorial to all his order, this investiture alone will adequately protect him, while employed in the peculiar function of his office.

That office consists in mincing the horse-pieces of blubber for the pots . . . . Arrayed in decent black; occupying a conspicuous pulpit; intent on bible leaves; what a candidate for an archbishopric, what a lad for a Pope were this mincer! (449-50).

The worn foreskin by the one who will slice the blubber into thin "bible leaves" for the try-pots protects him from the gore of his task. He has successfully donned the skin of the very animal he will now disassemble into thin strips to be tried and barreled and marketed for consumption. A form of religious ritual gathers around this devout deacon of dismemberment. The industrial task of reducing the whale to slices of blubber mingles with religious vestments, the mincing rod as the crook of an archbishop and the communion a confluence of body sacrifice and connection with the dead.

To be protected inside the skin of the very object, even person, one is to slice into pieces carries a primal energy and an ancient ritual sacrifice. The precious oil is to be used here to illuminate America's towns and cities. What can protect us in moments of cutting into may be the very substance of our object of dismantling. What insight attends such a de-cipherement? How might we be enshrouded in a skin of vital energy of the life principle itself? What Eros attends it?

Meditation

When has the life force or principle been most present in you?

August 20. Chapter 96: The Try-Works

The try-works are planted between the foremast and mainmast, the most roomy part of the deck . . . . Removing this hatch we expose the great try-pots, two in number, and each of several barrels' capacity. When not in use they are kept remarkably clean . . . . It is a place also for profound mathematical meditation. It was in the left hand try-pot of the Pequod . . . that I was first indirectly struck by the remarkable fact, that in geometry all bodies gliding along the cycloid, my soapstone for example, will descend from any point in precisely the same time (451).

As we shift from the whale's anatomy to the Pequod's physicality, we note the pots that will distill the whale mass into a liquid to be barreled, sealed, and stored in its belly until the ship returns to Nantucket. There exists a geometric and mathematical motion of universal certainty in the pots' precision, carrying something around their outside in centrifugal motion of descent in perfect accord with a mathematical formula. Precise, stable, open-mouthed, clean, waiting expectantly, the try-pots stand like sentinels ready to heat up and dissolve the next whale's blubbery segmented flesh.

Like alchemical cauldrons, the try-works are the locale for heating, melting, cooling and preparing the product of the whale ships' successful hunts. These pots become the locus of the voyage, where Leviathan is dissolved into its essential nature, a melting down of an unwieldy mass into a manageable consistency and volume. Perhaps they are the place in each of us where we cook something into a yielding substance we can control. Our try-pots are psychological and emotional places where we cook parts of our lives as well as the world's matter into manageable portions and then perhaps metabolize the two.

Meditation

What do you place in your emotional or psychological try-pots to cook into a controllable measure or commodity?

August 21. Chapter 96: The Try-Works

Here be it said in a whaling voyage the first fire in the try-works has to be fed for a time with wood . . . . In a word, after being tried out, the crisp shriveled blubber, now called scraps or fritters, still contains considerable of its unctuous properties. These fritters feed the flames. Like a plethoric burning martyr, or a self-consuming misanthrope, once ignited, the whale supplies his own fuel and burns by his own body. Would that he consumed his own smoke! for his smoke is horrible to inhale, and inhale it you must, and not only that, but you must live in it for the time . . . . It smells like the left wing of the day of judgment; it is an argument for the pit (452).

Once sufficiently heated, the try-pots will employ the whale's fried parts to consume itself in its own flames. Both martyr, who sacrifices him/herself for one's faith, and the misanthrope, who professes no love for human-kind, are conveyed as two extremes, both apt analogies of the whale's con-ditions. A terrible consequence is the horrific smell emanating from the self-consuming pieces of corpse. The smell of death pervades the try-pot atmosphere and the entire ship. It makes the process of fiery dissolution a ghastly task for the whalemen. Ishmael, comparing both task and smells with the coming apocalypse, ramps it up to another level of meaning. The analogy adds to this horrific industry.

An analogy breaches here: when one begins to consume one's self with the tinder of one's own heat, perhaps that act captures an apocalyptic moment in one's life. Signaling a self-destructive condition, the melting heat of one's own making may be the most hellish conditions one could possibly inflict on one's self. There are a multitude of ways we can consume our-selves with the passion of self-malice and self-inflicted wounds when we breathe in toxic vapors.

Meditation

Think back to when you engaged in heated self-consuming behavior.

August 22. Chapter 96: The Try-Works

The hatch, removed from the top of the works, now afforded a wide hearth in front of them. Standing on this were the Tartarean shapes of the pagan harpooneers, always the whale ship's stokers. With huge pronged poles they pitched hissing masses of blubber into the scalding pots, or stirred up the fires beneath, till the snaky flames darted, curling out of the doors to catch them by the feet. The smoke rolled away in sullen heaps . . . as to and fro, in their front, the harpooneers wildly gesticulated with their huge pronged forks and dippers; as the wind howled on, and the sea leaped, and the ship groaned and dived, and yet steadfastly shot her red hell further and further into the blackness of the sea and the night. . . (452-53).

If there is an infernal, scalding wildness in the Pequod's hunt, it takes place here in the melting pots of unbearable heat. Ishmael conveys a devilish image so reminiscent of the Italian poet Dante Alighieri's manic devils in their wildness and the darkness of the souls' despairing terrain of the *Inferno* who push the suffering shades underwater with spears and pitch-forks. The slow broth of the whales themselves provides the occasion for such demonic images of pitch forks, devils, "snaky flames" and diabolical actions to dissolve them. A potent violence is enacted on nature's matter from where a hellish atmosphere emanates.

Some of our behaviors can be violent, hellish and destructive. What we seek, what we reject, and what we wish to alter are all occasions for the try-pots we assemble on board our ship's deck, there to bring to a heated boil what we desire to dissolve, disintegrate, or denigrate in the consuming cauldron of self-absorbed and self-serving desires.

Meditation

What or who do you consistently stir with a pitch fork so that the heat of the flames under the try-pot will liquefy it or them?

August 23. Chapter 96: The Try-Works

So seemed it to me, as I stood at her helm, and for long hours guided the way of this fire-ship on the sea. Wrapped, for that interval, in darkness myself, I but the better saw the redness, the madness, the ghastliness of others. The continual sight of the fiend shapes before me, capering half in smoke and half in fire, these at last begat kindred visions in my soul . . . .

A stark, bewildered feeling, as of death, came over me. Convulsively my hands grasped the tiller, but with the crazy conceit that the tiller was, somehow, in some enchanted way, inverted. My God! what is the matter with me? thought I. Lo! in my brief sleep I had turned myself about, and was fronting the ship's stern, with my back to her prow and the compass (453-54).

Seduced by the fiendish scene in front of him, Ishmael is mesmerized by this altered reality; his own soul partakes of the demon shapes congesting around him. So altered by it and consumed by a dream state while at the rudder, he turns about and faces the ship's aft thinking it the prow. "Never dream with thy hand on the helm" (454), he enjoins us after he reverses himself in time to direct the ship away from destruction. Some force awakens him to near catastrophe so he can reclaim the ship's rightful direction and his own sanity.

"Look not too long in the face of the fire, O man!" (454) when one's hand is on the tiller of one's life; dreaming can be an expensive past time. Doing one's tasks, staying with the reality of one's responsibilities, remaining conscious, alert, attentive, and mindful are strategies to keep demons of destruction at bay and to avoid being dashed on the shoals of events. Duty before dreaming steadies the tiller.

Meditation

When, distracted by seductive or destructive images, did you drift off course? What were the consequences?

August 24. Chapter 96: The Try-Works

But even Solomon, he says, "the man that wandereth out of the way of understanding shall remain" (*i.e.* even while living) "in the congregation of the dead." Give not thyself up, then, to fire, lest it invert thee, deaden thee; as for the time it did me. There is a wisdom that is woe; but there is a woe that is madness. And there is a Catskill eagle in some souls that can alike dive down into the blackest gorges, and soar out of them again and become invisible in the sunny spaces. And even if he for ever flies within the gorge, that gorge is in the mountains; so that even in his lowest swoop the mountain eagle is still higher than other birds upon the plain, even though they soar (455).

Ishmael relates what amounts to an infernal underworld experience wherein he was completely reversed in life, absent right compass bearings, and pointed destructively in the wrong direction. Such a miscalculation almost capsizes the vessel entrusted to him. He entered the land of the dead and was seared by the fires of dissolution. He finds a rich analogy in the eagle in some souls who flies deep into a mountain gorge that is higher than the elevation of those birds who soar from a much lower altitude. These are the great souls of persons of a grander stature; they carry within them Solomon's wisdom. From all the descriptions of depth, Ishmael shifts to one of soaring heights.

Going off track, feeling one's life has become inverted or reversed by potent forces one confronts in life, can be both disorienting and dismembering. The world for a time makes little sense; one feels dazed, confused. Another side of who and what we are rises from fathoms down. In the process, something may need to die in us to correct our course. Grasping in hindsight one's desperation can right oneself.

Meditation

When has your life felt inverted, upside down or backward in a jumble of confusion? What righted it?

August 25. Chapter 97: The Lamp

See with what entire freedom the whaleman takes his handful of lamps—often but old bottles and vials, though—to the copper cooler at the try-works, and replenishes them there, as mugs of ale at a vat. He burns, too, the purest of oil, in its unmanufactured, and, therefore, unvitiated state; a fluid unknown to solar, lunar, or astral contrivances ashore. It is sweet as early grass butter in April. He goes and hunts for his oil, so as to be sure of its freshness and genuineness even as the traveler on the prairie hunts up his own supper of game (456).

By a set of analogies Ishmael extolls the purity of whale oil that illuminates the whalemen's lamps. He compares it to ale and game a land traveler stirs up for supper. This liquid is a treasure offered up by the whale to stave off darkness. The whaleman pilgrimages to the try-works, earlier the site of red devils with pitch forks, and fills his containers with the vital fluid, an elixir of purity and fecundity. Sacred qualities seem invested in the oil, a fluid of great value, and in its purity is without compare. The combined lights from each whaler's bunk Ishmael compares earlier to "some illuminated shrine of canonized kings and counselors" (456). Again he raises whaling to a noble stature.

What do we choose to illuminate and give comfort to in those darkened creases in our lives? What try-pots do we seek to replenish the light to our more dim and obscure places? Even more, what is the nature of the lamp we carry through our lives that helps us see what might otherwise remain invisible, unnoticed and seemingly irrelevant? The source of our illumination can determine what is made visible, what hidden. Periodically we may wish to refresh the source of our seeing.

Meditation

What lamp light source do you constantly return to in order to replenish your life and illuminate your current pilgrimage?

August 26. Chapter 98: Stowing Down *and Clearing Up*

Already has it been related how the great leviathan is afar off descried from the mast-head; how he is chased over the watery moors, and slaughtered in the valleys of the deep; how he is then towed alongside and beheaded; and how . . . . his great padded surtout becomes the property of his executioner; how, in due time, he is condemned to the pots, and, like Shadrach, Meshach and Abednego, his spermaceti, oil, and bone pass unscathed through the fire;--but now it remains to conclude the last chapter of this part of the description by rehearsing—singing, if I may—the romantic proceeding of decanting off his oil into the casks and striking them down into the hold, where once again leviathan returns to his native profundities, sliding along beneath the surface as before; but, alas! never more to rise and blow (457).

In what at first might sound like an objective summary of the business of whaling, Ishmael describes the brutal slaying and dismembering of the whale. Like the three kings who visit the Christ child at his birth, they, similar to parts of the whale, suffer through fire without being consumed by it. The cycle of the whale's life and death ends with the transformed animal, now in casks stored below deck, swimming again in liquid form, but with no promise of a breaching resurrection. The Christian story is imbedded herein as we witness in miniature the oil stored after the whale's carcass is crucified.

The deadly dangerous business of life is ensconced in the pursuit of what we seek, our dismembering of it, and the boon that leaches out from our prize's demise. Repetition is an undeniable mainstay of the process because what we pursue, enclose and treasure is what now moves below our decks. Murdering to dismantle and transform what we pursue places the transformed entity below our feet, alive and powerful.

Meditation

What object have or do you pursue in order to extract its treasure?

August 27. Chapter 98: Stowing Down *and Clearing Up*

But a day or two after, you look about you, and prick your ears in this self-same ship! . . . Hands go diligently along the bulwarks, and with buckets of water and rags restore them to their full tidiness. The soot is brushed from the lower rigging. All the numerous implements which have been in use are likewise faithfully cleansed and put away. The great hatch is scrubbed and placed upon the try-works, completely hiding the pots; every cask is out of sight; all tackles are coiled in unseen nooks . . . . then the crew themselves proceed to their own ablutions; shift themselves from top to toe; and finally issue to the immaculate deck, fresh and all aglow as bridegrooms new-leaped from out the daintiest Holland (458).

After the violence and bloody gore of dismembering a whale, which pollutes the ship's decks, a contrary effort of containing, storing the casks and clearing the horrid offal of leviathan is mandated. Disorder is restored to order, the signals of battle become scrubbed decks, stowed instruments of the hunt are cleaned and made invisible, and groomed whalemen appear polished as Dutch bridegrooms. One must feel a sense of achievement in such mighty and risky work as whales are first boiled into casks and now lie entombed in the Pequod's belly. A complete transformation has removed, and in many cases hidden, all traces of this violent enterprise.

The messes that life creates as well as the mess we each manufacture in the act of living, periodically call for a pause; we may devote days to rearranging the chaos of life into a cosmos of order. We find the place for each utensil or instrument used, restore our living/working space to order and prepare for what tasks before us may necessitate another mess in achieving similar or different goals.

Meditation

How do you reorder your life after a period of intense activity?

August 28. Chapter 98: Stowing Down *and Clearing Up*

[M]any is the time the poor fellows, just buttoning the necks of their clean frocks, are startled by the cry of "There she blows!" and away they fly to fight another whale, and go through the whole weary thing again. Oh! my friends, but this is man-killing! Yet this is life. For hardly have we mortals by long toilings extracted from this world's vast bulk its small but valuable sperm; and then, with weary patience cleansed ourselves from its defilements, and learned to live here in clean tabernacles of the soul; hardly is this done, when— *There she blows!*—the ghost is spouted up, and away we sail to fight some other world, and go through young life's old routine again.

Oh! The metempsychosis! Oh! Pythagoras. . . (459).

The analogy Ishmael sketches at chapter's end is one of the clearest expressions to link whale with world and whaling as a rich, nuanced analogy to life itself in the vast bulk of living and working within it. Life's messes often accompany our mission or vocation. Life is messy when we have our hands deep in it. We achieve a result, after which we dust ourselves off, only to find that we are being called to yet another adventure; that is the patterned round of life that brings it to blow once again. It sets our feet moving toward another skirmish with the whales of the world. His last exclamation has to do with the transmigration of the soul from one body to another.

"There she blows!" signals life breaching along the starboard or port of our voyage, where another pursuit looms to haunt us, to entice us and to invite us into its frey with all the attendant pathos that clings like barnacles to its skin. Life is like that: unexpected, dangerous, heating the blood, risky and worth responding to--the ancient shout of another spout insistent fore or aft. Whales mark life as both weal and woe.

Meditation

When last did you hear and respond to "There she blows!"?

August 29. Chapter 99: The Doubloon

When he halted before the binnacle, with his glance fastened on the pointed needle in the compass . . . . as the same riveted glance fastened upon the riveted gold coin there[;] he still wore the same aspect of nailed firmness, only dashed with a certain wild longing, if not hopefulness.

But one morning turning to pass the doubloon, he seemed to be newly attracted by the strange figures and inscriptions, stamped on it, as though now for the first time beginning to interpret for himself in some monomaniac way whatever significance might lurk in them. And some certain significance lurks in all things, else all things are little worth, and the round world itself but an empty cipher, except to sell by the cartload, as they do hills about Boston. . . (460).

Ishmael returns us to Ahab and the doubloon from Quito, Ecuador, the grand prize for whoever first sights the White Whale. But now the captain seems to see the coin for the first time and to wonder at its markings. The language of "fastened," "rivets" and "nailed firmness" offer a perspective that is "monomaniacal" and single-tracked. From here, Ishmael guesses, Ahab extracts a deeper layer of meaning: without significance as part of the properties of the world's matter, they lack value. Significance provides things stature in one's life. Otherwise the world's matter dwindles to commodities to be barreled and sold.

Without some meaning attached to the things of the world, life loses its luster. Discovering or creating significance in things affords our lives purpose and worth. Commodifying offers extrinsic value only, soon to be exhausted and forgotten. Interior significance yields value, importance and texture to life. Without it we die of desperate consumption trying futilely to fill the hole in ourselves with goods,

Meditation

By what process do things of the world gain significance for you?

August 30. Chapter 99: The Doubloon

Now this doubloon was of purest, virgin gold, raked somewhere out of the heart of gorgeous hills . . . . Nor, though placed amongst a ruthless crew and every hour passed by ruthless hands, and through the livelong nights shrouded with thick darkness which might cover any pilfering approach, nevertheless every sunrise found the doubloon where the sunset last left it. For it was set apart and sanctified to one awe-striking end . . . [as] one and all, the mariners revered it as the White Whale's talisman. Sometimes they talked it over in the weary watch by night, wondering whose it was to be at last, and whether he would ever live to spend it (460-61).

A talisman of great price, the doubloon is treated as a sacred object crucified to the main mast as a kind of beacon to the whalemen, reminding them night and day of the White Whale's absent presence. The gold coin signifies the White Whale below, serving as its valuable double-oon. No one dare steal it or deface it; as a powerful insignia, it carries the entire voyage's purpose on its shoulders and shines like a cunning little duplicate of the sun itself, illuminating every soul that approximates it. Ishmael speaks of it with a reverence surpassed only by his description of the White Whale. In the two images sun and moon coalesce. The doubloon carries a providential presence.

As a symbol for something sought after, the doubloon is not foreign to us. Its presence has intrinsic value as well as signals a desire, a way of being on board life's pursuits. We each may easily create a doubloon as a guiding symbol in our lives. Payoff or payment may not emerge for a lifetime, and even at its gain there is no guarantee it will be redeemed and spent. Perhaps the doubloon we choose is our own valued double that mirrors our deepest desires, meaning and purpose.

Meditation

Describe your doubloon as a symbol of what you quest after.

August 31. Chapter 99: The Doubloon

Before this equatorial coin, Ahab, not unobserved by others, was now pausing.

"There's something ever egotistical in mountain-tops and towers, and all other grand and lofty things; look here,--three peaks as proud as Lucifer. The firm tower, that is Ahab; the volcano, that is Ahab; the courageous, the undaunted, and victorious fowl, that, too, is Ahab; all are Ahab; and this round gold is but the image of the rounder globe, which, like a magician's glass, to each and every man in turn but mirrors back his own mysterious self. Great pains, small gains for those who ask the world to solve them; it cannot solve itself . . . . So be it, then, Born in throes, 't is fit that man should live in pains and die in pangs! So be it, then! Here's stout stuff for woe to work on (461-62).

The doubloon is one of the epic's richest symbols. As an image of the sun and a miniature of the earth herself, it resides in dramatic contrast to the Globe Theater where Shakespeare's plays were performed. The Globe is a mirror wherein Narcissus might see his own reflection. The doubloon doubles the mystery of every being's self that pauses to examine its luminescence. It invites a reverie in Ahab about what he quests after. Some ask too much of the world; it cannot solve its own mystery. The doubloon is a micro-mirror of the earth herself; man is born in pain and expires in death.

Moments like the one deployed above are infrequent for many of us. But in moments of deep meditation, we may discern with greater clarity. We might feel the fatality of life, its suffering into death, as well as recognizing and reconciling life's deepest wonders. "So be it" one may say in resignation or defiance. Perhaps life is allowed to defeat us, but we gather our strength and push on into a vale of tears.

Meditation

What is your attitude towards life's perils and suffering?

September 1. Chapter 99: The Doubloon

"No fairy fingers can have pressed the gold, but devil's claws have left their mouldings there since yesterday," murmured Starbuck to himself, leaning against the bulwarks. "The old man seems to read Belshazzar's awful writing. I have never marked the coin inspectingly. He goes below; let me read. A dark valley between three mighty, heaven-abiding peaks, that almost seem the Trinity, in some faint earthly symbol. So in this vale of Death, God girds us round; and over all our gloom, the sun of Righteousness still shines a beacon and a hope. If we bend down our eyes, the dark vale shows her mouldy soil . . . . This coin speaks wisely, mildly, truly, but still sadly to me" (462).

Starbuck's musings in the presence of the doubloon is his most eloquent speech of the entire voyage. The gold doubloon is like an eye or a mirror which reflects back to the gazer an interior image of his deepest nature. To approach the coin is to approach a silent golden oracle fixed to the mast as an omphalos of the world. The first mate recognizes that one's angle of vision mediates the world one inhabits. His reference to King Belshazzar in the Old Testament recalls the story of a mysterious hand that writes an enigmatic sentence on the wall of the king's chamber, which only the Hebrew sage Daniel is able to translate. The sentence is a divine menace against the dissolute Belshazzar (www.jewishencyclopeida.comarticles/2846/bels).

As an image that incites reverie, the doubloon doubles the perceiver; it allows us to see something of our inner nature and can speak to us what its eye discovers. It can take many forms in the world: a book, an incident, a painting, the voice of another, a dream, wherein we are placed in the presence of some parts of ourselves reflected, or echoed off the other. Something appears to illuminate our feelings.

Meditation

What image has the gold doubloon assumed in your moments of clarity?

September 2. Chapter 99: The Doubloon

"There's another rendering now; but still one text. All sorts of men in one kind of world, you see. Dodge again! here comes Queequeg—all tattooing—looks like the signs of the Zodiac himself. What says the Cannibal? As I live, he's comparing notes . . . .

. . . .

"Here's the ship's navel, this doubloon here, and they are all on fire to unscrew it. But, unscrew your navel, and what the consequence? Then again, if it stays here, that is ugly, too, for when aught's nailed to the mast it's a sign that things grow desperate. Ha! Ha! Old Ahab! the White Whale; he'll nail ye! This is a pine tree . . . . Oh, the gold! the precious, precious gold!—the green miser'll hoard ye soon!" (464-65).

Stubb watches off to the side as one-by-one the crew confronts the doubloon and deciphers its text with both projected images and words to uncover some analogy in themselves. The main mast of the ship powers its sails while the precious coin gives the crew direction and purpose as prize for spotting the White Whale. Stubb reads each man reading the doubloon and recognizes that even its sheer presence is a dangerous omen. He then compares Ahab himself to the doubloon and Moby Dick the force that will nail him, finally, to itself.

Our lives are surrounded by texts to be read. Often, no single interpretation will suffice to yield a fixed understanding. The passage above may inspire us to reflect on the manner and style of our interpretations and the way they reflect our own personal myth. We each develop and are shaped by our modes of analysis to make sensible the patterns of our lives. Without some coherent hermeneutic, we risk sailing rudderless across the seas of everyday encounters and adventures or remaining indolent in a breezeless sea.

Meditation

What pattern have you discovered to interpret your life's events?

September 3. Chapter 100: Leg and Arm *The Pequod of Nantucket, Meets the Samuel Enderby, of London*

"Ship, ahoy! Hast seen the White Whale?"

So cried Ahab, once more hailing a ship showing English colors, bearing down under the stern . . . .

. . . .

As good luck would have it, they had had a whale alongside a day or two previous, and the great tackles were still aloft, and the massive curved blubber-hook, now clean and dry, was still attached to the end. This was quickly lowered to Ahab, who at once comprehending it all, slid his solitary thigh into the curve of the hook . . . and then giving the word, held himself fast . . . . Soon he was carefully swung inside the high bulwarks, and gently landed upon the capstan head . . . [while] the other captain advanced, and Ahab, putting out his ivory leg, and crossing the ivory arm (like two sword-fish blades) cried out in his walrus way, "Aye, aye, hearty! let us shake bones together!—an arm and a leg!" (466-67).

Captain Boomer of the English whaleboat, Samuel Enderby, is the only other mortal Ahab meets who also pursued the White Whale. They both wear whale bone prosthetics and cross them in a ritual greeting. Ahab is hoisted on board the latter's ship by a blubber hook such that he seems to be both whale and captain. He appears as a Fast-Fish, now loose from the Pequod to meet another dismembered captain.

To meet someone who shares a similar wound as one's own, inflicted under similar circumstances of strife, is an astonishing moment of intimate connection. To greet affliction with affliction carries a scarred camaraderie. Often, little need be said on one level, yet a full conversation of shared circumstances is needed on another.

Meditation

When in life have you met your afflicted double?

September 4. Chapter 100: Leg and Arm *The Pequod of Nantucket, Meets the Samuel Enderby, of London*

"No, thank you, Bunger," said the English Captain, "he's welcome to the arm he has, since I can't help it, and didn't know him then; but not to another one. No more White Whales for me; I've lowered for him once, and that has satisfied me. There would be great glory in killing him, I know that; and there is a ship-load of precious sperm in him, but hark ye, he's best let alone; don't' you think so, Captain?"—glancing at his ivory leg.

"He is. But he will still be hunted, for all that. What is best let alone, that accursed thing is not always what least allures. He's all a magnet! How long since thou saw'st him last" Which way heading?" (472).

Captain Boomer responds to his Bunger in stating the one arm is all he is willing to sacrifice to the whale. He saw the fame and riches attendant on continuing to pursue Moby Dick but recognizes the risk of being further dismantled. The captain has earned the conviction that the White Whale might be best left to itself and assumes Ahab, in his own dismembered state, would assent. But the latter is like a sliver of metal dragged by the magnet of the White Whale. Having lost all freedom to either pursue it or leave it be, he is coerced by Fate. The two captains offer opposing dispositions to what attracts and afflicts them.

To be in the grip of the magnet of a force or image or desire that completely hijacks one's freedom is a deeply-imbedded human condition. The force of such an attraction compels our libidinal energy in one direction. We are swept along in its relentless force field and unwavering energy, often helpless to resist it effectively alone. Over time it can swallow one whole into the beast's belly.

Meditation

When were you possessed by a force that magnetized you to it?

September 5. Chapter 101: The Decanter

Ere the English ship fades from sight be it set down here, that she hailed from London, and was named after the late Samuel Enderby, merchant of that city, the original of the famous whaling house of Enderby & Sons . . . . How long, prior to the year of our Lord 1775, this great whaling house was in existence, my numerous fish-documents do not make plain; but in that year (1775) it fitted out the first English ships that ever regularly hunted the Sperm Whale . . . . Be it distinctly recorded here, that the Nantucketers were the first among mankind to harpoon with civilized steel the great Sperm Whale; and that for half a century they were the only people of the whole globe who so harpooned him (473).

This rich passage earmarks two elements for reflection. The first is the story's composition. In the first sentence Ishmael addresses us as reader-whalers in writing that before the Samuel Enderby of the previous chapter sails out of sight in the fiction, Ishmael the poet-scribe-historian wishes to accurately record its history. Thus, the time of the fictional historical event of the ship gamming with the Pequod and the narrative's creation are simultaneous. Fiction and history blend into one mythic conglomerate. History and fiction gam to produce a mytho-poetic artifact. The second element is the ancient action of whale hunting on Nantucket that considerably antedates British whaling.

If we think about our own identities, we can discern the way we create our histories in the very act of crafting it into a story. Our memory and imagination are capable of creating ourselves in time by fashioning a narrative that identifies and defines us. We may wonder if the stories of our lives are not the truer dimensions of our being than the events themselves. The latter become more "real" in the telling.

Meditation

Reflect on the way storying your life events offers it a fuller reality.

September 6. Chapter 101: The Decanter

Most statistical tables are parchingly dry in the reading; not so in the present case, however, where the reader is flooded with whole pipes, barrels, quarts, and gills of good gin and good cheer.

At the time, I devoted three days to the studious digesting of all this beer, beef, and bread, during which many profound thoughts were incidentally suggested to me, capable of a transcendental and Platonic application; and, furthermore, I compiled supplementary tables of my own . . . .

. . . .

But no more; enough has been said to show that the old Dutch whalers of two or three centuries ago were high livers . . . . For, say they, when cruising in an empty ship, if you can get nothing better out of the world, get a good dinner out of it, at least (476-77).

Ishmael is intent on not missing a single element in the business of whaling, even down to amassing "a detailed list of the outfits for the larders and cellars of 180 sail of Dutch whalemen" (476) which included 10,800 barrels of beer as well as vast amounts of pork, beef and butter for perhaps a three month whale hunt in frigid waters. The plentiful matter in the holds invites reveries of Platonic application. Moreover, tables of lists found elicit further tables in him as he is swept up by calculations. He resigns himself to a good meal for the voyage.

Nourishment while hunting on the sea of life's circumstances is essential and worth preserving. Whether one's decanter is empty or full, digesting all or part of the world's larder is essential to the hunt. Even if the belly of one's ship is empty, one can still hunt down a satisfying meal. The bread of life sustains one on several levels; to be nourished by it is essential in any quest.

Meditation

What nourishes you daily on your life's voyage? Is the diet sufficient?

September 7. Chapter 102: A Bower in the Arsacides

Hitherto, in descriptively treating of the Sperm Whale, I have chiefly dwelt upon the marvels of his outer aspect; or separately and in detail upon some few interior structural features. But to a large and thorough sweeping comprehension of him, it behooves me now to unbutton him still further, and untagging the points of his hose, unbuckling his garters, and casting loose the hooks and the eyes of the joints of his innermost bones, set him before you in his ultimatum; that is to say, in his unconditional skeleton.

But how now, Ishmael? How is it, that you, a mere oarsman in the fishery, pretend to know aught about the subterranean parts of the whale? Did erudite Stubb . . . deliver lectures on the anatomy of the Cetacea?. . . Explain thyself, Ishmael (478).

With characteristic hyperbole, Ishmael outlines his next strategy on the pilgrimage to whale knowledge by unlacing the leviathan's structure and form to reach its most basic boney foundation. His words are playful as he describes how he will "unbutton," "unbuckle," and "casting loose" all exterior clothing and hose so the innermost scaffolding of the whale's mystery can be laid bare. He questions himself in the second person as his own doubled Other on whether he has the authority or expertise to do so. His doubting himself in the past, however, has not deterred him from his heroic quest of discovery, which always includes a self-discovery.

Interiority can reveal an enticing other landscape, even cosmos, when we penetrate the exterior of someone or thing. Without such a deepened penetration into the fundamentals that support and give form to the world's matter, our understanding will not carry us beyond skin deep. Reaching inward and down, we discover in a revelatory moment another strata of meaning in the substances we believe matter.

Meditation

What in life do you wish to plumb the depths of for deeper knowledge?

September 8. Chapter 102: A Bower in the Arsacides

A veritable witness have you hitherto been, Ishmael; but have a care how you seize the privilege of Jonah alone; the privilege of discoursing upon the joists and beams; the rafters, ridge-pole, sleepers, and under-pinnings, making up the frame-work of leviathan; and belike of the tallow-vats, dairy-rooms, butteries, and cheeseries in his bowels.

. . . .

And as for my exact knowledge of the bones of the leviathan in their gigantic, full grown development, for that rare knowledge I am indebted to my late royal friend, Tranquo, King of Tranque, one of the Arsacides (478-79).

Ishmael sails to the basic inner structure of the whale to deepen into its very foundations, with Jonah as his guide and progenitor. The whale is described as both a house and a dairy farm, with joists and beams of structure mingling with butter and cheesed bowels, a sign of its skeletal and organic composition. To enter the frame of the whale, to meander through it in the spirit of Jonah, Ishmael turns to his tribal island friend Tranquo, leader of one of the islands of the Arsacides lying east of Papua, New Guinea in the Solomon Islands (www.wikipedia/solomonislands.com). Ishmael hosts an enormous number of analogies, relationships and knowledge bases from which to extract more complex levels of understanding of whale's interiority.

Perhaps at intervals the frame of our own understanding in pursuit of some essential quality of life is simply too constricted, narrow and prosaic; needed is a vaster landscape, a wider horizon, and even deeper waters to fathom. To dive beneath the skin of what we seek, engage, or encounter, we may have to step outside the familiar frame of knowing and enter foreign seas and atolls of interpretation.

Meditation

Where have you discovered other landscapes of understanding?

September 9. Chapter 102: A Bower in the Arsacides

The ribs were hung with trophies; the vertebrae were carved with Arsacidean annals, in strange hieroglyphics; in the skull, the priests kept up an unextinguished aromatic flame, so that the mystic head again sent forth its vapory spout; while, suspended from a bough, the terrific lower jaw vibrated over all the devotees, like the hair-hung sword that so affrighted Damocles.

It was a wondrous sight. The wood was green as mosses of the Icy Glen . . . . [and] the industrious earth beneath was as a weaver's loom, with a gorgeous carpet on it, whereof the ground-vine tendrils formed the warp and woof, and the living flowers the figures (479).

Ishmael confronts the overgrown and latticed skeleton of a great Sperm Whale in King Tranquo's jungle. The skeleton has been ritually carved with tribal markings that Ishmael cannot decipher. The lower jaw conjures the image of Damocles' sword. A 4th century BCE sycophant in the court of Dionysos II of Syracuse, Damocles is invited to witness what ruling demands. Damocles replaces Dionysus and enjoys being ruler until he notices a sword dangling from the ceiling, suspended by a horse's hair. Dionysus tells him that is what ruling is like. (www.about.com/ancient/ classicalhistory/swordofdamocles.com) Ishmael interposes the weaving shuttle made of the threads of vine tendrils so Nature can wrap her green ropes around the skeleton.

To make into a ritual object some element of nature is a deep instinct in us. Scrimshaw images carved on whale bones or wearing the tusk of an animal around one's neck as a talisman connects us to the natural order even as we might modify it to satisfy a ritual instinct in us. To transform an object from nature to culture is a poetic construction. We sense a deep connection to the natural order as artistic potential.

Meditation

What have you ritualized from Nature to enrich your life?

September 10. Chapter 102: A Bower in the Arsacides

All the trees, with all their laden branches; all the shrubs, and ferns, and grasses; the message-carrying air; all these unceasingly were active. Through the lacings of the leaves, the great sun seemed a flying shuttle weaving the unwearied verdure. Oh, busy weaver! unseen weaver!—pause—one word!--whither flows the fabric? what palace may it deck? wherefore all these ceaseless toilings? Speak, weaver!—stay thy hand! but one single word with thee! . . . . The weaver-god, he weaves; and by that weaving is he deafened, that he hears no mortal voice . . . (479-80).

This rich, visionary and mystical passage Ishmael's imagination conjures in the forest where the white skeleton of a great Sperm Whale rests in verdural repose. The leviathan from watery depths is enshrined in deep greens of the earth as vine-like tendrils intertwine around the majestic shape. The fiber, the woven carpet, continues to flow from life's loom, continually plaited of earth's threads into a fabric of the imagination; the whale is mythologized as a primitive god, originating in "the great world's loom" as a revelation. It suggests the entire world's landscape itself is a vast plait.

The loom of life can be deafening. So pervasive is its hum of spindles flying that all words uttered are immediately absorbed by the whirring machine. We are captured by the magic of the weaving and swallowed by its constant ferocious speed. Our own weaving as well can deafen us as the material factory of our own personal enterprise. We are being woven into a combination of fate, free will and destiny by an invisible presence that has its own patterns for us in mind. To perceive the weave of our life is to recognize deep patterns of our personal myth.

Meditation

When has your own life's weaving deafened you to your own words or to those of others?

September 11. Chapter 102: A Bower in the Arsacides

Now, amid the green, life-restless loom of that Arsacidean wood, the great, white, worshipped skeleton lay lounging—a gigantic idler! . . . the mighty idler seemed the sunning weaver; himself all woven over with the vines; every month assuming greener, fresher verdure . . . .

To and fro I paced before this skeleton—brushed the vine aside—broke through the ribs—and with a ball of Arsacidean twine, wandered, eddied long amid its many winding shaded colonnades and arbors. But soon my line was out; and following back, I emerged from the opening where I entered . . . . [but]naught was there but bones (480).

Ishmael's image weds Death in and to Life. Life is Death's companion. He also arouses the myth of Theseus entering the Labyrinth with Ariadne's saving thread to guide him into the mystery of such a timeless mythical marriage. The rich twining verdure of lush life in Nature encompasses the skeleton of death to create a wholeness in his soul. As he reaches the end of his line he is forced to retrace his steps through the skeleton, like a Jonah expelled from the whale's innards, to tell his tale. The skeletal whale weaves us to the world and back again, creating a network of relations and lines that tie us intimately to it.

Few are spared entering the belly of the beast, swallowed whole by Leviathan, there to confront the tension between life and death. This Jonah quality can be aroused in so many life situations when our existence is threatened—not just by physical death, but by any claim on our well-being that can dismember us. What Ariadne's line do we use in our journey down? What length do we sense is long enough to allow us a vision of the deepest recesses of our lives and then strong enough to guide us back to tell of our pilgrimage?

Meditation

In any conjunction of death in life, what thread guided you back out?

September 12. Chapter 102: A Bower in the Arsacides

The skeleton dimensions I shall now proceed to set down are copied verbatim from my right arm, where I had them tattooed; as in my wild wanderings at that period, there was no other secure way of preserving such valuable statistics. But as I was crowded for space, and wished the other parts of my body to remain a blank page for a poem I was then composing—at least, what untattooed parts might remain—I did not trouble myself with the odd inches; nor, indeed, should inches at all enter into a congenial admeasurement of the whale (481-82)

Ishmael prepares for chapter 103 as he ends this rich and perhaps most mythical chapter on the Sperm Whale's skeleton. His tone is playful and purposeful, as if he were returning from another land or waking from an extended dream. Now his own body becomes a text after describing the rich texture of the whale envined in verdurous tendrils. As an artist, Ishmael echoes Queequeg's poetic skin on which is drawn an entire cosmology. His mortal body's range of measurements and muse-inspired poetry doubles in miniature the longer, more ample epic text he is spinning out of himself, like Ariadne her thread. Marked now with whale numbers, he moves closer to inscribing and so doubling the whale's dimensions on himself.

What do we mark our body with so as not to forget it is an essential quality of our personal myth? If we pause for a moment to entertain our skin as parchment or paper, then what etchings do we wish to transcribe there or has the world marked us with: tattoos, surgical stitches, scars from previous wounds, birth marks—any and all of which are worthy and perhaps essential, not to be forgotten? Where we are marked is where our history mingles with the myth that attends these memories etched on the texted landscape of our skin-encased selves.

Meditation

Identify a body marking and tell the story of its creation.

September 13. Chapter 103: *Measurement of* the Whale's Skeleton

According to a careful calculation I have made, and which I partly base upon Captain Scoresby's estimate, of seventy tons for the largest sized Greenland whale of sixty feet in length . . . I say, a Sperm Whale of the largest magnitude, between eighty-five and ninety feet in length, and something less than forty feet in its fullest circumference, such a whale will weigh at least ninety tons . . . .

To me this vast ivory-ribbed chest, with the long, unrelieved spine, extending far away from it in a straight line, not a little resembled the hull of a great ship new-laid upon the stocks . . . .

The ribs were ten on a side. The first, to begin from the neck, was nearly six feet long. . . . The middle ribs were the most arched. In some of the Arsacides they are used for beams whereon to lay footpath bridges over small streams (483-84).

After offering numerous statistics on various whales, which at this juncture seems crucial in delineating the whale from a host of angles, Ishmael presents a fascinating comparison of the whale skeleton with a ship's structure. The analogy is rich when we recall the initial description of the Pequod dressed in whale finery and laced with whale bones and jaws. The gap between the bulk of a whale and that of a whaling ship pursuing it continues to contract, so that being in the belly of the whale is also to be on board its pursuer.

Attempting to know something by numerical calculation has a certain but limited value in both scope and depth. Like knowing facts and dates of historical events, it yields, finally, a stunted sterile story. Perhaps creating or discovering an analogy for what we are determined to understand can sail us closer to its essential qualities.

Meditation

Choose an event in your life and compare it by its likeness.

September 14. Chapter 14: The Fossil Whale

From his mighty bulk the whale affords a most congenial theme whereon to enlarge, amplify, and generally expatiate. Would you, you could not compress him. By good rights he should only be treated of in imperial folio . . . .

Since I have undertaken to man handle this Leviathan, it behooves me to approve myself omnisciently exhaustive in the enterprise; not overlooking the minutest seminal germs of his blood, and spinning him out to the uttermost coil of his bowels . . . . It now remains to magnify him in an archeological fossiliferous, and antediluvian point of view (486).

We discern in these chapters the epic task Ishmael has set for himself: not to slay whales but to describe their anatomy, physiology, history, mythology and theology in as heroic terms as possible. The writer's pen, not the whaleman's harpoon, is his cutting instrument of choice to fully imagine the whale from sperm to fossilized and historical plenitude. His is the work of scientist, historian, archeologist, mythologist and poet, combining these and other longitudes of knowing to arrive at a complete portrait of the elusive creature. The term "antediluvian" connects us with the Biblical narrative before the flood and anchors the whale again to Scripture.

What has called you to study it with such exhaustive and thorough questioning that you may have devoted a large segment of your waking life to its pursuit? It is a calling one has both heard and heeded in time to bring something to conscious awareness to add to the world's mighty bulk of knowledge. In so doing, what has your pursuit yielded that you are proud of having discovered, uncovered and relayed to others? What we pursue, what captures us, what we relate to, reflects our unique myth.

Meditation

Respond to either of the questions posed above.

September 15. Chapter 104: The Fossil Whale

Give me a condor's quill! Give me Vesuvius' crater for an inkstand! Friends, hold my arms! For in the mere act of penning my thoughts of this Leviathan, they weary me, and make me faint with their outreaching comprehensiveness of sweep . . . . Such, and so magnifying, is the virtue of a large and liberal theme. We expand to its bulk. To produce a mighty book, you must choose a mighty theme! No great and enduring volume can ever be written on the flea, though many there be who have tried it (486-87).

Ishmael's hyperbolic humor offers a rich reflection on his epic task as writer rather than as whaler. His subject matter is voluminous: the whale in all its bulky complexity. No small thinking or transcribing is up to the task he has set out for himself. He pauses for a moment in his efforts as a writer to survey his claim. To write a mighty book is part of the experience of whaling and of seeing on board this particular ship as it pursues the grand prize: the White Whale. If he chooses a less significant subject matter, his narrative will not have sufficient epic gravitas and immensity to endure. He must balance his life between harpoon and quill, both necessary for successful whaling. He seeks the quill of a high-flying condor to scribe the dimensions of his epic theme.

Each of us may have some epic task or dream to perform in life if we remain spacious enough to hear the call and courageous enough to heed it. Courage and a large heart as well as the audacity to cross disciplines of study are essential to pursue such a titanic enterprise. What we are called to will define us; what we refuse to respond to will outline our limits. To give ourselves over to what life seeks from us comprises our most important core experience to complete our narrative.

Meditation

What is it in life that calls to you, or has called you, that gives your life its richest purpose?

September 16. Chapter 104: The Fossil Whale

When I stand among these mighty Leviathan skeletons, skulls, tusks, jaws, ribs, and vertebrae, all characterized by partial resemblances to the existing breeds of sea monsters; but at the same time bearing on the other hand similar affinities to the annihilated antichronical Leviathans, their incalculable seniors; I am, by a flood, borne back to that wondrous period, ere time itself can be said to have begun; for time began with man. Here Saturn's grey chaos rolls over me, and I obtain dim, shuddering glimpses into those Polar eternities. . . .Then the whole world was the whale's; and, king of creation, he left his wake along the present lines of the Andes and Himmalehs (488).

Ishmael's reveries, stimulated by the bare bones of the whales and their enduring legacy, sends his imagination spiraling back into history and beyond, to pre-history and the origin of time. Whales existed as kings of the world, older than humankind, governing the globe with their majestic presence. "Who can show a pedigree like Leviathan?" (488), he asks rhetorically. Ubiquitous in time and space, the whale's presence on the planet dwarfs humans' longevity. In writing, Ishmael gains a perspective on history and creation itself, guided by whale bones. He alludes also to the flood of the world and Noah's ark, connecting once more the whale's history to Biblical epic.

To stand within a historical remnant of a past event or period, say, the Coliseum in Rome, or the early Etruscan huts or the site of a prehistoric excavation, is to calculate our brief moment on the planet as well as enlarge our historical imagination. When we sense the vast expanse of time behind us, as well as the eternal existing outside of time, we gain a sober sense of history as well as a broader contextual frame. The whale, for instance, becomes a humbling point of view.

Meditation

What context allowed you to see yourself within history?

September 17. Chapter 194: The Fossil Whale

I am horror-struck at this antemosaic, unsourced existence of the unspeakable terrors of the whale, which, having been before all time, must needs exist after all humane ages are over.

But not alone has this Leviathan left his pre-adamite traces in the stereotype plates of nature, and in limestone and marl bequeathed his ancient bust; but upon Egyptian tablets, whose antiquity seems to claim for them an almost fossiliferous character, we find the unmistakable print of his fin
. . . .

Nor must there be omitted another strange attestation of the antiquity of the whale, in his own osseous postdiluvian reality, as set down by the venerable John Leo, the old Barbary traveller.

. . . .

In this Afric Temple of the Whale I leave you, reader, and if you be a Nantucketer, and a whaleman, you will silently worship there (488-89).

Ishmael pulls from his word horde another vocabulary to attest to and match the ubiquitous whale in both time and space. His language offers an archeological roost from which to view its longevity and power of survival. Latinate words like "fossiliferous," "osseous," and "postdiluvian" attest to the magnitude of language needed to contain the cargo of his mighty theme. The whale has throughout history been adorned with words, stories, carvings, hieroglyphs, as well as addressed as a deity and lionized; we readers may worship at its temple.

We each tend to lift certain events, things, or people to an epic stature. We may even enshrine them, build a temple to them, worship them daily and dedicate our lives to their preservation. Identifying such presences is essential to grasping the terms of our personal myth.

Meditation

Identify the whale in your life you offer the most homage to.

September 18. Chapter 105: *Does the* Whale's Magnitude *Diminish?—Will He Perish?*

But still another inquiry remains; one often agitated by the more recondite Nantucketers. Whether owing to the almost omniscient look-outs at the mast-heads of the whaleships, now penetrating even through Behring's straits, and into the remotest secret drawers and lockers of the world; and the thousand harpoons and lances darted along all continental coasts; the moot point is, whether Leviathan can long endure so wide a chase, and so remorseless a havoc; whether he must not at last be exterminated from the waters, and the last whale, like the last man, smoke his last pipe, and then himself evaporate in the final puff (491).

Maintaining a sustained reflection on the whale's history, its mythology and mystical presence and now, its very survival, Ishmael continues his pursuit of the whale through the corridors of time and space. He continues to compare leviathan to humankind to suggest, in an ecological imagining, that the fate of the whale mirrors or doubles the fate of our species. Well before its emergence as a new awareness of the world's finite resources and its fragility, as well as the danger of so many living species being ground into extinction, Ishmael voices the real possibility of slaying all whales, and ourselves, into extinction.

Excessive and unconscionable devouring of the planet's resources may well end in our self-extinguishing recklessness. Denying an awareness of the intimate relationship of our life as a species being personally entangled with the earth's varied and abundant life forms' survival, is a gross act of greed, arrogance and selfishness whose consequences will one day breach to surprise us with devastating results.

Meditation

Describe your relation to the globe's resources and what forms of conservation you might or currently practice to preserve them.

September 19. Chapter 105: *Does the* Whale's Magnitude *Diminish?—Will He Perish?*

Wherefore, for all these things, we account the whale immortal in his species, however perishable in his individuality. He swam the seas before the continents broke water; he once swam over the site of the Tuileries, and Windsor Castle, and the Kremlin. In Noah's flood he despised Noah's Ark; and if ever the world is to be again flooded, like the Netherland's, to kill off its rats, then the eternal whale will still survive, and rearing upon the topmost crest of the equatorial flood, spout his frothed defiance to the skies (493-94).

Ishmael continues his epic vision of the whale's eternal presence and ubiquity around the globe. To approach the whale is to touch immortality itself, an eternal presence as an archetypal image in the temporal and finite embodied whale. Before land itself surfaced millions of years ago, Leviathan swam round the watery sphere. The places Ishmael cites reveal no limits to its rounded pilgrimage. It has sailed through Biblical waters as well, bridging history and myth. Ishmael then shifts from history to teleology by suggesting that the whale's song will be heard even if another flood should drown all land life. It will survive in proud defiance as a great bulk on the planet's once more watery surface. Even in a deluge, the whale remains unscathed.

We choose our divinities and immortalities, images of what we adore, worship and esteem, with religious fervor. We can imagine for a lifetime what is most indomitable for us, what melodies are closest to our own song, what helps us with life's demanding purposes. As with Ishmael, we choose what allows ourselves a sense of transcendence, even immortality, by identifying with its grandeur and immortal presence. Such images or ideas both sustain life and convey meaning.

Meditation

What image do you hold to be most eternal, transcendent and sacred?

Part V

The Trial in the Whale's Belly
Chapters 106-35

The temple interior, the belly of the whale, and the heavenly land beyond, above, and below the confines of the world, are one and the same.

The Hero With a Thousand Faces, 77.

September 20. Chapter 106: Ahab's Leg

And, indeed, it seemed small matter for wonder, that for all his pervading, mad recklessness, Ahab, did at times give careful heed to the condition of that dead bone upon which he partly stood . . . .

Nor, at the time, had it failed to enter his monomaniac mind, that all the anguish of that then present suffering was but the direct issue of a former woe; and he too plainly seemed to see, that as the most poisonous reptile of the marsh perpetuates his kind as inevitably as the sweetest songster of the grove; so, equally with every felicity, all miserable events do naturally beget their like (495).

Ishmael returns on his writing voyage from the anatomy of the whale's dimensions to the anatomy of the dismembered captain. Ahab's leg had splintered on his voyage to the deck of the Samuel Enderby; he now beckons the carpenter to fashion him a new one. Every step Ahab takes is a rhythmic dance between the life of his human leg and the dead thud of his whale bone prosthetic. In addition, he suffers now from a historical wound as it continues to duplicate itself in time present. Both horror and joy replicate their respective likenesses in Ahab's life, yet his will remains bent on concentrating almost exclusively on the wounds of his life and not on its wonders. Each begets its own likeness.

One of the richest symbols of literature is here fractured. If we entertain Ahab's stance symbolically, then each of us supports ourselves on existence's twin pillars of life and death, woundedness and wonderment, sorrow and joy. When we walk, our gait reminds us of this double mode of being wherein our death reflects our life and our life's mirror is death. This constant in all human existence is rejected by some, embraced by others, and remains unconscious for yet others.

Meditation

What images and emotions emerge when you meditate on your own death?

September 21. Chapter 106: Ahab's Leg

For, thought Ahab, while even the highest earthly felicities ever have a certain unsignifying pettiness lurking in them, but, at bottom, all heartwoes, a mystic significance, and, in some men, an archangelic grandeur; so do their diligent tracings-out not belie the obvious deduction. To trail the genealogies of these high mortal miseries, carries us at last among the sourceless primogenitures of the gods; so that, in the face of all the glad, hay-making suns, and soft-cymballing, round harvest-moons, we must needs give in to this: that the gods themselves are not for ever glad. The ineffaceable, sad birth-mark in the brow of man, is but the stamp of sorrow in the signers (496).

Ishmael seems to have as narrator absolute omniscience at this moment when he informs us of Ahab's most complex and innermost thoughts. The imaginal logic suggests that resting behind a world of phenomenal experiences wherein both sorrow and gladness are cast in their respective roles, nonetheless, when we back into the sourceless, prime event of the gods themselves, we uncover what seems an absolute truth applied to mortals and immortals alike: divinity itself experiences sorrow; the Olympian fields are not just a locale of sustained "archangelic grandeur" that we mortals reflect in duplicate design; they also carry the stamp of sorrow in our creators.

Behind our physical life is a deeper and nobler reality in which suffering and travail have been bequeathed to us to confront, contemplate and integrate as non-negotiable conditions of life. We are dismembered beings, inescapably; to deny it is to expose ourselves to even greater woes. In our mortalness we mirror the tempers of the gods. To live a life devoid of suffering is to delete an important dimension of our fragile identity as well as our indomitable grandeur.

Meditation

What have suffering and affliction taught you about your life?

September 22. Chapter 106: Ahab's Leg

That direful mishap was at the bottom of his temporary recluseness. And not only this, but to that ever-contracting, dropping circle ashore, who for any reason, possessed the privilege of a less banned approach to him; to that timid circle the above hinted casualty—remaining, as it did, moodily accounted for by Ahab—invested itself with terrors, not entirely underived from the land of spirits and of wails . . . .

But be all this as it may; let the unseen, ambiguous synod in the air, or the vindictive princes and potentates of fire, have to do or not with earthly Ahab, yet in the present matter of his leg, he took plain practical procedures;--he called the carpenter (496-97).

With its cryptic and mysterious prose, this passage hints at the core of Ahab's fractured self—the amputated leg that did much more than remove his limb; it gashed a deep ravine in his soul. Physical wound reverberates through his metaphysical self. That the origin includes "the land of spirits and of wails" both puns on wails as whales and exposes a feeling of dread in his being. But to the metaphysical anguish there attends also the physical practicality of replacing the splintered appendage, so he seeks out the carpenter to construct a new scaffold. Yes, the carpenter can weld a new leg in place but it will most likely never approach Ahab's deeper, eternally splintered soul.

Wounds of particular circumstances can slice through flesh and bone to dismember some essential coherence in our being. The wound may heal outwardly but leave the residue of a live coal smoldering within. To this gnawed part of ourselves that wails to be acknowledged and salved, we may require a spiritual solvent to reach far interior into the mangled and maimed spirit. Self-wounding continues the infection.

Meditation

What wound do you continue to carry that still festers and wails?

September 23. Chapter 107: The Carpenter

Seat thyself sultanically among the moons of Saturn, and take high abstracted man alone; and he seems a wonder, a grandeur and a woe. But from the same point, take mankind in mass, and for the most part, they seem a mob of unnecessary duplicates, both contemporary and hereditary. But most humble though he was, and far from furnishing an example of the high, human abstraction; the Pequod's carpenter was no duplicate; hence, he now comes in person on this stage.

. . . .

The one grand stage where he enacted all his various parts so manifold, was his vice-bench; a long rude ponderous table furnished with several vices, of different sizes, and both of iron and of wood (498).

Ishmael offers two varied perspectives on humankind: abstract in the singular, concrete in the manifold, the latter seeming to consist of a panoply of "unnecessary duplicates." The carpenter reveals himself as both concrete and singular. As an actor on the Pequod's stage of life, he brooks no resemblances. His task is singular, his persona unique. With his cavalcade of tools and his work bench as props, he rehearses his craft to repair anything when he repairs to his utensil-laden table. Ahab pays him a visit to have his splintered joist replaced with a solid duplicate.

In our own work we might explore how we duplicate no one in our style and manner of execution. Part of a unitary abstraction—humankind--each of us nonetheless approaches our work in unique styles using the tools of our trade, craft, assemblages, and talents. Attending to what in our mythic manner and strategies of work defines us most sharply, we can avoid being swallowed by anonymity into the masses. Our life tasks outwardly reflect our inner mythic motives, values and desires.

Meditation

What is most unique and original in the work you perform?

September 24. Chapter 107: The Carpenter

For nothing was this man more remarkable, than for a certain impersonal stolidity, as it were; impersonal, I say; for it so shaded off into the surrounding infinite of things, that it seemed one with the general stolidity discernible in the whole visible world; which while pauselessly active in uncounted modes, still eternally holds its peace, and ignores you, though you dig foundations for cathedrals. Yet was this half-horrible stolidity in him . . . an all-ramifying heartlessness;--yet was it oddly dashed at times, with an old, crutch-like antediluvian wheezing humorousness, not unstreaked now and then with a certain grizzled wittiness. . .(499).

Ishmael's convoluted language is full of imaginary twists in describing the carpenter. His rendition is grand, nuanced, humorous and playful, which reveals an entire worldview. We are in the presence of something much more than impressions of another person. The narrator catalogues many points of view of the carpenter's attitude to others, his humor, and the rich analogy created between himself and his wit, which would be at home "on the bearded forecastle of Noah's ark" (499). Nothing is outside of Ishmael's power to observe. His task as epic poet is to raise his narrative to elevated, biblical and historical levels.

To describe someone in nuanced and fresh ways is itself an art form. Done well, the other then lives in the imagination of the listener or reader in a profound and perhaps permanent way. An aura of immortality, of an undimmed impression, may gather around the description, capturing invisible qualities that move us closer to the truth of that character's narrative identity. Our own voyage as listener or reader is thereby enhanced in reading such persuasive descriptions.

Meditation

Describe yourself in the third person in elevated, nuanced terms.

September 25. Chapter 107: The Carpenter

He was a pure manipulator; his brain, if he had ever had one, must have early oozed along into the muscles of his fingers . . . .

Yet, as previously hinted, this omnitooled, open-and-shut carpenter, was, after all, no mere machine of an automaton. If he did not have a common soul in him, he had a subtle something that somehow anomalously did its duty . . . . And this it was, this same unaccountable, cunning life-principle in him; this it was, that kept him a great part of the time soliloquizing; but only like an unreasoning wheel, which also hummingly soliloquizes (500).

Somewhere between a machine and a man is the carpenter. Head and body are one unit, one flowing into the other. Devoted to his work to the seeming exclusion of anything else, the carpenter is competent, calm, cunning and careful. The life principle in him guides his skills as he talks to himself while humming at his work. He seems as well in perpetual motion, repairing, redoing, hammering things into a unity and talking as the sound of his spinning brain and subtle handiwork congeal—not a cog exactly—but a mainspring in a watch, sliding back and forth, helping him stay awake in performing his tasks.

One's own relation to his/her work might be best recalled through the carpenter and his craft. Like a smooth-running timepiece, he courses along certain grooves of movement in perpetual motion. We can become the work we perform, leaving no room for any other motions or meanings other than what occupies us as craft or trade. Small wonder, then, that when individuals retire, or because of illness can no longer work, they often recognize that their identity was totally cocooned in their occupation. Leaving one's job can mean being cast adrift on a sea of non-identity.

Meditation

Who/what are you apart from your work? What qualities come to mind?

September 26. Chapter 108: Ahab and the Carpenter. *The Deck—First Night Watch*

No fear; I like a good grip; I like to feel something in this slippery world that can hold, man. What's Prometheus about there?—the blacksmith, I mean—what's he about?

. . . .

Um-m. so he must. I do deem it now a most meaning thing, that that old Greek, Prometheus, who made men, they say, should have been a blacksmith, and animated them with fire; for what's made in fire must properly belong to fire; and so hell's probable. How the soot flies! This must be the remainder the Greek made the Africans of. Carpenter, when he's through with that buckle, tell him to forge a pair of steel shoulder-blades; there's a pedlar aboard with a crushing pack (502).

Ahab's presence is steeped in a mythic atmosphere. He conjures up the image of the titan Prometheus that the carpenter evokes. In the Greek myth he was the creator of the human race in the fires of the hearth. Fire is the animating heat, the element of life itself. The black soot is also an ingredient that forges an entire race of people. Ahab's imagination springs outward to include steel shoulder blades to shore up a tired "pedlar" whose pack is crushing him. The captain's imagination seems on fire as he seeks repair of his ivory leg; the double of his fleshy limb will be both physical and mythic.

The imagination has the capacity, when mythically inflected, to see into visible events analogous mythic figures and situations. We then can read phenomenal presences as mythic enactments of timeless gestures. Here traditions can collapse into one another and the world of everyday matter is suddenly laced with ancient stories and eternal figures of the soul passed down and inherited throughout history.

Meditation

Is there a figure from mythology that you identify with most strongly?

September 27. Chapter 108: Ahab and the Carpenter

"Well, then, will it speak thoroughly well for thy work, if, when I come to mount this leg thou makest, I shall nevertheless feel another leg in the same identical place with it; that is, carpenter, my old lost leg; the flesh and blood one, I mean. Canst thou not drive that old Adam away?

. . . .

It is, man. Look, put thy live leg here in the place where mine was; so, now, here is only one distinct leg to the eye, yet two to the soul. Where thou feelest tingling life; there, exactly there, there to a hair, do I. Is't a riddle?" (503)

Ahab's conversation transports us to the heart of the narrative in his depiction of two realities existing simultaneously in mutual embrace. Having his new ivory leg crafted provokes a meditation on his lost limb still having an existence juxtaposed to his new appendage. The soul can discern, believes the captain, two legs, two realities, one present and visible, one phantom and invisible. His observation opens to pondering the phantom reality lying beside the phenomenal world, eavesdropping on it. The soul sees in a dual way: the living and the dead, the present and the absent world. The "old Adam" is the dismembered limb.

What we may have lost, discarded or had removed does not ever leave us completely; its residue, its memory, carries its own palpable reality. It leaves its own trace, carries its own presence in the eye of the soul. We would live in two worlds always, then, which may be a way of understanding mythic consciousness. We live part of our lives within a phantom reality populated with spectral images that may at times haunt and control us. A felt sense of our past can be a powerful guide, like an ancestor or a White Whale, in our daily double lives.

Meditation

What phantom figure or figures from your past still influence you?

September 28. Chapter 108: Ahab and the Carpenter

But Ahab; oh he's a hard driver. Look, driven one leg to death, and spavined the other for life, and now wears out bone legs by the cord. Holloa, there, you Smut! bear a hand there with those screws, and let's finish it before the resurrection fellow comes a-calling with his horn for all legs, true or false . . . . What a leg this is! It looks like a real live leg, filed down to nothing but the core; he'll be standing on this to-morrow; he'll be taking altitudes on it . . . . So, so; chisel, file and sandpaper, now! (504-05).

Ahab leaves the carpenter to his sole task of shaping a new leg for him. The carpenter imagines Ahab burning through one leg after another such that the former cannot keep up with him in such demanding prosthesis production. He asks his helper to speed up the process as the two dig into their task. He also makes reference to Christ's second coming that he fears may happen before they finish their creations. His allusion adds to the captain's connection to Christ, as he earlier was described wearing a crucifixion on his face. The carpenter observes how much of a duplicate likeness has the new limb that Ahab will soon be supported by as he continues to quest after the White Whale. He and his assistant feel time's urgency to complete transforming whale bone into a mortal leg.

Part of our lives follows a ritual path constructed partially of the world's matter. We walk on one leg in the former and the second leg in the latter realm. We each comprise a duplicate of both realms, one literal, the other mythic, psychological, mystical or emotional. Both support us in essential ways. Being aware of both in some depth signals what may breach to the surface. Discerning what is artificial, what natural can assist us in knowing what something is in its essence.

Meditation

What part of your life that supports you daily is artificial, prosthetic?

September 29. Chapter 109: Ahab and Starbuck *in the Cabin*

According to usage they were pumping the ship next morning; and lo! no inconsiderable oil came up with the water; the casks below must have sprung a bad leak.

. . . .

"I was speaking of the oil in the hold, sir."

"And I was not speaking or thinking of that at all. Begone! Let it leak! I'm all aleak myself. Aye! leaks in leaks! not only full of leaky casks, but those leaky casks are in a leaky ship; and that's a far worse plight than the Pequod's, man. Yet I don't stop to plug my leak; for who can find it in the deep-loaded hull; or how hope to plug it, even if found, in this life's howling gale? Starbuck! I'll not have the Burton's hoisted" (506-07).

Now that the oil is seeping into the water in the holds, the Pequod begins to come apart, a process that will continue to story's end. Ahab, true to form, imagines the leaking casks as analogues to his own porous leaking. To underscore his monomania, he is willing to let the casks lessen their valued cargo so that his intense pursuit of Moby Dick continues uninterrupted. He will let fall to stern all the work and value of the cargo, inconsequential now in the face of his vengeance.

We understand how one can sacrifice much of value to pursue a single idea, desire or impulse, or how an affliction can consume one to the detriment of all other life values and treasures. A certain desperation attends such an impulse when all value trickles from one's life, leaving only the one thing to be pursued and conquered, or when one self-destructs through a consuming desire. Monomania shatters all boundaries in its singular pursuit.

Meditation

When have you, in an intense quest, risked everything of value?

September 30. Chapter 109: Ahab And Starbuck *in the Cabin*

But, mastering his emotion, he half calmly rose, and as he quitted the cabin, paused for an instant and said: "Thou hast outraged, not insulted me, sir; but for that I ask thee not to beware of Starbuck; thou wouldst but laugh; but let Ahab beware of Ahab; beware of thyself, old man."

"He waxes brave, but nevertheless obeys; most careful bravery that!" murmured Ahab, as Starbuck disappeared. "What's that he said—Ahab beware of Ahab—there's something there!" Then unconsciously using the musket for a staff, with an iron brow he paced to and fro in the little cabin; but presently the thick plaits of his forehead relaxed, and returning the gun to the rack, he went to the deck (507-08).

Starbuck's intention in visiting Ahab in his cabin is to shoot him and then turn the ship away from the threatening waters toward home. Instead, he leaves the cabin with the cautionary and prophetic words that Ahab must fear himself most. The captain reflects on this warning and finds truth in it. He becomes conscious for an instant that he himself may be the most destructive force to avoid. His thick plaited iron brow is described in much the same language as Moby Dick's own wrinkled forehead. The iron images that surround the captain underscore his unyielding hardness and brittle determination.

We need look no further than that double within ourselves, an interior Other, who can turn on us and exact the most devastating damage. Facing our own mono-maniacal instincts is the surest way to calm the powerful forces that can unleash afflictions on our own being and on those around us. Starbuck discerns that the enemy is not the White Whale but Ahab himself. The attitudes we carry from afflictions leveled at us by life's circumstances can be the most damaging.

Meditation

What situations have revealed to you your own destructive impulses?

October 1. Chapter 110: Queequeg in His Coffin

Poor Queequeg! . . . stripped to his woolen drawers, the tattooed savage was crawling about amid that dampness and slime, like a green spotted lizard at the bottom of a well . . . . How he wasted and wasted away in those few long-lingering days, till there seemed but little left of him but his frame and tattooing. But as all else in him thinned, and his cheek-bones grew sharper, his eyes, nevertheless, seemed growing fuller and fuller; they became of a strange softness of lustre; and mildly but deeply looked out at you there from his sickness . . . . And like circles on the water, which, as they grow fainter, expand; so his eyes seemed rounding and rounding, like the rings of Eternity (510).

Absent in the narrative for a considerable period, Queequeg breaches once more, this time as a sickly soul on the edge of death. He withers to a fraction of his original robust size, but his eyes grow into large orbs of lustrous light. Some quality of Eternity itself emerges in his eyes that expand "like circles on the water." The gap between the eternal and temporal realms appears to collapse; Queequeg has one foot in each domain as he diminishes in size while his eyes, enlarged, grow as faint as his life force.

Queequeg's disease transforms him as he contracts into his affliction. Illness pulls from us not only our strength, our vitality, but our physical self. To have a malady strike us down is to upset and scatter all the conventional daily certitudes we rely on to spur us along in our life's tasks that offer both meaning and purpose. To have that taken from us, to be beaten down by disease, can quickly reformulate our values and assumptions. Priorities may shift radically when an illness forces us to re-mythologize ourselves and our abilities.

Meditation

What has an illness, wound or affliction brought you to re-negotiate in your life?

October 2. Chapter 110: Queequeg in His Coffin

But now that he had apparently made every preparation for death; now that his coffin was proved a good fit, Queequeg suddenly rallied; soon there seemed no need of the carpenter's box; and thereupon, when some expressed their delighted surprise, he, in substance, said, that the cause of his sudden convalescence was this;—at a critical moment, he had just recalled a little duty ashore, which he was leaving undone; and therefore had changed his mind about dying; he could not die yet, he averred. They asked him, then, whether to live or die was a matter of his own sovereign will and pleasure. He answered, certainly (513).

Queequeg's illness descends on him suddenly and occasions the carpenter to craft his coffin. The savage seems fated to die and appears to acquiesce to it without any visible struggle. He settles into his measured coffin to make it easier for his body to be managed post mortem. Then, remembering a task left unfinished, he wills himself back to health to complete it. In his mythos, one certainly has a voice in one's living or dying. Queequeg is in touch with both at all times; to move between these contrary poles of existence is his personal choice.

Taken on another level, any of us can become dead to our life and foreclose on continuing through all manner of illness. Our vitality dissipates and we perform our duties like the living dead. But work that seems to offer us life and feelings of satisfaction can return us to a robust state if we respond to it. The presence of Queequeg within each of us can will us back to meaning and purpose. One memory may be more than sufficient to resurrect us. In moments of affliction we may be visited by a revelation that instructs us to continue, to reclaim ourselves for our world-work. We may then engage a resurrection of purpose.

Meditation

When have you been enlivened, even resurrected or revived, by a work or a task you feel called or re-called, to complete?

October 3. Chapter 110: Queequeg in His Coffin

With a wild whimsiness, he now used his coffin for a sea-chest . . . . Many spare hours he spent, in carving the lid with all manner of grotesque figures and drawings; and it seemed that hereby he was striving, in his rude way, to copy parts of the twisted tattooing on his body. And this tattooing had been the work of a departed prophet and seer of his island, who, by those hieroglyphic marks, had written out on his body a complete theory of the heavens and the earth, and a mystical treatise on the art of attaining truth; so that Queequeg in his own proper person, was a riddle to unfold; a wondrous work in one volume; but whose mysteries not even himself could read, though his own live heart beat against them (514).

As Queequeg is transformed from the brink of death to life, so too the wooden coffin made to house him is transformed into a sea chest, and later into a sealed life-buoy which will save one survivor of the Pequod. The transformation grows even more dramatic when he attempts to duplicate his bodily hieroglyphs onto the coffin's lid, in effect creating an aesthetic double of himself in images and markings. His inked body is translated from his parchment skin to wood to create an image at least as powerful as Ahab's whale bone jaw leg. Queequeg is a wondrous riddle of a book; his twisted double markings bring Ahab to call him "Oh, devilish tantalization of the gods!" (514).

Such a rich image of Self as a book appears on the pages in which is inscribed a riddle bound between the covers of an enigma. The way we duplicate ourselves in the world's matter is mysterious; we wish to carve some lasting image of ourselves onto the world's body, something those who follow us can point to and say "there s/he blows," right where we made a lasting impression in a legacy of our short existence.

Meditation

What marking do you wish to leave as a trace of yourself in the world?

October 4. Chapter 111: The Pacific

There is, one knows not what sweet mystery about this sea, whose gently awful stirrings seems to speak of some hidden soul beneath; like those fabled undulations of the Ephesian sod over the buried Evangelist St. John . . . . for here, millions of mixed shades and shadows, drowned dreams, somnambulisms, reveries; all that we call lives and souls, lie dreaming, dreaming, still; tossing like slumberers in their beds, the ever-rolling waves but made so by their restlessness . . . .

Thus this mysterious, divine Pacific zones the world's whole bulk about; makes all coasts one bay to it; seems the tide-beating heart of earth (515).

Ishmael's rich meditation on the Pacific Ocean is one of the most imaginative and over-arching in the voyage of words he crafts. It brings to his consciousness the nature of mystery as well as the mystery of Nature, with its countless teeming and often invisible life forms as well as the myriad wishes and dreams of mankind. In it inhabits as well the presence of divinity and in its size holds the entire planet in its expressive rolls. Perhaps too, he muses, it may be big enough to be the heart beat of the earth herself, so powerful are its natural rhythms.

To be moved by the natural order to enter a deep reverie on the mysterious matter contained therein is to marvel at its priceless presence. We see ourselves duplicated in the natural order, in history and in myth—all instances wherein we enjoy more deeply our connection with its divine aura. Nature calls us back to ourselves in our fullness and complexity as well as in our relation to all others, living and dead. For many, feeling at home in the world occurs most emphatically in the natural order, which assists us in re-ordering ourselves.

Meditation

Have you felt a deep connection with the ancestors of the past, perhaps sensed through Nature's order?

October 5. Chapter 111: The Pacific

Lifted by those eternal swells, you needs must own the seductive god, bowing your head to Pan.

But few thoughts of Pan stirred Ahab's brain, as standing, like an iron statue at his accustomed place beside the mizen rigging, with one nostril he unthinkingly snuffed the sugary musk from the Bashee isles . . . . and with the other consciously inhaled the salt breath of the new found sea; that sea in which the hated White Whale must even then be swimming . . . . His firm lips met like the lips of a vice; the Delta of his forehead's veins swelled like overladen brooks; in his very sleep, his ringing cry ran through the vaulted hull, "Stern all! the White Whale spouts thick blood!" (515-16).

Ishmael's observation runs an impressive gamut, from the nature god Pan and the serene Pacific to the vice lips of Ahab whose torment by the White Whale throbs more intensely in him as he moves closer to its habitation. He can feel its presence. Locked tight into his own affliction, the captain can allow nothing else to enter his nostrils but vengeance and destruction. His forehead pulses harder, with veins gorged with intense malice. In sleep he howls at his crew to be on the lookout for Moby Dick pulsing thick blood in his final breath.

To be consumed by hatred and vengeance is to constrict one's world down to a narrow taxed vein of experience. If one's intention is to conquer and destroy, then part of one's soul hardens to life's more expansive terrain. Present only is the growing energy of death, for one's obsessions can incarcerate the one avenging; freedom disappears from one's existence. One is hooked. We ask then: Who is worse off: the one pursued or the pursuer? Are they in fact one? Who is the actual prey?

Meditation

When and under what circumstances have you been constricted, even strangled by vengeful hatred that hardened you toward the world?

October 6. Chapter 112: The Blacksmith

[A]nd the houseless, familyless old man staggered off a vagabond in crape; his every woe unreverenced; his grey head a scorn to flaxen curls.

Death seems the only desirable sequel for a career like this; but Death is only a launching into the region of the strange Untried; it is but the first salutation to the possibilities of the immense Remote, the Wild, the Watery, the Unshored; therefore, to the death-longing eyes of such men, who still have left in them some interior compunctions against suicide, does the all-contributed and all-receptive ocean alluringly spread forth his whole plain of unimaginable, taking terrors, and wonderful, new-life adventures, and from the hearts of infinite Pacifics, the thousand mermaids sing to them—"Come hither, broken-hearted; here is another life without the guilt of intermediate death . . . (518-19).

His reflections on the misfortunes of the Blacksmith, Perth, that led him to lose his family, house and belongings because of alcohol, and his subsequent call by the sea, guide Ishmael into a deep-fathomed meditation on the sea's invitation to so many despairing souls, including himself. He refers to the oceans this time as "his" rather than "hers." The sea offers solace, another chance, renewal, a surface where mermaids, like sirens of the deep, entice souls to them as a substitute for suicidal despair. It also promises oblivion and anonymity, solace and liberation.

Less an escape than a renewal is offered by the vast watery immensity of the ocean; its cosmic and often tranquil surface, along with its deep fathoming, call to the soul and beckon to be resurrected and liberated from a static and meaningless or despairing existence. The sea challenges and cleanses, wipes the slate clean, revivifies the spirit and occasions a fresh beginning. It baptizes one into a new resolve.

Meditation

What experience of renewal have you had through water?

October 7. Chapter 113: The Forge

"I am past scorching; not easily can'st thou scorch a scar."

"Well, well; no more. Thy shrunk voice sounds too calmly, sanely woe-ful to me. In no Paradise myself, I am impatient of all misery in others that is not mad . . . . What wert thou making there?"

"Welding an old pike head, sir; there were seams and dents in it."

"And can'st thou make it all smooth again, blacksmith, after such hard usage as it had?"

"I think so, sir."

"And I suppose thou can'st smoothe almost any seams and dents; never mind how hard the metal, blacksmith?"

"Aye, sir, I think I can; all seams and dents but one" (520-21).

Ahab's keen interest in the blacksmith's skills in smoothing out dented metal will become more obvious in a moment. Presently he is more inter-ested in the nature of madness and misery and his own self-immolation in the throes of them. He has brought nails from the horseshoes worn by race horses, made of the hardest of metals, to forge into a harpoon head to slay Moby Dick. But Ahab is also interested in making smooth what life has dented and wounded. When life has used things hard, Ahab wonders if they can be restored, himself included.

We might reflect through Ahab's curiosity where the wrinkled surfaces, cracked seams and marked surfaces of our life can withstand a hammering back into their virginal smoothness. Life presents occasions, bruises, dents and rough surfaces that point often to deeper afflictions brought on by strife, suffering and surrender in whatever we hunt. Life marks us, dents our surfaces, torques and reveals where we encountered troubled waters as well as adversaries that reside below the surface. Living an unmarked life is impossible, suffering unavoidable.

Meditation

Where and when have you been dented, wrinkled and forged by life?

October 8. Chapter 113: The Forge

"Look ye here then," cried Ahab, passionately advancing, and leaning with both hands on Perth's shoulders; "look ye here—*here*—can ye smoothe out a seam like this, blacksmith," sweeping one hand across his ribbed brow; "if thou could'st, blacksmith, glad enough would I lay my head upon thy anvil, and feel thy heaviest hammer between my eyes. Answer! Can'st thou smoothe this seam?"

"Oh! That is the one, sir! Said I not all seams and dents but one?"

"Aye, blacksmith, it is the one; aye, man, it is unsmoothable; for though thou only see'st it here in my flesh, it has worked down into the bone of my skull—*that* is all wrinkles! . . . Look ye, blacksmith, these are the gathered nail-stubs of the steel shoes of racing horses" (521).

What originated as a request by Ahab for Perth to forge a harpoon head from the nails of race horses' shoes becomes a meditation on the dented, diseased forehead and bone of his skull. So fiercely has he tortured himself over the White Whales' destruction that his furrowed brow has forged into a crinkled paralysis, bone-deep. To smoothe it back to its original flatness requires skills beyond Perth's capacity. Ahab's wrinkled forehead cannot be forged anew. The agony of being dismembered has eternally creased him to the bone.

Body, mind and spirit are a unity, as Ahab's physiognomy reveals. What has tortured his mind now leaves its trace on his body. Our bodies often reveal the residue or traces of our sufferings; they can also be mirrors or doubles of our deeper, more invisible anguish and torments. As embodied wounded beings, we often reveal the visible consequences of sustained anguish and affliction. Some infirmities we may carry as a burden as well as a blessing our entire lives.

Meditation

Where on your body do you carry the memories of earlier strife and/or suffering, where dents and wrinkled surfaces persist and prevail?

October 9. Chapter 113: The Forge

"No, no—no water for that; I want it of the true death-temper. Ahoy, there! Tashtego, Queequeg, Daggoo! What say ye, pagans! Will ye give me as much blood as will cover this barb?" holding it high up. A cluster of dark nods replied, Yes. Three punctures were made in the heathen flesh, and the White Whale's barbs were then tempered.

"Ego non baptizo te in nomine patris, sed in nomine diaboli!" deliriously howled Ahab, as the malignant iron scorchingly devoured the baptismal blood.

. . . .

[T]he pole was then driven hard up into the socket . . . . This done, pole, iron and rope, like the Three Fates—remained inseparable, and Ahab moodily stalked away with the weapon; the sound of his ivory leg, and the sound of the hickory pole, both hollowly ringing along every plank (522-23).

One of the most dramatic and mythically-charged moments of the narrative is the wounded captain's ritualizing the creation of the harpoon he hopes to sink deep into the White Whale's flesh. The ritual gathers the three pagans from various lands, with Ahab as high priest who bonds them as a unity in a mockery of the Christian Trinity. He conjures the devil rather than the Father. Finally, the hollow sound of Ahab's gait, one of ivory, the other of wood, echoes their emptiness across the ship's planks. The weapon is now prepared, as is Ahab.

Forging weapons of defense or attack is not foreign to any of us. We forge them to strike back at who or what wounds or dismembers us. They take all manner of shapes and rationales, even blessings and baptisms. We baptize our harpoons to sanctify them and to justify our reprisals. No one is immune from this ageless pattern of revenge.

Meditation

What weapon do you forge to render afflictions on others or yourself?

October 10. Chapter 114: The Gilder

Penetrating further and further into the heart of the Japanese cruising ground the Pequod was soon all astir in the fishery . . . .

At such times, under an abated sun; afloat all day upon smooth, slow heaving swells; seated in his boat, light as a birch canoe; and so sociably mixing with the soft waves themselves, that like hearth-stone cats they purr against the gunwale; these are the times of dreamy quietude, when beholding the tranquil beauty and brilliancy of the ocean's skin, one forgets the tiger heart that pants beneath it; and would not willingly remember, that this velvet paw but conceals a remorseless fang (524).

A mild reflective description eases itself from Ishmael's reverie of tranquility as the ship sails into serene waters. Everything appears calm and dreamlike as the soft soothing sea holds the men in its gentle grasp, tending to them tenderly. However, just beneath the brilliant beauty of its skin beats a tiger heart with a wildness and a power that, unleashed, can transform any tranquil scene into a frothy chaos of destruction. Its paw is velvet, its fang a threat and its surface golden.

Becoming aware of these two opposite yet complementary realities may signal a wisdom and an absence of naivete. Not being lulled into such a maelstrom hidden by a benign exterior marks the difference between serving or succumbing to "the remorseless fang" at the depths of seemingly innocuous exteriors. The skin of a person or thing is just that: a skin-deep appearance which can disarmingly hide a more fierce reality. Such is the nature of all things mortal and natural. Always another, invisible dimension is present if we have the poetic cast of mind to discern its reality beneath a more blameless appearance.

Meditation

When have you encountered the once hidden remorseless fang of an otherwise calm and seemingly harmless exterior?

October 11. Chapter 114: The Gilder

Nor did such soothing scenes, however temporary, fail of at least as temporary an effect on Ahab. But if these secret golden keys did seem to open in
him his own secret golden treasuries, yet did his breath upon them prove
but tarnishing.

Oh, grassy glades! oh ever vernal endless landscapes in the soul; in ye,-
-though long parched by the dead drought of the earthly life,--in ye, men
yet may roll, like young horses in new morning clover; and for some few
fleeting moments, feel the cool dew of the life immortal on them. Would
to God these blessed calms would last. But the mingled, mingling threads
of life are woven by warp and woof; calms crossed by storms, a storm for
every calm (525).

Ishmael's continued lyric meditation touches on the sadness and the
sterling glory of life. The Gilder is one who traditionally is a craftsman
working with gold and silver. Here the artisan is nature herself. Ahab is
the instigator of the reverie which lurches into a lyric crescendo of grassy
glades which are not lost to the imagination but rediscovered as one sidles
toward death. To live fully is to feel the webbing of weal and woe in the
continuous warp and woof that comprises the world soul. There exists a
blessedness that pervades the created order and the souls of mortals—a
compromise between Eden and mortal earth.

A visionary expression of human life helps us remain unfixed from a single
vocabulary or worldview that denies its brethren. To feel the lives of fate
and the threading of calm and storm in the soul is to perceive a complete
life, where one can sense joy in its imperfection, a fullness in life's frailty
and even a glory in its gore.

Meditation

When have you become more fully conscious of life's rhythms in its pains
and pleasures, its gold and tarnish?

October 12. Chapter 114: The Gilder

Where lies the final harbor, whence we unmoor no more? In what rapt ether sails the world, of which the weariest will never weary? Where is the foundling's father hidden? Our souls are like those orphans whose unwedded mothers die in bearing them: the secret of our paternity lies in their grave; and we must there to learn it.

And that same day, too, gazing far down from his boat's side into that same golden sea, Starbuck lowly murmured:--

"Loveliness unfathomable, as ever lover saw in his young bride's eyes!—Tell me not of thy teeth-tiered sharks, and thy kidnapping cannibal ways. Let faith oust fact; let fancy oust memory; I look deep down and do believe" (525).

Ishmael's reverie continues into the golden core of the world's soul and mortal souls sailing within it. Some sense of being orphaned pervades the first part of his meditation. The father of our making lives in death where we must seek it; between birth and death feminine and masculine forces bind our soul life. Then Starbuck is heard to murmur words Ishmael records: the lovely lyric side of creation beyond and even beneath the snapping jaws of sharks. He sees deep into the ocean's depths a stubborn and eternal golden beauty that gives him faith in worldly goodness and in the immortal nature of the soul's dalliances.

Depth, verticality, a seeking beneath the ocean's skin for a reality of beauty worthy of belief and offering solace Starbuck voices. We each have glimpses that would "make us less forlorn" as Wordsworth's sonnet promises. In an instant we intuit the core of life's mystery and discern its lovely goodness. What does each of us see in the depth of the world, when our gaze leaves the horizon and casts down into the vast stillness?

Meditation

Gazing down into the world's depths, what rises to meet you?

October 13. Chapter 115: *The Pequod Meets* The Bachelor

As this glad ship of good luck bore down upon the moody Pequod, the barbarian sound of enormous drums came from her forecastle . . . . On the quarter-deck, the mates and harpooneers were dancing with the olive-hued girls who had eloped with them from the Polynesian Isles;

. . . .

And Ahab, he too was standing on his quarter-deck, shaggy and black, with a stubborn gloom; and as the two ships crossed each other's wakes— one all jubilations for things passed, the other all forebodings as to things to come—their two captains in themselves impersonated the whole striking contrast of the scene (527).

Two opposing worldviews converge when the Pequod crosses the wake of the Bachelor. The latter is bound home, filled with Polynesian beauties, the former sailing to its end in a hardened fixated pursuit of the White Whale. Festivities and distractions of delight on the Bachelor exclude Moby Dick's sightings, accompanied by a firm disbelief in its reality. The Bachelor is as shallow as the Pequod is deep. Both carry extremes and excesses of belief and non-belief. A suggestion arises here that one must first believe in the White Whale before he will appear to reveal his potent, even divine presence. Believing leads to seeing.

The White Whale requires belief no matter what we want to believe it is. What form we imagine it may determine its level of presentness. What we present in life through uncompromising, even obsessive belief, are the terms of the White Whale's phantom presence, the haunting shape of our deepest desires and most acute afflictions. We reflect on what we have pursued that wounded us and now struggles to heal. Our moods bespeak attitudes toward how we interpret the world.

Meditation

What is your White Whale that you have or have not pursued or been pursued by? Has it changed shape over time?

October 14. Chapter 115: *The Pequod Meets* the Bachelor

"Hast seen the White Whale?" gritted Ahab in reply.

"No; only heard of him; but don't believe in him at all," said the other good-humoredly. "Come aboard!"

. . . .

And thus, while the one ship went cheerily before the breeze, the other stubbornly fought against it; and so the two vessels parted; the crew of the Pequod looking with grave, lingering glances towards the receding Bachelor; but the Bachelor's men never heeding their gaze for the lively revelry they were in. And as Ahab, leaning over the taffrail, eyed the homeward-bound craft, he took from his pocket a small vial of sand . . . for that vial was filled with Nantucket soundings (527-28).

The Pequod witnesses its inverted double put distance between them. The former is full, contented and jubilant, the latter empty, discontented and somber, caught in the univocal grip of a single intention: to slay the White Whale. Nothing else matters. The Bachelor's denial of the whale's reality frees it from fear and any desire to hunt it. Ahab, always a surprise, reveals a vial of Nantucket sand, a symbol of his affection for home and perhaps an impulse to follow the Bachelor to its origin. His need to avenge his wound, however, prohibits him from giving an order to abandon his quest.

We can find ourselves split into two minds, contrary desires and intentions: to abandon what propels us forward in absolute intensity and to modulate our mission in life, or to pursue with full abandon what daimon goads us futilely forward with little possibility of success or conquest. The soul seeks its fulfillment even of a desire to destroy what afflicts us, even if such wounding leads to self-destruction. Nations as well as individuals can be hooked as hostages by such impulses.

Meditation

What desire that obsessed you for years have you abandoned?

October 15. Chapter 116: The Dying Whale

"Oh, trebly hooped and welded hip of power! Oh, high aspiring, rainbowed jet!—that one strivest, this one jettest all in vain! In vain, oh whale, dost thou seek intercedings with yon all-quickening sun, that only calls forth life, but gives it not again. Yet dost thou darker half, rock me with a prouder, if a darker faith. All thy unnamable imminglings float beneath me here; I am buoyed by breaths of once living things, exhaled as air, but water now.

"Then hail, for ever hail, O sea, in whose eternal tossings the wild fowl finds his only rest" (530).

Ahab's words continue to deepen into an encomium to the sea, sun and whales, now slain. It is also a dirge for the four dying whales. It expands to a description of whales, some of whom sport within the space of sea and sun, while others extinguish their "rainbowed jet" in death. A beauty and a cruel indifference are its trajectories of the sun. Yet the darker aspects of the whale carry a profounder faith. He considers all the presentations of a deep-down darkness active below the Pequod's keel and touches the mysterious grandeur of those life forms; they offer him momentary ballast and balance, as his elegant and potent prose describes.

We may try to comprehend something in our lives or in nature with calculations and measurements. But death and dying open up very different imaginal portals and corridors of understanding. Comprehension deepens with the mystery of life's forms; we may be shifted by a splendid solace on the main. Our hearts open to a vision of life's mysterious roilings towards what is unseen; we may find a kinship with Nature and hail it as brother or sister.

Meditation

What mystery in Nature has opened to you in its death or dying such that you were deepened and marked by its presence?

October 16. Chapter 117: The Whale Watch

Started from his slumbers, Ahab, face to face, saw the Parsee; and hooped round by the gloom of the night they seemed the last men in a flooded world. "I have dreamed it again," said he.

"Of the hearses? Have I not said, old man, that neither hearse nor coffin can be thine?"

. . . .

"Though it come to the last, I shall still go before thee thy pilot" . . . .
I have here two pledges that I shall yet slay Moby Dick and survive it."

"Take another pledge, old man," said the Parsee, as his eyes lighted up like fire-flies in the gloom—"Hemp only can kill thee."

"The gallows, ye mean.—I am immortal then, on land and on sea," cried Ahab, with a laugh of derision" (531-32).

The Parsee as prophet is Ahab's sinister double. After their exchange, they are "silent again, as one man" (532). He feeds the captain an image of immortality, at least according to Ahab's interpretation; his fantasy is that the hemp line refers to the hang man's noose. He then ignores or does not grasp the hemp line at his foot in the whaleboat. Unknowingly suffering an inaccurate interpretation, Ahab proclaims with excessive pride his immortality in this life, both on land and sea at the same time as his crew fastens a dead whale to the Pequod.

Easily done is our ability to convince ourselves of a desired reality that may have little foundation in the facts of our lives. We live, however, within elaborate fictions, "as if" realities, that stoke the fires of both our fears and desires. Immortality on many levels can convince us of our own invincibilities; when we truly sense our sustained vulnerability, we may need a White Whale to underscore such a reality.

Meditation

When have you felt invincible, untouchable and impregnable?

October 17. Chapter 118: The Quadrant

Now, in that Japanese sea, the days in summer are as freshets of efful-gences. That unblinklingly vivid Japanese sun seems the blazing focus of the glassy ocean's immeasurable burning-glass. The sky looks lacquered; clouds there are none; the horizon floats; and this nakedness of unrelieved radiance is as the insufferable splendors of God's throne. Well that Ahab's quadrant was furnished with colored glasses, through which to take sight of that solar fire . . . . At length the desired observation was taken; and with his pencil upon his ivory leg, Ahab soon calculated what his latitude must be at that precise instant (533).

Ishmael's language continues to carry a lyric sheen: "Freshets of effulgences" and a lacquered sky. All seems stripped bare as well, to expose the radiance of the nautical world in some ways mirroring the throne of God. What Ahab seeks is a sense of place, of location and of context. The sun is the center of all illumination and orients the Pequod through the quadrant's calculus. The benevolent world shines on him as he measures himself from the sun's position. A verdant calm descends on the voyage; Ahab seems satisfied at locating his position on the globe, but his feelings of dissatisfaction churn just below the surface.

On any quest, moments of stepping back to measure and inscribe one's latitude and longitude are necessary and prudent. Taking account of one's voyage by placing oneself at home somewhere may also inspire the question: "Is this the right voyage for me?" Nature herself can orient us within a larger purview so we can grasp our voyage's progress as well as its purpose and even determine if it should be canceled if we sense that while this voyage once served us, its shelf life has expired. An act of courage is needed to end-stop a journey whose purpose has dissolved.

Meditation

When have you taken out the quadrant to calculate your place in your life's voyage? Did your calculation bring a change in direction?

October 18. Chapter 118: The Quadrant

"Foolish toy! babies' plaything of haughty Admirals, and Commodores, and Captains; the world brags of thee, of thy cunning and might; but what after all canst thou do, but tell the poor, pitiful point, where thou thyself happenest to be on this wide planet, and the hand that holds thee: no! not one jot more! Thou canst not tell where one drop of water or one grain of sand will be to-morrow noon; and yet with thy impotence thou insultest the sun! Science! Curse thee, thou vain toy; and cursed be all the things that cast man's eyes aloft to that heaven . . . . Curse thee, thou quadrant!" dashing it to the deck, "no longer will I guide my earthly way by thee . . . . thus I split and destroy thee!" (534).

Scientific calculation fails him as a sufficient guide to the White Whale. It pulls one's gaze upward, not horizontally or down. Measuring one's place on the globe by means of the sun inadequately locates the white shape below the ocean's surface, like a moon in the depths. Ahab grasps instinctively that connecting with Moby Dick is not achieved by scientific or technical measurement. By dismembering the instrument, Ahab moves the hunt closer to completion. Hunting the White Whale is more akin to a metaphysical, not a physical, reckoning. It shares more ground with the medieval knights' quest for the Grail cup. Ahab's Science is too limited to discern Truth's geography.

Some moments in life reveal how calculation and prediction are essential. It can lead us to make reasoned decisions. But there are instances when measuring the physical realm with instruments of technology simply falls short. Clear reckoning might best surrender to a deeper knowing based on intuition and instinct, a gut feeling beyond reason's skyline. Some things in life are searched for and made present by a calculus of the imagination guided by a felt sense.

Meditation

When have you been guided by a fantasy or instinctive impulse?

October 19. Chapter 118: The Quadrant

Standing between the knight-heads, Starbuck watched the Pequod's tumultuous way, and Ahab's also, as he went lurching along the deck.

"I have sat before the dense coal fire and watched it all aglow, full of its tormented flaming life; and I have seen it wane at last, down, down, to dumbest dust. Old man of oceans! of all this fiery life of thine, what will at length remain but one little heap of ashes!"

"Aye," cried Stubb, "but sea-coal ashes—mind ye that, Mr. Starbuck—sea-coal, not your common charcoal. Well, well! I heard Ahab mutter, 'Here some one thrusts these cards into these old hands of mine; swears that I must play them, and no others.' And damn me, Ahab, but thou actest right; live in the game, and die in it" (535).

Starbuck witnesses the previous scene and Ahab's lurching gait as he sees into the future of this live coal of a captain that will in time decompose into a heap of ashes. His voice carries a determined despair. Stubb, too, is witness and shares with Starbuck what he overheard Ahab mutter: that Fate has dealt him a clear set of cards that he must play with and out. Some force prescribes his destiny, whatever he himself chooses. He knows he inhabits a space somewhere between choice and fate. How he plays his cards may possibly determine victory or death.

Not playing with a full deck, playing the cards one is dealt and playing one's cards close to one's chest are common expressions that acknowledge some invisible principle or presence in negotiating our lives. We may find the Joker in amongst those we have received from forces beyond our comprehension and we may wonder about the fairness or its lack in the cards we hold. The dealer is a character we may never glimpse but the cards we are assigned reflect our fate.

Meditation

Respond to "the cards" you have been dealt thus far in your life.

October 20. Chapter 119: The Candles

Warmest climes but nurse the cruelest fangs: the tiger of Bengal crouches in spaced groves of ceaseless verdure. Skies the most effulgent but basket the deadliest thunders: gorgeous Cuba knows tornadoes that never swept tame northern lands. So, too, it is, that in these resplendent Japanese seas the mariner encounters the direst of all storms, the Typhoon.

. . . .

"Here!" cried Starbuck, seizing Stubb by the shoulder, and pointing his hand towards the weather bow, "markest thou not that the gale comes from the eastward, the very course Ahab is to run for Moby Dick? the very course he swung to this day noon?" (536-37).

As Ishmael describes the Typhoon dropping suddenly out of the cloudless sky with little warning—even bearing down, not up to terrorize and destroy a town, so does he record Starbuck's coupling the damaging effects of such a whirlwind with Ahab's recent course adjustment so to heedlessly head into the seething seas of the White Whale. Typhoon and White Whale construct two stories: one dropping down from above, the other gathering energy from below. One portends the eventual irruption into view of the other; signals of the second are present in the destruction of the first.

Not infrequently are we given indicators of what may be through some disruption of our lives that places us on alert; one incident may prophecy what is impending. The first mimics what will or may be by means of what is. Sources in the threat or along one's side turn out to be an early warning device to prepare us for something more dire, especially if some change in our life's trajectory assumes a different relation to what we pursue.

Meditation

Has a major tack in your life coaxed the unexpected to the surface?

October 21. Chapter 119: The Candles

At the base of the main-mast, full beneath the doubloon and the flame, the Parsee was kneeling in Ahab's front, but with his head bowed away from him . . . .

"Aye, aye, men!" cried Ahab. "Look up at it; mark it well; the white flame but lights the way to the White Whale! Hand me those mainmast links there; I would fain feel this pulse, and let mine beat against it; blood against fire! So."

Then turning—the last link held fast in his left hand, he put his foot upon the Parsee; and with fixed upward eye, and high-flung right arm, he stood erect before the lofty tri-pointed trinity of flames.

"Oh! thou clear spirit of clear fire, whom on these seas I as Persian once did worship, till in the sacramental act so burned by thee, that to this hour I bear the scar; I now know thee, thou clear spirit. . ." (540).

Lightning, fire, terror, destruction, a chaos of seething Nature melds several worlds in flashes of white light and flames licking the air atop each of the three masts as Ahab communes with the clear spirit of air. He can only interpret this juncture of intense light as a guiding laser leading to Moby Dick. All vortexes into a singular interpretation. There is nothing else for Ahab than the white light of the whale that this cacophony of energy alighting on the spars of the ship's signals. Here the captain and the Parsee melt into and voice a common vision.

When we enter into an obsession or a possession, our manner of interpreting any and everything spirals into feeding and worshipping that one idea, a singular gripping reason for being. All is both altered and altared to serve the grand design of the obsession. Nothing would seem to be able to pry it loose; its monomaniacal force is contagious.

Meditation

Describe an obsession that overtook you with the force of a typhoon that guided your every thought and behavior and may still.

October 22. Chapter 119: The Candles

"All your oaths to hunt the White Whale are as binding as mine; and heart, soul, and body, lungs and life, old Ahab is bound. And that ye may know to what tune this heart beats: look ye here; thus I blow out the last fear!" And with one blast of his breath he extinguished the flame.

As in the hurricane that sweeps the plain, men fly the neighborhood of some lone, gigantic elm . . . so at those last words of Ahab's many of the mariners did run from him in a terror of dismay (542).

Ahab terrifies the crew with his fiery harpoon, his implement to slay the White Whale; he appears as Prometheus with the fired torch whose light pushes back the chaos of storm and night. He intimidates the entire crew with his prowess and seizes the moment to remind them of their oath taken earlier amidst the 3 crossed harpoons to pursue his dismemberer to earth's end. He symbolically blows out the flaming harpoon as a gesture of extinguishing their collective fired fear so they can confidently pursue their prey. The hunt continues to assume more mythic and other-worldly attributes fired in the heat of Ahab's fury.

Being overtaken by an obsession, especially one that emanates from being wounded, afflicted or dismembered, is powerful in its all-consuming presence. Satisfying that grudge can assume a stature larger than life itself. One risks everything to be avenged and may gather others around one in a sympathetic collective to inspire success. In the process, others share deeply one's affliction and can be subsumed by its energy. One's own judgment is suspended in the frenzy of the moment when one is called on to participate by swearing an oath to make another's cause his/her own.

Meditation

Have you found yourself part of a conspiracy to avenge another's wound, slight, or affliction of perceived injustice?

October 23. Chapter 121: Midnight—*The Forecastle Bulwarks*

"What's the mighty difference between holding a mast's lightning-rod in the storm, and standing close by a mast that hasn't got any lightning-rod at all in a storm? Don't you see, you timber-head, that no harm can come to the holder of the rod, unless the mast is first struck?. . . Not one ship in a hundred carries rods, and Ahab,--aye, man, and all of us,--were in no more danger then, in my poor opinion, than all the crews in ten thousand ships now sailing the seas. Why, you King-Post, you, I suppose you would have every man in the world go about with a small lightning-rod running up the corner of his hat, like a militia officer's skewered feather, and trailing behind like his sash" (544-45).

Stubb's harsh judgment is to convince Flask that what seems Ahab's immortality is an illusion and that the "fiery dart" he held put him in no more danger than any man not holding one. According to Stubb's logic, only if the main mast is struck by lightning would Ahab or any man holding a lightning rod be imperiled. Not all men need wear a lightning rod in their hat to protect themselves from the fiery elements in a storm. He calls on Flask to exercise good sense, even in a time of crisis that places their captain in such a dangerously vulnerable condition.

Good sense in a storm is an act of moral courage. One has to wonder at times, however, if it is enough. Good sense can anchor one in a storm, but Stubb wonders "whether the world is anchored anywhere" (545). Good sense can ground one, but is it of value if the globe itself free-floats? Something beyond good sense may of necessity be heeded. Perhaps faith, the miraculous, the invisibles, what sounds most practical, may be inadequate anchors in life's storms. Stubb is that voice in us that serves as a bellwether for what looms on the horizon.

Meditation

Is good sense in crises always sufficient for you in such situations? What might be an alternative?

October 24. Chapter 121: Midnight—*The Forecastle Bulwarks*

"Yes, when a fellow's soaked through, it's hard to be sensible, that's a fact. And I am about drenched with this spray. Never mind; catch the turn there, and pass it. Seems to me we are lashing down these anchors now as if they were never going to be used again. Tying these two anchors here, Flask, seems like tying a man's hands behind him . . . . I wonder, Flask, whether the world is anchored anywhere; if she is, she swings with an uncommon long cable, though. There, hammer that knot down, and we've done. So; next to touching land, lighting on deck is the most satisfactory . . . . Lord, Lord, that the winds that come from heaven should be so unmannerly! This is a nasty night, lad" (545).

Stubb's response to the chaos of the storm and its lightning is to do the work, follow orders, and thereby anchor one's self in one's duties, even when the world itself feels unmoored and swings dangerously. He and Flask fear the elements and struggle to shore up the ship against its ruin. Between the two men gathers an intimacy in the work, an authentic camaraderie that forms a small community in the storm. Stubb also senses that perhaps the Pequod will not drop anchor for the rest of the voyage, that it has crossed a watery threshold into another geography.

In the thick of threatening chaos we may form the most unusual alliances to bolster one another and find some security in another's company. Not being isolated amidst unmoored moments in our lives can bestow a gift on us from another. Such a communal support in performing a common task in dangerous circumstances can bestow great solace at a time of peril. Perhaps the most grounded we can be and enjoy is the presence of another in sympathy and human community. To see one's own condition in the face of another can foster courage. The Ishmael-Queequeg relation finds many iterations in the voyage.

Meditation

Did supporting another or being supported in a crisis encourage you?

October 25. Chapter 123: The Musket

The loaded muskets in the rack were shiningly revealed, as they stood upright against the forward bulkhead. Starbuck was an honest, upright man; but out of Starbuck's heart, at that instant when he saw the muskets, there strangely evolved an evil thought; but so blent with its neutral or good accompaniments that for the instant he hardly knew it for itself.

"He would have shot me once," he murmured, "yes, there the very musket that he pointed at me;--that one with the studded lock; let me touch it—lift it . . . . Loaded? I must see. Aye, aye; and powder in the pan;--that's not good. Best spill it?—wait. I'll cure myself of this. I'll hold the musket boldly while I think.--I come to report a fair wind to him" (548).

Starbuck's resistance to Ahab's monomaniac intent gathers energy when he steps below to the captain's cabin to report fair winds aloft. As he discovers, holds and examines the musket Ahab had earlier leveled at his first mate, Starbuck quickly senses how he might easily assassinate his captain and tack the Pequod towards New Bedford. Evil grows in him alongside opportunity. He thinks he can cure himself of such a destructive design by embracing the rifle, fully loaded and ready to be discharged. Part of him knows he is playing with fire.

When we experience injustice, madness, or destructive impulses in another and discover an opportunity to destroy it in the name of Justice, we approach a critical threshold. To act in the name of Justice can be overwhelming and conjure in us murderous impulses that prowl like natural tendencies or instincts. The mind may encourage such an instinct to uncoil. This dilemma may force us to revision our sense of Justice.

Meditation

Have you entertained murderous thoughts in the name of Justice?

October 26. Chapter 123: The Musket

"And would I be a murderer, then, if"—and slowly, stealthily, and half sideways looking, he placed the loaded musket's end against the door.

"On this level, Ahab's hammock swings within; his head this way. A touch, and Starbuck may survive to hug his wife and child again.—Oh Mary! Mary!—boy! boy! boy!—But if I wake thee not to death, old man, who can tell to what unsounded deeps Starbuck's body this day week may sink, with all the crew! Great God, where art thou? Shall I? shall I?"—

"Stern all! Oh Moby Dick, I clutch thy heart at last!"

Such were the sounds that now came hurtling from out the old man's tormented sleep. . . (549).

Starbuck's moral impasse at Ahab's cabin door intensifies the longer he wrestles with the conundrum obsessing him: to slay the monomaniac and liberate the Pequod to return home, or to let his revenge take from Starbuck and others what they love most. In his struggle, where he "seemed wrestling with an angel" (550), he feels God has deserted him. He cries out in the desert landscape, on the other side of which is Ahab's head rocking in agony in his hammock. He chooses, finally, to replace the musket where he found it and let the captain live.

If any of us would commit a violent act, even murder, to stop what we believe is a greater destruction, it must be done freely in our own principled way. Such a dilemma may be easily resolved by some tormenting thought by others. Where we may set the line for justice's sake reveals some core belief stemming from our personal myth. Such a choice may require immediate response or long premeditation. The weight of another's existence may depend on our resolution.

Meditation

Are there certain situations in which you would take another's life?

October 27. Chapter 124: The Needle

Muffled in the full morning light, the invisible sun was only known by the spread intensity of his place; where his bayonet rays moved on in stacks . . . .

Long maintaining an enchanted silence, Ahab stood apart; and every time the teetering ship loweringly pitched down her bowsprit, he turned to eye the bright sun's rays produced ahead; and when she profoundly settled by the stern, he turned behind, and saw the sun's rearward place, and how the same yellow rays were blending with his undeviating wake.

"Ha, ha, my ship! thou mightest well be taken now for the sea-chariot of the sun. Ho, ho! All ye nations before my prow, I bring the sun to ye! Yoke on the further billows . . . . I drive the sea!" (551).

Ahab glances fore and aft at the sun while the wake of the Pequod holds steady. He enjoys a certain self-stature wherein he guides, like Phaethon in Greek myth, his father Apollo's chariot of the sun. Ahab enjoys his image as that Greek figure's counterpart guiding his own chariot of the sea. He grows larger in self-stature by imagining that he pulls the sun behind him to illuminate all nations before him as he drives the sea forward in her swollen waves. Like a god he imagines himself.

We have moments of fancied grandiosity, of largeness, of being in control of forces and presences that in truth we do not, or only minimally. That same reality can be driven downward in moments of self-inflation when we live the illusion that powers beyond our reckoning are within our capacity to control, direct and domesticate. Sometimes the world aligns with our desires and wishes to such a powerful degree that we imagine ourselves a supreme commander.

Meditation

Have you discovered that something or someone you believed you controlled was not under your command?

October 28. Chapter 124: The Needle

Here, it must needs be said, that accidents like this have in more than one case occurred to ships in violent storms. The magnetic energy, as developed in the mariner's needle, is, as all know, essentially one with the electricity beheld in heaven; hence it is not to be much marvelled at, that such things should be. Instances where the lightning has actually struck the vessel . . . . the effect upon the needle has at times been still more fatal; all its loathsome virtue being annihilated, so that the before magnetic steel was of no more use than an old wife's knitting needle. But in either case, the needle never again, of itself, recovers the original virtue thus marred or lost (552).

A defining moment in the hunt occurs here in both the storm and its consequences. A breakdown arises in the energy of the needle on the Pequod and "the electricity beheld in heaven" (552). A major separation signals a shift in the journey as the impotent needle allowed the ship to sail in the opposite direction. This reversal portends a major alteration in the itinerary and in the energy of the captain's presence. He alone repairs the needle by replacing it in the compass, but the damage has been done. The voyage shifts direction from this bearing forward.

Losing direction, slipping out from under our bearings, or finding our "true north" has actually been pulling us south without our conscious awareness, can reveal our motion along a path that we recognize as not our own. All are feasible when our compass needle spins out of control. A life with a clear and controllable direction we may one day wake to discover is wrong, that we have been living our life in reverse or continually tacking into the wrong winds. Setting the needle true to our voyage, not someone else's, may be difficult but necessary if we are intent on living our own life, not another's.

Meditation

When has your life compass pointed you in the wrong direction?

October 29. Chapter 24: The Needle

With a blow from the top-maul Ahab knocked off the steel head of the lance . . . . Then, with the maul, after repeatedly smiting the upper end of this iron rod, he placed the blunted needle endwise on the top of it, and less strongly hammered that . . . . At first, the steel went round and round, quivering and vibrating at either end; but at last it settled to its place, when Ahab . . . stepped frankly back from the binnacle, and pointing his stretched arm towards it, exclaimed,--"Look ye, for yourselves, if Ahab be not lord of the level loadstone! The sun is East, and that compass swears it!"

. . . .

In his fiery eyes of scorn and triumph, you then saw Ahab in all his fatal pride (553-54).

With great fanfare and dramatic assurance, Ahab successfully replaces the impotent compass needle with one fully magnetic and pointing true north. Ishmael questions whether some of his captain's movements were displayed to intensify his control of the crew. Ahab takes full advantage of his repair to impress the whalemen so to fortify their courage in the hunt. In the process, however, he reveals an even keener self-pride both in "scorn" and "triumph." Ishmael calls it "a fatal pride" that points our compass to what he fails to accomplish.

Bravado can overwhelm and consume us in certain life situations when a skill we possess places us at the center of attention. A more authentic self may reveal a shadow side of who one is. Inflation often breaks down the borderline between who we appear to be and who we are. Our psychological tipping point may be in the breaths that follow our own highest sense of self-importance where the social compass needle points to us alone. A Fateful Pride can blind us to our limits.

Meditation

How do you attend to your own inflation when you see it clearly?

October 30. Chapter 125: The Log and Line

"Hands off from that holiness! Where sayest thou Pip was, boy?"

"Astern there, sir, astern. Lo! lo!"

"And who art thou, boy? I see not my reflection in the vacant pupils of thy eyes. Oh God! that man should be a thing for immortal souls to sieve through! Who art thou, boy?"

"Bell-boy, sir; ship's crier; ding, dong, ding! Pip! Pip! Pip! One hundred pounds of clay reward for Pip . . . ."

"Here, boy; Ahab's cabin shall be Pip's home henceforth, while Ahab lives. Thou touchest my inmost centre, boy; thou art tied to me by cords woven by my heart-strings. Come, let's down" (557).

Ahab discerns in the figure of the now-deranged Pip, who has been dismantled by his experience bobbing alone on the ocean where a vision of the deep's creatures infiltrated him, revealing an image of himself. The captain senses in the abandoned cabin boy who spouts gibberish a true reflection of himself, a twin, in the spirit of Narcissus gazing on himself, one who might just grasp his own sunken soul. But Pip's vacant eyes are absent his captain's reflection. The two as one will now share Ahab's cabin in a fantastic marriage, till death do they part.

When we meet and come to know someone who we feel is our brother or sister because we share a deep compatibility, such intimacy allows for an opportunity to reflect on some of our own traits as in a mirror starkly. The other person is and is not us. But some duplicated presence affords us a deeper insight into our own motives and manner of being. Our double is the Other of ourselves objectified in the world. Through the Other we can engage a deeper pattern of self-reflection. But we must guard against its turning to self-fixation.

Meditation

Describe a relationship in which you felt at one with Another as your reflection or intimate double or even "soul-mate."

October 31. Chapter 126: The Life-Buoy

[H]e had not long been at his perch, when a cry was heard—a cry and a rushing—and looking up, they saw a falling phantom in the air; and looking down, a little tossed heap of white bubbles in the blue of the sea.

The life-buoy—a long slender cask—was dropped from the stern, where it always hung obedient to a cunning spring; but no hand rose to seize it, and the sun having long beat upon this cask, it had shrunken, so that it slowly filled . . . . and the studded iron-bound cask followed the sailor to the bottom, as if to yield him his pillow, though in sooth but a hard one (560).

Preparation for the sightings of Moby Dick initiates a sacrifice: one sailor falls to the sea, followed immediately by a worthless life-buoy diminished by the sun and leaking all around. These two descend into the deep, one a "falling phantom," the other a worthless device intended to save lives but is now no more than a hard pillow for the whale watcher to permanently rest his head upon. This sequence will be reversed at novel's end when both Ishmael and a secure life-buoy spring and breach out of the sea to salvage the whaler-poet to tell his tale.

Initiation and sacrifice to inaugurate a major change in one's voyage, hunt, pilgrimage, or spiritual quest, suggests that the new journey must be paid for on some level in order to continue. Here, the fall of one promises the resurrection of its opposite. From disuse, the cask above shrinks to uselessness, like those heads Queequeg peddles in New Bedford; what once had value has diminished into insignificance. But its absence makes way for what is necessary to further the larger enterprise. Without the sacrifice, the journey may be end-stopped.

Meditation

When has the loss of a valued object allowed something else to emerge in its place so your life could continue to unfurl?

November 1. Chapter 126: The Life-Buoy

The lost life-buoy was now to be replaced; Starbuck was directed to see to it; but as no cask of sufficient lightness could be found, and as in the feverish eagerness of what seemed the approaching crisis of the voyage, all hands were impatient of any toil but what was directly connected with its final end . . . [so]they were going to leave the ship's stern unprovided with a buoy, when by certain strange signs and innuendoes Queequeg hinted a hint concerning his coffin.

"A life-buoy of a coffin!" cried Starbuck, starting.

"Rather queer, that, I should say," said Stubb.

"It will make a good enough one," said Flask, "the carpenter here can arrange it easily" . . . .

"Rig it, carpenter; do not look at me so—the coffin, I mean. Dost thou hear me? Rig it" (560-61).

The former life-buoy, dried from the sun, has sunk to the ocean's bottom, along with the phantom it was meant to save. Queequeg, healthy and whole once again, offers his coffin foot locker to replace it, in a gesture of generosity. It is an appropriate double since it combines life and death in one richly complex image. Created as a final resting place for the once-ailing islander, then transformed into his foot locker, it is once again transformed into a complete emblem of death and life, a saving object that will allow his brother, his double, Ishmael, to survive.

How something or someone can contain its opposite as a promissory note is one of life's deepest mysteries. We think of something crafted for one use transformed into one that runs contrary to the object's original intention. What at first portends and encapsulates death converts to a salvific presence to both sustain and renew life.

Meditation

When has the death of something or someone in your experience been the occasion for a major renewal of your or another's life?

November 2. Chapter 126: The Life-Buoy

"Cruppered with a coffin! Sailing about with a grave-yard tray! But never mind. We workers in woods make bridal bedsteads and card-tables, as well as coffins and hearses . . . . Hem! I'll do the job, now, tenderly. I'll have me—let's see—how many in the ship's company, all told? But I've forgotten. Any way, I'll have me thirty separate, Turk's-headed lifelines, each three feet long hanging all round to the coffin. Then, if the hull go down, there'll be thirty lively fellows all fighting for one coffin, a sight not seen very often beneath the sun! Come hammer, caulking-iron, pitch-pot, and marling-spike! Let's to it" (562).

Perth, the ship's carpenter, assumes the task of transforming Queequeg's coffin into a life-buoy double. A strange request he deems it, but he carries a philosophy that does not "ask the why and wherefore of our work." He sets to it, thinking that it might be able to save all aboard if the Pequod were to sink; he delightfully imagines how this one death/resurrection image could be sufficient in buoyancy to save the entire crew. It seems an impossible burden for the newly-minted mini-craft. Perth's creation will be something new under the sun. He calls to his companions, his tools, as he sets himself to the task "tenderly."

Each of us is at times given duties both within and beyond our skills to perform. We must draw a line at what tasks we are able and willing to tackle and which we allow to pass by. We may, like the carpenter, accept any and all jobs assigned to us, or we may occasionally pull up short from some because of moral, ethical or physical reasons or limits. We may also take on the task, find creative angles by which to accomplish it and make of it a work of personal art and achievement. Our own growth in life may require such moments.

Meditation

What kind of creative task have you refused? What task have you said yes to that challenged or exceeded your creative skills?

November 3. Chapter 127: The Deck

(Ahab to himself)
"There's a sight! There's a sound! The grey-headed wood-pecker tapping the hollow tree! Blind and dumb might well be envied now. See! that thing rests on two line-tubs, full of tow-lines. A most malicious wag, that fellow. Rat-tat! So man's seconds tick! Oh! how immaterial are all materials! What things real are there, but imponderable thoughts? Here now's the very dreaded symbol of grim death, by a mere hap, made the expressive sign of the help and hope of most endangered life. A life-buoy of a coffin! Does it go further?" (564).

Ahab's soliloquy carries several keen insights into his worldview. Fascinated by the paradox inherent in the construction of a coffin into a life-buoy, he ponders how immaterial is the world's matter. It does not preserve mortal life so much as it is home for eternity itself. Time and eternity mingle in his despairing imagination. He feels as if he has crossed over to the "dark side of earth" (564), away from the light of theory, which he holds suspect. In the hollow sound of the carpenter's hammer Ahab discovers the tick of time itself passing. He wonders if there is more to it than simply a transformed coffin.

We are made to deepen. The matter of the world can at certain moments fall away to yield what may feel imponderable, yet our spirit yearns for deeper, lower layers. At times of deep reflection, our fantasies can cluster into profound insights on the nature of our being. These precious moments of epiphany we might return to often to contemplate the truths they uncover. Something at the heart of the Christian myth may reside here, where death leads to life, not away from it. What is transformed may carry the miracle of resurrection and renewal.

Meditation

Describe a moment when some insight or truth about your own existence became clearer to you, crystallizing into a certainty.

November 4. Chapter 127: The Deck

(Ahab to himself)

"Can it be that in some spiritual sense the coffin is, after all, but an immortality-preserver! I'll think of that. But no, So far gone am I in the dark side of earth, that its other side, the theoretic bright one, seems but uncertain twilight to me. Will ye never have done, Carpenter, with that accursed sound? I go below; let me not see that thing here when I return again. Now, then, Pip, we'll talk this over; I do suck most wondrous philosophies from thee! Some unknown worlds must empty into thee!" (564-65).

Continuing with his soliloquy, Ahab develops his reflection, as does Narcissus in the most cogent myth of self-reflection. Something in the material world, the carpenter's task of transforming an object made for death into one that will sustain life, signals a deepening meditation. The hollow rat-a-tat of the hammer begins to unnerve him; it stirs up fantasies that fast become unendurable. He shakes himself free of this meditation by turning suddenly to Pip, whose own vision of the sea's immensity and of the fantastic creatures moving below the surface, including the miser-merman, Wisdom, brought him into madness. Ahab finds solace in the young cabin boy in contact with another world.

The highest takes solace in the lowest. Out of a certain madness comes wisdom. Seeking a deeper understanding, we may turn to the commonplace, the eccentric, the marginal and even the pathologized, for these can be the realms of soul-making. There truths unimagined before may haunt the depths. Life's revelation may erupt from the strangest sources; suddenly we inhabit a revelatory terrain. Such moments point us to how the madness of another may reflect our own nature.

Meditation

Where in life did you discover a truth in a most unusual source?

November 5. Chapter 128: *The Pequod Meets* the Rachel

Next day, a large ship, the Rachel, was descried, bearing directly down upon the Pequod, all her spars thickly clustering with men. At the time the Pequod was making good speed through the water; but as the broad-winged windward stranger shot nigh to her, the boastful sails all fell together as blank bladders that are burst, and all life fled from the smitten hull.

. . . .

"Hast seen the White Whale?"

"Aye, yesterday. Have ye seen a whale-boat adrift?"

"Throttling his joy, Ahab negatively answered this unexpected question;"

. . . .

The story told, the stranger Captain immediately went on to reveal his object in boarding the Pequod. He desired that ship to unite with his own in the search (566-67).

As the Pequod moves steadily toward the waters holding the White Whale, the Rachel descends on her with its own object of pursuit: the son of the ship's captain lost at sea pursuing a whale. Each seeks its own object of desire, one grieving the loss of a loved one, the other the vengeful assassination of its wounder. Love and hate mingle for a moment in the two captains' meeting: one sighting Moby Dick, the other seeing nothing of a whaleboat harboring the Rachel's son.

Love and hate, affection and acerbity conjoin in life, perhaps more frequently than we think. In love of what is lost comes a cry for communal support; in hate for what has afflicted us arises a negation of community. In hate grows obsession; in love, yearning. In love is a request for indulgence and support from others; in hate is monomania.

Meditation

When has both love and hate mingled in an act or decision you made?

November 6. Chapter 28: *The Pequod Meets* the Rachel

"My boy, my own boy is among them. For God's sake—I beg, I conjure"—here exclaimed the stranger Captain to Ahab, who thus far had but icily received his petition. "For eight-and-forty hours let me charter your ship—I will gladly pay for it; and roundly pay for it—if there be no other way—for eight-and-forty hours only—only that—you must, oh, you must, and you *shall* do this thing."

. . . .

Meantime, now the stranger was still beseeching his poor boon of Ahab; and Ahab still stood like an anvil, receiving every shock, but without the least quivering of his own.

"I will not go," said the stranger, "till you say *aye* to me. Do to me as you would have me do to you in the like case. For *you* too have a boy, Captain Ahab, though but a child . . ." (567-68).

Desperate in his grief, Captain Gardiner pours himself on the mercy and shared humanity of Ahab's power to double the grieving father's chance of locating his lost son. He asks to lease the Pequod for two days for his search, his son now lost in his own search for whales. But Ahab remains as unmoved as an anvil repeatedly rung by a hammer, so hardened is he to any outside interruption that would deflect him from his unconditional victory over Moby Dick. Nowhere is he more inhumane than this moment of rejecting the pleas of a grieving parent.

Life's purposes, desires, and strivings for achievement can narrow our moral vision and constrict our humanity into a selfish purpose. We raise our intent to the level of a god in our midst to worship at the altar of its demands. We can sacrifice all of greater value in our closed pursuit. Much of what makes us human can be sacrificed in our quest.

Meditation

Recall a pursuit you engaged that blocked from view all other aspects of your life as well as the needs of others.

November 7. Chapter 128: *The Pequod Meets* the Rachel

Hurriedly turning, with averted face, he descended into his cabin, leaving the strange captain transfixed at this unconditional and utter rejection of his so earnest suit. But starting from his enchantment, Gardiner silently hurried to the side; more fell than stepped into his boat, and returned to his ship.

Soon the two ships diverged their wakes; and long as the strange vessel was in view, she was seen to yaw hither and thither at every dark spot, however, small, on the sea . . . .

But by her still halting course and winding, woful way, you plainly saw that this ship that so wept with spray, still remained without comfort. She was Rachel, weeping for her children, because they were not (569).

The biblical story of Rachel weeping for her lost children overlays and shapes the confrontation of the two captains; one liquid in grief, the other steeled in his refusal to offer aid. One discerns from the zig-zag patterns of her hunt how aggrieved is the Rachel as she responds to the vaguest motion or unusual shadow on the waters. The ship itself weeps with the salty sea spray after her captain stumbles, dazed and in disbelief at Ahab's iron refusal of any compassion for his son's plight. Cast adrift once more, the Rachel blindly seeks her child in the wilderness of water.

Refused solace or aid when we feel ourselves powerless in the face of life's crises, our suffering magnifies. The human connection forged so swiftly by the presence of compassion for others more fortunate who offer us aid, or aid that we offer those grieving, establishes a community of care that is salvific in its ability to blunt the original trauma's power. When we are denied compassion, care or aid, we may easily slide into a full and dangerous despondency and zig-zag without direction.

Meditation

When have you offered aid to those rendered helpless or impotent?

November 8. Chapter 129: The Cabin

(*Ahab moving to go on deck; Pip catches him by the hand to follow.*)
"Lad, lad, I tell thee thou must not follow Ahab now. The hour is coming when Ahab would not scare thee from him, yet would not have thee by him. There is that in thee, poor lad, which I feel too curing to my malady. Like cures like; and for this hunt, my malady becomes my most desired health. Do thou abide below here, where they shall serve thee, as if thou wert the captain. Aye, lad, thou shalt sit here in my own screwed chair; another screw to it, thou must be" (570).

At first wishing Pip to be with him at all times after the cabin boy fell overboard and saw the wondrous sights of the abyss, Ahab now loosens the ties between himself and the crazed boy who carries something of the sea's deep mysteries within. Ahab further isolates himself in the cocoon of his own creation; his words echo Christ's own to his apostles that soon he would not be seen. While Pip is not a mirror for his malady, Ahab realizes, after citing philosopher Heraclitus' insight that "like cures like," that his malady reflects his "most desired health." He asks Pip to double for him in his cabin, to become the substitute or phantom captain, to occupy his chair and his authority.

Shedding what had at one time been essential to us comes in moments of renewed reflection. What serves us in one stage of our voyage may become a hindrance as we shift and tack into other winds of being. We may find ourselves realizing that what at one moment was curative has now become a malady. Letting go of what is necessary is always a sign of awakening and an acknowledgement that change has occurred wherein we divest ourselves of what is outmoded. Becoming fully conscious of our life tensions is a signal of development.

Meditation

When have you jettisoned something or someone you once needed because it no longer serves where you are in life?

November 9. Chapter 129: The Cabin

"Oh good master, master, master!"

"Weep so, and I will murder thee! have a care, for Ahab too is mad. Listen, and thou wilt often hear my ivory foot upon the deck, and still know that I am there. And now I quit thee. Thy hand!—Met! True art thou, lad, as the circumference to its centre. So; God for ever bless thee; and if it come to that,—God, for ever save thee, let what will befall". . . .

(Ahab goes; Pip steps one step forward.)

Hist! above there, I hear ivory—Oh, master! master! I am indeed down-hearted when you walk over me. But there I'll stay . . ." (570-71).

Ahab continues to address himself in the third person, as if he had vacated himself as he vacates Pip. In such a distant voice he is kinder to no one as he is to his cabin boy. The captain's voice is in a different register; it contains tender care for him and acknowledges the truth of Pip "as the circumference to its centre." Pip is the circumference to Ahab's center, forming a geometry that runs through the entire narrative. For himself, Pip hears but no longer sees, his Captain when his ivory leg strikes the boards of the deck above Pip's head. From circumference to center, they shift to a hierarchy of above and below through sound.

When we part from someone loved, what may emerge is another dimension of relating to what we've said farewell to. What residue remains is the memory of the loving relationship which may not be enough to sustain us. The once rich relationship now resounds in our memory as an important legacy of the myth that continues to form within. Losing who has sustained us may create even further isolation.

Meditation

Describe a shifted and now distant relationship with someone you were once intimate with. What quality of memory remains of it?

November 10. Chapter 130. The Hat

And now that at the proper time and place, after so long and wide a pre-liminary cruise, Ahab,—all other whaling waters swept—seemed to have chased his foe into an oceanfold, to slay him the more securely there; now, that he found himself hard by the very latitude and longitude where his tormenting wound had been inflicted . . . . now it was that there lurked a something in the old man's eyes, which it was hardly sufferable for feeble souls to see (572).

Such an important moment on the voyage occurs when Ahab returns the Pequod in both time and space to the very locale of his original dismem-berment. It is a signal instance in the hunt for the White Whale that only the day before was reported to have been seen by Captain Gardiner of the Rachel. Ishmael leaves open-ended what crosses over the captain's eyes on returning to the genesis of his original wound. The passage suggests that just this moment and this place has a propriety now in the voyage, having heard of Moby Dick's appearance as well as his soon-to-emerge majestic bulk as the Pequod bears down on its elusive prey.

Returning to a place of deep wounding, dismemberment and affliction can be devastating and incarcerating as we become captive once more to the original trauma. It can, however, also be an opportunity for liberation, of freeing ourselves from the shackles of what has caused a sustained re-sentment, revenge, bitterness or a partly-lived life. Wounds' origins consist as well of moments of great promise and healing potential or continued suppuration of the original infirmity.

We may continue to choose to keep the wound open, oozing, and thus more powerful, perhaps, than the original violation.

Meditation

Describe a significant experience of returning to the place of a deep afflic-tion. What were the consequences of this visitation?

November 11. Chapter 130: The Hat

In this foreshadowing interval, too, all humor, forced or natural, vanished. Stubb no more strove to raise a smile; Starbuck no more strove to check one. Alike, joy and sorrow, hope and fear, seemed ground to finest dust, and powdered, for the time, in the clamped mortar of Ahab's iron soul. Like machines, they dumbly moved about the deck, ever conscious that the old man's despot eye was on them (572).

Ahab settles deeper into a dismal gloom in the charged space and atmosphere of his wounding, now grown raw. His demeanor suggests that the original dismembering has re-opened and become revitalized , all because of the growing proximity of the White Whale before him and the original affliction behind him. All human emotion drains from each of the crew; they become a block of mechanical workers devoid of life or joy, as if each carries within himself the dismembered embittered self of their wounded leader. Ahab has magnified his full presence to that of a seared tyrant overseeing his vassals' every move. Yet he too is being watched, we learn, by the Parsee, whose hollowed eyes, "wan but wondrous" (573), track Ahab's every motion.

The power of a leader rests in his/her presence to create a mood or a collective disposition in the souls of all who are led by him/her. The spirit of each member of a particular tribe, city or nation can be re-formed or deformed by its leader's demeanor and emotional presence. One's leader can corrupt the souls of his/her citizens or raise them to new levels of hope and instill new courage into even the most timid among them. The role of a king, president or vicar carries great moral and ethical responsibility. The wounds leaders carry into their roles affect their capacity to lead and may afflict their subjects.

Meditation

Have you been placed in a leadership role? What did your own woundedness have on your abilities to perform your duties?

November 12. Chapter 130: The Hat

Nor, at any time, by night or day could the mariners now step upon the deck, unless Ahab was before them; either standing in his pivot-hole, or exactly pacing the planks between two undeviating limits,—the main-mast and the mizzen . . . .

He ate in the same open air; that is, his two only meals,—breakfast and dinner: supper he never touched; nor reaped his beard; which darkly grew all gnarled, as unearthed roots of trees blown over, which still grow idly on at naked base, though perished in the upper verdure (573).

Ahab's presence becomes, in this space of dismemberment and its lacerating memory in which the White Whale is present in his imagination, more mechanical, less human. He refuses to go below, intent instead on exacting a continuous ritual vigil in hopes of confronting once more Moby Dick near their battle's original site. His world constricts, his emotions narrow, his eating curbs, and his humanness largely dissolves. His own appearance he cares nothing for; a single-minded monomania infects all his parts, his routine hardens to unyielding steel and his relation to the natural order becomes that of a downed tree with gnarly roots and dying leaves.

Possession by one task, one idea, one thought, one emotion or one intention can contract one to a death in life. Qualities of one's fuller life expire as the one important act or thought sucks away everything extraneous to itself. Life ceases in its rich variety, a mechanism takes command and rules, much as a despot might demand unconditional allegiance. The soul surrenders to a self-imposed tyranny; in the process one sacrifices all semblance of freedom. The wound itself may enlarge to the size of a whale as one spirals down into total self-absorption.

Meditation

When in your life were you possessed by a particular identity that consumed you? Did something break you free?

November 13. Chapter 130: The Hat

Now, the first time Ahab was perched aloft; ere he had been there ten minutes; one of those red-billed savage sea-hawks which so often fly incommodiously close round the manned mast-heads of whalemen in these latitudes; one of these birds came wheeling and screaming round his head in a maze of untrackably swift circlings. Then it darted a thousand feet straight up into the air; then spiralized downwards, and went eddying again round his head.

But with his gaze fixed upon the dim and distant horizon, Ahab seemed not to mark this wild bird . . . (575).

As Ahab fixes himself with firmest fortitude on the deck. his gaze hammered to the horizon in anticipation of seeing the White Whale, a wild bird circles him in what some of the crew believe carries "some sort of cunning meaning" (575). The captain remains undistracted by its whirling, screaming flight, intent on attacking his head. Portents swirl around any action or event as the air seems charged with a cosmic energy. Unperturbed, Ahab remains resolute in his grooved gaze and behaves as if the bird did not exist.

Fixed almost obsessively on one image, vision or intention, one may be impervious to all of life's invitations, invasions or intrusions. Frozen in a mind set, paralyzed by one idea or purpose, or obsessed with pursuing and acquiring an object or goal, the soul can deflect and deny all other diversions or necessities of life, both those that threaten and those that emanate joy. Like Ahab, we can be incarcerated by a drive and halted by what provokes us to achievement. Fixity then blinds us to the subtle range of life's gifts or interests that would add richness. Like Narcissus, we remain self-fixated by a watery image.

Meditation

When have you been so engulfed by an intention or desire that it eclipsed all other dimensions of life?

November 14. Chapter 130: The Hat

"Your hat, your hat, sir!" suddenly cried the Sicilian seaman, who being posted at the mizen-mast-head, stood directly behind Ahab, though somewhat lower than his level, and with a deep gulf of air dividing them.

But already the sable wing was before the old man's eyes; the long hooked bill at his head: with a scream, the black hawk darted away with his prize . . . .

Ahab's hat was never restored; the wild hawk flew on and on with it; far in advance of the prow: and at last disappeared; while from the point of that disappearance, a minute black spot was dimly discerned, falling from that vast height into the sea (575-76).

As Ahab's gaze remains fixed on the horizon, the black hawk, emboldened, swoops down and hovers before the captain's face with talons poised above his head. The bird snatches his slouched hat and carries it to the horizon Ahab's gaze has been surveying. Not until it has all but disappeared from his vision does the thieving bird release the hat into the ocean, appearing as it falls perhaps no larger than the black punctuation that ends this sentence. A part of Ahab has been stolen and returned to the sea in the vicinity of his original dismemberment. The black dot of his hat may remind us of Pip's tiny head in the ocean.

Omens appear for and to those who are predisposed to discern them. They can appear as probes, both positive and negative, to usher in a future event accompanied by a mysterious yet palpable meaning. As portents, omens inflict the present with the future, give one a glimpse of something that is not yet, and open one to future possibilities, however briefly glimpsed.

Meditation

Point to an omen, a portent, or some sign in the present that was eventually realized more fully in the future. What in your life shifted?

November 15. Chapter 131: *The Pequod Meets* The Delight

The intense Pequod sailed on; the rolling waves and days went by; the life-buoy-coffin still lightly swung; and another ship, most miserably misnamed the Delight, was descried. As she drew nigh, all eyes were fixed upon her broad beams, called shears . . . serving to carry the spare, unrigged or disabled boats.

. . . .

"Hast seen the White Whale?"

"Look!" replied the hollow-cheeked captain from his taffrail; and with his trumpet he pointed to the wreck.

"Hast killed him?"

"The harpoon is not yet forged that ever will do that," answered the other, sadly glancing upon a rounded hammock on the deck . . . (577).

In the waters that Moby Dick inhabits, more signs of his wake appear, revealing his destruction. The Delight is a battered ship with one dead crew member and four others who are already buried at sea. The White Whale sheared five whalemen from her, traumatizing both captain and crew. Ahab approaches them soon after the deadly skirmish, anxious to know if the crew had successfully slain his object of pursuit. The captain's traumatic rejoinder is that no one is capable.

Such onslaughts in life are capable of shattering our resolve and fortitude to cope with an event that leaves us crushed and dismembered. The captain and his crew are both wounded and dispirited by a force of nature whose power seems boundless. We may feel the absolute value of life itself in simply surviving, as well as the grief of enormous loss, leaving one defeated and broken. When we confront our own White Whale, we sense the imminent danger of such power and authority that can breach with unanticipated fury to tear a hole in our life.

Meditation

When has enormous loss fundamentally changed you?

November 16. Chapter 131: *The Pequod Meets* The Delight

"Only *that* one I bury; the rest were buried before they died; you sail upon their tomb." Then turning to his crew—"Are ye ready there? place the plank then on the rail, and lift the body; so then—Oh! God"—advancing towards the hammock with uplifted hands—"may the resurrection and the life—"

"Brace forward! Up helm!" cried Ahab like lightning to his men.

But the suddenly started Pequod was not quick enough to escape the sound of the splash that the corpse soon made as it struck the sea; not so quick, indeed, but that some of the flying bubbles might have sprinkled her hull with their ghostly baptism (578).

The Pequod rests close to the Delight as a witness to the ritual burial of one crew member killed by the White Whale. The two ships share an intimate moment side by side as the Delight's captain raises a benediction, praying for the man's resurrection. The dead is lifted vertically on the plank that reminds us of Christ's cross being elevated after he was nailed to it. Ahab sees instantly that the Pequod is about to be sullied by the splashing water, a baptism of the dead. Fearing a bad omen, he tries in vain to distance his ship from the water rising up when the man enters the sea. The Pequod is tainted by the dead's waters.

Ominous incidents, as we interpret them for ourselves, occur on occasion in our lives. Forebodings can attend even the most commonplace events. Glimpses into unforeseen consequences of our actions or those of others may bubble up without provocation or warning. We read events as portents and assign meanings that help us comprehend them. We may also look back on our life events and discern their origins in a previous incident. Fate seems ever-present.

Meditation

When has an initial portentous event in your life completed itself in a future situation, condition or realization?

November 17. Chapter 132: The Symphony

It was a clear steel-blue day. The firmaments of air and sea were hardly separable in that all pervading azure; only, the pensive air was transparently pure and soft, with a woman's look, and the robust and man-like sea heaved with long, strong, lingering swells, as Samson's chest in his sleep.

Hither and thither, on high, glided the snow-white wings of small, un-speckled birds; these were the gentle thoughts of the feminine air; but to and fro in the deeps, far down in the bottomless blue, rushed mighty leviathans, sword-fish, and sharks; and these were the strong, troubled, murderous thinkings of the masculine sea (579).

Some portentous murdering life forms lurk just below the calm azure of a benevolent sea's skin. Masculine and feminine forces, presences and energies create their own organic cosmos in a symphonic whole of sky and sea; coalescence is their consequence. The visible appearances of nature's forces hide a deeper, more treacherous reality: the gliding phantoms of powerful primal life energies akin to thought mustered by the musings of the masculine waters. The normal attributes of sky as masculine and the sea as feminine are here inverted as the Pequod approaches the White Whale's haunting depths.

In such a lyric description of nature's benevolence as well as her treacherous creatures swirling invisibly below the surface, is an entire worldview written with great economy. Taking in and acknowledging both realities offers an image of unsentimental wholeness that does not blink from the reality of "murderous thinkings" of the sea. Holding the tension of these two enormous forces, both in complement and in opposition, creates a rich, overarching image of nature's primal power.

Meditation

Think of the passage above in relation to your own interior life. What analogies emerge that may link the two worlds for you?

November 18. Chapter 132: The Symphony

Tied up and twisted; gnarled and knotted with wrinkles; haggardly firm and unyielding; his eyes glowing like coals, that still glow in the ashes of ruin; untottering Ahab stood forth in the clearness of the morn; lifting his splintered helmet of a brow to the fair girl's forehead of heaven.

Oh, immortal infancy, and innocency of the azure! Invisible winged creatures that frolic all round us! Sweet childhood of air and sky! how oblivious were ye of old Ahab's close-coiled woe! . . .

Slowly crossing the deck from the scuttle, Ahab leaned over the side and watched how his shadow in the water sank and sank to his gaze, the more and the more that he strove to pierce the profundity (579-80).

Such a changed tone from earlier chapters appears as Ishmael's lyric description reveals how Ahab is in a transformative mood, becoming more with the natural order while leaving behind the acerbic world of revenge. He seems on the brink of yielding to a more gentle power even as he continues to carry in his head "that burnt-out crater of his brain" (580) and a splintered brow. Like a cinder he burns in a fever of profound pursuit; like Narcissus, he peers into the clear ocean's waters and observes his shadowed double sinking to his gaze; he clings to an unquenchable wish to penetrate the mystery of life itself.

Fevered to exhaustion by obsessions can consume us; we can be swallowed by a simple intention, desire and complete willfulness so there is nothing left but a hollow-eyed madness that devours our life. Such is the fierce power of single-mindedness that can incubate, incarcerate and even incinerate us, such that all freedom evaporates in the heat of longing. We may curl into "close-coiled" pain and desire, consuming one's self and those who surround him or her.

Meditation

Has an obsession at one point in your life threatened to devour you?

November 19. Chapter 132: The Symphony

But the lovely aromas in that enchanted air did at last seem to dispel, for a moment, the cankerous thing in his soul. That glad, happy air, that winsome sky, did at last stroke and caress him; the step-mother world, so long cruel—forbidding—now threw affectionate arms round his stubborn neck . . . [and] she could yet find it in her heart to save and to bless. From beneath his slouched hat Ahab dropped a tear into the sea; nor did all the Pacific contain such a wealth as that one wee drop (580).

Such a remarkable moment of unconditional intimacy between Nature's benevolent bounty and Ahab's wounded body. Not the dismembering force of Nature in the form of a whale but the caressing balm of a winsome air strokes the vibrant captain's being. Now something melts in him as it had in Ishmael so many pages ago. Blessings and healing energies emanate from Nature's mothering that builds in Ahab a softening that extracts a tear from him to mix his salty water with the briny Pacific. This moment of mutual and affectionate connection creates a "we(e)" drop, not an "I" drop in a communal confluence of emotions and shared presences.

Disconnected, alienated and separated are conditions we enter into and out of in a rhythm all our lives. But to come to a point of full acknowledgement that we are one with all, when the illusions of autonomy are snuffed out, is a moment of sweet freedom that liberates us from all trickeries of independence. Nature's own stillness heals one into wholeness with all other created life and non-life in a symphony of sympathy. Peace and serenity are its rich offshoots. A sense of blessedness descends on troubled souls to melt one into one's full humanity in communion with the healing balm of a benevolent world.

Meditation

Have you experienced a oneness with Nature and all others?

November 20. Chapter 132: The Symphony

Starbuck saw the old man; saw him, how he heavily leaned over the side; and he seemed to hear in his own true heart the measureless sobbing that stole out of the centre of the serenity around. Careful not to touch him, or be noticed by him, he yet drew near to him, and stood there.

Ahab turned.

"Starbuck!"

"Sir."

"Oh, Starbuck! It is a mild, mild wind, and a mild looking sky. On such a day—very much such a sweetness as this—I struck my first whale— a boy-harpooneer of eighteen! . . . Forty years of continual whaling! forty years of privation and peril, and storm-time! forty years on the pitiless sea! . . . for forty years to make war on the horrors of the deep! . . . I have not spent three ashore" (580).

Starbuck instantly senses some human qualities shading his captain when he leans over the ship's side to contribute one tear to the ocean's bounty to intermix his nature with hers. He draws closer to the captain in human sympathy. Serenity, not scathing rage, now surrounds Ahab, making him vulnerable, perhaps, to alternative actions. Now with a community of one other to share his history with, he opens himself to a nostalgic moment to recollect and trace his past path that led him for forty years wandering across ocean deserts.

When we find ourselves under the right weather conditions, some portal in us may gradually or suddenly open; in our human vulnerability and hunger for community we authentically reclaim what we had lost, where we were, where our destiny began to flow but perhaps clotted over time. In these instances we retrieve something of our life's vitality.

Meditation

Recall a benefit when you opened your past life to another.

November 21. Chapter 132: The Symphony

"Why this strife of the chase? why weary, and palsy the arm at the oar, and the iron, and the lance? how the richer or better is Ahab now? . . . Here, brush this old hair aside; it blinds me, that I seem to weep . . . . I feel deadly faint, bowed, and humped, as though I were Adam, staggering beneath the piled centuries since Paradise . . . . Close! stand close to me, Starbuck; let me look into a human eye; it is better than to gaze into sea or sky; better than to gaze upon God. By the green land; by the bright hearthstone! this is the magic glass, man; I see my wife and child in thine eye" (581).

Having suffered a deepening and more painful isolation from humanity as a consequence of his dismembered body and splintered soul on the cusp of confronting the White Whale, Ahab gazes outward for a closer look at his life in pursuit of the dismemberer. Instead of a mono-maniacal vision, he sees his own tormented humanity signaled from Adam on down to the present. Gazing into the orb of another's eye, however, Ahab reestablishes his soul with the larger human family through the images of hearth and home. Exhausted from his life's fierce tension, he yearns to melt, as Ishmael did early on, in the compassion willingly offered by his first mate; he reconnects with his own humanity.

Moments of purest clarity may visit us at any time in our life's pilgrimage. We turn back to gaze on our history and discern it with a depth perception missing before. We may see into our soul's abyss and recognize the nucleus of what has been driving us to destruction, what has palsied us in our pursuits. Perhaps we stretch out our hands to grasp the life-buoy of another; that one other suffices. Nature's abundant bounty can thaw our hearts and lift us out of self-absorption.

Meditation

Have you been pulled back from the brink of destruction by turning to the compassion of another, or has one turned to you for survival?

November 22. Chapter 132: The Symphony

"Oh, my Captain! my Captain! noble soul! grand old heart, after all! why should any one give chase to that hated fish! Away with me! let us fly these deadly waters! let us home! Wife and child, too, are Starbuck's—wife and child of his brotherly, sisterly, play-fellow youth; even as thine, sir, are the wife and child of thy loving, longing, paternal old age! Away! let us away!—this instant let me alter the course! How cheerily, how hilariously, O my Captain, would we bowl on our way to see old Nantucket again! I think, sir, they have some such mild blue days, even as this, in Nantucket" (581).

Starbuck seizes the moment in the midst of Ahab's grand epiphany and softened heart, which have separated him momentarily from the chains of wound and vengeance incarcerating him in his own emotional gaol. His first mate conjures for his Captain images of home, of *nostos*, of home-coming, so to lure the ship back to its origin. Overjoyed by his Captain's *metanoia*, his change of heart, Starbuck is prepared to pivot the ship's direction towards Nantucket, to deflect the present and to steer towards their respective families and climate that duplicates the present mild day of the heart.

A change of heart can be a miracle in the life of one bent on self-destruction that may affect only one person or an entire nation. Leaders will often confuse their personal desires with a more expansive common good by transposing the former on to the latter. In a moment of breakthrough, however, one may enjoy a moment of clear-hearted vision, especially when mirrored back to the person through the humanity of another. The heart may need only one witness for it to believe in radical change to occasion an instant of grace.

Meditation

When have you facilitated or witnessed the shift in another by helping to return that person to sanity and a feeling of serenity?

November 23. Chapter 132: The Symphony

"What is it, what nameless, inscrutable, unearthly thing is it; what cozening, hidden lord and master, and cruel, remorseless emperor commands me; that against all natural lovings and longings, I so keep pushing, and crowding, and jamming myself on all the time; recklessly making me ready to do what in my own proper, natural heart, I durst not so much as dare? Is Ahab Ahab? Is it I, God, or who that lifts this arm? But if the great sun move not of himself; but is an errand boy in heaven; nor one single star can revolve, but by some invisible power; how then can this one small heart beat; this one small brain think thoughts; unless God does that beating, does that thinking, does that living, and not I" (582).

Anguishing on the workings of the world as well as his place in the scheme of the created order, and wondering about the reality or illusion of free will, Ahab expresses one of his most profound meditations. He assumes that Starbuck is still his audience, but the first mate has already "stolen away" (582). Nonetheless, Ahab's confounded sense of his own actions, what his identity is and Fate's play in any human action, prompts him to wonder if God is at the treadle of the loom of everything that occurs in life and that we are all instruments of an inscrutable and invisible order that orchestrates every thought and act.

In various periods of our lives we may pause to question some basic daily assumptions we live by: our sense of freedom, purpose, meaning, life trajectory or agent of a grand design. These deeply imaginal and philosophic ponderings may appear at moments of crucial transitions wherein the myth we are living takes on a different beat and rhythm. Such insistence can humiliate us or humble us.

Meditation

When were you brought to question your own identity and purpose in life? What new awareness were you brought to?

November 24. Chapter 132: The Symphony

"By heaven, man, we are turned round and round in this world, like yonder windlass, and Fate is the handspike. And all the time, lo! that smiling sky, and this unsounded sea! Look! see yon Albicore! who put it into him to chase and fang that flying-fish? Where do murderers go, man! . . . But it is a mild, mild wind, and a mild looking sky; and the air smells now, as if it blew from a far-away meadow; they have been making hay somewhere under the slopes of the Andes, Starbuck, and the mowers are sleeping among the new-mown hay" . . . .

Ahab crossed the deck to gaze over on the other side; but started at two reflected, fixed eyes in the water there, Fedallah was motionlessly leaning over the same rail (582-83).

Having given impassioned voice to his own existential bewilderment that signals a shifting imagination, one he hopes will grasp the reality he has been pursuing, Ahab migrates to the sensate order of nature—the mild wind, the smell of the air, the wildness of the sky—and for a moment is appeased by it. But the absent Starbuck is replaced by Ahab's dark double, Fedallah, when the captain crosses the deck to gaze, like Narcissus, into the ocean's depth; he finds himself looking into the fixed orbs of his own dark Queequeg. The change in realities from one side of the deck to the other is dramatic and conclusive.

Two realities seem to exist in any moment of consciousness: a visible material one alongside an invisible inscrutable one. The former conceals the latter and, except for those moments of keen perception when the veil is pulled back in a revelatory instant and the invisible powers of the world soul emerge as the reality behind the phenomenal world, it remains beneath the shifting waters of consciousness.

Meditation

Have you experienced a moment when the world's veil was pulled aside to allow you a glimpse of a second reality?

November 25. Chapter 133: The Chase—First Day

That night, in the mid-watch when the old man—as his wont at intervals—stepped forth from the scuttle in which he leaned, and went to his pivot-hole, he suddenly thrust out his face fiercely, snuffing up the sea air as a sagacious ship's dog will, in drawing nigh to some barbarous isle. He declared that a whale must be near. Soon that peculiar odor, sometimes to a great distance given forth by the living sperm whale, was palpable to all the watch . . . . Ahab rapidly ordered the ship's course to be slightly altered, and the sail to be shortened (584).

After months of cruising the seas and killing whales, Ahab and his crew have sailed into the odors of the White Whale. Fixed in his pivot hole, from which he can prescribe a 360 degree motion, Ahab, like a dog, the animal who in the biblical story of Ahab licked his blood after he was slain in battle, can smell his object of pursuit carried by the air. After destroying both compass and sextant, he now relies solely on his animal sense to uncover the animal he has pursued without pause. He is the first to scent his prey and will shortly be the first to perceive it. He then slightly recalibrates the ship's sails and course in order to hone in precisely on the smell's emanation. Animal now hunts animal.

The pivot hole we stand in, fixed in the world, is different for each of us. It can represent a spot of security, of familiarity as well as a belief, a way of perceiving, a fastness to a point of view or a goal we seek without compromise, as well as a place from which we gaze on and gauge our world. It is the pivot point of our personal myth. Perhaps we set ourselves in it through where we have been dismembered, afflicted and are thus most vulnerable. From it we snuff the world through the desires we have and the substances we pursue.

Meditation

Identify the pivot hole your life settles into every day, from where you turn to perceive your world from a unique and secure point of view.

November 26. Chapter 133: The Chase—First Day

All sail being set, he now cast loose the life-line, reserved for swaying him to the main royal-mast head; and in a few moments they were hoisting him thither, when, while but two thirds of the way aloft, and while peering ahead through the horizontal vacancy between the main-top-sail and top-gallant sail, he raised a gull-like cry in the air. "There she blows!—there she blows! A hump like a snow-hill! It is Moby Dick!" . . . .

From this height the whale was now seen some mile or so ahead, at every roll of the sea revealing his high sparkling hump, and regularly jetting his silent spout into the air (584-85).

Ahab, to improve his view, has himself hoisted up the mast to claim a bird's-eye view of what is moiling through the waters ahead of him. He is the first to spot the "snow hill hump" that identifies the White Whale, which Ahab names in the story's first instance when the image of the whale and its being named are joined in the double exclamation: "There she blows!" It is an instant of epiphany, of discovery and of a fierce excitement that shrouds the ship and its crew. Moby Dick seems indifferent to the ship's bearing down on it as it spouts within view.

The long yearned for moment of discovery, of achievement in finally perceiving tangibly the White Whale one pursues ushers in a gush of excitement and vibrant satisfaction as well as anticipation. Each of us pursues a distinct White Whale: what we fear, are attached to, been afflicted by, addicted to, or that completes us in some primal way. Perhaps ambivalence and excitement are the two spouts that blow at this moment, their spray engulfing us when our life constellates around the white hump of our desires.

Meditation

When has something long-pursued finally come within reach?

November 27. Chapter 133: The Chase—First Day

"And did none of ye see it before?" cried Ahab, hailing the perched men all around him.

"I saw him almost that same instant, sir, that Captain Ahab did, and I cried out," said Tashtego.

"Not the same instant; not the same, no, the doubloon is mine. Fate reserved the doubloon for me. *I* only, none of ye could have raised the White Whale first . . . . He's going to sound! In stunsails! Down top-gallant-sails! Stand by three boats . . . . So; steady, man, steady! There go flukes! No, no; only black water! . . . Lower me, Mr. Starbuck; lower, lower,—quick, quicker!" and he slid through the air to the deck (585).

Ahab retrieves the doubloon he had nailed to the main mast as dividend for being the first crew member to sight Moby Dick. While Tashtego timidly challenges Ahab, the captain remains resolute that he alone was first to spot the object of their pursuit. Now he cries to be lowered quickly into the whaleboat to bear down on his prey. He calls for quickness and no hesitation when he takes complete charge of the hunt and insists the men move with dispatch to conquer the whale he believes is fated to be destroyed. "I only" carries an isolation and arrogance; it also doubles the line from the Book of Job in the Epilogue: "And I only am escaped alone to tell thee" (615).

Obsessions are powerful and unrelenting. They cancel out all other concerns when the soul is engulfed in the maw of obsession. All is in its service, as if the fixation itself took the form of a White Whale. Little space exists between the obsession's energy and its object; the two are welded into one attitude and action. The only motive present is to satisfy the obsession's unconditional demand: to conquer what obsesses.

Meditation

When/where were you devoured by an obsession that you pursued unconditionally? What were the consequences?

November 28. Chapter 133: The Chase—First Day

Like noiseless nautilus shells, their light prows sped through the sea; but only slowly they neared the foe. As they neared him, the ocean grew still more smooth; seemed drawing a carpet over its waves; seemed a noon meadow, so serenely it spread. At length the breathless hunter came so nigh his seemingly unsuspecting prey, that his entire dazzling hump was distinctly visible, sliding along the sea as if an isolated thing, and continually set in a revolving ring of finest, fleecy, greenish foam. He saw the vast, involved wrinkles of the slightly projecting head beyond . . . . and on either hand bright bubbles arose and danced by his side (586).

Ishmael places the subjects of his narrative in the third person, as if to distance himself from too much subjectivity so he can describe what it was like to approach this divinely-inflected leviathan. As the whaleboats draw near, the seas suddenly calm and all danger and vulnerability dissolve into the scene's serenity. A playful quality enters Ishmael's description wherein the White Whale seems a land animal covered in fleece with a wrinkled forehead tracing the lines of its bulk. Bubbles dancing and celebrating the whale's motion belies the terrible energy it is capable of unleashing in an instant; it is a moment of hierophany, of revelation and bespeaks a mythic presence.

Drawing nigh a divine natural force like the dazzlingly White Whale can disarm and foster a feeling of safety. Spangled play replaces deep and fathomless power in nature's intelligence. Nature fears nothing and will respond to the presence of others with persistent indifference. Being so close to such power and destructive energy can be intoxicating, like dwelling at the lip of a volcano or on the peaks of tall mountains when the weather is wild, or battling to survive in a raging storm.

Meditation

Have you come close to the natural order in its disarming serenity?

November 29. Chapter 133: The Chase—First Day

A gentle joyousness—a mighty mildness of repose in swiftness, invested the gliding whale. Not the white bull Jupiter swimming away with ravished Europa clinging to his graceful horns; his lovely, leering eyes sideways intent upon the maid; with smooth bewitching fleetness, rippling straight for the nuptial bower in Crete; not Jove, not that great majesty Supreme! did surpass the glorified White Whale as he so divinely swam . . . .

—[O]n each bright side, the whale shed off enticings. No wonder there had been some among the hunters . . . allured by all this serenity, [who] had ventured to assail it; but had fatally found that quietude but the vesture of tornadoes (586).

One of the most mythically-laden passages in the epic appears to contrast and enhance the White Whale against the backdrop of Greek and Roman narratives that expand the experience of the whale's potent majesty. The word "divinely" equates Moby Dick with the sacred—a glorious presence erupting from the sea to reveal itself in calm repose. The prose is lyric, lavish and learned. The White Whale's calm outer appearance belies a tornadic fierceness that could be unleashed when attacked by men confused into thinking it was conquerable.

To be in the presence of a divine object, person or figure in Nature can overwhelm us by its beauty and potential ferocity. When Nature reveals her bounty and beauty as well as her fury, we may feel swept into a vortex of attraction and terror. Contradictory impulses or possibilities constellate when we connect to its mystery. Its force can bewilder and beguile as well as entice. Grand repose may erupt into a furious urge to unravel those who approach to subdue it.

Meditation

Have you experienced the natural order in such a way that you detected a sacred or divine presence?

November 30. Chapter 133: The Chase—First Day

And thus, through the serene tranquilities of the tropical sea, among waves whose hand-clappings were suspended by exceeding rapture, Moby Dick moved on, still withholding from sight the full terrors of his submerged trunk, entirely hiding the wrenched hideousness of his jaw. But soon the fore part of him slowly rose from the water; for an instant his whole marbleized body formed a high arch, like Virginia's Natural Bridge and warningly waving his bannered flukes in the air, the grand god revealed himself, sounded and went out of sight. Hoveringly halting, and dipping on the wing, the white sea-fowls longingly lingered over the agitated pool that he left (587).

Ishmael continues to struggle with language that is sufficiently elevated to capture the grandeur and might of what emerges as revelation from the depths: as a hierophany the White Whale emerges from a different clime. Concealed at first, it fully reveals itself arching stiffly, perhaps bringing its magnificent fluke in the air to signal its intention to dive deep. As if to leave an indelible image in its absence, "the grand god" emerges in its powerful presence, then vanishes as quickly as it appeared in a movement of graceful submersion, with its angelic sea birds hoveringly marking its absence by the agitated pool.

Revelation of mystery is a profound and sacred instance in any of our lives. What we may initially only half-glimpse can become fully present to inspire awe, respect and not a little terror in those who gaze upon it. With any presence that surfaces from below, a deep psychological importance companions it. We may be changed for the rest of our lives by such an apparition from the deep when it connects us, even for a moment, with the mysterious waters of our own depths.

Meditation

Has it ever occurred that the deepest part of your own being was disturbed and manifested as a consequence of a strange presence?

December 1. Chapter 133: The Chase—First Day

"The birds!—the birds! cried Tashtego.

In long Indian file, as when herons take wing, the white birds were now all flying towards Ahab's boat; and when within a few yards began fluttering over the water there, wheeling round and round, with joyous, expectant cries. Their vision was keener than man's; Ahab could discover no sign in the sea. But suddenly as he peered down and down into its depth, he profoundly saw a white living spot no bigger than a white weasel, with wonderful celerity, uprising, and magnifying as it rose, till it turned, and then there were plainly revealed two long crooked rows of white, glistening teeth, floating up from the undiscoverable bottom. It was Moby Dick's open mouth and scrolled jaw (587).

Whiteness above points to whiteness below; what is above is so below as the Greek philosopher Heraclitus claimed. The white birds flock around Ahab because the object of his pursuit is directly below in the depths. All gathers in anticipation when the White Whale slowly enlarges in bulk as it rushes toward the surface. Ahab discerns such mounting magnification when he looks, again like Narcissus, over the side and sees something of himself reflected in the whale. The crooked rows of teeth mark the whale's imperfection, as is Ahab's ivory leg. Both man and leviathan embody distortion, affliction and doubling.

What is below us, out of sight, submerged in life, may embody what we seek resting just out of our grasp. The manner in which at a certain point it magnifies to loom large in our consciousness may signal that the pursuit nears an end, that the object of our quest is almost attainable and that we are it. Such a moment in life can excite, paralyze and provoke wonder if the sustained pursuit has been worth the cost.

Meditation

What was your response when something/someone you pursued was finally recognized as in part a distorted double of your own nature?

December 2. Chapter 133: The Chase—First Day

Now, by reason of this timely spinning round the boat upon its axis, its bow, by anticipation, was made to face the whale's head while yet under water. But as if perceiving this stratagem, Moby Dick, with that malicious intelligence ascribed to him, sidelingly transplanted himself, as it were, in an instant, shooting his pleated head lengthwise beneath the boat . . . .

The bluish pearl-white of the inside of the jaw was within six inches of Ahab's head, and reached higher than that. In this attitude the White Whale now shook the slight cedar as a mildly cruel cat her mouse (588).

Ishmael's language is purposely open-ended: "As if perceiving his stratagem" and "malicious intelligence ascribed to him" are tentative phrases that could easily accommodate another reading, an alternative angle of interpretation, as is true of so many passages and images. What fantasy one carries of the White Whale will yield other definitions of its nature and motives. Some instinct or purpose, however, seems to guide it to an intimate connection with the captain, as if the whale had something to whisper to its dismembered antagonist. At once playful and menacing, Moby Dick sports and explores in a social exchange with its pursuer in an attitude that holds the entire crew bedazzled while it scrambles to reach the safety of the ship's stern.

What is it to have what one has sought, regardless of motive, when one now moves purposefully towards it? Does it rob us of purpose? Does it threaten with its yielding? Does it engender fear in its fortitude? Now the relationship may shift radically when the object of our pursuit begins gently to turn the tables and approach us on its terms, outside our control. We may in this moment decide to renegotiate our relation to it.

Meditation

When has something/someone you pursued turned to pursue you?

December 3. Chapter 133: The Chase—First Day

And now, while both elastic gunwales were springing in and out, as the whale dallied with the doomed craft in this devilish way; and from his body being submerged beneath the boat, he could not be darted at from the bows . . . . then it was that monomaniac Ahab, furious with this tantalizing vicinity of his foe, which placed him all alive and helpless in the very jaws he hated; frenzied with all this, he seized the long bone with his naked hands, and wildly strove to wrench it from its gripe. As now he thus vainly strove, the jaw slipped from him, the frail gunwales bent in, collapsed, and snapped as both jaws . . . . bit the craft completely in twain and locked themselves fast again in the sea . . . (588).

So close to the object of his protracted hunt, Ahab is nonetheless incapacitated by the out-of-reach whale, who holds him in thrall from a position of relative safety. Hand-to-head combat ensues; Moby Dick holds the whaleboat between its crooked jaws, paralyzing to impotence Ahab and his men. Ahab grasps the lower jaw to free the whaleboat from its grasp, but succeeds only in rousing the whale to snap the boat in two, sending all its occupants sprawling across the ocean's surface. The scene begins to double the initial dismemberment.

To be in contact with our pursued object or situation in life, yet have no power or control over it once achieved, leaves one powerless, frustrated and perhaps enraged. What we pursue and finally gain is itself no cause for celebration, for it may remain outside our control. Moreover, it may turn to attack us at such a critical juncture, leaving us further wounded, paralyzed and defenseless. The thought may arise at such a moment: has this pursuit been worth the sacrifice and the payoff? Might our life been better engaged with more worthy intentions?

Meditation

When have you been incapacitated by what you so keenly sought? Did you yield to it or continue your pursuit?

December 4. Chapter 133: The Chase: First Day

Ripplingly withdrawing from his prey, Moby Dick now lay at a little distance, vertically thrusting his oblong white head up and down in the billows; and at the same time slowly revolving his whole spindled body . . . .

But soon resuming his horizontal attitude, Moby Dick swam swiftly round and round the wrecked crew; sideways churning the water in his vengeful wake, as if lashing himself up to still another and more deadly assault. The sight of the splintered boat seemed to madden him, as the blood of grapes and mulberries cast before Antiochus's elephants in the book of Maccabees (589).

The allusion to the Book of Maccabees refers to King Antiochus V warring against Judas Maccabees in the area of Beth-zechariah wherein the two armies faced off for a brutal battle. The elephants of Antiochus are made drunk on grapes and mulberry wine to provoke them to fight fiercely (First Maccabees 6. 15-37. www.books.google.com/books).

Like another Old Testament King, Ahab has released the infinite powers of Nature on his own head and those of his army of whalemen. Ishmael interprets the leviathan's behavior in terms of rage and the impulse to assault the ship and all on it but couches it in the language of "as-if."

The object, intention or condition one has devoted great planning and energy in pursuing can continue to intensify as the pursued transforms into the pursuer. So great may be its revealed strength, prowess and cunning that we may question the wisdom that spawned the initial quest. When the fury of what one initially thought was conquerable emerges, we may learn for the first time what force one has riled from the deep: a far stronger or more formidable presence.

Meditation

Were you surprised by the resistant force of something or someone you wished to control or conquer?

December 5. Chapter 133: The Chase—First Day

"Sail on the whale!—Drive him off!"

The Pequod's prows were pointed; and breaking up the charmed circle, she effectually parted the White Whale from his victim. As he sullenly swam off, the boats flew to the rescue.

Dragged into Stubb's boat with blood-shot, blinded eyes, the white brine caking in his wrinkles; the long tension of Ahab's bodily strength did crack, and helplessly he yielded to his body's doom for a time, lying all crushed in the bottom of Stubb's boat, like one trodden under foot of herds of elephants. Far inland, nameless wails came from him, as desolate sounds from out ravines (590).

The ship intervenes to separate the two antagonists in this first round of conflict; it saves the Captain from perishing. The word "sullenly" is surely Ishmael's own projection on the whale, which was not able to crush its pursuer. Close to defeat, Ahab lies in a broken heap in Stubb's whaleboat, like a fish pulled from the baleful brine of the sea, caked with its bitter salty residue. Deep within Ahab arise the sounds of "nameless wails" with a conscious pun on "whales," as those same sounds in the natural order might arise from hollow ravines. The captain appears to despair of conquering his adversary in one round.

Crushed and dismembered by what we have pursued with fierce and single-eyed conviction in life can sound despair deep in the soul. We can be claimed by the elements that surround our object of pursuit, desire, revenge or necessity. Such a failed achievement can undo and dis-assemble us, leaving us broken in despair. The soul languishes in such a heaped, but perhaps necessary, condition. We may need to confront such a situation in our lives to bring us life, even if it threatens our life. We may choose to call off the pursuit or double our efforts.

Meditation

When were you capsized while pursuing what you wished to destroy?

December 6. Chapter 133: The Chase—First Day

"The harpoon," said Ahab, half way rising, and draggingly leaning on one bended arm—"is it safe?"

"Aye, sir, for it was not darted; this is it," said Stubb, showing it.

"Lay it before me;-- any missing men?"

"One, two, three, four, five;--there were five oars, sir and here are five men."

"That's good.—Help me, man; I wish to stand. So, so, I see him! there! there! going to leeward still; what a leaping spout!—Hands off from me! The eternal sap runs up in Ahab's bones again! Set the sail; out oars; the helm!" (590-91).

Regaining his strength, defiant and unyielding, Ahab catches his second wind. He has learned nothing of the whale's unmatched force and ferocity; he fails to deliberate on whether continuing the pursuit is a wise choice for him, his men and his ship. The captain pushes leeward, towards "a leaping spout," his marker, while ignoring what he might have learned from the previous encounter. Moby Dick has issued fair warning with his spout misting across the bow, but the captain, caught in the tentacles of his wounded body and pride, believes the outcome of another confrontation will yield different results.

In our life pursuits, prudence can save us from falling into such reckless obsession to gain the treasure--the grail of our desires--no matter the cost. We step over a boundary from which there may be no return. Continued pursuit with abandon is a form of suicide, even though the fantasy we continue to nurture promises victory. An insane madness becomes our biggest hook to tether us to our obstinate desire. Our lust for success can become a larger whale than the one we pursue.

Meditation

When in life did your survival become dispensable and negotiable?

December 7. Chapter 133: The Chase—First Day

"What soulless thing is this that laughs before a wreck? Man, man! did I not know thee brave as fearless fire (and as mechanical) I could swear thou wert a paltroon. Groan nor laugh should be heard before a wreck."

"Aye, sir," said Starbuck drawing near, "'tis a solemn sight; an omen, and an ill one."

"Omen? omen?—the dictionary! If the gods think to speak outright to man, they will honorably speak outright; not shake their heads, and give an old wives' darkling hint.—Begone! Ye two are the opposite poles of one thing; Starbuck is Stubb reversed, and Stubb is Starbuck; and ye two are all mankind; and Ahab stands alone among the millions of the peopled earth, nor gods nor men his neighbors!" (592).

Ahab chastises Stubb who he believes could be a base coward had he not seen him perform courageously as a whaleman. Stubb has just made a trivial joke out of the captain's wrecked whaleboat lying in splinters on the Pequod's deck. To Stubb's frivolous remark that leaves him in Ahab's sight intrudes Starbuck with a contrary observation: not only is the wreck the result of Moby Dick's destructive force, not to be looked upon lightly, but it also carries a portent of impending destruction. Between the two mates Ahab sees the bookends of humanity, while the captain himself stands alone, isolated and unique.

While not exactly or purely a Stubb or a Starbuck, their two impulses towards interpretation signal how an experience may assume meaning for each of us, enhanced by how we envision it, make sense of it, or force it to fit the contours of our narrative identity. We each allot a certain meaning to our experiences so they have an order and comprehension within a larger frame: our personal myth.

Meditation

In a crisis, what manner of interpreting it do you gravitate towards?

December 8. Chapter 134: The Chase—Second Day

[L]ike as this pilot stands by his compass, and takes the precise bearing of the cape at present visible, in order the more certainly to hit aright the remote, unseen headland, eventually to be visited, so does the fisherman, at his compass, with the whale . . . . the creature's future wake through the darkness is almost as established to the sagacious mind of the hunter, as the pilot's coast is to him . . . . And as the mighty iron Leviathan of the modern railway is so familiarly known in its every pace . . . . even so, almost, there are occasions when these Nantucketers time that other Leviathan of the deep, according to the observed humor of his speed . . . (594-95).

Ishmael creates an elaborate correspondence between a pilot taking measurement of a coast to more accurately assess where the yet unseen line is, and whalemen who can discern where the now invisible whale will appear by using his visible wake as a tangible marker to tack towards where he will soon appear. He equates this latter ingenious ability to calculate the unseen motion based on what is visible, to the clocks that gauge the locomotive as it approximates the time it is predicted to arrive at its next station. Land and sea—the fixed and the fluid--are grasped by the same calculus of measuring the unseen by means of the seen.

Some events in life we measure according to their wakes or ephemeral traces, while others more land-secure can be gauged with more precise mechanical timing, beginning from where they are or were, and proceeding to where they will be. Such is our constant attempt to control, predict and order our lives. Within the leviathans we track, however, more latitude for deviation would appear to be present because their watery field allows for both surface *and* depth.

Meditation

When was a life prediction accurate, when well off the mark?

December 9. Chapter 134: The Chase—Second Day

The ship tore on; leaving such a furrow in the sea as when a cannonball, missent, becomes a plough-share and turns up the level field.

"By salt and hemp!" cried Stubb, "but this swift motion of the deck creeps up one's legs and tingles at the heart. This ship and I are two brave fellows! . . . Ha, ha! we go the gait that leaves no dust behind!"

"There she blows—she blows!—she blows! right ahead!" was now the mast-head cry.

"Aye, aye!" cried Stubb, "I knew it—ye can't escape—blow on and split your spout, O whale! the mad fiend himself is after ye! blow your trump—blister your lungs!-- Ahab will dam off your blood . . ." (595).

Stubb's rich metaphors uttered in the increasing frenzy of the chase offer new angles of vision on what is at stake in the moment. He refers to the monomaniac captain as the "mad fiend" in unwavering pursuit of the spouting whale. He also seems to have entered the titanic image of his captain in claiming that Ahab will clog the blood of the White Whale as "a miller shuts his watergate upon the stream" (595). When Stubb mentions hemp rope, we recall Ahab's belief that only hemp can kill him. He believes he is safe from such a fatality while on the high seas.

Our pursuits carry great energy to spur us on beyond our normal limits; the more manic they are, the more frenzied our quests that can inflate us in a titanic way; we believe nothing is big enough to trump our desires. A turbulent titanism leads entire countries into war in pursuit of imagined dangers or when White Whales are fabricated as believable fictions whose cost to a nation in pursuit can be exhaustive.

Meditation

What has a primary life pursuit forced or led you to ignore or forget?

December 10. Chapter 134: The Chase—Second Day

The hand of Fate had snatched all their souls; and by the stirring perils of the previous day; the rack of the past night's suspense; the fixed, unfearing, blind, reckless way in which their wild craft went plunging towards its flying mark; by all these things, their hearts were bowled along. The wind that made great bellies of their sails and rushed the vessel on by arms invisible as irresistible; this seemed the symbol of that unseen agency which so enslaved them to the race (595-96).

As has been done before in descriptions of the Pequod, Ishmael's language suggests the craft has a life of its own driven wildly by Fate as it plunges toward the White Whale's vaporous spout. Like men caught in the strong webbing of Fate itself, the Pequod too crashes forward in the grip of invisible powers. Pulled by an unseen magnetic force, men and craft are like metal files all pulled fixedly in one direction. "Fixed" and "fixity" are words normally ascribed to Ahab; now all seem to surrender to the driving attraction towards Moby Dick's gleaming wake. "Wild" and "reckless" suggest a loss of all boundaries as the vortex of the whale pulls them irresistibly toward it. By addressing "their souls," Ishmael seems to grow further detached from the crew.

Relentless, accelerating, like the energy pull of an addiction, one may feel fated to continually repeat behavior that debilitates. A rush to final judgment does nothing to deter the iron-like trajectory of one's desires. No obstacle is too big to dismantle the pursuit of what has afflicted one, like a god that at once persecutes and seduces. Such is the potency and pull of the White Whale each of us pursues. Life may seem to have meaning only when we discern its vertical spout on the horizon.

No member of our race escapes the magnetic pull of Fate. Both the Fate of race and the race of Fate are constants.

Meditation

What life event or condition do you believe you were fated to enter?

December 11. Chapter 134: The Chase—Second Day

They were one man, not thirty. For as the one ship that held them all; though it was put together of all contrasting things—oak, and maple, and pine wood; iron, and pitch and hemp—yet all these ran into each other in the one concrete hull, which shot on its way, both balanced and directed by the long central keel; even so, all the individualities of the crew, this man's valor, that man's fear; guilt and guiltiness, all varieties were welded into oneness, and were all directed to that fatal goal which Ahab their one lord and keel did point to (596).

The passage creates a spiraling vortex down, turning and pulling all with it in a motion of co-inherence wherein diversity is subsumed by an over-ranging force of unity. No more is there individuality. Fate moves like a spiral, consolidating all paths into a welded whole. The collective trumps any separateness. Thirty becomes one in the strange calculus of a willful scheme. All are part of a fixed keel of Ahab's design; free will is swallowed by one monomaniacal obsession. Such is the gravitational pull of keen emotion when bonded to vengeful purpose.

Individuals as well as nations can have their wills and freedoms co-opted by a single tyrant whose obsessive grand design can seduce every member of its citizenry. By a leader's claiming a common energy and crying for a united response to it, a people can yield their foothold on the actual facts by falling head-first into the fictional and the mythic, whose truth or falsehood is subsumed by a mass hypnosis. Nothing can move such a fixed obsession; only in its wake might a cooler measured response expose the catastrophe for what it is. To be lorded over by tyrannous designs is a malicious form of slavery.

Meditation

Where and when have you witnessed a single purpose or obsession coerce an individual, a group or an entire population?

December 12. Chapter 134: The Chase—Second Day

The triumphant halloo of thirty buckskin lungs was heard, as—much nearer to the ship than the place of the imaginary jet, less than a mile ahead—Moby Dick bodily burst into view! For not by any calm and indolent spoutings; not by the peaceable gush of that mystic fountain in his head, did the White Whale now reveal his vicinity; but by the far more wondrous phenomenon of breaching. Rising with his utmost velocity from the furthest depths, the Sperm Whale thus booms his entire bulk into the pure element of air, and piling up a mountain of dazzling foam, shows his place to the distance of seven miles and more . . . . in some cases, this breaching is his act of defiance (596-97).

Like a divinity emerging from deep in the ocean's heavenly depths, the White Leviathan surfaces as a sacred apparition as it shoots vertically out of the water in a gesture of mystical splendor. The language conveys the presence of a massive revelation. As one, the crew witnesses the wonder and the power of a manifestation that is as mysterious as it is terrifying in its awful grandeur. Its foamy presence reveals itself from seven miles away to the whalemen; it marks itself as a white stain on the surface of blue water, defiant in its divine apotheosis.

In rare moments we may experience a phenomenon in nature that resonates a deeper spiritual, even mystical presence. We may feel fear, terror and fascination as we stand in silent awe at both its beauty and its destructive capacity. Connected to its natural element, we are yet separate from it when it evokes a supernatural manifestation in its concentrated power. It may be of such force that its display transforms us even as its memory forms a large fluke print in our imagination.

Meditation

When has the phenomenal world of nature offered a glimpse of a supernatural force or presence?

December 13. Chapter 134: The Chase—Second Day

"Aye, breach your last to the sun, Moby Dick!" cried Ahab, "thy hour and thy harpoon are at hand!—Down, down all of ye, but one man at the fore. The boats!—stand by!"

Unmindful of the tedious rope-ladders of the shrouds, the men, like shooting stars, slid to the deck, by the isolated backstays and halyards; while Ahab, less dartingly, but still rapidly was dropped from his perch.

. . . .

As if to strike a quick terror into them, by this time being the first assailant himself, Moby Dick had turned, and was now coming for the three crews. Ahab's boat was central; and cheering his men, he told them he would take the whale head-and-head . . . (597).

Ishmael's language includes the sun and shooting stars; he struggles to invest the description with a more expansive cosmic frame to support an epic conflict wherein the planetary bodies are also engaged. Ahab's untamed and untrammeled hubris is a potent dynamic force in nature. His vengeance is both absolute and boundless in its titanism. Ishmael bears witness to the whale's turning and Ahab's resolve to "pull straight up to his forehead" (597), both brows wrinkled. Their mutual frenzy exactly mirrors the Narcissus of the other.

The vengeful impulse in the soul can cast off all caution, dissolve any sense of limitations and intensify a monomaniacal objective to destroy the other. A mirroring may grow from such an encounter in which no compromise or caution is part of either oppositional force's lexicon. A crescendo reaches an all-or-nothing intensity and invites total annihilation of self and other. Boundaries evaporate and the consequences of such absolutism promise mutual obliteration.

Meditation

Have you engaged in an intense all-or-nothing confrontation?

December 14. Chapter 134: The Chase—Second Day

[T]he White Whale churning himself into furious speed, almost in an instant as it were, rushing among the boats with open jaws, and a lashing tail, offered appalling battle on every side; and heedless of the iron darted at him from every boat, seemed only intent on annihilating each separate plank of which those boats were made . . . .

But at last in his untraceable evolutions, the White Whale so crossed and recrossed, and in a thousand ways entangled the slack of the three lines now fast to him, that they foreshortened, and, of themselves, warped the devoted boats towards the planted irons in him (597-98).

An intelligence of Nature is present in Moby Dick's strategy of using the lines connected to the harpoons sunk in his flesh to ensnare the whaleboats in his contracting web; their weapons bespeak their incarceration. He uses the harpoons to entangle and so confuse the crew by drawing their boats into a shortened unity. The weave crafted by the White Whale as a consequence of his own untraceable motions leaves a hint of his convoluted actions. The result can be seen as the whaleboats are tethered closer to where their harpoons hold in the flesh of the whale in an intimacy of antagonisms.

When we imagine this scene, we detect an irony in the harpoon's iron makeup. What is used to slay the other turns on the pursuers to transform them into victims of their own pursuit. Their weapons are what their prey uses to pull them dangerously closer to what they strive to assassinate. Each is now at once both pursuer and pursued, so tangled have their identities and their mutual destinies become. Both are now held by the harpoons in a webbing of ironic oneness. We think of when life itself presents us with such a tangled mess that we may mistake ourselves for the enemy and recognize the enemy in ourselves.

Meditation

Have you been a victim of your own harpoons cast into another?

December 15. Chapter 134: The Chase—Second Day

But soon, as if satisfied that his work for that time was done, he pushed his pleated forehead through the ocean, and trailing after him the intertangled lines, continued his leeward way at a traveller's methodic pace . . . .

As with Fedallah the day before, so Ahab was now found grimly clinging to his boat's broken half, which afforded a comparatively easy float; nor did it exhaust him as the previous day's mishap.

But when he was helped to the deck, all eyes were fastened upon him; as instead of standing by himself he still half-hung upon the shoulder of Starbuck, who had thus far been the foremost to assist him. His ivory leg had been snapped off, leaving but one short sharp splinter.

"Aye, aye, Starbuck, 'tis sweet to lean sometimes, be the leaner who he will; and would old Ahab had leaned oftener than he has" (599).

Broken into pieces, dismembered and disassembled, both Ahab and his boat are rescued from the maw of the whale that now cruises away from his damaged pursuers. He carries, however, the markings, the line traces of his battle with men behind him—visible tracks of the continuing strife. Again, Ahab, the wounded Fisher King with a sharp splintered leg, is dismasted in yet another doubling. Something breaks open in him; he speaks of himself in the third person as a double of himself in confessing that he should have leaned on others more often.

When wounds are inflicted on us from presences and forces well beyond our control and limits, they can break us open to a newly-discovered vulnerability, our human boundaries, and the blessings of others ready to step forward to aid us if we allow it. Our afflictions can humanize us or isolate us; they may bring us to our splintered knees.

Meditation

Has an affliction opened you to accept the aid of others?

December 16. Chapter 134: The Chase—Second Day

"Aye, and all splintered to pieces, Stubb!—d'ye see it.—But even with a broken bone, old Ahab is untouched; and I account no living bone of mine one jot more me, than this dead one that's lost. Nor White Whale, nor man, nor fiend, can so much as graze old Ahab in his own proper and inaccessible being.

. . . .

"Oh, oh, oh! how this splinter gores me now! Accursed fate! that the unconquerable captain in the soul should have such a craven mate!"
"Sir?"
My body, man, not thee. Give me something for a cane—there, that shivered lance will do. Muster the men. Surely I have not seen him yet. By heaven it cannot be! . . ." (600).

No sooner does Ahab willingly lean on another for support as substitute for his now missing prosthetic limb then he reveals the great split in him by re-asserting his indomitable and fixed will regarding Moby Dick. He carries the fantasy, undoubtedly from the prophecy of the Parsee, that only hemp can slay him; therefore, he believes he will remain untouched by the White Whale's attacks. He carries a god-like attitude about himself in his flawed grammar when he refers to himself as a double. The soul of the captain is invisible, the embodied Ahab a more visible story. He then frantically searches for the missing Parsee.

Even in the face of being dismembered, we can cling to a fantasy of invulnerability, a belief that pushes human boundaries far back or simply ignored. Such a titanic gesture places one in dicey territory with the world where we are embodied, limited and vulnerable. But if our soul is severed from our body, then grotesque exaggerations of our prowess can grow, untempered by a persistent fleshy finitude.

Meditation

Have you experienced a feeling of invulnerability and limitlessness?

December 17. Chapter 134: The Chase—Second Day

"*My* line! *my* line? Gone—gone? What means that little word?—What death-knell rings in it, that old Ahab shakes as if he were the belfry. The harpoon, too!—toss over the litter there,--d'ye see it?-- . . . this hand did dart it!—'tis in the fish! Aloft there! Keep him nailed—Quick!—all hands to the rigging of the boats— . . . . I'll ten times girdle the unmeasured globe; yea and dive straight through it, but I'll slay him yet!"

"Great God! but for one single instant show thyself," cried Starbuck; "never, never, wilt thou capture him, old man—In Jesus' name no more of this, that's worse than devil's madness. Two days chased; twice stove to splinters; thy very leg once more snatched from under thee; thy evil shadow gone—all good angels mobbing thee with warnings:--what more wouldst thou have?" (600-01).

Stubb has just relayed to Ahab that he saw the Parsee, the captain's dark double, tangled in Ahab's harpoon line and pulled under by the White Whale. Ahab's response questions whether his line is sunk sufficiently deep into the whale. His language is both defiant and colossal in its promise to sail round the globe ten times, if need be, to slay Moby Dick. Starbuck's countering voice interrupts his captain's resolve when he calls on the name of Christ and the angels to sway Ahab. Starbuck's cry is his last plea to cut the lines and return home.

Our obsessive pursuit of a goal against all contrary evidence points to further losses and afflictions, if not a permanent bankruptcy, as well as the power of addiction to an idea that consumes. Like an obsession, one can lose all proportion and clear perception in aching to satisfy a deep desire whose consequences are complete annihilation. We need in these moments a contrary voice to soberly assess our disorder.

Meditation

Have you been counseled by a voice contrary to your own desires?

December 18. Chapter 134: The Chase—Second Day

"Starbuck, of late I've felt strangely moved to thee; ever since that hour we both saw—thou know'st what, in one another's eyes. But in this matter of the whale, be the front of thy face to me as the palm of this hand—a lipless, unfeatured blank. Ahab is for ever Ahab, man. This whole act's immutably decreed. 'Twas rehearsed by thee and me a billion years before this ocean rolled. Fool! I am the Fates' lieutenant; I act under orders. Look thou, underling! that thou obeyest mine.—Stand round men, men. Ye see an old man cut down to the stump; leaning on a shivered lance . . . . 'Tis Ahab—his body's part; but Ahab's soul's a centipede that moves upon a hundred legs" (601).

Full of the language of doubling, Ahab reveals how split he is between his own humanity earlier reflected in Starbucks's eyes when the captain reconnected with all humanity through the orbs of his first mate. The other impulse goading him on is that he not at all free to pursue or not pursue the White Whale. Instead, he is simply an instrument of Fate itself as his commanding officer. More, his task has been outlined in an eternal realm and that hour is now upon him to achieve what was ordained "a billion years before this ocean rolled." Yet he knows Starbuck's admonition to cease this strife carries a truth.

A sense of events being fated in some way descends on all of us at moments in our lives. We distinguish most palpably forces that far exceed our strengths and make us the instrument of their purpose. Try as we may, there is little possibility of untangling from its powers. We may feel swept along, impotent to choose another path. We ride the currents of those specific circumstances that brook no options and turn from any spiritual or moral compass that might convert us.

Meditation

When have you believed you were fated to a certain course of life's actions or to accomplish a certain task reserved solely for you?

December 19. Chapter 134: The Chase—Second Day

"Believe ye, men, in the things called omens? Then laugh aloud, and cry encore! For ere they drown, drowning things will twice rise to the surface; then rise again, to sink for evermore. So with Moby Dick—two days he's floated—to-morrow will be the third. Aye, men, he'll rise once more—but only to spout his last! D'ye feel brave men, brave?"

"As fearless fire," cried Stubb . . . .

"The things called omens! And yesterday I talked the same to Starbuck there, concerning my broken boat. Oh! how valiantly I seek to drive out of others' hearts what's clinched so fast in mine!" (601).

Ahab struggles to justify what he believes he will achieve on the third day of the chase: conquering and annihilating the White Whale. Some ominous feature now enters the conversation before the final confrontation. Omens, Ahab believes, will be incarnated in the third instance when Moby Dick sinks below the surface, never to rise again. Then a major revelation on the captain's part: he seeks to exorcise from the hearts of others what he clings to in his own. He makes this profound observation, but does he believe it? He calls on his men's deepest courage to make the omen a reality.

In life's most important pursuits it is easy to sense that one has control of its terms and its resolution. One may smell victory in one more heroic push. If only one can persevere and sustain one's strength, all will be realized. Nations' leaders do this in war, but contrary to plans, the conflict may continue for years with victory always receding on the horizon. Keeping the hope of victory alive, one may rush to one's own destruction in full denial that victory is not immanent. Such a belief reveals the absolute power of myth to control an individual.

Meditation

When was a planned accomplishment or achievement denied you?

December 20. Chapter 135: The Chase—Third Day

"D'ye see him?" cried Ahab; but the whale was not yet in sight.

"In his infallible wake, though; but follow that wake, that's all. Helm there; steady, as thou goest, and hast been going. What a lovely day again! were it a new-made world, and made for a summer-house to the angels, and this morning the first of its throwing open to them, a fairer day could not dawn upon that world. Here's food for thought, had Ahab time to think; but Ahab never thinks; he only feels, feels, feels; *that's* tingling enough for mortal man! to think's audacity. God only has that right and privilege" (603).

The scene is of the earth born anew with a freshness of air that energizes Ahab and promotes his feeling function over thinking. He imagines in this last chapter of the epic a brave new world fit for angels. Feelings are the proper lot for mortals; thinking is for God alone. The captain seems to have reversed his point of view. Thought has obsessed him throughout the voyage up to this third day when feeling awakens and dominates his perceptions. Thought is divine while feelings are mortal. His one guide now is the White Whale's wake. *Wake* is a slippery word, implying both a trace in the water and the ritual to remember the dead; one marks out life, the other death.

A shift in disposition from a thinking to a feeling self shifts the keel of one's understanding of the world and tacks it in another direction. Feeling opens the world into a more poetic, even lyrical realm. Now the world's freshness as a felt experience is allowed in and enjoyed in a sensate way, with one's whole body. Not a concept but a felt reality of the world's beauty serves as a rudder to steer the ship of one's state of mind and being in a more immediate intimacy.

Meditation

Remember an experience you have had as a felt sense rather than as a concept or idea. Does feeling offer another level of understanding?

December 21. Chapter 135: The Chase—Third Day

"And by the eternal Poles! these same Trades that so directly blow my good ship on; these Trades, or something like them—something so unchangeable, and full as strong, blow my keeled soul along! To it! Aloft there! What d'ye see"?

"Nothing, sir."

"Nothing! And noon at hand! The doubloon goes a-begging! See the sun! Aye, aye, it must be so. I've over-sailed him. How, got the start? Aye, he's chasing *me* now; not I, *him*—that's bad; I might have known it, too. Fool! the lines—the harpoons he's towing. Aye, aye, I have run him by last night. About! about! Come down, all of ye, but the regular look outs! Man the braces!" (604).

In his zeal and armed with his instinctive calculations, Ahab has succeeded in accelerating past the White Whale's pace. He realizes that he has reversed roles with his prey. More than that, however, he draws a rich analogy between his own soul's journey and the ship's, wherein the sensibly-felt Trade winds propelling the Pequod have a correspondence in the energies that move his soul. Inside and outside, pursuer and pursued all conmingle in the vortex forming as the line between Moby Dick and Ahab tightens and blurs when he retraces his ground. The chase continues to contract.

Overshooting the mark and so missing it in one's enthusiasm creates a disappointment in that what one's goal is may now be behind rather than before one. Reversing directions may feel as if one is losing ground, but in fact it creates a paradox: retracing one's ground actually moves one forward to one's goal. At times what we assumed was before us to be achieved is in fact behind us to be retrieved.

Meditation

When in your life pursuits did you realize that your goal was no longer behind, but in front of you?

December 22. Chapter 135: The Chase—Third Day

Time itself now held long breaths with keen suspense. But at last, some three points off the weather bow, Ahab descried the spout again, and instantly from the three mast-heads three shrieks went up as if the tongues of fire had voiced it.

"Forehead to forehead I meet thee, this third time, Moby Dick! . . . The sails shake! Stand over that helmsman with a top-maul! So, so; he travels fast, and I must down. But let me have one more good round look aloft here at the sea; there's time for that. An old, old sight, and yet somehow so young; aye and not changed a wink since I first saw it, a boy from the sand-hills of Nantucket! The same!—the same!—the same to Noah as to me . . . . . Leeward! The White Whale goes that way; look to windward then; the better if the bitterer quarter" (605).

Ahab's language reveals that he knows the final showdown, the last encounter and confrontation, head to head, is at hand. His vision is young and old at once, both personal and universal. He looks round at the sea, his ship, his men, the White Whale and imagines the Pequod as the original ark and he Noah's double swinging the flood gates of the world submerged by God's desire, now opened, to double the world, but now without error. Fate seems to power the energies on board to carry him and his men to a final reckoning with the divine white phantom.

Moments of apocalypse can subdue us at life's critical moments of confrontation. In an instant we see with a broader lens in space and with a fuller historical vision in time. We can in this moment calculate clearly, pay close attention to particulars, while also seeing the larger latitude of such a poignant historical moment that enwombs the eternal within it. We may even sense the greatness of the instant, including our own, in all its terrible finality. One's vision expands to epic grandness.

Meditation

Describe a moment of apocalypse wherein you beheld greatness.

December 23. Chapter 135: The Chase—Third Day

Their hands met; their eyes fastened; Starbuck's tears the glue.

"Oh, my captain, my captain!—noble heart—go not—go not!—see, it's a brave man that weeps; how great the agony of the persuasion then!"

. . . .

"The sharks! The sharks!" cried a voice from the low cabin-window there; "O master, my master, come back!"

But Ahab heard nothing; for his own voice was high-lifted then; and the boat leaped on.

Yet the voice spake true; for scarce had he pushed from the ship, when numbers of sharks, seemingly rising from out the dark waters beneath the hull, maliciously snapped at the blades of the oars, every time they dipped in the water and in this way accompanied the boat with their bites . . . (606).

Like predators who seem to sense death which spans their clustering appearance, the sharks in concert seek to destroy the instruments of Ahab's whaleboat, filled with "tiger-yellow barbarians" (606). The sharks appear in concert with Moby Dick. Ahab and his harpooneers are singled out to confront their wrathful appetites. The sharks rise like demons from the ocean's depths to chew and chip away at Ahab's heroic attempt to engage and subdue the White Whale.

Every presence in life carries a dark double, a shadow, perhaps a pathology when motives are still unclear, even when the energy and calculations expended appear large and daring. These may arise on occasions when one realizes that the present has crossed a line; respect for a boundary once violated should be heeded. Turning back is not a failure but a homage to limits if one has the wisdom to yield.

Meditation

Have you in life turned back from or reconsidered a zealous pursuit?

December 24. Chapter 135: The Chase—Third Day

The boats had not gone very far, when by a signal from the mast-heads—a downward pointed arm, Ahab knew that the whale had sounded; but intending to be near him at the next rising, he held on his way a little sideways from the vessel; the becharmed crew maintaining the profoundest silence, as the head-bent waves hammered and hammered against the opposing bow.

"Drive, drive in your nails, oh ye waves! to their uttermost heads drive them in! ye but strike a thing without a lid, and no coffin and no hearse can be mine:—and hemp only can kill me. Ha! ha!"(607).

Images of "wrought steel," "hammered" and "nails" proliferate in a striking set of images of hardness, both metal and mettle. Ahab's mettle is severely tested in the tumultuous prologue to the White Whale's third and final rising. The captain feels invincible and immortal, with nothing to fear, no coffin in his immediate offing, for the prophecy is that only hemp rope can kill him. So long as he stays clear of the one substance, and assuming the prophecy is accurate, he can pursue Moby Dick with Fate's assurance of safety. Even the sea itself seems intent on beating Ahab back as a way to protect him. The captain is blind to the fact that the prophecy is true, his premise false.

In our fanatical pursuits it is not difficult to find thought, beliefs and intentions—all forms of fiction to convince ourselves to go on, to persevere--because of feelings of invincible power. Even when conditions become insurmountable, we may continue to cling to fantasies of being above it all, untouchable, armored from woundings; in such a state of mind, retreating never enters the equation. We hear "failure" or "retreat is not an option" that carries the same hubris.

Meditation

Have you entertained fantasies of invincibility? What was the outcome of such imagining?

December 25. Chapter 135: The Chase—Third Day

Suddenly the waters around them slowly swelled in broad circles; then quickly upheaved, as if sideways sliding from a submerged berg of ice, swiftly rising to the surface. A low rumbling sound was heard; a subterraneous hum; and then all held their breaths; as bedraggled with trailing ropes, and harpoons, and lances, a vast form shot lengthwise, but obliquely, from the sea. Shrouded in a thin drooping veil of mist, it hovered for a moment in the rainbowed air; and then fell swamping back into the deep . . . . [while] the waters flashed for an instant like heaps of fountains, then brokenly sank in a shower of flakes, leaving the circling surface creamed like new milk round the marble trunk of the whale (607-08).

As if a divine form were emerging suddenly and violently into view, Moby Dick surfaces in a breach of wonder trailing all the harpoon lines like the train of a white gown. Shrouded in mist, he appears as a supernatural presence displaying itself majestically. The water displaced by his mighty bulk flashes like fountains, which recalls the fountain that Narcissus stared into earlier: when Narcissus failed to comprehend the tormenting mild image in the fountain [he] "plunged into it and was drowned" (5). That image, now here in its tracing watery turmoil, is "the phantom of life" (5). The god of the depths has been fully roused, the phantom fully revealed, its apotheosis in full splendor.

It does happen that the magnitude and danger of what one may pursue, even if it is spoken of generally as life itself, suddenly shocks and all but dismembers our many desires. Life may turn to pursue us in its own particulars with its own blank, pleated forehead. Discovering what terms of existence arise from the deep in what we pursue can overwhelm and terrify, even swamping us in the waters of life.

Meditation

When has life seemed like a massive bulk of a whale you pursue?

December 26. Chapter 135: The Chase—Third Day

"Give way!" cried Ahab to the oarsmen, and the boats darted forward to the attack; but maddened by yesterday's fresh irons that corroded in him, Moby Dick seemed combinedly possessed by all the angels that fell from heaven. The wide tiers of welded tendons overspreading this broad white forehead, beneath the transparent skin, looked knitted together; as head on, he came churning his tail among the boats; and once more flailed them apart; spilling out the irons and lances from the two mates' boats, and dashing in one side of the upper part of their bows, but leaving Ahab's almost without a scar (608).

Furious at the harpoons that penetrate like metal nettles in his skin, the White Whale, *seemingly* with a careful intelligence, uses his tail to shatter and scatter two of the three whaleboats, rendering them useless splinters. But this time Ahab's boat is spared from another beating, as if the White Whale wished them all to see his intelligent prowess. As he ruins some and spares others, he also displays on his back, bound in whale lines, Ahab's dark double, the Parsee; his "half torn body" and "sable raiment frayed to shreds; his distended eyes turned full upon old Ahab" (608), who asks him where the second hearse is—the captain's.

The force of nature in her intelligence cannot be overestimated. Her cunning genius and prowess, when turned on those who would seduce and violate her nature, elicits a fierce and destructive recoil. Less malice than nature's own methods in the cyclic process of birth, growth, aging and death will not be surrendered to any man-made desires or artifices. Like a phantom presence, Nature's range of emotions can be nurturing and healing or destructive and overwhelming in its seeming indifference and randomness or in its precise intent to destroy.

Meditation

Have you experienced Nature's destructive force as a living animated presence? What allowed you to survive it?

December 27. Chapter 135: The Chase—Third Day

[A]nd Ahab was fairly within the smoky mountain mist, which, thrown off from the whale's spout, curled round his great Monadnock hump; he was even thus close to him; when, with body arched back, and both arms lengthwise high-lifted to the poise, he darted his fierce iron, and his far fiercer curse into the hated whale. As both steel and curse sank to the socket, as if sucked into a morass, Moby Dick sidewise writhed; spasmodically rolled his nigh flank against the bow. . . .

. . . .

[B]ut in that evolution, catching sight of the nearing black hull of the ship; seemingly seeing in it the source of all his persecutions; bethinking it—it may be—a larger and nobler foe; of a sudden he bore down upon its advancing prow, smiting his jaws amid fiery showers of foam (610-11).

The close encounter to which the entire epic has been heading occurs at this moment. The whale appears as an isolated hump in the water (en. wikipedia.org/wiki/Monadnock). Roles reverse; Ahab is the great wounder of the whale; both curse and harpoon enter Moby Dick at the same instant with great effect. The White Whale may recognize the Pequod as genesis of all its afflictions, according to Ishmael's perspective, and gathers his wrathful forces to attack it.

When the ardor in which we have pursued a goal suddenly assumes that same fervor towards us, one might pause to reflect. Mono-maniac designs are depicted in politics, religion, psychology and literature. All boundaries evaporate. Conquering, winning, subduing, mastering suck in all the air. Retreat, surrender, or compromise as alternatives are summarily dismissed. Madness reigns and projections control.

Meditation

When has an obsessive pursuit of yours bordered on madness?

December 28. Chapter 135: The Chase—Third Day

"The whale, the whale! Up helm, up helm! Oh, all ye sweet powers of air, now hug me close! Let not Starbuck die, if die he must, in a woman's fainting fit. Up helm, I say—ye fools, the jaw! The jaw! Is this the end of all my bursting prayers? all my life-long fidelities? Oh, Ahab, Ahab, lo, thy work . . . . Oh, his unappeasable brow drives on towards one, whose duty tells him he cannot depart. My God, stand by me now! . . . .

I grin at thee, thou grinning whale! . . . Oh, oh! oh, oh! thou grinning whale, but there'll be plenty of gulping soon! Why fly ye not, O Ahab!" (611).

As Ahab and his ocean-deep double grow more intimate in drawing closer to one another, like a shard of steel to a magnet, the captain sees himself mirrored more keenly in the leviathan. He speaks of himself continually in the third person as a double of himself. The language is saturated with doubleness. The captain prays for supernatural protection and courage as the whale bears down on the Pequod to splinter and sink its mighty bulk. Ahab reflects what he sees as a grinning whale speeding toward him by grinning back in mocking imitation of the Narcissus myth. As readers, we are asked to exist in a double reality in order to see with both literal and mythic eyes.

The above passage prompts a reflection on the nature of what it is we strive for in life, which here suggests we seek in the world's matter our own image. We search for a mirror reflection of who and what we are as well as what we dream of becoming. The burden, or the prize, or the burden that is the prize, is ourselves in depth in all our shadowed and noble aspects. A direct correspondence emerges in whatever success we are hell-bent towards. We both fear and desire its reality of depth in the same spirit that Narcissus approaches and pulls back from himself.

Meditation

Are you able to see your double in what most entices you in life?

December 29. Chapter 135: The Chase—Third Day

"The ship! The hearse!—the second hearse!" cried Ahab from the boat; "its wood could only be American!"

. . . .

"I turn my body from the sun. What ho, Tashtego! Let me hear thy hammer . . . . Oh, lonely death on lonely life! Oh, now I feel my topmost greatness lies in my topmost grief . . . . Towards thee I roll, thou all-destroying but unconquering whale; to the last I grapple with thee; from hell's heart I stab at thee; for hate's sake I spit my last breath at thee . . . ."

The harpoon was darted; the stricken whale flew forward; with igniting velocity the line ran through the grooves; ran foul. Ahab stooped to clear it; he did clear it; but the flying turn caught him round the neck . . . [and] he was shot out of the boat, ere the crew knew he was gone (612-13).

Ahab's curses beckon him towards the White Whale. His speech reveals that he knows the end is upon him, but not the terms of his termination. Sated with hellish hate and corrosive vengeance, Ahab defies the whale as he claimed earlier he would defy the sun if it insulted him; he kicks hard against Nature's forces that can flick him away like a pesky fly. The harpoon and its line then claim both whale and captain and wed them in the deep, like an umbilical cord from mother to infant. Not a breached birth but a breached death is Ahab's final reckoning.

When in our drive to conquer what has insulted us, something very incidental and self-generated may be the origin of our undoing. The infinitely small assumes a grand place in Fate's fabric. We may have acted as if nothing could harm or deter our efforts but we overlook the innocuous-appearing line running foul at our feet. We may reach a point of dissolution between who is hunter, who is hunted as they unite.

Meditation

Have you acknowledged yourself as a double of your object of revenge?

December 30. Chapter 135: The Chase—Third Day

And now, concentric circles seized the lone boat itself, and all its crew, and each floating oar, and every lance-pole, and spinning, animate and inanimate, all round and round in one vortex, carried the smallest chip of the Pequod out of sight.

. . . .

Now small fowls flew screaming over the yet yawning gulf; a sullen white surf beat against its steep sides; then all collapsed, and the great shroud of the sea rolled on as it rolled five thousand years ago (613-14).

Attacked and mortally wounded by the White Whale's wrath, the Pequod is sucked into the vortex created by the swirling Moby Dick and swallowed whole, pulling into the watery gravitational field every last chip of its enormous bulk. As the whirlpool subsides, small birds hover and scream their lament over the subsiding vortex of the energy field created by leviathan to demolish the whale ship. As the whirlpool slows, its trace diminishes, then disappears, erasing all remnants of the fierce fight between the human and natural orders. The ocean's ancient rhythm assumes its dominion once again, as it has done throughout time.

Very humbling is it to realize that all of our energy put into efforts for a lifetime can in one short instant be erased with almost no trace of its ever having happened, and worse, no story to preserve it. What seemed at one moment so crucial and monumental is in the next not even a ripple on the surface of life. The natural order has its own cadences and eternal ways, which may be temporarily interrupted by man's meddling or presence. But it soon regains that rhythm, deleting any sign of human significance. Whale as world reigns in the new silence.

Meditation

In your own pursuits, claims and achievements, have you made some lasting difference worth remembering in a poignant narrative?

December 31. Epilogue

"AND I ONLY AM ESCAPED ALONE TO TELL THEE"

—Job.

The drama's done. Why then here does any one step forth?—Because one did survive the wreck.

It so chanced, that after the Parsee's disappearance, I was he whom the Fates ordained to take the place of Ahab's bowsman, when that bowsman assumed the vacant post . . . and now, liberated by reason of its cunning spring, and, owing to its great buoyancy, rising with great force, the coffin life-buoy shot lengthwise from the sea, fell over, and floated by my side. Buoyed up by that coffin, for almost one whole day and night, I floated on a soft and dirge-like main . . . . On the second day, a sail drew near, nearer, and picked me up at last. It was the devious-cruising Rachel, that in her retracing search after her missing children, only found another orphan (615).

Guided by his shaman, Queequeg, and chosen by Fate, Ishmael finds himself in the role of a double of the Parsee in position and place. Thrown to the margins of the vortex, he is able to survive to tell the story, doubling the biblical event in the Book of Job as well as the story of Genesis of the flood. The sea cooperates in his survival with a calm surface; the lone survivor spends a full 24 hours on Queequeg's coffin life-buoy, which completes the cycle of life-death-life before being rescued as an orphan by the grieving Rachel.

Telling the story assures it immortality in place in time. Narratives themselves can order, arrange and offer coherent sense out of the most mysterious and initially incoherent of life's events in our narrative plots. The story bequeaths a communal life and form to what might be forgotten or remain formless. Telling our stories renews us.

Meditation

What part of your life do you want to transform into a coherent story?

Afterword

Like Dante, the pilgrim-poet before him, and in whose tracks he treads, Ishmael is called to carry the story of a quest that would not have been remembered without his traces on the page. At the same time, he has narrated himself into a new sense of identity by weaving his own history into the story he witnessed first-hand. His history has poetically merged with his narrative self.

In the spirit of a medieval quest, Ishmael keeps alive through his own remembered voyage the tradition of an ancient archetypal journey that has allowed us readers to be transformed in the act of reading and meditating on his supreme passages that we too booked passage on. The text he creates is our own Pequod, where a myriad set of life's deepest mythologies surface and mingle to create in its webbing a myth of America as well as a personal myth of one soul seeking through spiritual union a sense of his own identity and destiny.

The powerful myth woven by the writer coming into his own prowess as poet is matched by our readerly narrative identity that finds itself also enmeshed in the story of a search for the mystery of creation in both its life-giving and life-sacrificing demeanors. What has occurred will not be forgotten because of the memorable powers of storytelling that Ishmael employs in his vision of the mythology of Leviathan.

We are richer for its existence and perhaps in the voyage of reading itself, have grown closer to the winds that fill the sails of our own personal myth. Ishmael's story allows us a deeper fathoming of our own depths; for that reason alone the journey surely assumes abundant value for each of us who mustered the courage and risked signing on board our own unique Pequod. We heard and heeded The Call.

Whiteness

In you whiteness is the still flesh of
The circling globe
Magnet and lodestar
Fluke head hump spout.
Deeply silent in the slippery sibilant of
Ocean
Fluid-like: sperm oil blood spray of
Mist.
Just beneath the surface you glide
Reservoir of energy and shadow of depth.
Breaching between two worlds you are
For an instant upright—
So you speak the words of dark
Infinity.
We, washed in the after-spray
Of your cosmic foam in the
Slow bathe of a white double,
Put on your cloak of whiteness
And steal ourselves into
The chambers of history.[1]

---

1 Dennis Patrick Slattery, *Casting the Shadows: Selected Poems*, 73.

Bibliography

Adams, Michael Vannoy. "Madness and Right Reason, Extremes of One: The Shadow Archetype in *Moby-Dick.*" *Bucknell Review*, vol. 31, no. 2 (1988), 97-109.

———. "Getting a Kick Out of Captain Ahab: The Merman Dream in *Moby-Dick.*" *Dreamworks*, vol. 4, no. 4. (1984/85). 279-87.

Adamson, Joseph. *Melville, Shame and the Evil Eye: A Psychoanalytic Reading.* Albany: SUNY P, 1997.

Aristotle. *Poetics.* Trans. James Hutton. New York: Norton, 1982.

Armstrong, Robert Plant. *The Powers of Presence: Consciousness, Myth and Affecting Presence.* Philadelphia: U Pennsylvania P, 1981.

Arvin, Newton. *Melville. United States: The American Men of Letters Series.* New York: William Sloane Associates, 1950.

Bachelard, Gaston. *Earth and Reveries of Will: An Essay on the Imagination of Matter.* Trans. Kenneth Haltman. Foreword Joanne H. Stroud. Dallas: The Dallas Institute Publications, 2002. 61-64.

Barnum, Jill, Wyn Kelly and Christopher Sten, eds. *"Whole Oceans Away": Melville and the Pacific.* Kent, Ohio: Kent State UP, 2008.

Bates, Catherine, ed. *The Cambridge Companion to The Epic.* Cambridge, England: Cambridge UP, 2010.

Bickman, Martin. *American Romantic Psychology: Emerson, Poe, Whitman, Dickinson, Melville.* Dallas: Spring Publications, 1980.

Bodkin, Maud: *Archetypal Patterns in Poetry: Psychological Studies of Imagination.* London: Oxford UP, 1965.

Bond, D. Stephenson. *Living Myth: Personal Meaning as a Way of Life.* Boston: Shambhala, 1993.

Bradt, Kevin. *Story as a Way of Knowing.* Kansas City: Sheed and Ward, 1997.

Butcher, S.H. *Aristotle's Theory of Poetry and Fine Art.* London: Macmillan, 1902.

Calinescu, Matei. *Rereading.* New Haven: Yale UP, 1993.

Cameron, Sharon. *The Corporeal Self: Allegories of the Body in Melville and Hawthorne.* Baltimore: The Johns Hopkins UP, 1981.

Campbell, Joseph. *The Hero With a Thousand Faces.* Bollingen Series XVII. Novato, California: New World Library, 2008.

———. *The Power of Myth.* New York: Doubleday, 1988.

Coleridge, Samuel Taylor. *Biographia Literaria. The Collected Works of Samuel Taylor Coleridge*. Ed. James Engell and W. Jackson Bate. Bollingen Series LXXV. Princeton: Princeton UP, 1984.

Coles, Robert. *The Call of Stories: Teaching and the Moral Imagination*. Boston: Houghton Mifflin, 1989.

Cotkin, George. *Dive Deeper: Journeys with* Moby-Dick. Oxford: Oxford UP, 2012.

Coupe, Laurence. *Myth. The New Critical Idiom*. London: Routledge, 2009.

Cowan, Bainard: *Exiled Waters:* Moby-Dick *and the Crisis of Allegory*. Baton Rouge: Louisiana State UP, 1982.

———. "Ishmael's Sabbatical." *What is a Teacher? Remembering the Soul of Education Through Classic Literature*. Ed. Claudia Allums. Dallas: The Dallas Institute Publications, 2013. 131-46.

Cowan, Louise. "Introduction: Epic as Cosmopoesis." The Epic Cosmos. Ed. Larry Allums. Gen. Editor, Louise Cowan. Dallas: The Dallas Institute of Humanities and Culture, 1992. 1-26.

Davis, Merrell and William Gilman, eds. *The Letters of Herman Melville*. New Haven: Yale UP, 1960.

Davis, Clark. *After the Whale: Melville in the Wake of* Moby-Dick. Tuscaloosa: U Alabama P, 1995.

Delbanco, Andrew. *Melville: His World and Work*. New York: Knopf, 2005.

Donovan, Frank. *The Odyssey of the Essex*. New York: David McKay Co, 1969.

Doty, William. *Myth: A Handbook*. Tuscaloosa: U Alabama P., 2004.

Dreyfus, Hubert and Sean Dorrance Kelly. *All Things Shining: Reading the Western Classics to Find Meaning in a Secular Age*. New York: Free Press, 2011.

Edinger, Edward. *Ego and Archetype*. Boston: Shambhala, 1992.

———. *Melville's* Moby-Dick: *An American Nekyia*. New York: New Directions, 1978.

Foster, Thomas C. *Twenty-five Books That Shaped America*. New York: Harper-Collins. 2011.

Gentile, John. "The Pilgrim Soul: Herman Melville's *Moby-Dick* as Pilgrimage." *Text and Performance Quarterly*. Vol. 29, No.14. October 2009. 403-14.

———. Director. *Moby-Dick* by Herman Melville. Adapted by John Gentile and Henry Scott. Still Well Theatre, Kennesaw State University, Kennesaw, Georgia. April 15-20, 2008.

———. *Moby-Dick* by Herman Melville. Adapted by John Gentile. Directed by Henry Scott Festival International de Theatre. Universitaire de Casablanca, Morocco. July 10-15, 2009.

———. *Moby-Dick* by Herman Melville. Adapted by John Gentile. Directed by Marium Khalid. Lifecycle Building Center, Atlanta, Georgia. April 10-May 12, 2013.

Goldner, Loren. *Herman Melville: Between Charlemagne and the Antemosaic Cosmic Man. Race, Class and the Crisis of Bourgeois Ideology in an American Renaissance Writer.* New York: Queequeg Publications, 2006.

Gottlob, Stephanie and Yuji Oka. "Spiral Praxis: A New Universal Bodymind Flow System for Contemporary Life." *Somatics: Magazine-Journal of the Mind/Body Arts and Sciences.* Volume XVI, Number 4, 2012. 34-43.

Herman, Daniel. *Zen and the White Whale: A Buddhist Rendering of Moby-Dick.* Bethlehem, PA: Lehigh UP, 2014.

Heyford, Harrison. "Unnecessary Duplicates: A Key to the Writing of *Moby-Dick.*" *Herman Melville,* Moby-Dick. Ed. Hershel Parker and Harrison Hayford. New York: A Norton Critical Edition. Second Edition, 2002.

Hillman, James. *Archetypal Psychology. Uniform Edition of the Writings of James Hillman.* Vol. 1. Putnam, CT: Spring Publications, 2013.

———. *Revisioning Psychology.* New York: Harper Perennial, 1976.

Irwin, John T. *American Hieroglyphics: The Symbol of Egyptian Hieroglyphics in the American Renaissance.* Baltimore: John Hopkins UP, 1983.

Job. The Jerusalem Bible. Garden City, New York: Doubleday, 1966. 729-78.

Jonah. The Jerusalem Bible. Garden City, New York: Doubleday, 1966. 1494-96.

Jung, C.G. *The Archetypes and the Collective Unconscious.* Second Edition. Bollingen Series XX. Volume 9,i of *The Collected Works of C.G. Jung.* Trans. R.F.C. Hull. Princeton: Princeton UP, 1971.

———. *Symbols of Transformation: An Analysis of the Prelude to a Case of Schizophrenia.* Second Edition. Vol. 5. Princeton: Princeton UP, 1967.

———. *The Spirit in Man, Art and Literature.* Trans. R.F.C. Hull. Vol. 15 of *The Collected Works of C.G.Jung.* Princeton: Princeton UP, 1966.

Kalsched, Donald. *The Inner World of Trauma: Archetypal Defenses of the Personal Spirit.* London: Routledge, 1996.

Keen, Sam and Anne Valley-Fox. *Your Mythic Journey: Finding Meaning in Your Life Through Writing and Storytelling.* New York: Jeremy Tarcher/Putnam, 1989.

Keller, Catherine. "Leviathenic Revelations: Melville's Hermenautical Journey." *Face of the Deep: A Theology of Becoming.* London: Routledge, 2003. 141-55.

Kirk, G.S. *Myth: Its Meaning and Functions in Ancient and Other Cultures.* Sather Classical Lectures. Vol. 40. Berkeley: U California P, 1973.

Lewis, C. Day. *The Poetic Image.* London: Jonathan Cape, 1951.

Lincoln, Bruce. *Theorizing Myth: Narrative, Ideology and Scholarship.* Chicago: U Chicago P, 1999.

Marovitz, Sanford E. and A.C. Christodoulou, eds. *Melville "Among the Nations": Proceedings of an International Conference*, Volos, Greece, July 2-6, 1997. Kent, Ohio: The Kent State UP, 1998.

May, Rollo. *The Cry For Myth.* New York: Norton, 1991.

McGinn, Bernard. "Ocean and Desert as Symbols of Mystical Absorption in the Christian Tradition." *Journal of Religion*, vol. 74, no. 2. 155-81.

Melville, Herman. *Moby-Dick; or, The Whale.* Collector's Edition. Introduction by Clifton Fadiman. Norwalk, Connecticut: The Easton Press, 1977.

———. *Battle-Pieces and Aspects of the War: Civil War Poems.* New York: Da Capo Press, 1995.

Metzger, Deena. *Writing for Your Life: A Guide and Companion to the Inner World.* San Francisco: HarperSanFrancisco, 1992.

Miller, David. "Orestes: Myth and Dream as Catharsis." *Myths, Dreams and Religion.* Ed. Joseph Campbell. Dallas: Spring, 1970. 26-47.

Moore, Thomas. *Care of the Soul: A Guide for Cultivating Depth and Sacredness in Everyday Life.* New York: HarperCollins, 1992.

Neihardt, John G. *Black Elk Speaks: Being the Life Story of a Holy Man of the Oglala Sioux.* Premier Edition. Albany: SUNY P, 2008.

Nickerson, Thomas. *The Loss of the Ship Essex, Sunk by a Whale.* Nathaniel Philbrick (ed). New York: Penguin Classics, 2000.

Olney, James. *Memory and Narrative: the Weave of Life-Writing.* Chicago: U Chicago P., 1998.

Olson, Charles. *Call Me Ishmael: A Study of Melville.* San Francisco: City Light Books, 1947.

Paracelsus: Selected Writings. Jolande Jacobi,ed. Trans. Norbert Guterman. Bollingen Series XXVIII. New York: Pantheon Books, 1958.

Parker, Hershel and Harrison Hayford, eds. Moby-Dick *as Doubloon: Essays and Extracts (1851-1970).* New York: Norton, 1970.

Parker, Hershel and Harrison Hayford, eds. *Moby-Dick. A Norton Critical Edition. Second Edition.* New York: Norton, 2002.

Penn Warren, Robert, ed. *Selected Poems of Herman Melville.* New York: Barnes and Noble, 1970.

Pardes, Ilana. *Melville's Bibles.* Berkeley: U California P, 2008.

Philbrick, Nathaniel. *Why Read Moby-Dick?* New York: Viking, 2011.

————. *In the Heart of the Sea: The Tragedy of the Whaleship Essex.* New York: Penguin, 2000.

Plotinus, *The Enneads.* Trans. Stephen MacKenna. Burdett, NY: Larson Publications, 1992.

Robertson-Lorant, Laurie. *Melville: A Biography.* Boston: U Massachusetts P., 1996.

Sanborn, Geoffrey. *The Sign of the Cannibal: Melville and the Making of a Postcolonial Reader.* Durham: Duke UP, 1998.

Schultz, Elizabeth A. *Unpainted to the Last:* Moby-Dick *and Twentieth Century American Art.* Lawrence, Kansas: U Press of Kansas, 1995.

Severin, Tim. *In Search of* Moby-Dick: *The Quest for the White Whale.* New York: Basic Books, 2000.

Slattery, Dennis Patrick. "The White Whale and the Afflicted Body of Myth." *The Wounded Body: Remembering the Markings of Flesh.* Albany: SUNY P, 2000. 131-58.

————. "*Moby-Dick* and the Myth of Narcissus: Seeing Into and Seeing Through." *A Limbo of Shards: Essays on Memory, Myth and Metaphor.* New York: iUniverse, 2007. 213-223.

————. "Watery Worlds, Watery Words: Ishmael's (W)rite of Passage in *Moby-Dick. New Orleans Review,* vol. 11, 2 (Summer 1984). 62-66.

————. *Harvesting Darkness: Essays on Literature, Myth, Film and Culture.* New York: iUniverse, 2006.

————. "Speaking, Reflecting and Writing: The Myth of Narcissus and Echo." *South Central Bulletin,* No. 4, Winter, 1983. 217-20.

———. "The Narrative Play of Memory in Epic." *The Epic Cosmos*. Ed. Larry Allums. General Editor, Louise Cowan. Dallas: The Dallas Institute Publications, 1992. 331-52.

———. "Narcissus, Echo and Irony's Resonance." *Psychology at the Threshold*. Dennis Patrick Slattery and Lionel Corbett, eds. Carpinteria, California: Pacifica Graduate Institute Publications. 67-84.

———. A Lecture on *Moby-Dick* and Human Embodiment to an interdisciplinary group of scholars at the American Acupuncture Institute, Columbia, Maryland, September 19-21, 1986.

———. "*Moby-Dick* and the American Mythos." *Zion's Herald,* January/February 2006. 13.

———. *Riting Myth, Mythic Writing: Plotting Your Personal Story.* Cheyenne, Wyoming: Fisher King Press, 2012.

———. *Creases in Culture: Essays Toward a Poetics of Depth.* Cheyenne, Wyoming: Fisher King Press, 2014.

———. *Casting the Shadows: Selected Poems*, Kearney, NE: Morris Publishing, 2001.

Slochower, Harry. "The Quest for an American Myth: *Moby-Dick*." *Mythopoesis: Mythic Patterns in the Literary Classics.* Detroit: Wayne State UP, 1970. 223-45.

Spanos, William V. *The Errant Art of Moby-Dick: The Cold War, and the Struggle for American Studies.* Durham: Duke UP, 1995.

Sten, Christopher. *The Weaver God, He Weaves: Melville and the Poetics of the Novel.* Kent, Ohio: The Kent State UP, 1996.

———. *Sounding the Whale: Moby-Dick as Epic Novel.* Kent, Ohio: Kent State UP, 2011.

———. *Savage Eye: Melville and the Visual Arts.* Kent, Ohio: Kent State UP, 1991.

Strachan, Gordon. *The Bible's Hidden Cosmology.* Edinburgh, England. Floris Books, 2005.

Tarnas, Richard. "*Moby-Dick* and Nature's Depths." *Cosmos and Psyche: Intimations of a New World View.* New York: A Plume Book of the Penguin Group, 2007. 239-41.

Taylor, James. *Poetic Knowledge: The Recovery of Education.* Albany: SUNY P, 1998.

Turner, Frederick. *Epic: Form, Content, and History.* New Brunswick, New Jersey: Transaction Publishers, 2012.

Vaihinger, Hans. *The Philosophy of "As If": A System of the Theoretical Practical and Religious Fictions of Mankind.* Trans. C.K. Ogden. The International Library of Psychology Philosophy and Scientific Method. London: Routledge, 1968.

Vincent, Howard. *The Trying-Out of* Moby-Dick. Boston: Houghton Mifflin, 1949.

Von Franz, Marie-Louise. *Projection and Re-collection in Jungian Psychology: Reflections of the Soul.* Trans. William H. Kennedy. Chicago: Open Court P, 1995.

———. *Alchemy: An Introduction to the Symbolism and the Psychology.* Toronto: Inner City Books, 1980.

Wagner, Robert D., Jr. *Moby-Dick and the Mythology of Oil: An Admonition for the Petroleum Age.* 2010.

Watts, Alan W. "Western Mythology: Its Dissolution and Transformation." *Myths, Dreams, and Religion.* Ed. Joseph Campbell. Dallas: Spring, 1970. 9-25.

Westman, Heinz. *The Structure of Biblical Myths: The Ontogenesis of the Psyche.* Wilmette, Illinois: Chiron, 1991.

About the Author

Dennis Patrick Slattery, Ph.D. has been teaching for 45 years, the last 20 in the Mythological Studies Program at Pacifica Graduate Institute in Carpinteria, California. He is the author, co-author, editor or co-editor of 24 volumes, including six volumes of poetry: *Casting the Shadows: Selected Poems*; *Just Below the Water Line: Selected Poems*; *Twisted Sky: Selected Poems*; *The Beauty Between Words: Selected Poems* with Chris Paris; and *Feathered Ladder: Selected Poems* with Brian Landis. He has co-authored one novel, *Simon's Crossing*, with Charles Asher. Other titles include *The Idiot: Dostoevsky's Fantastic Prince. A Phenomenological Approach*; *The Wounded Body: Remembering the Markings of Flesh*. With Lionel Corbett he co-edited and contributed to *Psychology at the Threshold* and *Depth Psychology: Meditations in the Field*. With Glen Slater he co-edited and contributed to *Varieties of Mythic Experience: Essays on Religion, Psyche and Culture. A Limbo of Shards: Essays on Memory, Myth and Metaphor*. His more recent books include *Day-to-Day Dante: Exploring Personal Myth Through the Divine Comedy*; *Riting Myth, Mythic Writing: Plotting Your Personal Story*. With Jennifer Selig, he co-edited *The Soul Does Not Specialize: Revaluing the Humanities and the Polyvalent Imagination* and *Reimagining Education: Essays on Reviving the Soul of Learning*. He wrote *Creases in Culture: Essays Toward a Poetics of Depth*. His most recent books are *Bridge Work: Essays on Mythology, Literature and Psychology* and *Road, Frame, Window: A Poetics of Seeing. Selected Poems of Timothy Donohue, Donald Carlson and Dennis Patrick Slattery*. He has also authored over 200 essays, book and film reviews in books, magazines, journals, newspapers and online journals.

He offers (w)riting retreats in the United States, Europe and Ireland on exploring one's personal myth through the works of Joseph Campbell and others. www.dennispslattery@pacifica.edu; dslattery@pacifica.edu.

About the Photographer

Focusing on active lifestyle, documentary, and the abstract, Vincent Shay is an award winning photographer & videographer from San Luis Obispo, California. For more information about Vincent Shay visit:

www.vincentshayphotography.com